PITIRIM A. SOROKIN
ON THE
PRACTICE OF
SOCIOLOGY

Edited and with an Introduction by

BARRY V. JOHNSTON

THE UNIVERSITY OF CHICAGO PRESS

Chicago and London

Barry V. Johnston is professor of sociology at Indiana
University Northwest. He is author of *Pitirim A. Sorokin:
An Intellectual Biography,* published in 1995 by the
University Press of Kansas.

The University of Chicago Press, Chicago 60637
The University of Chicago Press, Ltd., London
© 1998 by The University of Chicago
All rights reserved. Published 1998
Printed in the United States of America

07 06 05 04 03 02 01 00 99 98   5 4 3 2 1

ISBN (cloth): 0-226-76828-7
ISBN (paper): 0-226-76829-5

Library of Congress Cataloging-in-Publication Data

Sorokin, Pitirim Aleksandrovich, 1889–1968.
    On the practice of sociology / edited and with
an introduction by Barry V. Johnson.
        p.   cm. — (The Heritage of sociology)
    Includes bibliographical references and index.
    ISBN 0-226-76828-7. — ISBN 0-226-76829-5 (pbk.)
    1. Sociology. I. Johnston, Barry V. II. Title.
III. Title: Pitirim A. Sorokin on the practice of
sociology. IV. Series.
HM61.S673   1998
301—dc21   97-32778
                                                CIP

♾ The paper used in this publication meets the minimum
requirements of the American National Standard for
Information Sciences—Permanence of Paper for Printed
Library Materials, ANSI Z39.48-1992.

Contents

Acknowledgments

Preparation of this work was facilitated by a number of generous colleagues, friends, and institutions. Larry Nichols's original translations, constructive counsel, and encouragement have enhanced the volume. I am grateful to Vincent Jeffries and Fred Wacker for their valuable insights and comments on earlier drafts of the introduction. Significant suggestions by Robert K. Merton and Donald Levine sharpened the focus of the text. Indiana University Northwest supported the project, and the staff of Tutt Library at Colorado College gave gracious logistical assistance. To Laurel I give my love and gratitude; and to her, Blake, Ian, and Caitlin I dedicate this volume.

Introduction

Pitirim Sorokin's Science of Sociology and Social Reconstruction: An Intellectual Journey

William Kolb opened his 1951 review of *Social Philosophies of an Age of Crisis* with a probing question on the fate of the great Russian-American sociologist Pitirim Alexandrovitch Sorokin:

> Who reads Sorokin? Whatever the answer to the question, sociologists generally are not included in the attentive group. To be sure *Social Mobility* and *Contemporary Sociological Theories* are frequently cited by sociologists and are used by them in teaching and research. But the *Dynamics* and all its progeny . . . are lost in sociological limbo. They are no longer even criticized, simply ignored. (Kolb 1951, 267–68)

Forty-seven years later, one may still wonder: Why read Sorokin? For many sociologists, his name invokes memories of controversy and anger. Others see a pioneer who opened new fields of study, animated scholarly controversies, and wrestled with the ultimate questions of life. But who was Sorokin, and what is his relevance for the sociological enterprise? It is curious that so many could ask such questions about one of the discipline's founders and elder statesmen.

The first half of this introductory essay probes Sorokin's scholarly development and career. An exegesis of his general and special sociologies is the focus of the second. For now, it can be said that he was one of the most erudite, insightful, and critical figures in the chronicles of sociology. Over six decades he published thirty-seven books (which received at least forty-two translations) and more than four hundred articles. Don Martindale contends that this makes Sorokin the most prolific sociologist ever (1972, 5). However, it is the value of his publications that makes him of interest.

Sorokin's Career: An Overview

Sorokin was a pioneer and an outcast. His early American works opened new vistas onto rural sociology, social stratification, and theory. They provided an elegant standard for scientific sociology and won him the founding chairmanship of the sociology department at Harvard University. A continuous innovator, he next pushed toward a new integral theory of history in his four-volume magnum opus, *Social and Cultural Dynamics* (1937–41). In this work he explored the vast expanse of human affairs and outlined the surfacing crisis of modernity, issues toward which he directed the last two decades of his scholarship. At the Harvard Research Center in Creative Altruism he analyzed the global crisis and developed a blueprint for social reconstruction. His pioneering interest in these topics, combined with a prophetic and combative style of disagreement, drove him to the margins of a discipline hungry for acceptance as a science and eventually into exile from it. However, in the 1960s, several of his classic works were reissued and two *Festschrift* volumes were published (Allen 1963; Tiryakian 1963), moving the pendulum in the opposite direction. And the best was yet to come: in April 1963, rank-and-file sociologists acclaimed Sorokin president of the American Sociological Association in the association's first successful write-in campaign (Johnston 1987, 103–22). Fittingly, when Sorokin died in 1968, it was with the dignity of an accomplished scholar.

The enduring value of Sorokin's work was captured by the dissident sociologists who wore "Sorokin Lives!" buttons at the 1969 meeting of the American Sociological Association. These dissenters found Sorokin's crisis studies to be prescient; his works touched the very essence of the society against which they were protesting. Sorokin lived for them because he understood human pain and its relationship to social structure. His analysis was compelling because it captured what could be done in society and attempted to move others toward that vision. At times Sorokin was as they were: intemperate, challenging, difficult. However, as a master of his craft, he left behind a discipline that grew and was enlivened by his presence.

Sorokin's complexity and remarkable productivity make it difficult to embrace his oeuvre in a short essay. However, we begin with an examination of the three self-proclaimed stages in his intellectual development: Christian-pietistic, positivistic-progressive, and integral. For the sake of clarity I have added two derivative yet distinctive stages in his work: crisis sociology and the sociology of social and moral reconstruction (Sorokin 1963, 39–41, 73–76, 204–5; Schneider 1984, 149–59; Costello 1993, 97–125).

The Christian-Pietistic Period

Pitirim Sorokin was the peasant son of a Komi mother and a Russian father. He was born on the Komi homelands in 1889 and passed his early years under conditions that would have broken a lesser man.[1] After his mother's death when he was just three years old, he and his older brother, Vassiliy, wandered with their father, Alexander, from town to town in search of work. Alexander, who died when Pitirim was ten, was a craftsman who repaired and built Orthodox churches. As a result, Pitirim's youth was spent with priests and religious laity. Early on, Orthodox ritual and theology mixed with vestiges of Komi paganism to shape his view of the world. While secular and naturalistic studies stimulated his mind, the liturgy and rituals of the church disciplined his spirit. His religious commitment deepened with long periods of prayer and fasting, retreats to the wilderness for contemplation, and the practice of Christian asceticism. As his knowledge of the spirit deepened, Sorokin became a popular "teacher-preacher." His homilies were helpful to his fellow peasants, who often sought his advice on spiritual and practical matters.

Sorokin would later observe that "the moral precepts of Christianity, especially the Sermon on the Mount and the Beatitudes, decisively conditioned my moral values not only in youth but for the rest of my life. The roots of the Harvard Research Center in Creative Altruism, established by me in 1949, go back to these precepts of Jesus learned in my boyhood."[2] Religious training and Komi traditions conditioned the young Sorokin's thinking more deeply than he could then know. However, his spiritually driven views would soon be shattered by rebellions, revolutions, and imprisonments. The transformation began in 1903.

The Positivistic-Progressive Period

Sorokin's formal education expanded when, at age fourteen, he won a scholarship to the distant Khrenovo Teachers Seminary. This conser-

1. Sorokin left at least three autobiographical accounts: Sorokin 1924, Sorokin 1963, and "Sociology of My Mental Life," in Allen 1963. The most comprehensive biographical account is in Johnston 1995.
2. The Sermon on the Mount and the Beatitudes forecast happiness for those without wealth or comfort on earth: "Blessed are the poor, the sorrowful, the meek, the hungry, the merciful, the faithful, the peacemaker, and the pure of heart, for they all shall be comforted and rewarded" (Sorokin 1963, 41; cf. Mt 5:3–11). The remainder of the Sermon guides one toward a good spiritual and social life: Overcome anger, conquer lust, love your enemies, do not lie or judge others, pray, and follow the Golden Rule. In this sermon, Jesus also gave his followers the Lord's Prayer.

vative Orthodox seminary, which trained teachers for the synod's elementary schools, had unanticipated effects on Sorokin. There he was transformed from a callow teenager into a politicized intellectual and revolutionary. By age sixteen he was active in the Social Revolutionary Party and a strong voice in opposition to the czar, which eventually led to his expulsion from the seminary. He was first arrested in December 1906 and during his imprisonment celebrated his eighteenth birthday. The experience was surprisingly positive for Sorokin. The jail had a library, and there he began reading the political works of Mikhaylovsky, Lavrov, Kropotkin, Marx, Bakunin, Tolstoy, and Lenin. To these he added translations of works by Darwin and Spencer. Long conversations with other prisoners planted in him the seeds of new political ideas, an increasing disenchantment with monarchy, and a search for an ideological foundation for revolution. These were indeed weighty issues for the narrow shoulders of an eighteen-year-old.

Upon his release, Sorokin became an organizer for the Social Revolutionary Party in the Volga region of northern Russia. But czarist pressures soon drove him to St. Petersburg, where he continued his education. Lacking a gymnasium degree, he went to night school and prepared for the entrance examinations to the university. He passed these in May 1909 and over the next five years studied first at the Psycho-Neurological Institute and later at the University of St. Petersburg. In the process, the simple Christianity of a Komi peasant was sociologically transformed.

The Russian Masters

Sorokin's formal introduction to sociology came from E. V. de Roberty and M. M. Kovalevsky at the Institute. De Roberty, a Durkheimian, held that interaction was the basic unit of social behavior and sociological study. As products of interaction, social acts were irreducible to biological or psychological characteristics. Interaction also shaped thought and in the process produced language, through which humans defined the world, constructed identities, and developed knowledge that they used for cooperation, organization, and survival. Like Comte, de Roberty spoke of three modalities of thought: analytical-scientific, religious-philosophical, and artistic-aesthetic. While all were present in any given historical epoch, one dominated and shaped the cultural and individual mentality of the time. From de Roberty, Sorokin learned the basic assumptions of the sociological canon.[3]

3. De Roberty's modalities differ from Comte's in that his artistic-aesthetic does not correspond to Comte's metaphysical. Interestingly, two of Sorokin's principles of ulti-

Through Maksim M. Kovalevsky's teachings and two-volume text *Sociology*, Sorokin became deeply interested in social order and the dynamics of historical change. This teacher was a Comtean positivist, seriously engaged with the doctrines of progress and evolution. In him Sorokin saw how a disciplined mind used the comparative historical method to handle complexity and form historical generalizations. Kovalevsky's *Contemporary Sociologists* (1905) likely served as Sorokin's model for *Contemporary Sociological Theories*.

As the Institute's first chairman of sociology, Kovalevsky cast the discipline as both a theoretical and an applied undertaking. He encouraged an empirical, problem-oriented, historically grounded perspective. Theory and practice were sociology's twin pillars, and Kovalevsky provided Sorokin with a role model as a scholar-activist.

It was from the great scholar of law and morality Leon Petrazhitsky that Sorokin learned the dynamics of social organization. For Petrazhitsky, law was the foundation of social order, channeling basic emotions and biological drives into sets of rights and duties that prescribed and proscribed behaviors. Laws were also more coercive than were moral directives. While the imperative that the rich should give to the poor placed a moral obligation on the rich, for example, it did not mean that the poor could demand a portion of a rich person's wealth. But law institutionalized morality and specified the rights and duties of each party; it was imperative and attributive. The subject of a duty was required to perform it, and the subject of a right could demand gratification. By distributing rights and duties at the macrosociological level, laws specified the contents of a society's political, social, and economic institutions.

Petrazhitsky grounded law in the social psychological fabric of human nature. He also provided Sorokin with a rich model of order, power, and the role of collective mentalities as agents of civilizational change. More important, he taught Sorokin the theoretical and practical importance of altruism in social life. Petrazhitsky was deeply concerned with the relationship between justice and charity, and his "politics of law" sought to reconcile them. Sorokin's later interests in altruism and social improvement were similar to his (Gurvitch 1932, 103–4).

At the Institute and the University, Sorokin also studied with Vladimir Bekhterev and Ivan Pavlov. He sensed that these early behaviorists and competitors for priority in the discovery of the conditioned reflex

---

mate reality and cultural types—sensate and ideational—parallel those of de Roberty and Comte, and he used them in a similar manner.

were onto something foundational about human behavior. Indeed, their ideas—particularly Pavlov's—strongly influenced his 1922 ethnography of the great Russian famine, *Hunger as a Factor in Human Behavior* (reprinted 1975); his 1925 work, *The Sociology of Revolution*; and his two experimental studies of perceptions and rewards, published in the early 1930s (Sorokin 1932, 720–37; Sorokin, Tanquist, Parten, and Zimmerman 1930, 765–82). The last of these works appears as chapter 11 of this volume.

Sorokin received his undergraduate degree in 1914. Sociology was not yet offered at the University, so he continued studying with his masters through the faculty of law and economics, where sociology was taught as the theoretical basis for law. In 1916 he earned the magistrant of criminal law degree, specializing in penology and constitutional law. However, the Revolution delayed his thesis defense until 22 April 1922, and by 1919 a sociology department had been established at the University. After several additional years of study and teaching, he defended his two-volume *Sistema Sotsiologii* (published in 1920) for his doctor of sociology degree. Sorokin described these as years of great intellectual growth and development:

> Along with my enrichment of knowledge . . . I continued the work of integrating [it] into a unified, . . . consistent system or *Weltanschauung*. Philosophically, the emerging system was a variety of empirical neopositivism or critical realism based upon logical and empirical scientific methods. Sociologically, it represented a sort of synthesis of Comtean-Spencerian sociology of evolution-progress corrected and supplemented by the theories of . . . the Russian social thinkers, and . . . other western social scientists. Politically, it was a form of socialist ideology founded upon the ethics of solidarity, mutual aid, and freedom. All in all it was an optimistic *Weltanschauung*. . . . I did not foresee then that this scientific, positivistic, and progressively optimistic *Weltanschauung* would soon be found wanting by the crucial test of historical events. (Sorokin 1963, 75–76).

Despair

The time between 1914 and 1922 witnessed Sorokin's effort to combine intense academic work with gut-wrenching and dangerous political activities. In late 1916 Russia faced rising unrest in its cities and villages, a failing war effort, inflation, poverty, and hunger. With the autocracy in decline, Pitirim dedicated himself to Russia's survival. This campaign resulted in more arrests and brought him to the forefront of revolutionary activity. When the czar was deposed in 1917, he became a prominent political figure and the personal secretary to

Aleksander Kerensky in the short-lived post-Czarist government. It has been asserted that as holder of this office, Sorokin may have possessed greater political power than any other sociologist in the history of the discipline. As second in command of the July-to-November government, he had an office in the Winter Palace from which "he selected future ministers, [and] took an active part in all the events of those stormy days." It has also been reported that Sorokin was asked by a delegation of Komi representatives to become president of an independent Komi republic (Doykov 1996, 7).[4]

All of this came at great social and personal cost. The country was in ruin and Sorokin's life in constant danger. The Revolution had taken the lives of his two brothers and his three closest teachers: de Roberty was murdered in Tverskaia in 1915, Kovalevsky died in Petrograd in 1916, and Petrazhitsky committed suicide in Poland in 1917.

His sorrows deepened in 1918, when it became clear that his hopes for Russia had failed. With Lenin firmly in power, Sorokin was again on the run and would serve three longer and more brutal terms in Bolshevik jails. During his final imprisonment, Lenin ordered him shot. The petitions of key political figures led instead to Sorokin's pardon and eventual voluntary exile. This sixteen-year period of political activism ended on 22 September 1922, when Sorokin and his wife, Elena, left Moscow for Germany. By this time his sociology, politics, and philosophy were again changing. As he noted,

> World War I had made some fissures in the positivistic, "scientific," and humanistic *Weltanschauung* I held before the war. The Revolution of 1917 enormously enlarged these . . . [and] forced me . . . to sternly re-examine my prewar *Weltanschauung*. . . . This reconstruction took place slowly during five years in Communist Russia and then, after my banishment, in Europe and the United States. . . . It resulted in what I now call the *integral system* of philosophy, sociology, psychology, ethics, and values. Some indications of it are already noticeable in my Russian *Sistema Sotsiologii*. . . . [But] in their mature form the basic principles of integralism are systematically stated in my volumes published in the last three decades. (Sorokin 1963, 204–5)[5]

---

4. The claim to the greatest political power most likely resides with the philosopher and sociologist Thomas G. Masaryk, who was the first president of Czechoslovakia from 1918 to 1935. While widely known as a philosopher, he was also an active sociologist. See Kolegar 1967, Roucek 1938, and Masaryk 1970.

5. By "the last three decades," Sorokin means 1933 to 1963. The first date signals the year by which the major part of the research and writing for *Dynamics* was underway. The second date marks the publication of *Long Journey*.

Scientific Sociology and the Rise to a New Prominence

Sorokin's transition from empiricism to integralism was, as he observed, a slow one. Indeed, it took more than a decade. During this time the Sorokins moved from Berlin to Prague, where, as guests of President Thomas G. Masaryk, Pitirim taught at Charles University. The couple would likely have settled there had Sorokin not received an invitation from Edward C. Hayes and E. A. Ross to give a series of lectures in the United States on the Revolution.[6] Soon he found himself aboard the *Martha Washington* on his way to New York and another new beginning.

The émigré scholar arrived in New York City on 3 November 1923. After two months of working on his English and giving lectures at Vassar, he traveled the circuit of midwestern colleges, lecturing and looking for employment. Through Ross and F. Stuart Chapin he landed a job at the University of Minnesota. There, from 1923 to 1929, he became famous as an empirical-positivistic sociologist and wrote six books: *Leaves from a Russian Diary* (1924); *The Sociology of Revolution* (1925); *Social Mobility* (1927); *Contemporary Sociological Theories* (1928); *Principles of Rural–Urban Sociology,* with Carle C. Zimmerman (1929); and the first of the three volumes of *A Systematic Source Book in Rural Sociology,* with Zimmerman and Charles J. Galpin (1930). Reviews of the first two books showed Sorokin to be a controversial figure but one not to be ignored. The works on social mobility, rural sociology, and sociological theory defined their respective fields at the time and established Sorokin as a force to be dealt with in American sociology.

Leaves is an autobiographical account of Sorokin's revolutionary experiences between 1917 and 1922, while *The Sociology of Revolution* analyzes these uprisings as social events. Following a Pavlovian model, Sorokin conceptualizes human action in revolutions as a complex of primal and contradictory drives. Humans desire peace and war, express love and hate, and yearn for independence and domination. Normally these primitive urges are channeled by social structures into acceptable forms. But the first stage of revolution destroys the social

---

6. See Nichols 1996a. In this article, Nichols reveals the heretofore unknown story of how Ross and Sorokin became acquainted, a process he traces to a letter from Sorokin to Ross dated 16 December 1921 and two letters from Sorokin to Ross dated 26 July 1922 and 6 January 1923. While the invitation to come to the United States and lecture was probably unexpected (Sorokin 1963, 202), it was not spontaneous. Sorokin had established a scholarly relationship with Ross, a subtheme of which was a possible visit to the United States. Nichols's account amends that given by Sorokin and in my earlier treatment of this event (Johnston 1995, 20).

fabric and sets the primal urges free. With social disorder comes the second stage: violence and destruction. Terror and coercion, signs of the third stage, are then used to recondition behavior and form a new social order. In this final stage, suppression continues until the new social reflexes are so strong that additional conditioning is no longer needed. Sorokin uses this approach to analyze the Russian Revolution and, to a lesser extent, the revolutions of France, Germany, England, and Egypt. He concludes that revolution is an undesirable form of social change that often undermines the very reforms it seeks and as such should be avoided rather than advocated.[7] "The Perversion of Human Behavior in Revolution," chapter 18 of this volume, describes this process and its consequences.

Sorokin's next book, *Social Mobility*, was the first of his nonpolitical volumes in English. It made a major contribution to sociology and is often cited as a pioneering work in the study of social stratification. It also established Sorokin as a scientific sociologist. The data in *Mobility* were culled from an exhaustive cross-cultural search of the literature along with independently compiled information. Sorokin uses these data sets to explore core issues in stratification and mobility, among them the origins, universality, and types of stratification systems; the social, biological, and psychological characteristics of social classes; the types and dynamics of selection and mobility; ascription and achievement processes in stratification and mobility; and the consequences of social mobility. In his analysis, Sorokin develops several concepts that would structure future discourse in mobility studies: horizontal and vertical mobility, open and closed systems, and the mobility of strata and individuals. (For an overview of these ideas, see chapter 12 in this volume.) Unfortunately, the sociological development of this subfield was delayed by a lack of data and a sharp turn in the study of stratification toward field studies such as *Middletown* and *Yankee City*. Nonetheless, *Social Mobility* established Sorokin's intellectual priority in this area.

Contemporary Sociological Theories is Sorokin's most widely read, cited, reissued, and translated work. It offers a panoramic walk through the "forest of sociological theory," in which live nine major species (or schools) of sociological thought. Each of these, while tolerating multiple perspectives, consists of a theoretical system defined by a shared definition of reality and agreement on the key variables that

7. While some praised this work, it did not fare well among many sociologists; see Park 1926 and Grierson 1926. Both reviewers felt the book lacked objectivity and failed to advance a sociological understanding of revolution.

explain sociocultural phenomena. The purpose of *Theories* is to assist both novice and specialist in separating the "strong trees and beautiful flowers" from the "sterile plants and weeds." With this goal in mind, Sorokin describes major works in the nine traditions and gives readers a sense of their value. Strong theories, he says, study social action using inductive approaches, measurable concepts, systematically gathered data, statistical analysis, and multicausal explanations. Not surprisingly, these methods are in keeping with Sorokin's conception and practice of sociology.

In the underbrush of Sorokin's forest live the life-draining weeds of the discipline. Here one finds speculative philosophers and philosophers of history in communion with those who favor case analysis over statistical methods. Here also are scholars who agonize endlessly over the nature of sociology, pile words upon words, and contribute little to knowledge. The most virulent weeds of all are the "sociological preachers," condemned by Sorokin for their negativity, their pretensions of omniscience, and their tendency to create problems in the acceptance of true sociologists. This underbrush, says Sorokin, had to be replaced with a scientific garden; *Theories* would save sociology from intellectual dead ends and provide direction for its acceptance as a science. It was in this spirit that Sorokin evaluated the contributions of the schools.

His next book, *Principles of Rural–Urban Sociology,* was cast in the theoretical framework advocated in *Theories.* It was also the first of his coauthored English works with Carle C. Zimmerman, a lifelong colleague and friend. Intimately tied to it was the three-volume *Systematic Source Book in Rural Sociology* (1930–32). This compendium of theory and research begins with a theoretical interpretation of rural life from ancient to modern times and concludes with a systematic analysis of social organization, mobility, and stratification. The global scope of the data and analytical sources yields a foundation for generalization not bound by the narrow corridors of space and time conventionally walked by sociologists. The second volume of the *Source Book* offers an institutional analysis of rural life through a cross-cultural and extensive time series of observations on the family, the economy, education, morality, art, religion, and politics. The final volume quantitatively describes psychosocial, demographic, and biological characteristics of rural populations and concludes with a theoretical discussion of rural–urban relationships. Unprecedented in the 1930s, the scope of data and the institutional foci of these three volumes adumbrated the approach and contents of *Social and Cultural Dynamics.*

As impressive as their work was, Sorokin and Zimmerman were

unable at first to find a subsidy for its publication. But they did obtain a small grant on the condition that the three volumes be cut to one and published as a textbook. In 1929 *Principles* appeared and raised the practice of rural sociology from a culture-bound, empirically underdeveloped, and value-laden field of study to the "dignity of a natural science" (Anderson 1929, 328). The scope and theoretical character of the materials, the unprecedented data base, and the method of analysis make this work distinctive. *Principles* explores rural and urban existence through a social structural analysis that results in a true sociology of rural life. It avoids oversimplification and introduces readers to sociology as a generalizing science capable of nomothetically analyzing patterned and repetitive aspects of social life separated in time and space. The cross-cultural data also permit the authors to correct faulty generalizations of previous researchers. Finally, Sorokin and Zimmerman avoid the textbook pitfalls of entertaining simplicity and sociological preaching.

The publication of *Principles* and later the *Source Book* resulted in a synergism that transformed rural sociology both within and outside the University of Minnesota. There, Sorokin and Zimmerman became the teachers of teachers, developing a group of students whose works became important and influential.[8] In the process, they raised rural sociology from the stigma of provincialism and provided an exemplar for an empirically driven science of rural life at Minnesota. This exemplar was the basis of the "Sorokin-Zimmerman sociological school." Focused on social change, this school was antievolutionist, grounded in the Western intellectual tradition of the nineteenth and early twentieth centuries, and distinctive in its cross-cultural data base and methods of statistical analysis. For its members, scientific sociology had to be practical and useful; when done correctly, it guaranteed a quality of knowledge that could soften problems endemic to social change (Zimmerman 1973, 103–5).

Theories, the works in rural sociology, and *Mobility* demonstrated for students and practitioners the form and nature of scientific sociology. Unhappily, they also alienated three powerful groups of American sociologists. Sorokin's use of the term "sociological preacher" was particularly unfortunate. Many early presidents of the American So-

8. Among them were T. Lynn Smith, who wrote *Sociology of Rural Life;* Charles Price Loomis, who with J. Allen Beegle coauthored *Rural Social Systems* and *Rural Sociology: The Strategy of Change;* Paul Landis, who wrote *Rural Life in Process;* and Edgar A. Schuler, Nathan Whetten, Otis Durant Duncan, and Fred Frey, all of whom published widely in the field.

ciological Society were deeply concerned about public morality, social policy, and sociology. More than a few of them—Lester F. Ward, Franklin H. Giddings, W. I. Thomas, William G. Sumner, Albion Small, George E. Vincent, Edward C. Hayes, James P. Lichenberger, Ulysses G. Weatherly, and Charles L. Gillian—either had ministers as fathers or grandfathers or had themselves engaged in ministerial careers. In addition, there were five influential clergymen among the founders of the ASS. Undoubtedly, they were embarrassed and angered to be identified among the weeds of the discipline (Hinkle and Hinkle 1954, 1–17).

In a less strident manner, Sorokin had also offended those who engaged in speculative philosophy and the philosophy of history by claiming they were not even a part of the garden. What they did was not, in his estimation, sociology.

Finally, the powerful scholars of the Chicago School received from Sorokin neither their accustomed praise nor even prominent consideration. Their emphasis on ethnography and the case approach was in his judgment less valuable than statistical methods, which replaced simple ideographic description with more powerful nomothetic understandings. In *Mobility,* the works of Robert Park, Ernest Burgess, Ellsworth Faris, W. I. Thomas, and William Ogburn are relegated to footnotes or mentioned only among long lists of books concerned with the study of an issue. In *Theories,* Park and Burgess are identified with a Simmelian formalism that Sorokin stops just short of calling a sterile flower. He does call Albion Small's works on Marx and Gumplowicz "poorly informed and naive" in the first case and "loose and misleading" in the latter (Sorokin 1928, 520). Ogburn's theory of culture lag is judged as questionable and most likely incorrect. Thomas's four wishes receive passing attention in the text, while his book *The Unadjusted Girl* and his study (with Florian Znaniecki) *The Polish Peasant in Europe and America* are acknowledged in a footnote. The works of Faris are also mentioned only in footnotes and those of Louis Wirth and G. H. Mead not at all. Such disregard and caustic criticism continued in the *Source Book* and *Principles.* Indeed, it catalyzed decades of tension between Sorokin and those who practiced sociology in the Chicago tradition (Sorokin 1963, 224–29).

However, the late 1920s was a period of growth and change in sociology, and Sorokin's books were widely read and used to teach growing numbers of undergraduate and graduate students. While this gave him visibility and prominence, the works themselves were theoretically and methodologically innovative at a time when sociologists were looking for new ideas and direction. *Mobility, Theories, Princi-*

ples, and the *Source Book* made definitive contributions to major sub-fields and established Sorokin as a power in American sociology. It was on the basis of these works that he came to the attention of Harvard's president, Abbott Lawrence Lowell, and was invited to become the founding chairman of the Department of Sociology. In just seven years Sorokin had risen from the rank of émigré scholar to one of the most respected positions in the discipline.

The Integralist Stage

Harvard challenged Sorokin. Even before his arrival, he had written to Lowell to ask for an early sabbatical "in order to complete a work more important than any of my previous publications, the work which I hope to make worthy of the high standards of the works of the Harvard scholars" (Sorokin 1929; Sorokin 1963, 235–51; Johnston 1995, 54–83). Already established among the doyens of the discipline, Sorokin was now reaching for a place in the pantheon of scholars, and *Social and Cultural Dynamics* would be his vehicle. Success in this venture required more than an encyclopedic knowledge of history and erudite analysis; this work would have to be brilliant and grounded in a powerful set of explanatory principles that in a single stroke could account for a broad range of human experiences across space and time. Sorokin was seeking a major theoretical breakthrough grounded in a new epistemology. He would discover the dynamic principles driving social change.

Sorokin had been thinking about this possibility since 1928, and even then it had produced anxiety. By 1930, the anxiety gave way to apprehension and later to acceptance: "Come what may, it is better to fail in the achievement of a great task than to be successful in the accomplishment of a pedestrian purpose;" he eventually noted (Sorokin 1963, 235). Harvard demanded excellence, and from Sorokin's moments of doubt came a recommitment to seek greatness in the face of possible self-destruction (Sorokin 1963, 247).

In 1937, the first three volumes of *Dynamics* appeared. While each contains a massive amount of comparative quantitative data, they are not works of scientific sociology. Volume 1 develops a technical language defining cultural integration, cultural systems and congeries, and cultural mentalities. These concepts are then used to describe quantitative fluctuations in forms of art, music, literature, and architecture over 2500 years of Western civilization and comparable stretches of other civilizations. Volume 2 similarly describes fluctuations in systems of reasoning and truth (such as science, vitalism, and animism), ethics (absolutism, relativism), and law. The third volume focuses on variations in systems of social relations (family, government, economy), wars, revolts, and revolutions. In each of these areas, Sorokin finds fluctuations in substance but no intensifying advancement from primordial forms to higher levels of achievement and integration. Indeed, he uses his finding of a trendless flux to attack the idea of a progressive, linear evolution culminating in a modern age of science and progress.

Regrettably, reviews of the 1937 volumes were mixed, and the book fared poorly at Harvard and in the sociological community.[9] More important for our purpose, volume 4 of *Dynamics,* which contains the most powerful argument and evidence for Sorokin's integralism, was not published until 1941. By then, few sociologists were interested. In this volume, we learn that integralism is an epistemology, a theory of human nature, and a philosophy of history. While each of these elements is analytically distinct from the others, they combine in Sorokin's presentation of complex cultural supersystems and give great insight into the dynamics of society and of history.

Integralism as a system of truth and human nature posits that humans are three-dimensional creatures: they possess a body, a mind, and a soul. Each dimension knows the world differently and supports a distinctive epistemology. The body experiences reality through the senses and knows the world empirically. The mind seeks knowledge through reason and understands the world rationally. The soul, or supersensory capacity, develops from intuition, grace, and God's revelation. Through this third dimension, humans grasp the sublime or transcendent truths of their existence.

While all these capacities are present in every human society, Sorokin theorizes, one is always dominant over the others, accounting for differences in social life in different periods. In sensate cultures, for example, members develop a system of scientific thinking committed to progress that shapes their social organization and historical experience. Similarly, cultures can be based on the truths of faith, or of rationality. Sorokin's theory of cyclical social change thus focuses on ages dominated by rational, empirical, spiritual, or mixed cultural mentalities and their cultural supersystems. He tests this model against the historical experiences of Western and other societies. The results, he says, indicate the need for deeper, integral understanding of human

9. *Dynamics* was a major publishing event of 1937. The *New York Times* and the *New York Herald Tribune* gave it prominent coverage in their book review sections, including large pictures of Sorokin. The Book-of-the-Month Club chose the work as its July selection, and it was the most widely reviewed sociological work from the period 1937–42; see Tibbs 1943. For a comprehensive discussion of the reviews and Sorokin's replies, see Johnston 1995, 114–23.

history. Past attempts to comprehend the psychosocial world using only one system of truth were always incomplete. The integral system binds the three dimensions of truth in a way that more closely approximates their presence in historical experience. Therefore, it is a more complete way of understanding history. Similarly, integral concepts of society and personality are more satisfying than those of earlier models because they better reflect and incorporate the heterogeneity of their essences. Through integralism, we come to know ourselves, the social structures we make, and the world we live in more completely.

Indeed, it was the insights of integralism and his historical analysis that drove Sorokin to consider the problem of social crisis and reconstruction. However, *Dynamics* also signaled the next step in the development of his general sociology, one that had begun in the *Sistema Sotsiologii,* in which he had put forward a well-developed theory of social structure and organization. With *Dynamics,* he now set in place the long-missing theory of social change and used it as a bridge to his crisis and social reconstruction studies of the 1940s through 1960s.

Integralism was pivotal for Sorokin because it combined all the worldviews he had previously embraced. Clearly, his Russian years had been split between those based on the truths of faith and those founded on the truths of science, which came together only after he had for many years been practicing the empirical-positivistic sociology that made him famous in the United States. At the same time, he increasingly realized the limits of empiricism and sought a worldview more inclusive of the characteristics of humanity, society, and history. In this quest he broke with empiricism and became an integral sociologist. This transition would cast Sorokin as a philosopher of history, a weed in the sociological garden.[10]

Prophetic Sociology and the Crisis of Modernity

From his analysis of the Western historical experience, Sorokin concluded that this civilization had passed through the stages of sensate, ideational, and idealistic supersystems twice and was now in the declining period of a third sensate era. As in the past, these were times of destruction and crisis. But the evidence from *Dynamics* suggested a crisis more terrifying and dangerous than earlier ones. One global war and a series of major revolutions had already taken place, and

10. For more on Sorokin's integralism, see Ford 1963, 33–66; Allen 1963, 371–89; Ford 1996; and Sorokin 1957. In the review that opened this essay, Kolb reached the same conclusion about Sorokin's transformation, although he did not make the ironic connection to *Contemporary Sociological Theories.*

the world was embroiled in what would become the second global confrontation. In addition, the moral fiber of society was weakening. People were losing faith in the objectivity and value of their systems of truth, justice, and law. Codes of right and wrong were no longer valued as appropriate standards for conduct; instead, they had become devices by which the rich and powerful could consolidate their privileges and manipulate disadvantaged underclasses. Even more dangerous was the growing sense that only the childlike and the dull treated others with honesty and respect. The wily citizen of the modern age sought advantage, not fairness, in interpersonal relationships. This ethos undermined civility and eroded the foundations of relationships. Knowledge, too, had become instrumental and pragmatic at the personal and group levels. Love of learning, aesthetics, and creativity declined as people became increasingly trained rather than educated. Rationality pervaded human relationships, and people became frighteningly comfortable in an overly rationalized world. There was a crisis of the human spirit that promised as much damage as the new weapons of mass destruction. This was a time of crisis that required the skills of the scholar and the activist. It was this conviction, predicated on *Dynamics,* that moved Sorokin to become a prophetic sociologist.

His commitment to prophecy was clearly tempered by his skills as a sociologist. Early on, Sorokin had perceived a connection between descriptive/nomothetic science and prescriptive ethics. While the ethicist was concerned with what ought to be, and the scientific sociologist with what is, their work could be linked. The practical ethicist often lacked the knowledge of social life necessary to develop effective protocols for specific situations. The sociologist, meanwhile, could provide information about the contextual understandings through which moral principles are transformed into appropriate actions. The possibility of this conceptual partnership motivated Sorokin (and other sociologists) to improve the discipline as a science. He believed that just as dealing with biological facts had made for better medicine, discovering social facts and making them widely known would enable scientists and ethicists to reduce human injustice and help society live more wisely. Progress in social and moral reconstruction would be greatly enhanced by such an arrangement (see "Sociology and Ethics," chapter 21 of this volume).

In this spirit, Sorokin labored to educate specialists and citizens about the modern crisis and to stimulate commitment to improvement. In 1941, he published volume 4 of *Dynamics,* as well as *The Crisis of Our Age* and the "Declaration of Independence of the Social Sciences" (see chapter 5). These works were followed by *Man and Society in*

Calamity (1942) and two articles on the nature of conflict and reconciliation: "The Cause and Factors of War and Peace" (1942) and "The Conditions and Prospects for a World without War" (1944), chapters 19 and 20 in this volume. *Crisis* condenses and popularizes *Dynamics*, while *Calamity* is a study in the sociology of disasters. Along with the war studies, these books were attempts to inform and mobilize people for social action. They combine analysis with moral injunctions and wrap Sorokin in the cloak of prophetic sociology.

Robert W. Friedrichs's conception of changes in the sociological tradition is particularly appropriate for analyzing Sorokin's transformation from priestly to prophetic sociology (Friedrichs 1970, 57–110). In Friedrichs's terms, priestly practitioners are committed to a sociology modeled on the natural sciences. They practice rites of value neutrality, venerate objective analysis, and suspect blasphemy in all forms of knowledge other than the empirical. They surrender themselves to the exegesis of order and the divination of empirical laws for predicting the future. Priestly sociologists also use a special language (mathematics), serve long novitiates in graduate schools mastering the liturgy and rituals of research, and form a community committed to empirical truth (Fitch 1958, 368–70). They are often the interpreters between laity and literati because the former lack the expertise to understand the methods and findings of the latter. This dynamic encourages dependency, and, paradoxically, these priests often ask followers to accept their findings on faith (Bendix 1951, 190).

Prophets are driven by other goals. Their sociology goes beyond science to the improvement of society. They are value-committed critics, activists, and polemicists. The prophetic tradition in social theory extends from Comte and the "Prophets of Paris" to Karl Mannheim, Pitirim Sorokin, Robert Lynd, Robert MacIver, and Louis Wirth (Friedrichs 1970, 74).

Sorokin's prophetic works sent clear messages to both lay and professional readers: There is a modern crisis, as described and analyzed in *Dynamics* and the jeremiad *Crisis*. Sensate culture is only one of several forms that modern life might take; *Dynamics* describes earlier, successful ways of living that could also serve as models for our future. However, we are not determined by these. An alternative is the integral society, which fuses the strengths of past civilizational forms into a more viable and creative whole. This type of civilization could replace functional rationality with substantive direction and moral relativity with absolute values.

For Sorokin, epistemology and morality are intertwined. Sensate epistemology and science can produce no eternal truths, he says, just probabilities; hence, as a system of knowing, even its fundamentals are in continuous flux. Yesterday's truths are tomorrow's myths. It follows that any system of morality based on this form of understanding is relative and predicated on all things remaining constant. Since this is hardly ever the case, the basis for morality is also constantly in flux. Integralism provides a more inclusive epistemology and consequently a more stable basis for understanding and morality; allowing moral relativity to be replaced by a set of absolute values. Consequently, Sorokin reasons, one could expect a more peaceful and fulfilling way of life. The question he left dangling was, How does this come to be so? At this point Sorokin had no answer, but he did have ideas. These were later developed and promoted through the Harvard Research Center in Creative Altruism.

As a prophetic sociologist, Sorokin became isolated from the profession, but not entirely unwillingly (Becker 1950, 196–98). To him mainstream sociology had begun to seem exceedingly empirical, methodologically dominated, and sterile. Furthermore, by 1944, his situation at Harvard had changed. Talcott Parsons had become chairman of sociology, and in 1946 he led a successful movement that did away with the department. The new Department of Social Relations held little interest or opportunity for Sorokin. By then, however, his professional goals had moved beyond activism toward the theoretical study of social reconstruction.[11]

The Sociology of Moral and Social Reconstruction

Above all else, Sorokin was a sociologist, and his interest in the Harvard Research Center in Creative Altruism was a product of his professional concerns. As Lawrence T. Nichols shows in his translation of Sorokin's study of Tolstoy as a philosopher (chapter 8 of this volume), the two men shared a major set of convictions about the nature of the world, humanity, and how life is best lived. These basic values were grounded in their shared ethnicity and philosophy, a Russian worldview committed to the importance of feelings over rationality and science; the centrality of the soul and of God; the importance of love; and the values of peace, equality, and altruism.

Indeed, in this model, God, love, and happiness are the roots of personal and social peace. They are also the answers to the four most enduring questions in philosophy: (1) What is the essence of the world?

11. Sorokin's prophetic sociology is only one element in his replacement and this great change. For more comprehensive accounts of these events, see Johnston 1986 and Nichols 1996b.

(2) What is the essence of the "I"? (3) What is the relationship between the "I" and the "not-I"? (4) Who am I, and how am I to live? The essence of the world is God. The essence of the "I" is the soul. The relationship between the "I" and the "not-I" is the difference between wisdom and knowledge. Wisdom comes from the knowledge of God and the growth of the soul. The "not-I" is the world of knowledge (facts, analysis, theory), which tells us of many things but little of the ultimate concerns of existence. Finally, one should live happily, and true happiness comes from connection to God and to others. We connect through love, which nourishes the soul and bonds the one to the many. When individuals and groups actualize their spiritual natures, they are happy and at peace. When cultural and social arrangements become obstacles to spiritual realization, suffering and conflict result.

Sorokin recognized that these tenets were incorporated in most of the world's major religions. Indeed, he ends *Crisis* by asserting that this is the direction the prophets and their followers should take. Had he stopped there, many of his critics and supporters would have been correct: Sorokin was looking for a new ideational or idealistic age of faith and had become a modern Jeremiah, exhorting us to prepare for the coming Kingdom of God. But Sorokin the sociologist recast his philosophy in academic terms: A common denominator of the essence of the world, the "I," wisdom, and proper living is love. It ties humans to one another and to the transcendent, promotes a commitment to wisdom, and enables one to live a life of connection and happiness with others. In consequence, it promotes peace and reduces suffering, raising an interesting psychosocial question: How does one cultivate the growth of love personally, in primary and secondary groups, in community, and in society, thereby increasing amity and reducing conflict?

In short, Sorokin was looking for an answer similar to that put forth by his countryman Peter Kropotkin in *Mutual Aid: A Factor of Evolution.* Based on his historical and naturalistic studies, Kropotkin asserts that the evolution of animals and the ethical and social progress of humans results not from struggle but from learning to cooperate and help others. Love and related emotions were, to Sorokin's mind, the foundation for such prosocial behavior. Consequently, increasing them promoted mutual aid and the progressive evolution of humankind (Jaworski 1993, 72). The social implementation of this goal became the focal concern of the Harvard Research Center in Creative Altruism.

The opportunity for Sorokin to pursue this interest was provided in 1942 by Eli Lilly, who was convinced that the sociologist could

successfully determine the direction for the moral and intellectual re-
generation of society. At the time, Sorokin was preoccupied with other
works and did not contact Lilly until 1946. He then proposed an institute where scholars could study the modern crisis and find ways of
avoiding catastrophe. Lilly promptly responded by pledging financial
support for the venture.[12] The first grant was for $20,000, which Soro-
kin used to formulate a mission statement, commission original studies
of altruism, and begin his study *The Reconstruction of Humanity*
(1948). This book served as the Center's exemplar and guided its
fourteen-year research program.

Sorokin's initial studies show that love and altruism had been
largely ignored by psychologists and sociologists. These professionals
regularly focused on negative social acts (crime, family violence, discrimination) but stigmatized the study of prosocial behavior and love
as nonscientific exercises in sociological preaching. The Center, however, was committed to discovering the nature of these entities and to
learning how to produce, accumulate, and use them to nurture better
individuals and more cooperative social relationships. The results of
Sorokin's efforts were reported in a number of books and articles, most
notably. *Altruistic Love: A Study of American Good Neighbors and
Christian Saints* (1950), *Explorations in Altruistic Love and Behavior:
A Symposium* (1950), *Social Philosophies of an Age of Crisis* (1950),
S.O.S.: The Meaning of Our Crisis (1951), *Forms and Techniques of
Altruistic and Spiritual Growth: A Symposium* (1954), *The Ways and
Power of Love* (1954), and *Power and Morality: Who Shall Guard
the Guardians?* (1959). An overview of the Center's philosophy, theoretical concerns, publications, research findings, and aspirations was
published as "Studies of the Harvard Research Center in Creative Altruism" (chapter 23 of this volume). These were Sorokin's efforts as
an applied sociologist to develop practical algorithms for human improvement and social reconstruction.

Sorokin's General and Specific Sociologies

Many of Sorokin's early works defined the character of the discipline
and demonstrated how sociologists think and do research. His greatest

12. Sorokin's recollection of this event in *Long Journey* is blurred and imprecise.
He reported receiving an unsolicited letter in the winter of 1946 offering him a large
sum of money to advance the altruism project. The letter was signed by a man unknown
to him—Eli Lilly (Sorokin 1963, 276). But he apparently confused the 1942 and 1946
contacts: existing archival records show that Lilly was the first to contact Sorokin but
that Sorokin himself raised the question of research support.

efforts (for example, *Social Mobility, Contemporary Sociological Theories,* and the works in rural sociology) provided templates for practitioners and had the desired effect of creating malleable disciplinary boundaries to be expanded and surpassed by future generations. For these he is rightfully remembered. But other of his groundbreaking efforts have been overlooked; including his general sociology, which advanced the discipline's early efforts to create a common lexicon and taxonomy. These basic scientific tools were essential to standardizing the asking and answering of sociological questions. Similarly, his pioneering efforts in crisis and altruism studies have been forgotten or ignored. Yet his works in the former area offer important insights into modernity and group dynamics, and those in the latter adumbrate directions now taken in the study of conflict resolution, the sociology of emotions, and the study of prosocial behavior.[13] As such, they opened new horizons for innovation and added grist for the sociological mill. These studies represent part of Sorokin's historic contributions to the field and offer possible directions for future research.

A General Sociology of Order and Change

Sorokin's earliest systematic thinking on social order and change is found in his doctoral dissertation, the two-volume *Sistema Sotsiologii.*

13. Although the technical language identifying many of these areas of study has shifted over the years, Sorokin's place in their lineage is clearly acknowledged. The *World Encyclopedia of Peace* recognizes his pioneering contributions to war and peace studies: *Dynamics* is cited along with the work of Quincy Wright as laying the foundation for the modern study of war (Laszlo and Yoo 1986, 2:533). While Sorokin's notion of value gap and integration as major factors underlying war and peace was contested earlier, this integrationalist view has gained support in recent studies of conflict and its resolution. Modern integrationalists argue that the decline in wars among European nations resulted largely from an assimilation of common economic, political, and social values and institutions. Indeed, it is this bonding of culture and organization that has made war increasingly less likely in Europe; outside of Europe, however, cultural integration lags, making conflict more likely. Interestingly, the world has become divided into zones of peace and war based, in part, on cultural similarities and differences.

Later in the *Encyclopedia* Sorokin is recognized as a significant figure in the history of peace studies and his *Crisis* is cited as a major contribution to the psychology of peace and peace research (Laszlo and Yoo 1986, 2:411–12 and 4:123, 127, 132). Similarly, Rapoport 1974, 263, identifies Sorokin along with Wright and Lewis F. Richardson as the most prominent pioneers of early peace research.

In other areas, Gordon W. Allport cites Sorokin's contributions to the empirical study of sympathy, and Peter Lenrow locates him in the early tradition of altruism and sympathy studies (Allport 1985, 13; Lenrow 1978, 264). He is also recognized by Beverly Cuthbertson-Johnson, David D. Franks, and Michael Dornan (1994, 17, 70, 200–202) for his contributions to the study of love, the relationship of love to social identity and role acquisitions, and the relationship of emotions to sociocultural context.

As a work of science, it signaled the end of his formative stage and reflected the influence of his Russian masters. The *Sistema* was planned as an eight-volume series in general sociology. The first two volumes (the only ones published) focused on social "analytics" (structure). These were to be a prelude to the longer study of social "mechanics" (process). There is no English translation of the *Sistema* at this time, but the volumes have been summarized by Wsevolod W. Isajiw, whose interpretation Sorokin read and endorsed in 1950 (Isajiw 1950, 290–319). Isajiw notes that the first half of *Society, Culture, and Personality* reproduces the framework of the *Sistema* almost literally (Isajiw 1950, 292).

In both of these works, Sorokin presents his orientation to sociology before his exegesis of social analytics. Not surprisingly, this orientation reflects the positivistic-progressive (scientific) stage of his development. He posits that sociology is a science constructed along the lines of the natural sciences and as such focuses on society as it is, avoids questions of what ought to be, and studies observable, measurable phenomena. It does not dwell on wishes or emotions but on concrete actions. Sociological objectivity demands abandoning the monistic belief that the laws of nature and of society combine into a single, harmonious force. These laws are different, and even though the method of determining them is the same, a distinctive sociological theory is required.

Sociology's basic unit of study is human interaction and its consequences. Other disciplines examine specific types of interaction (economic, religious, and so on), but sociology concerns all of them as well as the characteristics common to all of them. It explains how they combine to form social systems and the consequences these systems have for their participants. In scientific terms, if all the institutional forms of interaction are equal to N, then sociology is the discipline of N and $N + 1$. These and other of Sorokin's early thoughts on the discipline are found in "The Boundaries and Subject Matter of Sociology" (1913) and "Sociology as a Science" (1931), chapters 1 and 3 of this volume. These articles demonstrate his first formulation of the issue while still in Russia and his pre-*Dynamics* orientation at the beginning of his tenure at Harvard.

Sorokin's comprehensive theory of interaction combines two complementary activities. The first is a three-dimensional theoretical sociology consisting of social analytics, social mechanics, and social genetics (an investigation of the historical patterns of societal development). The second, applied sociology, involves the implementation of the discoveries of theoretical sociology to ameliorate problems created by social change.

The Character, Importance, and Forms of Interaction

Interaction occurs when the behavior of an individual is the result of the action of another individual (or individuals). Sociology focuses on such external acts, studies their impact on other observable acts, and ends with an external act. According to Sorokin, the sociologist's task is to understand the what, the why, and the connections among actions. This does imply studying such nonobservable entities as aspirations and motivations, but Sorokin insists that interpretive inquiry be kept to a minimum.

The constitutive elements of social interaction are well known: two or more people, who condition one another's behavior; their actions; and the vehicles that transmit their actions. Vehicles are the conductors through which meanings, values, and norms are objectified and transmitted—for example, language and writing, signs, gestures, and rituals.

Sorokin observes that a large number of need-oriented interactions provide the foundation for social institutions. In turn, a system of institutions constitutes a complex network of need satisfactions called a society. When people agree on how to live and how to satisfy their desires in a given environment, they organize and cooperate. When they differ, they split into interest groups and compete, or else they form separate societies. Thus, interaction is the basic force from which all groups originate and the mechanism through which dynamic collective life is expressed.

Sorokin next describes types of interaction and the groups with which they are commonly associated. Solidary interactions involve actors who share common values and behaviors and cooperate to reach goals; the groups that result are typically primary groups. Antagonistic interactions reflect opposing values and competition. They are frequently manifested in formal, goal-oriented, compulsory relationships in which authority is exploitative, ideologies develop to legitimate the exploitation, and there is hostility among group members. Between these two extremes we find the contractual interactions of secondary groups. These groups combine cooperation and competition along with affective and instrumental behaviors. Formality dominates, the interactions are limited to defined times and places, and behavior lacks spontaneity. Such contract-based relationships are typically short-lived but make up much of social life in advanced societies.

Further on, Sorokin cautions readers that while each form of interaction has concrete examples—a family, a conscript army, and a commercial enterprise, respectively—one should think of them as forms of interaction, not concrete groups. To confuse them with real historical groups obscures the fact that these forms of interaction are present at different times in the fabric of all groups (Sorokin 1947, 93–119). Hence the classification of groups should be grounded in a different set of characteristics.

The Characteristics of Groups and Personalities

The second volume of *Sistema* opens with an overview of social groups, moving from the simplest to the most complex. For Sorokin, groups have a real existence and bind people through functional and causal bonds. Such bonds can be based on kinship, race, gender, religion, ethnicity, or social class, each of which promotes different antagonisms and solidarities. Each group conditions the behavior of its members differently, and a complex of memberships locates an individual in social space.

Sorokin discusses three types of groups, distinguished by the number of ties that members share: the elementary-unibonded group, the cumulative-multibonded group, and the complex social aggregate. The most important elementary units are the biological and sociocultural groups that we join at birth—those based on race, gender, territory, kinship, wealth, religion, and language. They determine our position in a web of social relationships that shapes the cultural content of our life-world.

The most important cumulative-multibonded groups are those that bind elementary groupings to maximize social power and competitive advantage. Size, resources, and organization are key factors here. Multibonded groups can be open or closed, solidary or antagonistic. If they are solidary, members share well-integrated, consistent imperatives for behavior and enjoy stable, long-lasting relationships. Conversely, antagonistic multibonded groups are affected by contradictory norms that undermine consistent social actions and threaten viability. Persistence is also influenced by the group's adaptiveness to a particular historical time and place. "Typical" multibonded groups are well adjusted to their sociohistorical and territorial environments; their "atypical" counterparts are not.

The third level of organization is the complex social aggregate, or national population. Sorokin defines it as the social-geographical space occupied by a substantial number of unibonded and multibonded groups. The characteristics of the national population are found in the overlapping of these groups. If we think of each group as a circle, the boundaries of the population (society) will be determined by the space enclosed within all the circles.

When discussing the basic structure of and relationships among elementary groups, cumulative groups, and complex social aggregates, Sorokin was fond of using a chemical analogy. Cumulative groups result from the combination of different elementary groups in the same way that chemical compounds result from the bonding of different elements. Clearly the number of possible combinations, chemically and sociologically, is vast. As in chemistry, some sociological elements will be in a great number of compounds, while others are only in a few. In addition, some compounds are stable and long-lasting, and others are more volatile and short-lived. Such is also the case in the sociological universe. The most important elementary units combine in many different ways to form complex sociocultural entities. Again, depending on the combination, place, and time, some will be more stable and long-lasting than others. In Sorokin's construction, these stable multibonded groups persist while their unstable counterparts do not.

To determine the structure of a society, one must know what unibonded and multibonded groups are involved; how stable (typical) or unstable (atypical) the combination is for its territory and time; which multibonded groups are solidary and which are antagonistic; which groups are open and which are closed; and which groups are most important for the continuity of the society. It is also important to know the rate at which group membership changes as well as the types of old groups that have disappeared and new ones that have taken their place.

Sorokin ends the discussion of group characteristics by considering the relationship between social structure and personality. Here he asserts that personality is socially constructed and its contents are determined by the groups to which an individual belongs. Each group provides imperatives for behavior and through them forms a slice of a person's mentality or ego. Hence there are as many egos as there are groups and combinations in which the individual participates. Behavior is the net result of group pressures and imperatives. If pressures are consistent, then behavior is purposive and unambiguous. If social imperatives are contradictory, the individual experiences ambivalence and indecisiveness but acts in compliance with the strongest of the contradictory forces. This behavior, in Paretan terms, could easily be irrational but consistent with a person's preferences. It follows that when one's position in a system of social coordinates changes, his or her ego and actions will also change. This is the condition of humanity,

and Sorokin maintains that it is senseless to speak of the problem of
the individual and society because the content of personal identity is
constituted in and coterminous with a network of social relationships.
Thus, Sorokin concludes, "as previously we have expressed the group
in terms of individuals, so now we have defined the individual in terms
of the group; in this we have elucidated the phenomenon from two
sides and have closed the circle . . . broken in the beginning but unbro-
ken in reality" (Isajiw 1950, 319). That is, the individual and the group
are both constituted in the process of interaction.[14]

The Internal Dynamics of Social Structure

The *Sistema* continued to evolve in the United States. It became the
foundation of Sorokin's introductory course on social organization
and change at Minnesota and of his Sociology A at Harvard. It reached
maturity in *Society, Culture, and Personality,* in which it was expanded to explain how groups regulate members' behavior.

This process, says Sorokin, requires a system of rules differentiated
by demand for compliance as well as the power of sanctions. The
group's core meaning and values are expressed and protected in a body
of law-norms. Drawing on the ideas of Petrazhitsky, Sorokin proposes
that these rules distribute obligatory rights and duties among interacting parties. While most people obey them out of commitment to
the values they convey, a few lack such wisdom, and compulsory enforcement becomes necessary. Sanctions are then enforced by fellow
members or agents of authority in a bureaucracy or the state. All organized groups use law-norms to protect core values and maintain order.
These norms coexist with other forms of social control, including un-
official law-norms (alternative norms), which emerge because formal
laws often lag behind social changes that make them obsolete or in
need of fine-tuning. For example, "Thou shalt not speed" may be interpreted variantly in different places and at different times of the day
even though the official rule is clear. So official laws often develop a
range of toleration that makes them more adaptive to particular situations. In addition, many social relationships are only minimally regulated by law-norms. For example, among family and friends, most behavior is guided by customs and folkways, which may through time
modify or replace the law-norms.

Unlike law-norms, folkways and customs are imperatives that urge
a form of behavior rather than entitle someone to demand that con-

---

14. The *Sistema* ended with this section on personality but was followed by a commentary from V. V. Sapov.

duct. Moral norms such as those provided by the Ten Commandments and the Sermon on the Mount are cases in point. They are driven only by the ethical standards of the actor, while law-norms have other means of enforcement.[15]

More analytically, Sorokin uses Petrazhitsky's concept to explain order in groups and institutions. Law-norms separate behavior into three classes—required, recommended, and prohibited—and carefully specify behaviors at all levels of society. At the macrosociological level, for instance, the state organizes proscriptions based on demand for compliance and severity of violation into felonies, misdemeanors, and torts. All social groups (primary or secondary) and institutions also develop authority structures. The rights and duties of each member determine where she or he fits in the stratified group. The law-norms crystallize who is in control of key institutions such as the economy, the family, or a university. Therefore, the structure and dynamics of each group, institution, or national population is the mere consequence of the operation of law-norms. Sorokin concludes that from the division of norms into obligatory, recommended, and prohibited flows a precise definition of rights, duties, functions, and roles that identifies the status of groups at all levels of society and yields a system of stratification and social control. Petrazhitsky's concept thus provides an elegant, integrated, and powerful principle for understanding organization and action at all levels of sociocultural integration.

The Classification of Groups

Continuing his chemical metaphor, in *Society, Culture, and Personality* Sorokin again classifies groups as elementary or unibonded groups (UBGs) and multibonded or compounded groups (MBGs). All groups are integrated by two forces: causal-functional integration, based on the intensity of identification and relationships maintained by members; and meaningful integration, stemming from the commitment to core values, meanings, and norms. UBGs are those integrated by a single system of meanings, norms, and values based on the biosocial and sociocultural characteristics that identify their members. MBGs are those integrated by two or more systems of meaning into more complex units. Table 1 contains examples of each type of group and allows us to grasp their interrelationships. In this classification scheme,

---

15. Sorokin also discusses technical norms, which tell us how to do something, and norms of etiquette or fashion. These are congeries of norms that are important in different contexts but must be substantially transformed to become law-norms.

TABLE 1. Classification of Groups

I. Important Unibonded Groups (Centered around the Main Values)	II. Important Multibonded Groups (Made by a Combination of Two or More Unibonded Values)
A. Biosocial characteristics 1. Race 2. Gender 3. Age	
B. Sociocultural characteristics 4. Kinship 5. Territorial proximity 6. Language (nationality) 7. State 8. Occupation 9. Economics 10. Religion 11. Politics 12. Scientific, philosophical, aesthetic, educational, recreational, ethical, and other ideological values 13. A nominal group of the elite: leaders, geniuses, and historical persons	1. Family 2. Clan 3. Tribe 4. Nation 5. Caste 6. Social order 7. Social class

Sorokin shifts from social ties and action to shared meanings as the key factor in social structure.

There are two problems inherent in this classification: the variety of MBGs is enormous, so little would be gained from a total inventory; and the logical classes of meaning and the boundaries of social groups are not identical (in other words, the same meanings are frequently shared by a number of different groups). Therefore, the classification scheme needs further refinement. Sorokin accomplishes this by focusing on historically significant MBGs. He asks: What groups in complex social aggregates have actually been permanent and powerful, and what core values, norms, and meanings have typified them in different historical periods and settings? Based on this approach, he identifies the types listed in the table and argues that they have shaped the main lines of social differentiation and guided human destiny for some time.

Sorokin extends his formulation and builds on his chemical analogy when he writes of affinities among multibonded groups. In chemistry, affinity refers to the attraction between elements that causes them to form compounds easily. But chemistry, he says, has advanced to the point at which the main combinations of affined elements are well

known; social science has not. Sorokin therefore explores groups affined in one-to-one combinations through bonds of race, gender, age,
kinship, and territory (Sorokin 1947, 239–41). From these, he suggests
a model of increasing complexity based on the most common and important MBGs. This model consists of two series: one including the
family, the clan, the tribe, and the nation; the other, consisting of the
caste, the estate, and the social class. The typicality of these MBGs
across historical space and time makes them modal structures and
yields important insights into patterns of social organization and personality. According to Sorokin, however, previous attempts to analyze
these groups lacked precision and accuracy. His specification of basic
elements and combinations allows more rigor and clarity of analysis
and consequently a better model of social structure and organization.

Sorokin begins his work on complex MBGs with the most fundamental yet most complex of the biosociological units, the family. It
compounds lifelong ties of kinship, age, gender, race, territory, language, culture, religion, occupation, and economics. The family is the
only true all-embracing community. Its unique structure and functions
shape the lives of billions of people and thereby strongly influence
broader sociocultural processes (Sorokin 1947, 246–47).

The next level of kinship organization, the clan, appears regularly
across a broad spectrum of human experience. It combines a number
of families of shared race, territory, language, culture, and ownership
of cooperative economic ventures. Clans are less solidary than families
because they combine sibs, so the relationship to a common ancestor
is less immediate. Clans are also relatively closed groups with a strong
sense of unity, cooperation, and continuity. They represent a common
form of nomadic and agrarian social organization.

Tribes consist of two or more clans bound by dwelling area, culture,
and kinship. They often operate as primitive states rather than as families. They are more open than clans as well as less solidary, larger, more
formally organized politically, and more specialized economically than
the groups that compose them. They represent a significant form of
prenational social organization.

Kinship as the basis for social organization stops with the tribe, at
which point increasing numbers and diversification of ties leads to the
appearance of states and nations. But what distinguishes a state from
a nation? In its primordial form, says Sorokin, the state was similar
to the clan and the tribe, and its power was coterminal with that of
these groups. Only later did it become an entity in and of itself. This
process was triggered by population growth and the need for a more
complex order, which required a formal system of laws and an organi-

zational structure capable of meeting challenges to collective survival. Although the state fulfills these functions, it is not an MBG but a socio-cultural grouping that maintains a set of relationships within an MBG. In contrast, the nation is a three-bonded group defined by territory and language that includes the state as the central element in its organizational and operational structure. The nation is the largest of MBGs and paradoxically is held together by the least complex bonds of structure.

Sorokin next turns to castes, estates, and social classes. These stratified groups have organized economic life, status, and power in a number of large and important societies. Even though its basis has been outlawed, caste is still a basic element of social structure and personal identity in India. A caste is a closed, endogamous group with high solidarity, fluid organization that is bound by ties of race, kin, territory, language, occupation, and religion. Caste life is directed by sacred law, so religion is the foundation for the system. All of the castes have their own occupations, whose interplay is regulated at the community level. In short, caste is an important social marker that places the Hindu in a network of social relations structured by an elaborate system of etiquette, privilege, and obsequiousness.[16]

Estates are hereditary groups that are more open and exogamous but less stable and solidary than castes. While they represent phenomenon of the state, their influence in Western societies has declined over the centuries, and for the most part they have been replaced by social classes.

Social class is one of the most troublesome concepts in the sociological lexicon. Sorokin maintains that no existing theory—including those of Marx, Veblen, Sumner and Keller, Warner and Lunt—rendered an adequate definition or classification of classes. His sociological chemistry, however, allows analysts to isolate eight defining features of them. Classes are (1) legally open but socially semi-closed; (2) typical; (3) solidary; (4) antagonistic to other social classes; (5) organized, in varying degrees, to pursue common interests; (6) conscious, in differing degrees, of their own existence and unity; (7) characteristic of Western society in the eighteenth, nineteenth, and twentieth centuries; and (8) held together by two unibonded ties (occu-

16. Sorokin observes that the caste concept had been picked up by many students of race relations in America; see, for example, Dollard 1937 and Davis, Gardner, and Gardner 1945. However, others had argued that the two systems were fundamentally different. Oliver C. Cox, for instance, regularly wrote on race and caste as ways of obscuring the basic fact that black exploitation was grounded in social class considerations (Cox 1945, 1948).

pational and economic) and one tie of social stratification (that is, they define their social boundaries by contrasting their rights and duties to those of other social classes).

The major elements of a social class are economic, occupational, and legal. These determine the objective positions of members and are affined (Sorokin 1947, 272). In other words, poverty (economic position) easily coalesces with manual labor (occupational position) and with comparative disfranchisement (legal position). Conversely, wealth affines with creative mental work and privileged status. When affined groups become organized, they form social classes and develop class consciousness. Historically, such consciousness grows in step with organization, and classes differentiate. Sorokin also adds a cultural dimension to the class model when he notes that membership produces moral, physical, mental, and behavioral similarities among members. This process results in a stronger consciousness of kind and reinforces the boundaries of class, strengthening the sense of "we" and "they."

Over the last two hundred years, notes Sorokin, there have been four major social classes: proletarians, peasants and farmers, a dwindling class of large landowners, and capitalists. Much of modern history has been written around the axes of their alliances and antagonisms. Classes are beyond question one of the defining forces of the modern era, but they are not the only divisive structure in society. Stratification also operates within and between UBGs and divides society by race, gender, ethnicity, age, religion, and political power. These differences imply a continuing struggle for wealth, power, and privilege in which some groups rise and others fall.

Social stratification also divides populations along horizontal lines into strata. Some have all the characteristics of social groups; these Sorokin calls "real strata." Others consist of aggregates sharing only a status and a role set (for example, serfs), which he calls "as-if strata." The third type of stratum is statistical and created as an artifact of measurement and description. Such strata could result from dividing the economically active population into quintiles based on income or from simply assigning names to artificial divisions, as W. Lloyd Warner did with his six social strata. For Sorokin, however, only the first two types of strata are theoretically significant.

Multibonded stratification can also involve more complex double, triple, and quadruple strata. Double-bonded strata evolve in a population when a group's superiority or inferiority is based on both its economic and its political position. If dominance and disadvantage are based on religion, wealth, and politics, triple-bonded strata result.

Once the characteristics of the upper stratum are defined, those of other levels can be determined by observation, analysis, and historical record. It is clear that Sorokin's organization of stratified groups derives from his classification of biosocial and sociocultural unibonded groups and their evolution into a variety of more complex groups.

Sorokin's taxonomy provides a real stratigraphy for sociology. It allows the analyst to break down complex structures of inequality and see how differentiation and combination operate to produce real and as-if strata and groups. Using his taxonomy, one can also locate any individual in the complex social space of his or her historical time. Grounding stratification in his sociological chemistry allows Sorokin to move up and down the web of social organization with a clarity and precision he believed to be lacking in many other conceptual schemes. His definitions can be applied to all populations and used to compare hierarchies in different contexts of social space and time.

Types of Societies

Sorokin's discussion of social structure culminates in his attempt to develop a number of societal types. His ideal classification involves eleven characteristics of a population: (1) its main UBGs and as-if organized groups;[17] (2) the number and kind of MBGs; (3) how each group is stratified; (4) which groups are open, closed, or intermediate; (5) which are centralized and decentralized; (6) which MBGs and strata are solidary-affine or antagonistic-disaffine internally; (7) which groups are typical for their time and place; (8) the relative power of each group and stratum; (9) which groups are solidary and antagonistic with one another; (10) the structure and function of a group; and (11) its characteristic meanings, values, and norms (Sorokin 1947, 296–97). When these data are supplemented by a knowledge of mobility and culture, one has an adequate basis for classification.

But Sorokin asserts that while his approach is more comprehensive than those of others (including Durkheim, Spencer, and Le Play), the data do not exist for its empirical construction. Therefore, it is an abstracted model for an idealized taxonomy to which sociology should aspire. Indeed, he acknowledges: "It is beyond this work to give such a complete classification. . . . The outline of its nature suffices . . . [and] for the present we shall denote only types of societies that are

---

17. By an "as-if organized group" Sorokin means a large number of people of the same race, gender, or age category who may feel and act like an organized group but do not interact with one another or share common institutional structures (for example, all American Indians).

important enough and distinct enough to be described specifically. Each . . . is widely used in historical, sociological, and anthropological disciplines . . . [and] in their totality are more real and adequate than those given by current, largely artificial classifications" (Sorokin 1947, 301).

Sorokin next contrasts urban and rural societies that have no single dominant group to those that do. These societies also manifest different sociocultural atmospheres, lifestyles, and psychologies (Sorokin 1947, 302). The egalitarian type is less centralized, less regimented, and more democratic than its counterpart. Access to authority and social mobility is more open, and less social distance separates the strata. In recent history, this form of society is less common than that with a central dominant group.

Societies of the dominant form are classified on the basis of the MBGs from which power and authority flow. Sorokin discusses seven types: societies dominated by families, tribes, castes, estates, social classes, nation-states, and theocracies. Whatever the secondary differences between MBGs, each of these types is controlled by a central group from which a line of power flows. Sorokin concludes that these groups do not represent all possible types but are the most typical and widespread (Sorokin 1947, 306).

In closing, Sorokin cautions that until more data are available, this is the best he can do. Each of the types is derived from real structures and fits a description widely used by historians and social scientists. Furthermore, because of their typicality, no history, anthropology, or sociology can be written without reference to them (Sorokin 1947, 306). He expresses a hope, however, that as data accumulate, sociologists will strive for that fine-grained classification suggested by his eleven-dimensional design. With it should come a more precise model for directing cross-cultural and historical research.

Interestingly, Sorokin postulates that locating sociocultural phenomena in space and time requires different concepts than those of the natural sciences and mathematics. In their place he uses the ideas of social space and time. Plainly, social scientists see important differences in space that are irrelevant to physical scientists. One hundred acres can consist of a concentration camp, the grounds of the White House, or the center of the Vatican, each of which contains a different mixture of meanings, vehicles, and actors. Thus locating sociocultural phenomena in space requires determining the position of their meanings in the realm of meanings, the place of their vehicles in the universe of vehicles, and the positions of individuals or groups in the universe of social agents. The node of articulation among these categories determines a phenomenon's sociological location as well as its relationship to other sociocultural phenomena. For the physical scientist, however, one hundred acres is one hundred acres, regardless of its social definitions.

Social time is also not homogeneous; indeed, even social disciplines construct it differently. Economists speak of operational time, psychologists of mental age. Among philosophers, it means different things in the works of Kant, Aristotle, Berkeley, and Bergson. These differences and other qualities of social time are discussed in the essay that Sorokin coauthored with Robert K. Merton (chapter 14 in this volume). The two of them observe that in the social world, calendrical time calibrates and marks few social events. Instead, social groups frequently reckon time to fit the rhythms of their activities and rarely confine time measured by behavior into solar equivalents of years, weeks, or days. Thus, time varies by the social structure in which it is reckoned, and as such the ebb and flow of human life is best considered within that context. Sociologists gain little from a uniform approach calibrated in standard units.

Sorokin first unfolded his notions of space and time in *Dynamics* and more fully expressed them in *Sociocultural Causality, Space, Time* (1943). These constructions aid sociologists in discovering patterns of social events and relationships among them. They also promote a broader, more helpful sociological context in which to consider the dynamics of social change.

Cultural and Social Change

With a structural cornerstone in place, Sorokin expanded his general sociology to include social and cultural change. While both elements are typically braided in studies of social transformations, Sorokin emphasizes cultural factors as the determining and propelling force in this process (Sorokin 1963, 482–88). For him, culture encompasses ideological, behavioral, and material elements incorporated into the actions of millions of people in the course of daily life. But how do such elements form cultural systems?

In *Dynamics,* Sorokin details four sources of integration: spatial adjacency, common association with an external factor, causal-functional, and logico-meaningful. Of these, only the last two are sociologically important. Causal-functional integration occurs on a continuum. At one extreme, cultural elements are so closely connected that a change in one affects all or many of the rest; at the other, a change in one has no discernable impact on the others because not all elements are connected. Sorokin calls unrelated elements "cultural congeries." They are associated with one another only by proximity or an external factor and hence are not sociologically significant.

Although causal-functional analysis provides valuable insights into cause–effect relationships, the study of logico-meaningful integration is more important for sociohistorical understanding. The essence of the logico-meaningful method involves discovering the central principle that permeates all components of a culture, gives sense and significance to each, and in this way makes a cosmos from a chaos of apparently unintegrated fragments (Sorokin 1937, 1:32). This method allows one to understand cultural integrity in the same way that a properly trained mind sees the unity in Euclid's geometry or in a Bach concerto. Sorokin's suggestion that logico-meaningful knowledge is superior to cause–effect understanding raised concerns from empirical sociologists and led to debates of the concept.

Through his logico-meaningful analysis of history, Sorokin isolates three major types of culture. The pure forms are called ideational and sensate; the third, a mixture of the other two, is termed idealistic. Sorokin notes:

> Each has its own mentality; its own system of truth and knowledge; its own philosophy and *Weltanschauung;* its own type of religion; . . . its own forms of art and literature, its own mores, laws, code of conduct; its own predominant forms of social relationships; its own economic and political organization; and finally, its own type of *human personality,* with a peculiar mentality and conduct. (Sorokin 1937, 1:67)

The determining characteristic of each cultural type is the principle of ultimate truth and reality that shapes its institutions and fuses their character, meaning, and personality.

In ideational cultures, ultimate reality flows from nonmaterial, everlasting being. The preeminent needs and goals of the individual are spiritual and realized through supersensory capacity. There are two subclasses of the ideational mentality: ascetic and active. The ascetic form involves seeking spiritual goals through a denial of the world and the flesh. In its extreme form, a person loses oneself in unity with the deity or the ultimate value. Active ideationalism entails striving to remake the world according to one's spiritual values. Advocates of this form struggle to convert others to their image of God and ultimate reality.

In sensate cultures, ultimate reality comes through the senses. In such societies, the supersensory appears to be an illusion, and spiritual indifference permeates the culture. Needs and ends are physical in nature and quenched by exploiting the environment. Sensate mentality, the opposite of ideational, takes three forms. The active sensate satisfies needs by responsibly manipulating the physical and cultural worlds. The passive sensate is shortsighted and based on a nonreflective misuse of natural and cultural capital: the world exists to meet wants; therefore use it. Even less disciplined is the cynical sensate, following any instrumental route to satisfaction. Sorokin holds sensate cultures in less esteem than ideational ones except for the pseudoideational type, in which reality is mostly sensate and needs predominantly physical. Unhappily, these needs go largely unsatisfied because of a lack of technology, and poverty is routinely endured. A band of primitive people exemplifies this type.

Many cultures fall between the ideational and the sensate, and Sorokin views most as poorly integrated. The exception is the true idealistic culture, in which reality is many-sided and human needs are both spiritual and material, with the former dominating. The vitality of this culture springs from its multidimensional orientation to reality: the known world results from the interplay of spiritual and empirical truths.

Sorokin searches the histories of Greco-Roman and Western civilizations—and, to a lesser degree, those of the Middle East, India, China, and Japan—for actual examples of these cultural types. He describes changes in their truth systems, art, scientific discoveries, and other social institutions and concludes that all cultures move through ideational, idealistic, and sensate periods separated by transitional times of crisis. Over the last 2500 years, Western culture has followed this rhythm, passing through the sequence twice and was now living in the declining phase of a third sensate epoch.

Sorokin describes this cycle of change as a result of two forces: the doctrine of immanent determinism and the principle of limits. Social systems, like biological ones, change according to their inherent potentialities. Immanent determinism asserts that the internal dynamic organization of a system establishes its capacity for change. Systems, however, have limits, and as they become more and more sensate—moving toward the extreme cynical sensate—they reach these limits. In dialectical fashion, ideational countertrends are then produced that grow stronger as the system polarizes and start to move the culture toward an idealistic form. The dissonant changes reverberate throughout the culture and violence increases as the system takes on a new configuration.

Sorokin next asks why these changes happen as they do. Again, he returns to the idea that the character of a culture is determined by the principle that underlies its system of truth and reality. Historical analysis reveals that ideational systems rest on the foundations of spiritual truth, sensate systems on the authority of the senses, and idealistic cultures on the truths of reason. None of these principles alone, however, provides absolute truth. If a system of truth and the culture it maintains were absolutely true, there would be no historical rhythms; conversely, if a system were completely false, it would not last. Therefore, because the superrhythms continue to occur, each system of truth and its corresponding culture must only partially satisfy human needs and demands for truth. Each, however, contains elements necessary for the adaptation of humankind to physical, social, and cosmic milieux. Truth systems change because each type of knowledge has strengths and weaknesses. When one dominates, it forces out others and prevents a holistic understanding of the world. The longer a mentality dominates, the more anomalies that accrue. That is, people become increasingly aware that their system is too narrow to explain important aspects of life, and the authority and value of the dominant mentality is increasingly called into question. Soon other means are needed to address those aspects of culture and cosmos not satisfactorily handled by that mentality. Unhappily, the superrhythms of ideational, idealistic, and sensate mentalities could go on forever, with humans never realizing ultimate truth.

Sorokin's solution to this endless cycle is the pursuit of integral truth, a body of knowledge that embraces all three forms of knowing. It "combines the empirical truths of the senses; the rational truths of reason; and the superrational truths of faith" (Sorokin 1941, 762–63). Integral truth gives us a more inclusive and valid grasp of reality. It also broadens our understanding and deepens our knowledge of the other forms of knowing.

In integral philosophy Sorokin also brings together the religious, scientific, and rational aspects of his own experience. Culture and humankind change, he says, because of a need for a more adequate knowledge to deal with life's major challenges. Sensate knowledge gives us science, technology, and physical comfort but tells us little of the spirit. The truths of faith address those issues but leave us relatively helpless in the face of nature. As each type of culture tries to provide what is missing, it changes. Integralism, however, binds the truths of science, reason, and spirituality into a comprehensive whole. It provides the means of obtaining a satisfying framework to comprehend life, cosmos, and the role of humanity in each (Sorokin 1941, 746–61).

Sorokin knew that integralism would struggle for acceptance in a sensate age. His contemporaries acknowledged mathematics and logic as fruits of reason and natural science as a product of the senses but considered the truths of intuition, inspiration, and revelation more questionable. Sorokin thus demonstrates how these sources had led to discoveries in mathematics by Poincaré and Birkhoff; in science by Newton and Galileo; in creative art by Mozart and Beethoven; in philosophy by Plato, Nietzsche, and Kant; and in religion by Muhammad and St. Paul. He concludes *Dynamics* with a plea for integral understanding and with dismal predictions about the future of Western society, which he believed to be in a crisis-ridden and dangerous transitional period of increasing violence, revolutions, and wars. He warns that major changes in values and understandings would be necessary if we were to survive. Accordingly, his subsequent research began to focus on that transition, as he published *The Crisis of Our Age, Man and Society in Calamity,* "A Neglected Factor of War," "The Cause and Factors of War and Peace," and "The Conditions and Prospects for a World without War."

The Sociology of Crisis

The Crisis of Our Age offered a warning, a call to action, and an agenda for social change. As Sorokin's popularized abridgment of *Dynamics,* it told a new audience that this was not a simple crisis. It went well beyond the economic, political, and intellectual changes of the last half-century; it affected all aspects of life and produced a rate of change and disorganization much more rapid and pervasive than its predecessors had. But the crisis was not the Spenglerian death knell of Western civilization. It was instead a massive change that challenged humanity to bring forth a new social system free of the problems that were destroying the old one.

In *Crisis,* Sorokin rejects Spengler's notion that cultures die but allows that they are not eternal. Between these extremes lie the cyclical fluctuations documented in *Dynamics.* Now, he asserts, all the major institutions of the Western supersystem are undergoing transformation, and these changes correspond with increases in war, criminality, mental illness, and violence. All signs indicate a turning point. But what, he asks, will this entail, and how can society most effectively adjust?

For Sorokin, a knowledge of history is essential for meeting the challenge. The slow decline of medieval ideational culture and the gradual rise of a sensate paradigm had resulted in two centuries of the mixed ideational type. In the sixteenth century, the shift was completed and a sensate paradigm stabilized and dominated Western experience for four hundred years. Now that order was crumbling as a nascent system took form, and society was bracing for another paradigm shift—one in which the sensate system would be replaced by an ideational, ideological, or possibly integral paradigm.[18]

Sorokin predicts that in the disintegration of sensate culture, many people will die but most will survive. Many of these will change their value system, social purpose, and direction. The vehicles of sensate culture—its technology, material wealth, buildings, communication systems, and other elements of infrastructure—will become the vehicles of a new cultural form. That is, the new values tied to these objects will redefine their purposes. Also, not all of the sensate supersystem will disappear. Remnants will survive in those areas of life in which their contributions were constructive; thus science, technology, engineering, medicine, agriculture, and related efforts will continue to benefit from sensate knowledge and methods. But instead of being *the* system, the sensate paradigm will be *one* of the systems of truth.

Analogously, says Sorokin, there will be a shift of talent in society. Many people of genius will leave scientific work, and the science of discovery will be largely replaced by a science of application. The best minds can then explore previously neglected areas, and great progress will result in philosophy, the fine arts, law, ethics, and other less cultivated fields of development. In the process, each of these fields will assume the more vital and creative forms of the emerging order. Such far-reaching changes will produce temporary increases in social and moral disorganization, as individuals struggle to cope with the new age. As anomie increases, quality of life will decline. Fortunately, this decline will be temporary, and as more people embrace the new system of values, culture, and social arrangements, the transitional period will end.

Sorokin suggests that these changes will be less painful if society accepts certain historical truths. First, change is a typical response to an aging system, and sensate culture is only one of the available options. Second, before discarding it, we must institutionalize what is valuable and abandon what is not. Among the results he expects are a new approach to what it means to be human; a new and more comprehensive epistemology; a restructuring of many social institutions; and a recasting of social relationships and organization in light of new values. The archetype for these changes is integralism, which Sorokin

---

18. In his discussion of the modern crisis and transformation, Fritjof Capra draws heavily on Sorokin, whom he credits with a clear notion of paradigm shifts and their role in social change. Capra, like Sorokin, believed we were facing a major reorientation of civilization (Capra 1982, 21–55).

advocates as the paradigmatic foundation for the emerging social order. Through it, he argues, the required changes can be productively and cooperatively achieved.

The darker side of this metamorphosis of Western civilization is also discussed briefly in *Crisis* and more completely in *Man and Society in Calamity* as well as in Sorokin's war articles. *Calamity* is a work in the Malthusian tradition that focuses on the emotional, cognitive, behavioral, and demographic consequences of famine, pestilence, war, and revolution. Combined with *Crisis,* it offers a comprehensive treatment of these transitional dislocations. But the major scholarly contribution of *Calamity* is its factually based, analytically driven disaster theory of social change.

Sorokin explores the etiology of these disasters to determine their essential and supplementary causes. For example, the essential cause of pestilence is infection. Its virulence is enhanced by supplementary ambient conditions that increase the viability of the pathological organism and by sociocultural circumstances favorable to its spread: high population density, poor sanitation, famine, ignorance, war, and lack of vaccinations and medicines. Famine's essential cause is the inability to produce, purchase, or equitably distribute adequate food supplies. Its impact is exacerbated by poor land, lack of water, pests, and social factors such as inadequate technology, invasion, war, and revolution.

Wars and revolutions share the same etiology but operate within different sociopolitical boundaries. Each is the consequence of the disintegration of a common value system that holds together a society (revolution) or binds two or more societies into a peaceful unity (war). These conflicts are intensified by famine, plague, more powerful military technology, and growing nationalism. Interestingly, the occurrence of a war stimulates revolution, and vice versa.

Unquestionably, combined disasters are more intractable and devastating to a society. But what, asks Sorokin, are the patterns of combination? One calamity frequently fuels another. Historically, pestilence is the least affined of these misfortunes, while famine is often associated with war, revolution, and plague. It can lead to war and revolution when a society lacks the resources to alleviate poverty and its attendant hunger; when there is a large gap in resources between the poor and the rich; when the rich are poorly armed and organized; and when the norms, values, and laws that hold the society (or societies) together have disintegrated. Sorokin claims that if the value system remains strong, people will cooperate. Thus, all four conditions must be present if war or revolution is to result from famine.

Sorokin also finds that wars and revolutions promote each other and regularly catalyze famines and epidemics. This leads him to conclude that they are the most common sources of social calamities.

Sorokin detects two historical strategies for coping with disasters. The most typical and least ennobling involves letting them run their course, a strategy that results in a high toll of misery and death. Less frequently, people rationally and cooperatively address the essential and supplementary causes of the cataclysmic event(s) and develop survival strategies. For example, a well-integrated society can maintain a sociopolitical structure capable of controlling the causes of pestilence, war, and revolution. Because the tragedy inherent in the latter two of these is so great, and they so often catalyze famine and plague, Sorokin focuses on them.

Based on his study of 967 wars fought between 901 and 1925 along with similar studies of revolutions reported in *Dynamics* (1937, 259–508), he finds that as the gap between the values systems of combatants increases, the violence of war and revolution becomes more intense and destructive. Conversely, the causes of these calamities are often eliminated when a social order is based on a common value system that transforms possible combatants into allies. Value integration will prevail, he asserts, if current changes lead nations to adopt an integral system of values and social organization. "The Cause and Factors of War and Peace" and "The Conditions and Prospects for a World without War" (chapters 19 and 20 in this volume) present the foundation for Sorokin's survival model.

The key to this model is attaining an integral society. By this Sorokin means one that incorporates a holistic approach to humanity, knowledge, values, and social organization. Integral epistemology promotes a wider understanding of the world and of the nature of being human. Through the three-dimensional universe of body, mind, and soul and the corresponding ways of knowing, a broader base for sharing and understanding is created. Reality is not the simple product of a nationalistic consensus or a single epistemic preference; instead, it fuses diverse humankind into a unified manifold of experience. In such a world, humans are again treated as incarnations of the divine and manifestations of the absolute, not mere bodies to be used as means to an end. The expanded epistemology helps one to see and feel the similarity between self and other. Such awareness promotes more inclusive values and moves us beyond pragmatic and functional goals in the quest for substantive and wise ends. In the process, the system of contractual social relations is replaced by more cooperative forms. These changes at simple levels of social life (dyads, triads, primary and secondary groups) eventually transform social institutions (economy, polity, education, religion) and reshape society. Cooperation, not conflict, becomes the foundation of the new social order, and finding new ways to cooperate will move humanity to a more peaceful and fulfilling world.

Sorokin's crisis works linked a social mission to his theory of order and change. But the studies stopped short of offering a method that would move humanity in the direction of peace. Exactly what strategy would promote the realization of an integral society? The answer came in *The Reconstruction of Humanity,* the Sorokinian exemplar for the new age.

The Sociology of Social Reconstruction

Sorokin opens *Reconstruction* with three chapters exploring often praised yet ultimately ineffective ways of creating a peaceful world. Later, in summarizing his findings, he would write:

> None of the prevalent prescriptions against international or civil wars
> . . . can eliminate nor notably reduce these conflicts. . . . Tomorrow the
> whole world could become democratic and yet wars and bloody strife
> would not be eliminated because democracies happen to be no less bel-
> ligerent nor strife-infected than autocracies. . . . The same goes for edu-
> cation. . . . Since the tenth century . . . education has made enormous
> progress . . . and yet the international wars and bloody revolutions . . .
> have not decreased. On the contrary, in the most scientific and most
> educated twentieth century they have reached an unrivaled height and
> made this the bloodiest century among all. . . . The same goes for reli-
> gious changes . . . not backed by increased altruization of persons and
> groups. Without a notable increase in unselfish, creative love (as ideally
> formulated in the *Sermon on the Mount*) . . . in overt behavior, in social
> institutions and culture, there is no chance for a lasting peace. (Sorokin
> 1963, 271–73)

The solution he proposes to the crisis of modernity is an integral society, and the mechanism for its attainment is the altruization of humanity (see Sorokin 1948, 7–56).

Amitology: A Sociology of Peace

Writing in 1951, Sorokin defines amitology as the applied science that develops the human capacity for love, friendship, and mutual aid (cooperation) in personal and social relationships. The guiding assumptions of amitology are integral. Humans, as the creators of a complex social life, have added to the inorganic and organic worlds the superorganic realm of culture, which ties them to a total reality. Through it, they seek the supreme integral values: the unity of social peace, harmony with nature, and the growth of the soul. The means to these ends is altruism. Finding ways to make humankind more altruistic would become the task of the Harvard Center in Creative Altruism.

According to Sorokin, humans become more altruistic by practicing love in all of their social relationships. Their capacity to love grows as they give the superconsciousness (soul) increasing control over the conscious mind. Love in turn drives social actions toward more prosocial and cooperative forms. World religions serve as rich sources for norms to direct such actions and deepen altruistic potential.

Particularly useful, for Sorokin, are the Ten Commandments and Sermon on the Mount. These are more than biblical injunctions; they are principles for character development. If society wants to eliminate social problems and evil, says Sorokin, then it must promote the development of better people. This strategy has been frequently overlooked by social scientists, who emphasize the darker side of behavior. Yet the Sermon and Commandments provide norms and values for living a good life. Under their influence, for example, parents will care for children in ways that nurture their development. Politicians will avoid creating unjust legislation. Scientists and inventors can work for the common good. All businesspeople, laborers, and mechanics can altruistically fulfill their daily roles and in the process contribute to the prosocial ethos of society. Sorokin views culture as the product of millions of small individual acts. If each of us simply avoids the selfish abuse of our functions, then the world will be improved. But if we each attempt to altruize our actions, then the world will be enriched.

The Center would develop a methodology for the production and use of love (and the related emotions of compassion, sympathy, and empathy) in all social relationships. The result would be a safer, more temperate society that nurtured human development and promoted less violent and more constructive interpersonal relationships.

The Harvard Research Center in Creative Altruism

The Center's blueprint for social reconstruction is contained in Sorokin's personal studies and those he edited, funded, and encouraged.[19]

19. The most helpful of these are the *Symposium* volumes (Sorokin 1950, 1954) and Maslow 1959. The first of these studies discusses the forms of love and their interrelationships; how love is produced, accumulated, and distributed; how love grows; love's measurable dimension; and its relationship to creativity and genius. There are also interesting essays on biological factors in altruism and peace research; different psychological approaches to love, hate, and friendship; and empirical studies of prosocial and antisocial behavior. The Maslow volume includes essays by such notables as Ludwig von Bertalanffy, Paul Tillich, Gordon Allport, Theodosius Dobzhansky, M. F. Ashley Mon-

The complete amitological program also includes ideas from the volumes cited previously, numerous articles, and the works of others.[20] This cumbersome mountain of material resists easy summarization. What follows is an integrative framework, beginning with personal altruistic preparation and moving up through the levels of social complexity from dyads to primary and secondary groups, communities, and society. The works of Sorokin most concerned with these issues are *The Ways and Power of Love, Forms and Techniques of Altruistic and Spiritual Growth: A Symposium,* and *Power and Morality: Who Shall Guard the Guardians?*

Sorokin's program draws from such cross-cultural studies as Roger Godel's exploration in *Forms* of Eastern and Western sciences, religions, and ontologies. Godel compares the two methods of apprehending empirical and ultimate reality, each of which has its strengths. The Hindu turns inward and the Westerner outward in pursuit of scientific knowledge and religious experience. In the realm of religion, both approaches leave the seeker waiting in quiet supplication for the presence of God; in that of science, they had remained on separate paths until Western scientists began their exploration of the subatomic world and learned the limits of objectivity (Godel 1954, 3–12). Quantum physics confirms that each is a valid but partial route to knowledge and that they are stronger and more productive when combined.[21] Godel's essay supports integralism as a theory of human nature and as an epistemology. The truths of the senses and those of the spirit intertwine and yield a more inclusive grasp of the natural and the sublime. Thus combining many cultural experiences expands knowledge and awareness more than following a single avenue of understanding.

Western religions have also developed physical techniques that promote the growth of the soul. In *Forms,* Anthony Bloom examines the spiritual exercises of Orthodox Christian monks, while Pierre Marinier explores prayer. The linking of body, mind, and soul is strengthened by Orthodox monks through mortification, meditation, and a set of physical postures that Bloom describes as "Christian Yoga" (Bloom

---

tague, F. S. C. Northrop, and Erich Fromm. Each explores different aspects of altruism and prosocial behavior. *Forms* contains many of the works briefly touched on in this essay.

20. There are several helpful works that cover this large corpus of research and commentary; Matter 1974; Bierwiler 1973 and 1978; and Johnston 1995, 189–220.

21. Of particular interest on this important point is Sorokin 1956, chapter 12, in which he discusses sociology's failure to incorporate the lessons of subatomic physics into its methodology. As a result, he asserts, it blindly applied an objectivist philosophy of science no longer credible among many scholars.

1954, 93–108). These practices prepare the mind and the body to experience the transcendent. Mortification, which disciplines the body directly and the mind and soul indirectly, prepares one for meditation and worship. Fasting, vigils, hard labor, and chastity each produce different effects: fasting, for instance, increases intellectual acuity, while thirst is conducive to progress in prayer. Meditation calms the mind, puts the spirit to work, and produces beneficial effects on the body. Finally, Bloom describes several physical postures that provoke special mental states. These exercises build awareness of the complexities of human nature and the relationships among its elements. Attentive awareness to one element promotes realization of the others, and this synergistic process yields a fullness, a desire to seek the transcendent in oneself and in others. The quest fosters enhanced awareness of our integral natures.

Prayer, however, has been more typical of religious and particularly Christian experiences. It is an exercise and discipline that focuses attention on God and produces physical and psychological benefits. Its somatic effects are of particular interest to Marinier, but he also describes prayer as means to moral recovery and heightened awareness of reality. Prayer, for him, is a transcendental universal in the pursuit of grace and holistic development (Marinier 1954, 145–64).

These and other essays in *Forms* teach one to discipline the flesh, transcend the ego, and develop the soul. The techniques described are only a few of those used by Jewish, Christian, Muslim, and Buddhist seekers to enhance their spiritual and altruistic capacity. As methods of character development, they motivate members to overcome egoism and ego-centered altruism, a primitive altruistic form in which people give in order to get and serve others so as to be served. It does not require transcendence of ego or result in a richer form of altruism. However, spiritual practice enables neophytes to increase the intensity, duration, adequacy, extensiveness, and purity of their love and prosocial behaviors. In the process, they advance toward a more exceptional altruism.[22]

22. Sorokin expected that few people would become exceptional altruists, but he encouraged this type of spiritual and social growth. Among the five observable dimensions of love that he delineates are extensiveness, which refers to range. Its zero point is pure egoism, and it increases as we come to love others: family, fellow citizens, humanity. Hate is the zero point for love's intensity; we approach its maximum when we give what we value most to or for another. Duration measures how long love lasts, and purity refers to the motivation for love: Is it ego- or other-driven? Adequacy has to do with its effect on its objects: Does love free and enrich them or make them dependent? In the first case, it is adequate; in the second, not. Sorokin conceptualizes each variable

Altruization techniques begin with the individual but can also improve social relations in primary, secondary, and larger social contexts. For example, J. Mark Thompson's essay in *Forms* considers inimical relationships in small groups of students. His research demonstrates that sustained acts of kindness by adversaries regularly transformed hostile dyadic relationships into congenial ones (Thompson 1954, 401–17). Other contributors to the volume examine strained, often angry, relationships in the larger and more formal context of a mental hospital, with a focus on patients and nurses. They find that the tensions inherent in therapeutic relationships were greatly reduced when each group worked to imaginatively take the role of the other. As empathy increased, nurses moved beyond clinical indifference to compassion. Similar empathetic efforts by patients resulted in less hostility and more responsiveness. The longer they persisted, the better things became and the more effective the nurses were in the care of their charges (Hyde and Kandler 1954, 387–99).

These studies are illustrative and do not exhaust the range of the Center's research and publications on such subjects. Indeed, Sorokin broadens and deepens the discussion of altruistic techniques in several volumes, including *The Ways and Power of Love*. In this work he argues, behavioristically, that prosocial group dynamics are enhanced when the behavior of the young is channeled by sanctions toward generosity; when these sanctions are consistently and broadly reinforced by group opinion and action; when all groups consciously and immediately use proven methods to reduce animosity and conflict; when prosocial norms and values are regularly rewarded; when empathy is encouraged by the controlled living of deprivation (asceticism-mortification); and when creativity, prayer, exploration for faults, and binding vows of charity and selflessness are encouraged. As these behaviors are repeated, habituated, and institutionalized, group actions at all levels become more altruistic and peaceful.

Two exceptional examples of these and other practices in use at the community level are found in the Center's studies of the Mennonites and the Hutterites. The Mennonites were an excellent choice because they ranked high on all of Sorokin's dimensions of love. Their altruism was extensive and broad in scope; it went well beyond the community to the nation and the world. It was intense and pure, meaning that Mennonites performed significant acts of assistance without expecta-

---

as existing on a continuum from 0 to 100. The extraordinary altruist will have a score of 500; the pure beast, 0. For more discussion of the dimensions of altruistic development, see the *Symposium* volume (Sorokin 1950, 3–24).

tion of reward. These behaviors were institutionalized in their cultures and inculcated by socialization in the personalities of the young. In the process, altruism became a stable and durable component of their culture. Mennonite altruism empowered people to grow and become independent; thus it was adequate in Sorokin's meaning of the term. But what else could they teach us about communal altruism?

The Mennonite community, Sorokin's collaborators note, is devout in prayer and believes that good works are essential for salvation. These commitments bind its members together and extend their altruism beyond the brethren to all who experience loss and suffering. They maintain hospitals, orphanages, credit unions, homes for the elderly, cooperatives, insurance companies, and burial societies for Mennonite and non-Mennonite alike (Krahn, Fretz, and Kreider 1954, 309–28).

They are also remarkable on the basis of their worldwide charity. During World War I, 200,000 Mennonites contributed $2.5 million for emergency assistance in foreign lands. By World War II they had become more organized and raised almost $13 million to alleviate foreign suffering (Krahn, Fretz, and Kreider 1954, 320). Their projects targeted mothers and children and those not served by other relief efforts. There were no exclusions on the basis of race, class, or political sympathies. The projects were staffed and administered by volunteers who regularly involved their home congregations with the needy. The congregations frequently sent additional food, clothing, tools, and medicines. There were also children-to-children projects through which young Mennonites sent clothing, school supplies, small toys, and books to less fortunate youngsters.

What motivated people to do these things, and how was their altruism institutionalized and passed to new generations? An answer is found in Eberhard Arnold's essay on the Hutterites in Paraguay (Arnold 1954, 293–307). Hutterites are direct descendants of the Swiss Anabaptists, and their altruism arises from the Bible. The young members of the group learn early that their time and resources are to be used in the work of God. These values carry over into special relief projects and neighborly assistance. As Arnold reports, adult role models are the key to socialization. They demonstrate egoless behavior, personal responsibility, cooperation, and Christian love. Adults give children freedom yet provide a clear set of behavioral prescriptions and proscriptions. Their examples are reinforced by older children, who take responsibility for younger ones. Peer groups are never exclusive, provide normative reference points, and sanction behavior but always leave open clear paths on which the unruly can return to full membership. The family, however, is the most important means for internalization of the community ethos. In it children learn all required life skills. The examples of parents and others demonstrate that marriage is a commitment to loyalty, love, responsibility, and mutual aid that bonds mates into an insoluble spiritual and physical unity. The Society of Brothers gives members in late adolescence the opportunity to leave for education and other experiences. Afterward, each freely decides whether or not to return to the community. Most do, and they assume their positions as role models for the next generation.

These studies suggest several important things about altruism: religion provides powerful mechanisms for ego transcendence, moral development, and social responsibility; humans are capable of organized altruism that extends beyond the primary group to socially and geographically distant others; altruistic communities can survive in a sensate age of individualism; such communities are historically viable and persist from generation to generation; and organizational models for altruistic communities already exist.

Altruistic Transformations in Complex Societies

Sorokin's next concern was whether altruism could be institutionalized at the highest levels of sociocultural integration. In *Power and Morality: Who Shall Guard the Guardians?*, he and Walter A. Lunden deal with obstacles that nation-states face in becoming more humane and altruistic. The book first provides a history of power and corruption, covering iniquity by monarchs, democratic and fascist political leaders, captains of industry, and even Catholic popes whose authority extended over foreign states. The authors find today's rulers not unlike their predecessors but more dangerous because nuclear energy gives them the capacity for greater mischief. The monopolistic control of weapons of mass destruction results in infinitely greater power—a power that society is challenged to control for the common good.

Sorokin and Lunden put their hopes in a government of scientists, sages, and saints. The technical complexity of today's world, they say, requires greater intellectual skill than was characteristic of earlier politicians. As this trend accelerates, politicians will be increasingly replaced by scientists. But will this mean better government, or simply one oligarchy replacing another? Existing statistical evidence shows no significant differences in intelligence between criminals and noncriminals and no systematic, long-term relationship between technical progress and peace. Therefore, they conclude, it is unlikely that a shift to a scientific elite, in and of itself, will improve the current situation.

What scientists lack is the wisdom of the sage. Society now needs leaders who are pansophic intellectuals capable of integrating scientific understanding into a broader framework of moral principles for social reconstruction and progress (Sorokin and Lunden 1959, 169). The pansoph must combine scientific wisdom with ethical leadership and strive to replace moral relativism with a system of cross-culturally valid moral norms. Unhappily, scientific learning has not been accompanied by moral literacy, and moral standards remain circumscribed by the boundaries of culture. The interdependence of today's world demonstrates that parochial tribal morality and its nationalistic expressions are obsolete and dysfunctional. Consequently, world leaders will be challenged to develop a moral code that can bond all nations into a principled community. This requires a heterogeneous governmental elite (Sorokin and Lunden 1959, 175).

Such a moral transformation necessitates the participation of global religious leaders and exceptional altruists, who must be more ecumenical than those of the past and must promote moral education suitable for a global population. Clearly, great religious leaders have changed the path of history. The demands for a new international moral order now require today's leaders to rise to the levels of past historical accomplishments (Sorokin and Lunden 1959, 175–189).

Sorokin and Lunden conclude that the guardians of the guardians will serve as the moral leaders of the new global community and in the process transform sensate government into an integral form. If they can deliver a few decades of peace, then the most dangerous part of the declining sensate transition will pass and a solid foundation for an emerging integral order will be in place. And, they add, history requires that the new elite assume increasing control as soon as possible and work to frame the new civilization (Sorokin and Lunden 1959, 184–93).

Epilogue

The Sorokinian oeuvre is remarkably broad, and the altruism studies clearly represent more than a pious hope for the future of humanity. They apply amitological research to practical problems and use integralism as the model for social reconstruction. At the Center, Sorokin combined his studies of history and social change with a program for human improvement. A careful reading of the works he produced there demonstrates his skills as social scientist, historian, and applied sociologist. Such a range of interests and skills is uncharacteristic for most practitioners of the craft. Furthermore, because Sorokin crossed the boundaries of several disciplines and specialties, he became in the minds of many a philosopher, and more specifically a philosopher of history. Near the end of the review that opens this volume, William Kolb outlined the importance of this role:

> To ignore the contemporary philosopher of history is to risk the loss of our sociological souls. . . . The picture of modern society which these men present has tremendous relevance. Atomization, fragmentation, alienation, bureaucratization, terror, the loss of human choice—all are realities of our time. We need to know if these phenomena are the inevitable results of attempting to organize a society on the basis of individual freedom and dignity, or if there can be a viable social order in which arbitrary authority, coercion, and the violation of human beings are at a minimum. The predictions of the philosophers of history are conservative. . . . We must accept these predictions or show that a sociology of possibility . . . can find conditions in which freedom and order are not incompatible. (Kolb 1951, 268)

Sorokin advanced an agenda for the sociology of possibility. His early works pushed the boundaries of established specialties and opened new fields for research and theoretical development. Integralism and the historical explorations in *Dynamics* and its progeny were bold attempts to extend the sociological frontier beyond its comfortable realm of discourse. In these works Sorokin struggled to isolate the energizing elements of social change and discover the patterns of Western history. To escape the cycle of growth, decline, and crisis, Sorokin envisioned the possibility of an integral society and explored the ways in which it could come into being. This search led to the altruism studies, which heralded later developments in the systematic study of emotions, altruism, and prosocial behaviors. Yet few scholars looked beyond the surface of the Center's pioneering work for a sociological core. Even Lewis Coser asserted that these studies "do not warrant analysis in a work devoted to sociological theory" (Coser 1977, 491).

Plainly, pioneers are a lonely and often endangered breed, but they are also necessary. As the celebrated world historian Arnold J. Toynbee observed,

> It is, of course, as an intellectual pioneer that Sorokin has made his mark on the history of thought about human affairs. A pioneer condemns himself to be corrected and surpassed . . . his trails will be progressively straightened out, . . . [and] his axe's blaze marks on tree trunks will be replaced by neon signs. All these improvements will overtake his path-finding work. . . . [But] there is one thing that [successors] cannot do [to the] discoverer. They cannot supersede him. Even Daniel Boone's

trail . . . still lives today in the radar beam that a pilot follows in navigating his plane from Washington, D.C., to St. Louis. (Toynbee 1963, 4)

As a pioneer, Sorokin opened new sociological vistas. He also had a solid understanding of sociology—one that today's practitioners may find helpful during a period of theoretical eclecticism and disciplinary uncertainty. In his critical study of American sociologists, Robert Bierstedt observed that Sorokin's place in sociological theory is secure:

> He gave sociology a scope and significance that, except in Ward, was nowhere approached by his predecessors. For him sociology is no mean and petty discipline, . . . but a strong and vital inquiry into the processes of society and history. . . . Many of his insights are spectacular. One always knows that one is in the presence of a man who knows what sociology is. . . . Sorokin gave size to sociology. (Bierstedt 1981, 347)

Sorokin's contributions are now part of the fabric of contemporary sociology. Edward Shils deftly conveyed his relationship to the unfinished business of the discipline when he wrote of the prejudice and promise inherent in Sorokin's legacy:

> The one writer who knew all of European sociology was Professor Pitirim Sorokin, one of the most erudite of men. In his *Systematic Source Book in Rural Sociology,* he brought more concrete European sociology to America than any writer, but it passed unnoticed by the general run of sociologists. . . . His *Social Mobility* was a pioneering inventory; it was duly noted but it was uninfluential in its own time. . . . His *Sociology of Revolution* was disregarded by his contemporaries . . . and it was condemned by the oncoming generation of the thirties. . . . In general, except in the cases of Robert Merton and Arnold Anderson, Professor Sorokin's erudition and acumen failed to transmit itself to the generation which was trained in the thirties and forties. The failure was partly a matter of an idiosyncratic rhetoric and a disputatious and rivalrous temperament, partly a matter of the misfortune of being a premature refugee. Cast too soon out of his motherland into a world not yet ready, his idiom was never harmonized with the idiom of his contemporaries. The importance of his work remains for the future to discover. (Shils 1980, 108)

The essays that follow extend from Sorokin's Russian years to his presidency of the American Sociological Association. In many of them, he stimulates, irritates, and challenges his readers to open their minds to new horizons. Those who accept the challenge will participate with a master of the craft in a sociology of possibility.

References

Pitirim A. Sorokin's works appear in a separate bibliography at the end of this book.

Allen, Philip J., ed. 1963. *Pitirim A. Sorokin in Review*. Durham, N.C.: Duke University Press.

Allport, Gordon W. 1985. "The Historical Background of Social Psychology." In *The Handbook of Social Psychology*, ed. Gardner Lindzey and Elliot Aronson. New York: Random House.

Anderson, Nels. 1929. "Review of *Principles of Rural–Urban Sociology*." *New Republic* 60: 328.

Arnold, Eberhard C. H. 1954. "Education for Altruism in the Society of Brothers in Paraguay." In *Forms and Techniques of Altruistic and Spiritual Growth: A Symposium*, ed. Pitirim A. Sorokin, 293–307. Boston: Beacon Press.

Becker, Howard. 1950. *Through Values to Social Interpretation*. Durham, N.C.: Duke University Press.

Bendix, Reinhard. 1951. "The Images of Man in the Social Sciences: The Basic Assumptions of Present Day Research." *Commentary* 11: 190.

Bierstedt, Robert. 1981. *American Sociological Theory: A Critical History*. New York: Academic Press.

Bierwiler, Kay. 1973. "Sorokin's Studies into Creative Altruism." *Journal of Human Relations* 21: 178–93.

———. 1978. "Pitirim Sorokin's Research in Altruism." Ph.D. diss., State University of New York at Albany.

Bloom, Anthony. 1954. "Yoga and Christian Spiritual Techniques: Somatopsychic Techniques in Orthodox Christianity." In *Forms and Techniques of Altruistic and Spiritual Growth: A Symposium*, ed. Pitirim A. Sorokin, 93–108. Boston: Beacon Press.

Capra, Fritjof. 1982. *The Turning Point: Science, Society, and the Rising Culture*. New York: Simon and Schuster.

Coser, Lewis A. 1977. *Masters of Sociological Thought*. 2d ed. New York: Harcourt Brace Jovanovich.

Costello, Paul. 1993. *World Historians and Their Goals: Twentieth Century Answers to Modernism*. DeKalb, Ill.: Northern Illinois University Press.

Cox, Oliver C. 1945. "Race and Class: A Distinction." *American Journal of Sociology* 30: 360–69.

———. 1948. *Caste, Class, and Race*. New York: Monthly Review Press.

Cuthbertson-Johnson, Beverly, David D. Franks, and Michael Dornan. 1994. *The Sociology of Emotions: An Annotated Bibliography*. New York: Garland Publishing.

Davis, Allison, Burleigh B. Gardner, and Mary R. Gardner. 1945. *Deep South: An Anthropological Study of Caste and Class*. Chicago: University of Chicago Press.

Dollard, John. 1937. *Caste and Class in a Southern Town*. New Haven: Yale University Press.

Doykov, Yuri. 1996. *Modern Thought of P. A. Sorokin*. Arkhangelsk: Arkhangelsk Regional Studies Museum—Emigration History Research Center.

Fitch, Robert E. 1958. "The Scientist as Priest and Savior." *Christian Century* 75: 368–70.

Ford, Joseph B. 1963. "Sorokin as Philosopher." In *Pitirim A. Sorokin in Review*, ed. Philip J. Allen, 33–66. Durham, N.C.: Duke University Press.

———. 1996. "Sorokin's Methodology: Integralism Is the Key." In *Sorokin and Civilization: A Centennial Assessment*, ed. Joseph B. Ford, Michael Richard, and Palmer Talbutt, 83–92. New Brunswick, N.J.: Transaction Books.

Friedrichs, Robert W. 1970. *A Sociology of Sociology*. New York: The Free Press.

Godel, Roger. 1954. "The Contemporary Sciences and the Liberative Experience of Yoga." In *Forms and Techniques of Altruistic and Spiritual Growth: A Symposium*, ed. Pitirim A. Sorokin, 3–12. Boston: Beacon Press.

Grierson, J. 1926. "Review of *The Sociology of Revolution*." *The American Journal of Sociology* 7: 399.

Gurvitch, Georges. 1932. "Petrazhitsky, Lev Iosifovich." In *The Encyclopedia of the Social Sciences*, ed. E. R. A. Seligman and A. Johnson, 12: 103–4. New York: Macmillan.

Hinkle, Rosco C., and Gisela J. Hinkle. 1954. *The Development of Modern Sociology*. New York: Random House.

Hyde, Robert H., and Harriet M. Kandler. 1954. "Altruism in Psychiatric Nursing." In *Forms and Techniques of Altruistic and Spiritual Growth: A Symposium*, ed. Pitirim A. Sorokin, 387–99. Boston: Beacon Press.

Isajiw, Wsevolod W. 1950. "Pitirim Sorokin's *Sistema Sotsiologii*: A Summary." *American Catholic Sociological Review* 17: 290–319.

Jaworski, Gary Dean. 1993. "Pitirim A. Sorokin's Sociological Anarchism." *History of the Human Sciences* 6: 61–77.

Johnston, Barry V. 1986. "Sorokin and Parsons at Harvard: Institutional Conflict and the Origins of a Hegemoic Tradition." *Journal of the History of the Behavioral Sciences* 22: 107–27.

———. 1987. "Pitirim Sorokin and the American Sociological Association: The Politics of a Professional Society." *Journal of the History of the Behavioral Sciences* 23: 103–22.

———. 1995. *Pitirim A. Sorokin: An Intellectual Biography*. Lawrence, Kans.: The University Press of Kansas.

Kolb, William L. 1951. "Review of *Social Philosophies of an Age of Crisis*." *American Sociological Review* 16: 267–68.

Kolegar, Ferdinald. 1967. "T. G. Masaryk's Contributions to Sociology."
Journal of the History of the Behavioral Sciences 3: 27–37.

Krahn, Cornelius, J. Wenfield Fretz, and Robert Kreider. 1954. "Altruism
in Mennonite Life." In *Forms and Techniques of Altruistic and Spiritual
Growth: A Symposium,* ed. Pitirim A. Sorokin, 309–28. Boston: Beacon
Press.

Laszlo, Ervin, and Jong Youl Yoo, eds. 1986. *The World Encyclopedia of
Peace.* New York: Pergamon Press.

Lenrow, Peter. 1978. "Dilemmas of Professional Helping: Continuities and
Discontinuities with Folk Helping Roles." In *Altruism, Sympathy, and
Helping: Psychological and Sociological Principles,* ed. Lauren Wispe.
New York: Academic Press.

Marinier, Pierre. 1954. "Reflections on Prayer: Its Causes and Psychophysio-
logical Effects." In *Forms and Techniques of Altruistic and Spiritual
Growth: A Symposium,* ed. Pitirim A. Sorokin, 145–64. Boston: Beacon
Press.

Martindale, Don. 1972. "Pitirim A. Sorokin: Soldier of Fortune." In *Sorokin and Sociology: Essays in Honour of Pitirim A. Sorokin,* ed. G. C.
Hallen and R. Prasad, 4–42. Agra, India: Satish Book Enterprise.

Masaryk, Thomas G. 1970. *Suicide and the Meaning of Civilization,* trans.
William B. Weist and Robert G. Batson. Chicago: University of Chicago
Press.

Maslow, Abraham, ed. 1959. *New Knowledge in Human Values.* New
York: Harper and Brothers.

Matter, Joseph A. 1974. *Love, Altruism, and the World Crisis: The Challenge of Pitirim Sorokin.* Chicago: Nelson-Hall.

Nichols, Lawrence T. 1996a. "Intergenerational Solidarity in the Creation
of Science: The Ross–Sorokin Correspondence, 1921–1931." *Journal of
the History of the Behavioral Sciences* 32: 135–50.

———. 1996b. "Sorokin and American Sociology: The Dynamics of a
Moral Career in Science." In *Sorokin and Civilization: A Centennial Assessment,* ed. Joseph B. Ford, Michael Richard, and Palmer Talbutt, 45–
64. New Brunswick, N.J.: Transaction Books.

Park, Robert. 1926. "Review of *The Sociology of Revolution.*" *Annals of
the American Academy of Arts and Sciences* 123: 230.

Rapoport, Anatol. 1974. *Conflict in Man-Made Environments.* Manchester:
Penguin Books.

Roucek, Joseph S. 1938. "Masaryk as Sociologist." *Sociology and Social
Research* 22: 412–20.

Schneider, Louis. 1984. "Pitirim A. Sorokin: Social Science in the Grand
Manner." In *The Grammar of Social Relations: The Major Essays of
Louis Schneider,* ed. Jay Weinstein, 149–59. New Brunswick, N.J.:
Transaction Books.

Shils, Edward. 1980. *The Calling of Sociology and Other Essays on the
Pursuit of Learning.* Chicago: University of Chicago Press.

Sorokin, Pitirim A. 1929. Letter of 16 October to A. Lawrence Lowell. President Lowell's papers, Harvard University Archives, Pusey Library.

Thompson, J. Mark. 1954. "Experimentation with the Technique of Good Deeds in Transformation of Inimical into Amicable Relationships." In *Forms and Techniques of Altruistic and Spiritual Growth: A Symposium,* ed. Pitirim A. Sorokin, 401–17. Boston: Beacon Press.

Tibbs, A. E. 1943. "Book Reviews of *Social and Cultural Dynamics:* A Study in *Wissensoziologie.*" *Social Forces* 21: 473–80.

Tiryakian, Edward A., ed. 1963. *Sociological Theory, Values, and Sociocultural Change.* Glencoe: The Free Press.

Toynbee, Arnold J. 1963. "Sorokin's Philosophy of History." In *Pitirim A. Sorokin in Review,* ed. Philip J. Allen, 3–36. Durham, N.C.: Duke University Press.

Zimmerman, Carle C. 1973. "My Sociological Career." *Revue Internacionale de Sociologie* 9: 103–5.

I

SHIFTING VISIONS
OF SOCIOLOGY

1

The Boundaries and
Subject Matter of Sociology

To define the field of sociology, as with any science, means to select the category of facts that are the object of its study—in other words, to establish a special point of view on a series of phenomena that is distinct from the point of view of other sciences.[1]

No matter how diverse the definitions by means of which sociologists characterize the existence of social or superorganic phenomena, all of them have something in common, namely, that the social phenomenon—the object of sociology—is first of all considered the interaction of one or more kinds of center, or interaction manifesting specific symptoms. The principle of interaction lies at the base of all these definitions; they are all in agreement on this point, and their differences occur further on, regarding the character and form of this interaction. We shall now support what has been said with examples.

The most popular and widespread definition of sociology, as the science of the organization and evolution of society, already presupposes by its very character the category of interaction, because society is inconceivable without the interaction of the individuals who compose it.[2]

It is obvious that the "constancy of relations" that Spencer emphasizes as the characteristic sign of society, or the superorganic phenome-

Originally published, in Russian, in pamphlet form (St. Petersburg: Obrazovanie, 1913). Translated by Lawrence T. Nichols.

1. On this point it is impossible not to concur with E. V. de Roberty, L. Gumplowicz, S. L. Frank, and others who quite correctly point to the equivalence of "defining the object" and "establishing a special point of view." See de Roberty, "Sociology and Psychology," *Annales de l'Institute International de Sociologie* 10: 108; Frank, *Philosophy and Life* (St. Petersburg: Zhukovskago, 1910), 284–85; Gumplowicz, "The Program of Sociology," *Annales* 1: 104.

2. See, for example, A. Comte, *The Course of Positive Philosophy* (Paris: Bailliere, 1864), vol. 4, chap. 1; M. M. Kovalevsky, *Contemporary Sociology* (St. Petersburg: Pantalieva, 1905), vol. 1, chap. 1; Charles A. Ellwood, "Marx's Economic Determinism," *American Journal of Sociology* 12 (July 1907): 35–46.

non, is only another term designating the very same principle of inter-action.[3]

"In 'community,' in the 'superorganic' phenomenon" says E. V. de Roberty, "we see nothing other than the prolonged, uninterrupted, many-sided, and unavoidable interaction that establishes itself in every constant and nonaccidental aggregate of living beings."[4]

The social phenomenon, or society, "exists where several individuals stand in interaction," says G. Simmel.[5]

Nor does Gumplowicz view the matter otherwise, with only this difference: to the category of the elements of interaction he brings the group but not the individual. "As the social phenomenon," he says, "we understand the relationships arising out of the interaction of human groups and contacts."[6]

"Every aggregate of individuals that is in constant contact constitutes society," in the opinion of Durkheim. Compulsion, the characteristic feature of the social phenomenon, obviously already presupposes interaction.[7]

The "intermental" process of Tarde and its forms—imitation, opposition, and accommodation—are only other words to designate the very same principle of interaction in all its diversity.[8]

Stammler also does not wish to say anything different when he states that the logical precondition of social life is the presence of external compulsory rules, that "social life is the life of the people that is regulated by an external form." We see the very same thing in his disciple Natorp.[9]

Novicow, who considers "exchange [*l'échange*] as the basic phenomenon of human association," designates this process of interaction with a different word.[10]

3. Herbert Spencer, *Foundations of Sociology* (SPB, 1898), 1:277ff.

4. E. V. de Roberty, *A New Statement of the Questions of Sociology* (Sitiva Publishers), 49 and elsewhere; *The Sociology of Action* (Paris, 1908), chap. 1.

5. G. Simmel, *Soziologie* (Leipzig: Dencker and Humblot, 1908), 5–7; *A Sociological Sketch* (Johansen Publishers), 31–39.

6. L. Gumplowicz, *Outlines of Sociology* (Moscow: Popov Publishers, 1899), 105, 106, 113, 116, 265, and elsewhere.

7. E. Durkheim, *On the Division of Labor in Society* (Odessa, 1901), 221; *The Rules of Sociological Method* (Paris, 1907), chap. 1.

8. G. Tarde, *Studies in Social Psychology* (Paris: V. Giard & E. Briere, 1898), chap. 1.

9. R. Stammler, *Economy and Law* ("The Source" Publishers [Leipzig: Veit and Co., 1906]), 1:91ff; P. Natorp, *Social Pedagogy* (Bogdanov Publishers [Stuttgart: Fromann, 1904]), 76ff.

10. J. Novicow, "Exchange: The Fundamental Phenomenon of Human Association," *Revue internationale de sociologie* 11 (1911).

We see the very same thing sharply formulated by Giddings, Draghicesco, Bouglé, Espinas, Vaccaro, Fouillee, de la Grasserie, Ward, and others.[11]

Indeed, in the same way, it is clear that without interaction there would not and could not be any kind of aggregate, association, society, or, in general, social phenomenon, since there would be no relationships of any sort.

Of course, this consensus about the generic substratum of every social phenomenon does not in the least predetermine the diversity of opinion about subsequent concepts of interaction. Nevertheless, in order to strengthen the argument that the interaction of centers of one kind or another constitutes the existence of the social phenomenon and the object of sociology, and in order to gain a full understanding of this conception, the following questions, at least, must be answered:

1. If the process of interaction is to be considered the social phenomenon, among what or among whom must this process occur?

2. If this question is resolved in one way or another, then it must further be asked whether or not the duration of interaction is important to the conception of the social phenomenon. Should it be assumed that the social phenomenon can be seen only in durable and constant interaction or that it arises in every interaction, no matter how brief or casual?

Without precise answers to these questions, especially the first of them, the concept of "interaction" (and, in the same way, that of "the social phenomenon") becomes meaningless. The reason is that interaction, as is well known, is not a process that is specific to some defined type of phenomenon but is a global one that is characteristic of all forms of energy and that displays itself even in "the law of gravity" or "the law of equality of action and reaction." Therefore, it is clear that if one wishes to make interactions the special object of social science, it is necessary to indicate specific symptoms [*differentia specifica*] of this global and, in a sense, generic process that can distinguish this form of interaction from its remaining forms and can thereby consti-

---

11. F. H. Giddings, *Principles of Sociology* (Johansen Publishers [New York: Macmillan, 1994]), 3, 28, 30, 160–65, and elsewhere; D. Draghicesco, *On the Role of the Individual in Social Determinism* (Paris: Alcan, 1904), 136–90; C. C. Bouglé, *Egalitarianism and Sociology* (Paris: Alcan, 1908); A. V. Espinas, *The Social Life of Animals* (SPB, 1898), 79ff, 108ff; M. A. Vaccaro, *The Sociological Bases of Law and the State* (Paris: V. Giard & E. Briere, 1898), 63ff; A. Fouillee, *The Sociological Elements of Morality* (Paris, 1905), vol. 2, chap. 1, chap. 2, 143ff; R. de la Grasserie, "On Psychosociology," *Revue de sociologie* (1912), nos. 3 and 4; Lester Ward, *Pure Sociology* (Paris, 1906), 21 and chap. 10 ("Synergy").

tute the social phenomenon as a special form of being in the world and the object of a special science.

It is deeply regrettable that many sociologists do not even pose this question, as though it were about something self-evident. At the same time, however, there are numerous attempts to answer the given questions in one way or another. The most important forms of these answers fall into three types: *(a)* those that distinguish special centers of this interaction that are not found in its other forms; *(b)* those that indicate special characteristics of social interaction that distinguish it from other categories; and, finally, *(c)* those that simultaneously combine both modes. The last of these distinguish social interaction from the generic concept as a special form by indicating its specific characteristics and by indicating its interacting units (centers). Thus, through each type, one can define a special category of social interaction and so also define the object of sociology. Let us illustrate each type.

Type A. It is possible to say, for example, that social interaction will only be that in which the interacting centers (units) are biologically indivisible units. In this case, the field of sociology would encompass not only the human world but also that of animals and plants ("zoosociology" and "phytosociology").[12] Its problem would be knowledge of all forms of interaction between the designated centers.

Following this type, it is possible to posit another, taking as similar centers only people. This in fact is the one that most representatives of social science follow. In this case, the problem of sociology would include knowledge of all forms of intercourse among people. Simmel's concept of the social phenomenon can serve as a concrete example of this type. "Society," he says, "exists everywhere that several individuals are in interaction, no matter what the consequences." From this point of view, even war is a social fact. "I am genuinely inclined to regard war as the ultimate case of socialization," he says.[13]

Type B. Side by side with this example, another is possible, one that defines the social phenomenon by indicating specific characteristics of the process of interaction. The general feature of all constructions of this type consists in defining social interaction as psychological interaction. In this case, it is not the character of the centers of interaction that serves as the principle constituting social interaction but rather the

12. See W. Wagner, "Sociology in Botany," *Nature* (September 1912), in which the principles of phyto- and zoosociology are stated, the corresponding problems of phytosociology are presented, and an evaluation of such efforts is given.

13. Simmel, *A Sociological Sketch*, 34–37. See also the article of F. Puglia in *Annales de l'Institute de Sociologie* 2, 69–72.

psychological reason for interaction—independent of the interaction itself—among whatever sort of centers it occurs. "Every interaction that has a psychological reason is social interaction"—such is the formula for this type.

Upon this general principle, shared by a great many sociologists, we have a series of theories that differ from one another in minor details. That social interaction is psychological interaction is an idea unanimously shared by Espinas and Giddings and Tarde and de Roberty and Petrazhitsky and Tönnies and Kelles-Kraus and so on. Some of these theorists, however, see social interaction in every psychological interaction, while others see it only in psychological interaction with specific symptoms. It is possible to place such figures as, for example, de Roberty in the first group.[14] Others—including Espinas, Letourneau, Giddings, Gumplowicz, Tönnies, Makarevicz, and so forth—regard as the social phenomenon only psychological interaction that manifests either a striving for mutual use and mutual service, or "consciousness of kind," or "common interest," or common purpose.

"Societies," says Espinas, "are groups in which individuals, though distinct, are normally united by psychological bonds—that is, by ideas and mutual impulses." To this feature he adds the indicator "mutual exchange of services" as the characteristic sign of society.[15] And since these symptoms are found also in animal societies, this gives him the right to include the animal world within the field of sociology.

Similar to the foregoing views are the concepts of society (or the social phenomenon) of such figures as Giddings, who sees "pure association" where there is "consciousness of kind" that carries over into "the love of camaraderie."[16]

From the point of view of Tarde, social interaction is intermental (psychological) interaction having an imitative character, the polar extremes of which are opposition and accommodation.[17]

Without presenting further illustrations, we now turn to the third type of definition of social interaction, which consists in a combination of both of the previous modes.

Type C. There are a great many variations on this type. Some theorists—for example, Durkheim and Stammler—understand as the ob-

---

14. De Roberty, *A New Statement,* 49; *New Ideas in Sociology* 1: 5.

15. A. V. Espinas, "To Be or Not to Be," *Revue philosophique* (1904): 466–68; *The Social Life of Animals,* 79, 107, and elsewhere.

16. Giddings, *Principles of Sociology,* 445ff.

17. G. Tarde, *Studies in Social Psychology,* 59–61; "Psychology and Sociology," *Annales de sociologie,* 10: 78; *The Laws of Imitation* (Paris: Alcan, 1890), 68, 89, and elsewhere.

ject of social science the interaction of people (centers here are people) but only that in which external compulsion is found. "A social fact," says Durkheim, "is every form of activity, whether sharply defined or not, capable of exerting external pressure on an individual."[18] Stammler agrees with him in this regard, with his focus on the "external regulation of joint human life."

Others, such as Spencer, understand as the object of sociology (society) interaction among people that involves a constancy of relationships. A third group, including Makarevicz, Gumplowicz, Letourneau, and Tönnies, considers the social phenomenon to be interaction among people that displays a striving for a "common purpose." ("Society is found where two or a greater number of individuals strive to attain a general purpose," says Makarevicz.)[19] Or society is found where there is a "general interest." (Society is "a group concentrated around a general interest of some sort," writes Gumplowicz.)[20] Some figures, such as Makarevicz and Tönnies, distinguish *Gemeinschaft* and *Gesellschaft [communité* and *société]*, understanding by the latter terms groups of people striving for some common purpose, or groups constructed on a contractual basis, and so forth.[21] The family usually has the quality of *Gemeinschaft;* a commercial company, the quality of *Gesellschaft;* and so on. To this same type must be added numerous constructions of the object of sociology akin to those of Ward, de Greef, Palante, Novicow, Worms, Puglia, Ostwald, and others.[22]

Without reproducing further views, we see already from the foregoing synopsis—which has attempted to concisely, adequately, and vividly characterize and systematize numerous and diverse efforts to define the object of sociology—that sociologists have not yet achieved full agreement on this question and that the very conception of sociology remains vague. This diversity of views becomes still greater when we direct our attention to the distinctive efforts to construct social science "that for the most part have been presented by the Germans

18. Durkheim, *The Rules,* 19.

19. J. Makarevicz, *Einfuhrung in die Philsophie des Stratrafrechts* (Stuttgart: Enke, 1906), 36.

20. Gumplowicz, *Outlines of Sociology,* 222.

21. See F. J. Tönnies, *Gemeinschaft und Gesellschaft* (Leipzig: Fues, 1887); "Sociology and Psychology," *Annales* 10: 290–97. "The Fundamental Notions of Pure Sociology," *Annales* 6: 65ff.

22. See Ward, *Pure Sociology,* vol. 1, "Sociological Essays"; G. de Greef, *Sociology: The General Structure of Societies* (Brussels: Larcier, 1908), 8, 41, 62; G. Palante, *An Essay in Sociology* (Paris: Alcan, 1910), vols. 1 and 2; J. Novicow, *The Mechanism and Limits of Human Association* (1912), passim; Puglia, 69–72; W. Ostwald, *Die Energetischen Grundlagen der Kulturwissenschaft* (Leipzig: Klinkhardt, 1909).

under various names, such as "social philosophy," "the science of culture" [*Kulturwissenschaft*], "the science of ends" [*Zweckwissenschaft*], "the science of spirit" [*Geisteswissenschaft*], and so forth.[23]

Even though, in the impartial opinion of Puglia, it is impossible not to reproach many sociologists for frequently passing by the given problems—the precise definition of the object of their science—it would be unfair to deprive sociology of the title of science because of the absence of a generally accepted object of study. Its position in this regard is not worse, and perhaps better, than the position of other social sciences and "the science of spirit." When we take philosophy and the disciplines close to it—logic, psychology, ethics, aesthetics, history, economics, politics—we can say that all of these still await their own definitions, despite their venerable age. This being so, the problem if attentively followed leads not to an easy and cheap rejection of the "scientific character" of this or that discipline but to an effort to give a clear answer to the problems of "dubious" science and to the possibility of helping to resolve this situation.

The next question that we must answer is, To which of the foregoing three types should we give preference in defining the object of sociology?

It is hardly necessary to demonstrate that a speedy solution to this problem depends little on which of the given modes we select, because when all is said and done, each of these modes leads to type C. Each does so for the simple reason that the character of the centers of interaction and the character of the same process of interaction are not distinct from each other but are inseparably joined. It is possible to say that the character of the process of interaction is clarified by the character and features of its centers (the "substantial" point of view). If a pair of centers, *a* and *b* (for example, two rocks), have different features from centers *c* and *d* (for example, two animal organisms), then by the same token it is clear that the features of the processes of interaction will be different between *a* and *b* on the one hand and *c* and *d* on the other. It is also possible to state the reverse—that the character of the centers is a function of the features of the process of interaction ("logical relationships"), that the centers are only junctions in which the currents of processes of interaction cross one another.

As we conclude this article, it is desirable to touch also on one particular point that has elicited and elicits in our day no small amount of controversy, namely, the relationship between sociology and psy-

---

23. See R. Stammler, *Theorie der Rechtwissenschaft* (Halle: Buchhandlung des Waisenhauses, 1911).

chology (individual, collective, and the psychology of peoples [*Volker-psychologie*]). A great many sociologists, proceeding from the fact that sociology studies psychological interaction, have drawn two basic conclusions: (1) that sociology must lean upon psychology, and (2) that sociology is nothing other than collective psychology.

After attentive analysis of these controversies, however, it is impossible not to recognize that they are based, in large part, either on a misunderstanding on the one hand or on an imprecise formulation of arguments on the other. Thus, the controversy about whether sociology must lean on psychology—that is, whether in Comte's classification of sciences, psychology should follow biology (Ward, Tarde, Giddings, Palante, Mill, Spencer, de Greef, and others) or sociology should follow biology (and psychology is a derivative science leaning on biology and sociology, as geology leans on physics and chemistry)—leads to another controversy about how we should study and explain social phenomena and their evolution. Should we proceed from the characteristics of individual consciousness (individual psychology as the basis), or should we proceed from the fact of interaction and explain individual consciousness itself as a social phenomenon (sociology or collective psychology as the basis)? In the first case, individual psychology provides the correct point of departure: we try to explain social facts by means of analysis of their characteristics, as a totality of integrated individual consciousness or as their summation. And since individual psychology occupies itself with the analysis of these states of consciousness, we must conclude that it is the basis of sociology. In the second case, we would say that the very same characteristics of individual consciousness are not something found everywhere, independent of social surroundings and interaction, but on the contrary are simply the junctures or foci where diverse processes of interaction cross one another. Therefore the properties and character of these latter processes define the very character and composition of individual psychology. From this it follows that one should proceed not from analysis of the properties of individuals but from analysis of the process of interaction (or social intercourse). The features of the latter will explain the features of the former. Such is the position of "sociologism."

As is evident from this explanation, the controversy by its very nature leads to the question of which mode is methodologically preferable. Such a statement of the question already simplifies the problem considerably. It is possible to use, we think, either one or another method, but if we use the first, we must establish two important points or introduce two corrections. If by following the first point of view

consistently we ignore the very process of interaction as an autonomous factor, then we meet with two difficulties: (1) the inexplicability
of the genesis of spirit and (2) the inexplicability of how the logic of
the objectification of spirit differs from the logic of individual consciousness. Indeed, if the entire secret consists in explaining the characteristics of individual consciousness, then how shall we explain its development? By what power can consciousness become constantly more
complex, richer, and more splendid? Or, if it is by nature "formed by
itself," how can it progress without any reasons or factors? It is clear
that from a logical point of view, this explanation is unacceptable, first
of all because it involves some sort of miracle (autogenesis). Second,
it is unacceptable because it is a Malerov explanation—"Opium lulls
one to sleep, because sleep is its characteristic"—which is no explanation at all.

In view of this, the second perspective considerably improves the
matter by pointing to the process of interaction as the factor that explains the transformation of individual consciousness. This position
presents an advantage not only from the logical point of view, as a
hypothesis that fully clarifies the "unexplained," but also finds support
in purely empirical conditions: *(a)* In the fact that when personality is
more or less isolated from social intercourse and its complex and diverse aspects, it not only does not develop, regardless of the rich incli-
nations of its consciousness, but, on the contrary, "runs wild". *(b)* In
the fact that like consciousness itself, its fundamental features (for example, the differentiating and synthesizing faculty of consciousness,
memory, understanding, will) are only a direct reflection of the characteristics of the process of social intercourse: the law of differentiation
and integration of societies, the law of preservation. The continuity
and superindividual being of societies and so forth are also inexplicable
without this process of social intercourse, which is affixed to any aspect of consciousness.[24] And *(c)* in the fact that where interaction is
complex and intensive, there individual psychology is also complex
(an argument based on the method of concomitant variations).

On the other hand, the products of social interaction are hardly
a mere summation of the characteristics of individual consciousness.
Whether we take law, or language, or myths, or religion, or science,
in their objectified forms, all are inexplicable as an arithmetic sum of

24. On this relationship, see the works of de Roberty, Durkheim (*The Elementary
Forms of Religious Life* [Paris: Alcan, 1912]), and in particular Draghichesco (*On the
Role of the Individual,* 112–271), who gives a systematic explanation of these positions.
Also see G. Simmel, *Religion* (Moscow, 1909).

the characteristics of individual consciousness.[25] If we are skeptical about theories that explain the formation of the state through the individual powers of "heroes," then still less can we believe in theories of individual creation of these aspects of culture. And here the second theory has the advantage that, by pointing to interaction itself as a factor that transforms quantitative differences into qualitative ones, it greatly assists in clarifying the given phenomena. From this perspective, "social reality is a social bond, having a psychological reason and realizing itself in the consciousness of individuals, that leads at the same time through its composition and continuity to its limit. This social spirit, which from the sociological point of view is civilization, is also, from the historical point of view, the world of values, as opposed to the world of things that forms the object of the physical sciences."[26]

With regard to the position that sociology must be merged with social or collective psychology, it is necessary to keep the following points in view. Many have already proposed substituting the term "collective psychology" for "sociology," in view of the vagueness of its object. We would have nothing against this change, if they could show us that the subject of collective psychology is clearer. However, we have not received that from them, and thus we do not find a basis for such a change, because in that case we would exchange one unknown x for a not-better-known y.

Examining that which in point of fact is given under the name "collective psychology," we should quickly recognize it as a division of sociology. Thus, from Siegel's point of view, collective psychology studies psychological interaction, such as that among "heterogeneous" individuals, that has a weak organic bond (for example, a crowd, the theater-going public, conventions, and so forth). By virtue of this, interaction here acquires different forms than in aggregates of "homogeneous and organic unions." This, in the opinion of Siegel, serves as a basis for the formation of a special science, collective psychology, that is distinct from sociology, which specifically studies the interaction of

25. On the relation to language, myth, and the instinct of work, see W. Wundt, in particular *Elements of Folk Psychology* (Leipzig: Kroner, 1912), 1–11; Lazarus; Steintahl; and the article of Simmel, "The Concept and Tragedy of Culture," *Sociology:* 21. On the relation to instincts, see Lucien Lévy-Bruhl, *Morality and the Science of Mores* (Paris: Alcan, 1903). On the relation to religion, see E. Durkheim, *The Elementary Forms of Religious Life.* On the relation to science, see E. V. de Roberty, *The Constitution of Ethics* (Paris: Alcan, 1900), *The Sociology of Action,* and *Concepts of Reason* (1912).

26. Kozlowsky, *"La realite sociale," Revue philosophique* (1912): 171.

"homogeneous" individuals and the "organic bonds" among them.[27] Such is also the point of view of de la Grasserie, in whose opinion the object of collective psychology is casual, unorganized aggregates that are neither formed nor differentiated nor coordinated—in a word, aggregates in which there is no constancy of relationship in the interaction of individuals. Aggregates of this type are the object of social psychology.[28]

In the opinion of Tarde, collective psychology is intermental psychology, in contrast to intramental and extramental psychology. The first of these, which studies "suggestion [*suggestion*] proceeding from one mind to another in a normal condition," is also, in essence, sociology.[29]

In the opinion of LeBon, collective psychology is a science that studies "the spirits of races."[30] Most Italians also distinguish social psychology from sociology and collective psychology. Thus, according to the view of Rossi, collective psychology is a science that studies psychological interaction found in casual aggregates (in "the crowd") and proceeding on the ground of synesthesia [*sinestesia collettiva*]. Social psychology studies "the spirit of the people or the race"—that is, the spirit of stable aggregates; while sociology is the crown of this and other sciences, which has as its object "social interaction [*il concorso sociale mutuamente consentito*], at first unconscious-automatic and then more and more conscious."[31]

Thus do F. Squillace, Colmo, Groppali, and others look at the matter. Without uselessly expanding the number of different understandings of collective psychology, it is already obvious from what has been said that the subject of collective psychology is no clearer than the subject of sociology.

In view of this, in order to define the relationship of the former to the latter, we must decide what we mean by collective psychology. If its problem is the study of all basic forms of psychological interaction—that is, the same thing that sociology studies, according to our definition—then obviously it is the gist of sociology, and one of these names will be superfluous. But it does not matter at all which one; the question is not about a word but about the very character of a science.

27. See Siegel, *The Criminal Crowd* (SPB, 1896), 3–17.
28. R. de la Grasserie, "On Psychosociology," *Revue de sociologie* 3 (1912): 167ff.
29. Tarde, "Psychology and Sociology," 78–79.
30. Gustave LeBon, *The Psychological Laws of the Evolution of Peoples* (Paris: Alcan, 1907), "The Spirit of Race."
31. P. Rossi, *Collective Psychology* (Milan, 1900), 213; *Sociology and Collective Psychology*, 2d ed., 99–112, 145–49.

If by collective or social psychology we mean that which Siegel, de la Grasserie, LeBon, Tarde, Rossi, Squillace, and others mean, then obviously it will be clearer under the heading of sociology, as the science that studies all basic forms of psychological interaction.

In this way, in our opinion, the controversy over the relationship between psychology and sociology is resolved.

2

Some Contrasts between European and American Sociology

Any attempt to draw a clearly cut line between European and American sociology as forming two organic systems, each conspicuously different from the other but harmonious and coherent within itself, is a very hopeless enterprise, faulty in its very nature. It is the purpose of this paper merely to illustrate contrasts and similarities in the general development of sociology in recent times. . . .

Let us begin with several exterior differences in the growth of sociology in Europe and America during the last seventy or eighty years. A conspicuous difference in this respect is that in America sociology has grown as a child nursed by the universities and colleges; while in Europe its modern start, since August Comte, and development have in a considerable degree taken place outside of the universities and colleges. Indeed a number of the founders of the principal modern sociological systems in Europe never occupied the position of a teacher in university at all. Among these were, for instance, Herbert Spencer, A. Gobineau, Otto Ammon, B. Kidd, J. Novicow, P. Lilienfeldt, K. Marx, G. Ratzenhofer, N. K. Mikhaylovsky, P. Lavrov, A. Coste, H. de Tourville, E. Demolens, P. Rousier, K. Loentieff, and others. Others occupied a temporary professorship not in the capacity of a professor of sociology but of a professor of natural science or a discipline widely different from sociology. Such was the connection with a college which August Comte, E. de Roberty, G. de Greef, F. Le Play, L. Gumplowicz, G. Simmel, M. Kovalevsky, G. Tarde, E. Durkheim, R. Worms, V. de Lapouge, Morselli, and many others had. Sociology was, so to speak, only their "hobby" and not what they were employed to teach in the university. Only quite incidentally a few of them occasionally gave a series of sociological lectures in various "free colleges"—schools not included in the system of regular colleges supported by the governments—or perhaps gave in the regular universities some sociological,

Originally published in *Social Forces* 8 (September 1929): 57–62. Reprinted by permission of the publisher.

some non-obligatory course—a "hobby-course"—not included in the regular college curriculum. In the United States the situation was very different. Here sociology emerged, from its very beginning, as a university or college discipline. Long before any European university had a sociological course, a series of American universities introduced sociology as a regular course in the university curriculum. As early as 1876 W. G. Sumner gave his course in sociology at Yale; in 1890 sociology was given by F. H. Giddings in Bryn Mawr [College]; it was introduced in 1885 at Indiana, in 1889 at Kansas, in 1890 at Johns Hopkins, in 1891 at Harvard, and in 1898 at Chicago Universities.[1]

This difference also continues to exist at the present moment: although the number of universities and colleges in Europe where sociology has been introduced as a regular course has considerably increased since the time of the War and revolutions, nevertheless this number is still much below that of the United States. In Europe sociology still remains an extra-university discipline not recognized by the majority of the universities; in the United States the universities and colleges which do not have it are the exceptions.

Since up until the last few years sociology in Europe was not taught in colleges, there was no need for an existence of the textbooks in sociology. Since in America sociology was adopted very early by the colleges, this made necessary the preparation of the college textbooks. Hence the fact that while American literature in sociology has been composed largely out of the textbooks, in Europe the textbook literature has occupied a relatively insignificant place in the total sociological literature of that continent. Up to 1906–10, in European sociological literature there were almost no books written for the special purpose of serving as texts. At the best there were few works remotely approaching to the text type, as for instance L. Gumplowicz's *Grundriss der Soziologie* (1885), or G. de Greef's *Introduction à la sociologie* (1885), Morselli's *Sociologia generale* (1898), Th. Achelis's *Soziologie*, R. Eisler's *Soziologie* (1903), E. Waxweiler's *Esquisse d'une sociologie* (1906), and two or three other similar works. But even these were not written with the purpose of serving as texts and represented either a summary of other, more substantial works by the same authors or a popularization of sociological works for the general public at large. The bulk of sociological works produced in Europe has been composed almost entirely out of monographic works; works which

---

1. See A. Small, "Fifty Years of Sociology in the United States," *American Journal of Sociology* 21: 732ff. Giddings, however, developed his beginnings from the editorial offices of *The Springfield Republican*.

have not cared to be popular or suitable for students but have cared, principally, to be a contribution to the science of sociology. In America the situation has been rather the opposite. The energy of the American sociologists to a much greater extent has been spent in the production of the textbook literature. Before 1906–10, American sociology already had a series of books written for texts and with the characteristics of texts. Samples of these are *Introduction to the Study of Society* by A. Small and G. Vincent (1894); *Principles of Sociology* by F. H. Giddings (1896); Giddings's *Elements of Sociology* (1898); *Outlines of Sociology* by L. Ward (1898); *Text-Book of Sociology* by J. C. Dealey (1903); *Introduction to Sociology* by A. Fairbanks (3rd ed. 1903); *Elements of Sociology* by F. W. Blackmar (1905); *Foundations of Sociology* by E. A. Ross (1905); *Sociology and Social Progress* by T. N. Carver (1907); and *General Sociology* by G. E. Howard (1907). The situation is similar at the present moment. The yearly production of sociological literature in America is still represented by textbook literature—this to a degree incomparably larger than that of Europe.

This difference is even more significant than it appears from its exterior form. In the first place it explains why the American sociological textbook literature is the best in the world. No other country can rival the United States in this field—not only quantitatively but also qualitatively. Even now, in spite of the appearance of several European textbooks in sociology, they are neither so well rounded, so full of information, nor so well adapted for the textbook requirements as are many American sociology texts. This is true both of the texts in general sociology and of special sociologies, be it rural and urban sociology, social psychology, criminology, cultural anthropology, social evolution, and so on.

However, this superiority of the American textbooks has had its drawbacks. The point is that the textbook always puts some limitations on the originality of the work. A good textbook must always be well proportioned, and no one part of it can be very much developed. Again, any good text contains a great deal of truism and platitude, current and popular opinion. Any text requires from its author not so much creative originality as a competent survey of existing theories and material well known to the specialists but unknown to the students. Textbook writing is somewhat in conflict with the writing of original monographs, which tend to say something new and important and to say it distinctly and in a developed form. The more a sociologist is busy with the writing of texts, the less he has time and energy for the production of original monographs; for, as a rule, monographs require enormous energy, patience, meditation, creative mind, and much research. This is almost impossible for a scholar busy with the writing of texts. In addition, one engrossed too much in textbook production is likely to acquire habits of thinking stamped by "the textbook intellectual level," which, as a rule, is much below the intellectual level of a monograph. Add to this the various commercial and similar considerations which tend to lower the level of the textbooks still more. Likewise, the habit of publishing and financing in inexpensive editions numerous important monographs has not been established in the American scene. All this explains why American sociological literature, although unrivaled in the field of texts, at the same time can scarcely be said to be unrivaled in the field of real scientific contributions to sociology—in the field of new, original, and fertile theories, in the field of real enrichment of our knowledge of social phenomena. It is certain that American sociology has made its contribution in this field also, and we shall see that this contribution has been rapidly increasing, but, as yet, it has not been so great as to be unrivaled. If one would survey the most important original theories in the field of sociology which have been set forth during the last fifty years, it is likely that any of the large European countries—France, England, Italy, Germany, Russia—has serious reasons to maintain that its contribution to sociology has been, at least, not less than that of the United States of America. And it is probable, also, that each of these countries would be able to confront the three or four outstanding American sociologists (in the field of original contributions) of the last fifty years by the same or an even greater number of equally outstanding sociologists. Such is the essence of this difference.

The next important point of difference between the sociologies compared is as follows. Though the last twenty years have been marked in Europe by an establishment of special institutes for sociological research, such as the Solvay Institute in Belgium or the Köln Institute and the Institut für Betriebs-soziologie in Germany or Le Play House in England, nevertheless, the number of such institutions in Europe has been very limited, and the research opportunities have been very scarce (mainly on account of a lack of funds, in the war and postwar conditions). In the United States the situation in this respect has been, for the same period, incomparably more favorable. In various forms—beginning with various experimental stations and ending with various research institutes in the field of social phenomena—this country has, at the present moment, an incomparably greater number of such institutions and spends incomparably larger funds for various branches of research in the field than any or perhaps than all European countries taken together. This naturally results in the much more rapid progress of sociological research in this country than in European countries. At the present moment, American sociology has already such an enormous and valuable amount of special research material that even very few of the American sociologists themselves have an adequate idea of its richness and significance, and not a single American author of a text in general sociology has tried to any significant degree to use it. At the present moment, the American situation is characterized by "a lack of the missing link" between the textbook literature and that of special research. This "missing link" is an elaboration of new inductive theories, principles, and generalizations based on the data of special researches. If this is done in the future, and if Europe does not keep pace with America in the field of research, this may lead to the future ascendancy of American over European sociology.

Let us now consider another difference. Putting aside the works of the outstanding European and American sociologists and taking the bulk of the ordinary sociological works of both continents, we cannot but notice a conspicuous difference between their character. The bulk of the sociological works in America are marked by their quantitative and empirical character while the bulk of the sociological literature of Europe is still marked by an analytical elaboration of concepts and definitions, by a philosophical and epistemological polishing of words. Putting the same idea in negative form it may be said: The bulk of the sociological studies in America is very rich in quantitative and empirical materials and is somewhat poor in fine and elegant thinking; the food is rich but it is not quite finely digested. In Europe the bulk of the studies show fine thinking with all the exquisiteness of epistemology and logic, but the wheels of this fine thinking are moving in the air on account of the lack of concrete and carefully studied material. The result is, in the American case, the domination of the material over its investigator and the limited vista of the investigator, who often behind the trees of his material does not see the forest. In Europe the result of the fine intellectual machinery working in the air is a kind of scientific sterility, an unfertile word-polishing which does not get us any further. Indeed, consider hundreds and thousands of various special bulletins, theses, papers, surveys, and so on published annually in America. They are full of figures, diagrams, case studies, tables, correlation coefficients, indices, newspaper clippings, and other forms of empirical materials. And yet, among all these studies, one rarely finds a really thoughtful study, with fine and elegant logic and with logical and epistemological discriminations; a clear mastership over the facts studied, a broad horizon, a large mental perspective, a solid background, and adequate generalizations are the exception. The bulk of the studies are rather of a routine, I would say even of an automatic, character. Living in an age where everything from a car to a Victrola record tends to become automatic, our studies follow the same tendency. Every professor of sociology or psychology or political science in this country through whose hands have passed dozens of master's and doctor's theses, who has read hundreds of various surveys and case studies, who has gone through dozens of various bulletins and research studies published by various research institutions knows that the enormous bulk of these works were prepared almost half-automatically. To send a questionnaire or to compile the data from superficial interviews and other sources of a survey; to tabulate them; to apply Pearsonian or other formulas of correlation—that is the usual procedure in a great many of the studies. Having performed these or even still simpler operations, the authors describe the results often without any particular knowledge and carefulness, and the study is ready. All this is done half-automatically—just following the usual routine without any attempt to penetrate into or to ask of the validity of the material, its adequacy, the validity or spuriousness of the correlation, the real significance of the formula applied and the adequacy of the results received, their similarity or discrepancy with the results of similar studies, the survey of these other studies, and so on and so forth. In nonstatistical studies one commonly meets defective logic, a poor knowledge of the field, an ignorance of the studies made before, a superficiality of the thinking, lack of originality, clumsy methodology, etc. In spite of the ability to make an automatic application of the Pearsonian formula, studies often show a violation of the fundamental laws of logic and a lack of any understanding of the fundamental laws of induction. Shall we wonder that under such circumstances a considerable bulk of these researches do not rise above a purely clerical, half-automatic work, with all the limitations, provincialisms, and faults of such works? This is what I mean by the domination of the material over its investigator, lack of fine thinking, and loose logic of these researches. Such is one of the most common defects of a considerable part of the American researches which must be overcome if we are to have genuine scientific researches instead of pseudoscientific stuff whose value is very questionable.

In Europe, with regard to logic and fine thinking, the situation seems to be better. Whether this is due to the fact that these studies have very sparse concrete material which by virtue of its sparseness cannot dominate the investigator and urges him to compensate for the lack of material by polished speculation; or whether it is due to a greater attention paid in European universities to logic, philosophy, and epistemology, which give a refinement to thinking; or whether to the fact that many European sociologists came to sociology from philosophy, logic, epistemology (e.g., Simmel, Durkheim, de Roberty, Wundt, and many others) or at least were well trained in these disciplines—whatever may be the cause, the discussed art of a more elegant thinking in European sociological works, in German, French, Italian, and Russian, can scarcely be questioned. As a sample, take for instance the recent works of L. von Wiese, O. Spann, Th. Litt, K. Breisig, C. Brinkman, W. Sauer, Gerhard Lehman, Th. Geiger, A. Walter, F. W. Jerusalem, H. L. Stoltenberg, Max Scheler, Max Hausenstein, and Hans Freyer in Germany; or the works of M. Halbwachs, C. Bouglé, G. Richard, Mauss, Fauconnet, Hubert, and others in France. As a rule, one almost always finds in these works a thinking with all the delicacies of epistemological discriminations, though quite commonly one finds in these works very little "real meat."

There are some exceptions to the difference discussed, but the difference itself seems to be quite tangible and real. From this standpoint it is very useful for a European sociologist to come to this country and to plunge himself into the study of the bulk of special researches existing and to learn the method, the technique, and the results of these researches. On the other hand, it is advisable for an American sociologist to peruse carefully European sociological works in order to acquaint himself with the fine points of its elegant art of thinking. The study of philosophy, logic, epistemology may also help a great deal in this respect. So much for this point.

The last general difference between the sociologies compared is that European sociological works show a somewhat better knowledge of history generally and the history of social thought particularly, and the historical method is somewhat more and more skillfully used than in the American sociological works. Glance through the bulk of the European sociological works and you will see that they, as a rule, open with a developed or short historical survey of the preceding theories in the field; they are full of references to historical facts; they use wide historical confrontations and historical material, especially that from the history of law and juridical codes, institutions, and sources. In America such a procedure is relatively rare. The majority of the texts, and often even treatises, either do not have any references at all to the predecessors or, at the best, have a few scanty references to American sociologists—mostly other textbook writers. Putting the thing in a humorous way, we can say that the bulk of American sociological works tacitly imply that there was nothing or very little before 1890, when sociology definitely appeared in America. Of course a few sociologists like Comte and Spencer there were, but they were about all. As a rule, a knowledge of the history of social thought has been very meager in America; this applies to the bulk of the sociologists. As a result, the classical works of sociology in their original or translations—be it the works of Comte or Spencer, Buckle or Durkheim, Tarde or Max Weber, Condorcet or Ibn Khaldūn—Vico or Plato, Aristotle or Confucius—as a rule are unknown to the bulk of the teachers in sociology or are known only from some secondary sources and in a very inadequate form. A knowledge of the classical works in sociology and social sciences has not been required from the candidates for master's or doctor's degrees in sociology. This explains the short historical memory of American sociological works.

Concluding this superficial characterization of the American and European sociologies, it should be emphasized that the above contrasts and parallelisms are to be taken only as very approximate and rough; nevertheless, I hope that they are not misleading. From the above one can see that as far as the American sociology is concerned, its present situation is rather cheerful in comparison with the situation in Europe. If the American sociologists would try further to reinforce themselves in the weak points indicated; if their energy more and more will be given to the research monographs instead of being given to the manufacturing of the texts; if in addition the bulk of them would try to avoid the "merry-go-round" in superficial "preaching" generalities and would plunge themselves in the painstaking and deep study of specific problems; then, with the favorable financial and other situations in this country, and with a realistic bent of American mind, there are all the reasons to expect the flaring up of American sociology to a new and higher level. This is the more true because of the fact that in some fields of special sociology, for instance in rural sociology, America already occupies this position of leader, not only in textbooks but in monographic literature.

3

Sociology as a Science

I

Since, by the grace of our president, I have to talk on the nature and subject matter of sociology and its relationship to other social sciences, I shall begin with a critical remark intended to clear the ground for a subsequent construction. This remark consists in the claim that most of the existing definitions of sociology appear to me unsatisfactory. The samples and reasons follow.

Sociology has been defined as the science of culture. Such a definition hardly defines, since culture is a broad term and nearly all of the social sciences—economics, history, jurisprudence, philology, political science, science of arts and literature—are sciences of culture. The definition is far too loose and does not differentiate sociology from other social sciences at all. It stops where it should begin its task and analysis.

Again, sociology has been variously defined as the science of human relations, of the phenomena of social interaction, of social forms, of group interpretation, or simply as the science of society. So far as such definitions stop at these points and do not try to show how and in which way sociological study of these phenomena differs from a study of the same phenomena by all the other social sciences, these definitions are open to the same objection of lack of any precision. They fail to go far enough to differentiate properly sociology from the other social sciences, all of which also study human relations, social interaction, social forms, and society. Whether you take economics, or history, or the science of law, or political science, or ethics, or any of the social disciplines, they all deal with these phenomena.

Some of our colleagues have tried to find the proper field of sociology in the so-called "group interpretation," of social facts. I am afraid their "property claim" will also be disputed. If "group interpretation" means that sociology deals with groups rather than with individuals,

Address given at the Eastern Sociological Conference, 25 April 1931. Originally published in *Social Forces* 10 (1931): 20–27. Reprinted by permission of the publisher.

then obviously it does not differ from most of the social sciences, since they also deal with groups and associations. Political science deals with the state, municipality, community, Congress, Parliament, court, and other groups and institutions. Economics deals with corporations, trusts, cooperative groups, various associations, social classes, and other groups. The same is true of history, which deals with all kinds of groups; of the science of language, religion, arts, and whatnot. "Language group," "Roman Catholic Church," "Gothic or classical art," and so on imply neither an individual nor a mere sum of individuals but groups as integrated social bodies. If by group interpretation is meant that sociology explains social phenomena as a result of group activities, then again it must be said that hardly any social science interprets social phenomena as a result of the activity of isolated individuals but always as a result of group activity.

Mutadis mutandis, the same can be said of sociology as a science of society and some other definitions. So much for a criticism; now, for a construction.

II

Any satisfactory definition of sociology will show first, that sociology studies a set of social phenomena either not studied systematically by any other social science or studied by sociology from a point of view different from that of the other social sciences; and second, that the class of phenomena studied and the standpoint from which they are studied are logically consistent and scientifically important. Let us take, first, the sociological standpoint.

In the observation of any set of phenomena, our attention may be directed either to the traits and relationships *peculiar* to this set or to the traits and relationships *common* with many other sets. Studying any phenomenon—physical, chemical, biological, social, psychological—we may busy ourselves either with marking the characteristics which belong to our phenomenon only, which are not found in any other phenomenon and consequently are unique and unrepeated in time or space; or we may concentrate on marking the traits in which the phenomenon studied is similar to other phenomena, which therefore are repeated in time or in space or in both. The first standpoint is *individualizing;* the second, *generalizing.* The disciplines in which the first viewpoint predominates are individualizing sciences, like all historical disciplines; those in which the second viewpoint predominates are generalizing sciences, like physics, chemistry, and general biology. The individualizing disciplines are concerned predominantly with a description of the unique—unrepeated—phenomena and relationships, in all their concreteness; the generalizing sciences, with a description of uniformities and formulation of laws—that is, the sets of relationships repeated either in time series, or in space, or in both. The inner structure, the scope, and the methods of these two types of sciences are profoundly different—almost opposite, as it has been brilliantly shown by Cournot, W. Windelband, and H. Rickert. Since that is so, the first thing which every sociologist has to decide in defining the nature of sociology is as to whether sociology is to be an individualizing or generalizing science. Without a solution of this pre-problem, there is no possibility of arriving at a clear and logically consistent concept of sociology. On the other hand, the decision predetermines all the essential traits of sociology, which would be profoundly different in both cases. In my opinion sociology is and should be a generalizing science. It has been a generalizing discipline in the conceptions of all great sociologists from Confucius, Plato, Aristotle, Ibn Khaldūn, and Vico to August Comte, Herbert Spencer, Tarde, Durkheim, and Pareto, and it should be because such a discipline is needed among social sciences and because otherwise it would be identical with history—that is, nonexistent, *de facto*. Such is my choice. When it is properly understood it becomes evident at once that through this generalizing standpoint it radically differs from all the *historical* social sciences. The contrast is as great as it could be. In contradistinction from any historical discipline, busy mainly with the unique and unrepeated aspects of social phenomena (like the history of Rome, of China, of the Roman Catholic Church, of Abraham Lincoln, of Yale University, and so on—each subject being a unique phenomenon not repeated either in time or space), sociology is interested only in those aspects of social phenomena and their relationships which are repeated either in time or in space or in both; which consequently exhibit some uniformity or constancy or typicality. Historical sciences paint the individual picture of the unique phenomenon studied (a certain person, institution, social object, social constellation of certain conditions); sociology gives either an abstract formula (law) which describes (quantitatively or otherwise) a repeated uniformity (or the degree of variability) in the relationship between two or more societal variables or a *type* as a composite photography of the repeated social phenomena of a certain kind. This difference sharply differentiates sociology from all historical disciplines.

III

When this cardinal point is well understood, the nature of general as well as special sociologies becomes easily comprehensible. Under these conditions, the task of *general* sociology may consist evidently in nothing but a study of those traits and relationships which are common to all social phenomena. To be common to all social phenomena means to be given in any social phenomenon wherever and whenever it exists or to be repeated any time and anywhere where any social phenomenon is given. Through this subject matter, general sociology radically differs from all the other social sciences. None of them studies this problem, and none is competent to study it, as long as it remains a special social science. Each of these other social disciplines studies only its special variety of social phenomena: economics, the economic variety; political science, the political variety; and so on. But insofar as all these varieties are subclasses of the same general class of social phenomena, they all must have, side by side with their specific characteristics and relationships, some traits and relationships common to all of them; otherwise they cannot belong to the general class of social phenomena and cannot be styled by a common name of the social sciences. Schematically, this can be expressed in the following way. Let the following varieties of social phenomena consist of the following elements and relationships:

> economic: a, b, c, n, m, f, e
> political: a, b, c, h, d, j, p
> religious: a, b, c, g, i, q, r
> and so on

Granting that all the other varieties of social phenomena have the same common elements and relationships—a, b, c—these a, b, c would compose the field of general sociology. An isolation, description, analysis, and classification of these common elements and relationships is the subject matter of general sociology. This field is not studied by the other social sciences, on the one hand; on the other, for its study there must exist a separate discipline. The logical requirement of adequacy and the principle of the economy of effort urge imperatively the existence of such a discipline. The logical adequacy requires that where there exist N subclasses of a certain class of the phenomena, the number of the scientific disciplines for their study has to be $N + 1$. If there are two subclasses of organisms—plants and animals—there must be not only botany and zoology but the third discipline—general biology—which studies the traits common to all organisms. If there are n

varieties of the physical phenomena—sound, electricity, etc.—there must be and there is, besides special physical disciplines each of which deals with one variety, an additional part—general physics. Besides a discipline which studies, say, the female sex of *Homo sapiens,* and a discipline which studies its male sex, there must be a discipline which studies the traits common to both sexes. Otherwise, if the traits belonging only to one variety are ascribed to the whole class of phenomena (for instance, specific traits of plants to all organisms), the theory will be inadequate or fallacious. If, on the other hand, each special discipline dealing with a special variety of the given class of phenomena would repeat all the traits common to the whole class, the theory would also be inadequate and immensely wasteful from the standpoint of the economy of effort. Suppose that a special discipline dealing with a certain variety of matter—for instance, with Lucky Strike cigarettes—would begin seriously to contend that "Lucky Strikes gravitate in direct ratio to the mass and in inverse ratio to the square of the distance," that in their field "the action is equal to the reaction," and so on, enumerating thousands of laws of physics and chemistry and general biology valid not only for the Lucky Strikes but for matter generally and for all organisms, you can easily see that such a discipline would be a caricature on a scientific discipline and besides exceedingly wasteful from the standpoint of the economy of our efforts. Any real scientific achievement has always consisted in a reduction of numerous valid partial regularities to one more general valid regularity. Newton's law of gravitation was a great achievement because it embraced in one formula an infinitely great number of the partial uniformities and showed that this law was applicable not only to the Lucky Strike or to a more narrow field, as it was in Kepler's law, but to all matter. The same can be said of the social sciences. If each of them would repeat in application to its special variety the statements applicable to all varieties of social phenomena, such a discipline would be not far from our "science of the Lucky Strike."

One more remark before I pass to special sociologies. Many people seem to mix the above concept of general sociology with a vague synthetic philosophizing. They think that such a concept of sociology does not make out of it a special science but makes a kind of a "synthetic hodgepodge" or encyclopedia of all social sciences. I emphatically stress that such a conclusion is utterly wrong. Instead of a long analytical disapproval of this fallacy, let me briefly allude to its nature. The director or bookkeeper or treasurer of a firm deals with the whole firm, in contradistinction to the various employees, each of whom deals only with a small portion of the firm's business and activity. Shall we conclude from this that the functions of the director, or bookkeeper, or treasurer are "encyclopedic" and not special? Go to any firm or to any school of business administration and you can easily learn a simple truth: though their specialty involves dealing with the firm as a whole, nevertheless, their functions are highly specialized, much more so than the functions of a worker who does only one kind of operation. This shows that there are many kinds of specialties and among them a highly qualified specialty of "isolation, description, analysis, and classification (or management) of the traits and relationships of all classes or divisions of 'the firm' of social phenomena." This means that sociology in the above sense is a very special science but its specialty is different from that of the other social sciences. So much for the subject matter of general sociology.

IV

You know well that side by side with general economics there are a number of special economics, like economics of transportation, banking, agricultural economics, etc. The same is true of political science, psychology, and some other disciplines. Similar is the situation in sociology. Side by side with general sociology there exist and should exist a number of *specialized* sociologies. As to their standpoint, it is the same in regard to their particular fields as that of general sociology to its field—that is, the viewpoint of a generalizing discipline. As to their subject matter, it is a study of the traits and relationships common not to all social phenomena (this is the field of general sociology) and not to one variety of social phenomena (that is the field of the other social sciences), but repeated uniformities and relationships given between two or more varieties of different social phenomena or between the social and nonsocial phenomena. As you see, the subject matter of the special sociologies is "interstitial." The relationships between various forms of economic phenomena are studied by economics. The same is true of the relationships between various forms of the political phenomena studied by political science. We know well, however, that in social reality the economic phenomena are not isolated from the political; they interact and influence one another. Many economic conditions affect forms of political organization and processes, and vice versa. If economics is competent to study the economic phenomena, and political science, the political phenomena, neither one of these disciplines is logically competent or is entitled to study these interstitial problems. They, by virtue of their nature and definition, are beyond either economics or political science. They do not belong to their field. The same may be said of hundreds of other interstitial problems. Relationships between business cycles and vital processes; economic conditions and criminality; the suicide movement and religion; religion and economic organization; forms of recreation and forms of law and morals; heredity and genius; the racial factor and inventiveness; geographic factors and economic phenomena; climate and civilization; temperature and social rhythms—these and thousands of other problems are interstitial. There is no science among the other social sciences within which these problems fall. Meanwhile, they have to be studied. For their study there logically has to be a discipline. On account of the nature of sociology, these problems fall logically within its territory. They logically should belong to its special branches. And as a matter of fact they have belonged to them since long ago. Some time ago, there appeared geographical sociology, with its repeated study of the uniformities in the relationship between social and cosmic conditions; biological sociology, as a study of the relationship between biological factors and social phenomena; economic sociology, as a study of relationships between economic and political, religious, and other social phenomena; demographic sociology, busy with the relationships between the vital and various social phenomena; sociology of religion, trying to find out the relationship between the religious and the other varieties of social phenomena; sociology of arts; political sociology; and so forth.

These special sociologies have been existing, and [figure 3.1] shows that my concept of sociology logically and naturally fits the existing facts. Its logical "should" coincides with the factual "is." Such a coincidence is one of the best tests of the validity of a concept.

It is to be stressed that in outlining the field of the special sociologies, I have in view the logical nature of these fields and their problems but not the specialty of men who study them. These interstitial problems may and have been studied by doctors, farmers, emperors, professors of economics, philosophy, theology, and many others. The point is the logical nature of the problems which do not and cannot fall within the field of the other social sciences except sociology but not the vocation of the man who studies them. Newton wrote his famous *Principia* and the same Newton wrote his less famous commentaries on Apocalypse. From the fact that both of these works were written by the same man, famous naturalist, does not follow that both works belong to the same science of physics or theology. One logically falls within the field of physics; the other, within that of theology. Many great sociological studies were made by the nonsociologists *ex officio*

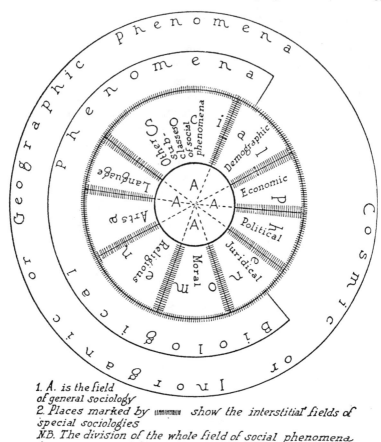

1. *A.* is the field of general sociology
2. Places marked by ▦▦▦ show the interstitial fields of special sociologies
N.B. The division of the whole field of social phenomena into a number of fields of social sciences is only illustrative

Figure 3.1

(Le Play, Ibn Khaldūn, Malthus, and so on) and vice versa; some of the sociologists *ex officio* (e.g., G. Tarde, E. Durkheim) made very important contributions to the fields of other sciences, like constitutional law, psychology, etc. The logical nature of a problem and its belonging to the field of a certain science is one thing; and by whom, according to a man's occupational status, the problem is studied is quite another thing. One should not mix them.

According to the logical nature of the problems discussed, many portions of such works as Plato's *The Republic*, Confucius's *Texts of Confucianism*, Aristotle's *Politics*, Ibn Khaldūn's *Prolegomènes*, Dante's *De Monarchia*, Montesquieu's *The Spirit of Laws*, Adam

Smith's *The Wealth of Nations,* Malthus's *Essay on Population,* and so on are nothing but a variety of either general or specialized pure sociology.[1]

Such in outline appears to me the logical nature of general and specialized sociologies, their standpoints, and their subject matters. This concept is logically consistent; it gives to sociology not only a system but inner coherency and unity; it makes sociology a special science in a particular sense; it is supported by the factual history of social thought and the present status of sociology; and last but not least, it clearly and definitely separates sociology from all the other social sciences, so far as a separation of various disciplines exists and is plausible.

The accompanying diagram depicts the concept given visually and may be helpful for a more concrete representation of the above.

---

1. This shows, by the way, that the usual idea that sociology is a young science born with August Comte is utterly fallacious. Sociology, as a matter of fact, is as old as almost any other science. Only the clumsy word "sociology," invented by Comte, is young.

4

Conclusion: Retrospect and Prospect

It is time to finish our walk over the field of sociology. We have crossed it from border to border in various directions. It is certain that we have not studied its secondary features as attentively as perhaps we should have. It is certain also that we could not study in detail the character of the small sociological houses built by individual sociologists. Nevertheless, we have explored the most important features of the field sufficiently well to have an approximately accurate idea about its present situation. Let us briefly sum up our impressions.

First, the field is divided into many areas with different methods of cultivation of sociological knowledge. Consequently, the knowledge itself grows in an elementary and somewhat anarchical way. The whole field reminds one of a half-wild national forest rather than a carefully planned garden. Shall we regret such a situation? The answer is that some improvement in the general planning for the whole field is probably desirable. Nevertheless, the planning and standardizing must not be overdone. An artificial standardization in sociology is especially dangerous. It may lead to a degeneration of real sociological knowledge into dry and lifeless scholastics. The complex nature of social phenomena makes rather necessary a variety of the approaches and methods of study. Attacking them with various methods and from various scientifically sound standpoints we have more chances to know them than by attacking with only one standardized method and from one standardized standpoint. Some sociologists are worried about the lack of such a uniform standard, and some nonsociologists often indicate this feature as an evidence that there is no such science as sociology. We must not be troubled much with these worries and criticisms. If the critics know something about the nonsociological cultural sciences like law, economics, history, political science, psychology, and so on, they must recognize that these disciplines are approximately in the same state of wilderness in which sociology is placed. Only those

Originally published in *Contemporary Sociological Theories: Through the First Quarter of the Twentieth Century* (New York: Harper and Row, 1928), 757–61. Reprinted by permission of the publisher.

of these "scholars" who do not know their specialty beyond a couple
of textbooks, or beyond their own block in the whole field of these
sciences, can believe that they are standardized and well "combed."
As a matter of fact, each of these sciences is in about the same state
of "wilderness" as sociology. Therefore we may advise the critics that
they would be better silent in this respect. "*Medice cura te ipsum*,"
we can say to them. So much about this point.

The second conspicuous feature of the explored field is that it is
rich with "sterile flowers" and "weeds." Speculative discussions about
what sociology is; what it ought to be; what culture is; whether society
is a bio-organic, psycho-organic, superorganic, or mechanic system;
whether culture is a psychical or nonpsychical phenomenon; what the
difference is between cultural, social, psychosocial, and psychological
phenomena; what progress is; what the relationship of society and the
individual is; and so forth and so on are examples of what is styled
"sterile flowers" in sociology. Many sociological works have factually
consisted in a mere speculation over these and similar problems and
have not gone further. They have taken the "antechamber" of sociology for its whole building. Besides, even these introductory problems
have been often outlined in the vaguest and the most unsatisfactory
way. Shall we wonder that such "sociologies" have not given us any
real knowledge of social phenomena, except a lot of somewhat indefinite words piled one upon another? Shall we be surprised that after
reading such "sociologies" many people of thoughtful mind should
have assumed a negative attitude toward such a "science"? They are
right as far as this "word piling" is concerned. They rightly say: "Instead of a long and tedious reasoning of what sociology is, show it in
fact." "Instead of a discussion over how sociology ought to be built,
build it." "Instead of flapping around the introductory problems of
the science, give us something certain; show us your causal formulas,
and give us a single real analysis of the phenomena." They seem to be
right in their criticism, as far as these "sterile flowers" of sociology
are concerned.

Now come the "weeds." Their first variety is represented by "the
preaching and evaluating judgments" in the field. Many a "sociological" work in its bulk is but a book of prescriptions of what is good
and what is bad, what ought to be done and what ought to be avoided,
what is progress and what is regress, what reforms are to be made to
save "the world" from its evils, and so on. As this preaching job does
not require any serious study of the facts, a great many incompetent
persons have pretended to be omniscient doctors who know how the
world is to be saved and give their "prescriptions" about war eradica-

tion, birth control, labor organization, the sex and race problem, and so forth. In this way, all kinds of nonsense have been styled, published, circulated, and taught as "sociology." Every idler has pretended to be a sociologist. Shall we wonder that this again has discredited sociology greatly? In view of the heterogeneity of scientific and evaluative judgments, and in view of the radical difference between a study of the facts as they are and moralizing on what they ought to be, it is rather evident that this "weed" should be eradicated from the field of scientific sociology and planted where it belongs.

Other "weeds" are different, but also harmful. An insufficient study of the facts in time and space; a mania for generalizing a certain conclusion far beyond the factual basis on which it is built; an ignorance of the theories and studies made by others and in preceding times; a failure to make from a certain hypothesis all the important conclusions and to verify them as to whether they are corroborated in space and time; a failure to test an invented hypothesis seriously—such are some of these "weeds." Shall we wonder that even the best theories in sociology are fallacious to a certain extent? A slight attempt to test them shows at once either that their factual analysis is wrong, or that their generalization is overdrawn, or that a purely fictitious correlation is accepted for a real one, or that the conclusion is one-sided. Under such conditions, it would naturally be expected that sociology would remind one of a "museum of scientifically pathological theories," as Professor Petrazhitsky rightly says. The reading of this book has shown this. It is needless to say that these "weeds" must be eradicated, too.

This criticism does not mean, however, that in this field we have found only sterile flowers and weeds. By no means. We have seen in each district a considerable number of potentially strong trees, fine plants, and beautiful flowers. I say "potentially" because they are considerably overgrown by the weeds and sterile flowers that need to be cleared away from them. This being done, they may be the pride of every scientific gardener. In so far as this, sociology is not only going to be a science but already *is* one; but only within the mentioned limits. In order to broaden these limits, we must evidently avoid a repetition of the above mistakes. This is the task of the younger and the future generations of sociologists.

Finally, one inference is to be made from the above survey. There are a great many theories devoted to a discussion of what sociology is and what is its subject matter. It is not my intention to enter into a discussion of the problem. My intention is to indicate that instead of a speculation over the problem, many an author would have done better by studying the development of sociological theories for the last fifty years. Such study shows something very instructive in this respect. In the first place it shows that several definitions of sociology are in contradiction with the real movement of sociological studies. For instance, if we must accept the definition of the formal school, almost all the above studies would have to be excluded from sociology. What would remain would represent something so insignificant that it scarcely would deserve the name of a sociology or any other science. With a corresponding change, this may be said of some other definitions of sociology. In the second place, the development of sociology begins to show more and more clearly what its subject matter is. It seems to be a study, first, of the relationship and correlations between various classes of social phenomena (correlations between economic and religious; family and moral; juridical and economic; mobility and political phenomena; and so on); second, that between the social and the nonsocial (geographic, biological, etc.) phenomena; third, the study of the general characteristics common to all classes of social phenomena. All the surveyed schools are busy with either the establishment of correlations between various classes of social phenomena or between the social and the nonsocial phenomena, or with an elaboration of the formulas which describe their most general features.[1] Whether a sociologist likes this or not, such seems to have been the real subject matter of sociological theories. More than that, this subject matter becomes more and more clear as we proceed from the beginning to the end of the period studied. It is not my purpose to develop and substantiate this conception of sociology and its subject matter. I have

1. It is easy to understand that both components of the subject matter of sociology are logically inseparable. Where we have to study N classes of phenomena, there logically should be $N + 1$ classes of sciences. Each of N special sciences studies the characteristics of its special class of phenomena; the additional $N + 1$ science would study the characteristics common to all N classes. Two fundamental classes of organisms, plants and animals, require the existence of botany, which studies the specific characteristics of plant organisms; zoology, which deals with animal organisms; and general biology, which studies the characteristics common to both classes of organisms and their relationship. Likewise, if social phenomena are classified into the classes $a, b, c, d, \ldots n$, each class being studied by a special social science (economics, political science, law, etc.), besides N special sciences there should be an $N + 1$ science which would study the general characteristics common to all N classes of social phenomena and the relationship or correlation between them. Such is the logical reason for an existence of sociology in the defined sense. And such has really been the subject matter of sociological theories for the period studied. See a brilliant analysis of the above in Leon Petrazhitsky, *Introduction to the Theory of Law and Morals* (St. Petersburg: Erlikh Publishers, 1907), 80–81; see also P. Sorokin, *Sistema Sotsiologii* 1:30–36.

done it elsewhere. Through indicating the above fact, I want only to draw the attention of the sociologist to what has been the real subject matter of sociological theories. This may prevent many a wild speculation over the problem and may be useful for those who are inclined to study this type of topic. In addition, I shall observe only that this conception agrees with the best definitions of sociology, though differently worded, and with the nature of really existing sociology. Being a mere inference from the survey, it is less speculative and more inductive than many other definitions, and therefore it is likely to be more accurate than many other definitions set forth by various authors. Sociology has been, is, and either will be a science of the general characteristics of all classes of social phenomena, with the relationships and correlations between them; or there will be no sociology.

5

Declaration of Independence
of the Social Sciences

Three Guesses

The times we live in are profoundly revolutionary. The epochal crisis of our sensate culture and society is unfolding before our very eyes. My statement a number of years ago that a crisis had begun which would attain an extraordinary scale presently was denied by many a critic; at the present time, only the blind can continue such denial. The extraordinary crisis is here in all its stark reality. The central issue of our times is not totalitarianism versus democracy, or capitalism versus communism, or internationalism versus nationalism, or pacifism versus militarism; still less is it Hitler or Stalin versus Churchill or Roosevelt. All these conflicts are mere sideshows. Living, as we do, at the beginning of the end of the sensate phase of our culture and society, in a period of profound transition, the issue is sensate culture and society versus the fundamentally different ideational or idealistic culture and society.

Such a crisis means a complete re-examination and re-evaluation of all the values, without exception, of the contemporary culture and society. From our science and philosophy, religion and fine arts, ethics and law, up to all forms of social, economic, and political organization, present-day values are subjected by the Supreme Court of History to merciless trial. Contemporary sociology and the social sciences are not exempt from this acid test. The verdict of this court is final and cannot be appealed. No one can predict with certainty what the verdict will be in regard to contemporary sociology and the social sciences. One can, however, offer a guess based on certain reasons. When it is given explicitly as a guess, and nothing more, nobody is misled, whether it be lucky or poor. Whichever it is, history will determine.

Paper delivered at the meeting of the American Sociological Society, Chicago, 29 December 1940. Originally published in *Social Science* 16 (July 1941): 221–29. Reprinted by permission of the publisher.

This point made clear, I am going to offer three guesses in this matter, hoping they will prove lucky, as some of my previous conjectures have turned out to be. The first guess anticipates the character of the verdict of history *re* contemporary sociology and the social sciences. The second guess concerns the reasons for this verdict as they will be formulated by the Supreme Court. The third guess foresees the kind of corrective discipline that is likely to be prescribed for sociology and the social sciences if they are to pass into the values of the culture to come.

First Guess: Anticipation of the Verdict

As to the verdict of the Supreme Court of History in the matter of contemporary sociology and social science generally, it is going to be something like a grade D, given to a student, representing neither complete failure nor satisfactory attainment. A student receiving such a mark is put on probation, with the provision that if he can improve, he will be passed. So will history deem that sociology and social science in the first half of the twentieth century were on probation.

Second Guess: Anticipation of the Reasons for the Verdict

The reasons given by the Supreme Court of History to justify its verdict are likely to be the following: Sociology and social science of the first half of the twentieth century were obsessed by an ambition to be copies of the natural sciences. Because of this obsession, they did not create referential principles adequate for a study of sociocultural phenomena nor develop methods fit for such a study. In addition, they discarded the referential principles and methods used by the great social thinkers of the past. Knowing little the real character of the natural sciences, and understanding still less their methods, sociologists and social scientists ascribed to the natural sciences conceptions and methods which the latter either have never employed or have long since discarded. They failed to see that if sociology and the social sciences were identical with the natural sciences in referential principles and methods, there would be no need for any "social physics" or "social mechanics" or "natural science sociology." In that case real physics, chemistry, mechanics, or biology would take care of the study of sociocultural phenomena, and no amateurish pseudophysics or pseudobiology would be necessary. All such homemade duplications of the natural sciences would be simply useless monstrosities devoid of the virtues of natural science and of understanding of sociocultural phenomena as distinct from inorganic and organic phenomena.

As a result of this imitative obsession, sociology and the social sciences of the first part of the twentieth century were neither natural science fish nor social science flesh. They did not have any consistent principles and methods of their own, nor could they fruitfully apply the concepts and methods of the natural sciences to sociocultural phenomena. From this fatal blunder all the specific defects of these disciplines followed.

A. They had more methods and more heterogeneous sets of principles than any natural science, yet they yielded very meager results in real cognition of sociocultural phenomena.

B. Being under a delusion that the natural sciences are based upon sensory observation and sense data only, sociology and the social sciences tried to base all their conclusions upon sense observation and upon nothing else. This peculiarity was called by different names, such as "operational or instrumental method," "pure empiricism," "behavioristic and objective study of sociocultural phenomena," "quantitative and sociometric method," "logico-experimental and inductive procedures," and the like. Obsessed by this delusion, these disciplines either vetoed or neglected reason and intuition as sources of cognition generally and of sociocultural cognition in particular. Any logical and epistemological analysis of sociocultural problems was declared to be merely a "tyranny of words" or "fruitless armchair philosophy" or "sterile tautology." Logic was replaced by semantics; mathematics, by numerology. Intuition, in all its forms, was branded as mere superstition; logical and intuitional truths, as stupid survivals of the past. As a result the social sciences have become, to a considerable degree, a warehouse of heterogeneous facts, mechanically collected and mechanically processed through various patented techniques of social research believed automatically to give valid propositions.

C. They collected a vast ocean of "facts" and stored away a most astounding mass of information about this, that, and everything—from poverty and crime, the sex life of the Melanesians, and the Freudian libido up to fascism, sunspots, chromosomes, quintuplets, electrons, and almost everything imaginable and unimaginable. But in spite of this collection, only a few generalizations and correct formulas of uniformities in sociocultural processes were discovered. What they produced was either *(a)* a distorted repetition of formulas developed in the natural sciences, which neither concerned sociocultural phenomena, as distinct from physical and biological phenomena, nor gave any understanding of sociocultural reality; or *(b)* they manufactured many a homemade generalization of very precise character that invariably turned out to be invalid; or *(c)* at the best, they restated in a vulgarized form many generalizations discovered by the great social thinkers of the past, to whom, ordinarily, they acknowledged no indebtedness.

Carried away by their imitative belief that scientific research consisted just in fact-finding and fact-collecting, sociology and the social sciences collected without discrimination so many facts, of such heterogeneous nature, that soon they were lost in the jungle of these facts. They did not know what to do with them, and, despite the collection, they understood the sociocultural phenomena as little as, or perhaps even less than, before. To alleviate this intolerable situation, they started a large number of bibliographies, then bibliographies of bibliographies, and bibliographies of bibliographies of bibliographies.

Compiled ordinarily by first-year graduate students forced to pile up mechanically everything they incidentally came across, these bibliographies could not solve the difficulty. None of the social scientists could plow through the tens of thousands of titles, mainly of valueless works, given in the bibliographies. They prided themselves, however, on the preciseness of the strictly alphabetical order of the titles and on the lower than "probable" frequency of typographical errors. In this way, standardized routine triumphed over any competent, thoughtful, and nonstandardized analysis of the valuable works in the field.

Having banished logic and thought, the social sciences now found themselves in the dilemma of having no means with which to organize an intractable mass of incidental and diverse facts. Lacking principles to order it into a logical, consistent system, they had only the binding of the book as a bond between unrelated chapters, only the paper of the page to hold together the motley array of facts printed upon it. Instead of searching for binding and integrating principles, they appointed sets of special "Committees for Integration and Standardization" of the respective sciences by fiat of the majority of their members. In this way, they standardized introductory texts, special courses, the size of the books, the number of pages to be read by the students, and so on, all with great precision, allowing, however, "the standard deviation within probable error" for any nonconformist teacher. Thus, logical consistency was replaced by mechanical standardization; logical unity, by the "space–time continuum" of the book or page; concentrated thought, by the "operational method" of tinkering with tabulating machines, questionnaires, and surveys; scientific discovery, by the majority vote of the members of the Committees for Integration, Standardization, and Hard-Pressure Promotion of the respective disciplines. The triumph of purely factual, nonspeculative, antilogical, and anti-intuitional social science was almost complete.

No less disastrous were the results of the banishment of all forms of intuition, as a source of truth and knowledge, from the sacred precincts of sociology and the social sciences. Having cut off this most important and most penetrating source of cognition in general, and of sociocultural cognition in particular, the social sciences became more and more platitudinous in their standardized superficiality. Their creativeness progressively dried up. Their understanding of sociocultural reality thinned out. They failed to make great discoveries; their generalizations became increasingly either a painful elaboration of the obvious; or a mere epitome of the counted telephones, quintuplets, income taxes, letters mailed, yards of canvas used for painting, number of books published, arrests made, babies born, and millions of other tabulations; or a progressive approximation to the wisdom of knowing more and more about less and less; or, finally, just a jungle of contradictory theories concerning which nobody could say which were true and which were false.

When this danger was noticed, the social sciences attempted to counteract it in their usual mechanical way.

First, they introduced a hierarchy of ranks among the social scientists, beginning with the superfellows and superresearchers, passing to the fellows and full-fledged researchers, then to the subfellows and subresearchers, and ending with the lower ranks of the active, contributing, and tolerated members. It was assumed that the infallibility and validity of the theories of each rank were in very close positive correlation with the position of each rank in this hierarchical pyramid.

Secondly, they organized several Supreme Councils of Research, whose dicta were assumed to be infallible. References to the decisions of these Star Chambers of Social Science replaced actual tests of the validity of theories offered.

Thirdly, in addition to all these mechanical simulacra of real value and validity, the social sciences declared that there were certain techniques of scientific research which delivered automatically the truth to anyone who used them. They renewed the Baconian myth of the existence of infallible techniques. This revived mythology helped for some time. During a few decades, the rank and file of social scientists believed indeed in the infallibility of the technique of the mental test, of the coefficient of correlation, of the standard deviation and probable error; of the technique of psychoanalysis and interviewing; of the technique of the case method in fieldwork and of the field method in casework; of the technique of measurement of all kinds of barometers—econometric, psychometric, sociometric, and ethicometric—each capable of predicting anything from the future trend of mankind up to the fluctuation of the price of pig iron to A.D. 2000 or the size of the population of the United States or Siam in A.D. 2344. As a part of these techniques, a legion of very complex formulas and symbols was introduced, and the sacred technical rites of the operational, instrumental, semantic, sociometrical, psychoanalytic, and other methods were established.

For a time this device worked beautifully. Social scientists became feverishly busy with mastering, applying, and computing the results of these marvelous techniques. The social science journals and books began to be filled with complex diagrams, figures, formulas, and sacred symbols, awe-inspiring for all noninitiated mortals and as enigmatic as undecipherable hieroglyphics. Like the inscrutable sacred symbols of the ancient religions and the incomprehensible utterances of the oracles, they increased enormously the prestige of the social sciences.

Unfortunately, in the course of time, scientists and mortals began to notice that many an infallible prediction derived by an infallible technique proved all too fallible. Many a predicted trend did not take place; many a trend not anticipated occurred. Many a supposedly watertight theory turned out to be a flat error; many a conclusion, false. Thus the charm of the magical techniques was broken. Then was it seen that many of these techniques were founded upon the sand; that still others secured their misleading exactness at the cost of approximate validity.

D. As a mere consequence of this unfortunate situation, sociology and the social sciences failed also from a purely practical standpoint. In contradistinction to the natural sciences and the social sciences of many previous periods, they were unable to eliminate any important social evils or to contribute to human welfare. They were incapable of offering any systematic plan of sociocultural reconstruction. The measures offered by them in the name of science proved either useless or harmful. The more economists tampered with economic conditions, the worse economic conditions became. The more criminologists interfered in the prevention and repression of crimes, the more crimes grew. The more educators experimented with educational problems, the more superficial and less thoughtful became the students. The more political scientists interfered in the matters of political reconstruction, reorganization of government, and establishment of international peace, the worse the government regimes turned out, the more internal disorders and revolutions increased, and the bigger and more frequent wars became. The more advice they gave as to how to save democracy and liberty, the faster democracy and liberty vanished. The more they began to discuss marriage and the family, the more divorce and the disorganization of the family grew. It would perhaps be unfair to attribute these results to scholars and to social science, yet these results testify well to the inefficacy and superficiality of the practical advices of the social sciences. Their positive plans for reconstruction were either only perfectly platitudinous, finicky, unimaginative, and Lilliputian measures; or a vulgarized variation of the plans created by the social thinkers of the past, deprived of their inspiration, made pedestrian and unfit for existing conditions; or a series of most bizarre plans neither charming because of their grandeur nor capable of realization.

In most cases the plans of sociocultural amelioration and reconstruction offered by various factions of social scientists were but a reiteration of the programs and platforms of ignorant politicians and political factions. In the name of science, the social theorists who were affiliated with the communist or Nazi political factions noisily offered the communist or Nazi creed. In the same name of science, the theorists who were affiliated with conservative Tories offered the Tory plans of social amelioration. The very diversity and contradictoriness of such plans—all offered as the last word in social science—were incontrovertible evidence of ignorance and of inability to construct a scientific plan obligatory for all. By reiteration of the haphazard, grossly ignorant, and usually selfish plans of politicians, the social sciences discredited themselves still more.

Finally, as already mentioned, they could offer no scientific plan of reconstruction because they could not foresee the future trends and development of sociocultural processes. Most of their forecasting, from theories of bigger and better progress in the nineteenth century up to scientific forecasting of business and social trends in the twentieth, proved erroneous. In a historical movement toward war, the social sciences saw only enduring peace; while revolutions brewed, they were promising streamlined order; on the eve of an economic crash and long-time depression and impoverishment, they envisaged seventy-seven fat years of prosperity in which economic fluctuations would become less and less violent. This parade of misinformation by the social sciences marked a decline in their prestige.

These vices of sociology and the social sciences of the first half of the twentieth century, together with others left unmentioned, are sufficient to justify a verdict of "guilty," with subsequent banishment either into the kingdom of oblivion or into the morgue of history. However, the Supreme Court of History, mindful of the noble penological principle *in dubio pro reo,* will find that there were some mitigating circumstances which justify putting sociology and the social sciences on probation.

If within the next generation the social sciences are able to free themselves from most of the vices recorded against them and succeed in modifying their behavior in the particular way indicated below, they will be pardoned and permitted to pass into culture and society in good standing. The conditions for the reformation of the social sciences, as set by the Court, are the following.

Third Guess: The Reformation and Declaration of Independence of the Social Sciences

Sociology and the social sciences will abandon their insane ambition to be pseudomechanics, pseudophysics, or pseudobiology. They will reclaim their lost primogeniture to be a science studying sociocultural phenomena directly, with their own system of referential principles fitted to the peculiar nature of sociocultural reality. More specifically, this reformation means the following fundamental changes in sociology and the social sciences of the first part of the twentieth century.

A. They will fundamentally revise their system of truth and knowledge, which is almost exclusively the truth of senses, based upon sensory observation, with the testimony of the sense organs as the only and supreme arbiters of the true and the false. This truth of senses must be replaced by a more adequate integral system of truth, consisting of the organic synthesis of the truth of senses, truth of reason, and truth of intuition, each mutually checking and supplementing the others. Considering that the true sociocultural reality is a manifold having at least three different aspects—nonrational or empirical, rational, and metaempirical and metarational—the truth of senses must give cognition of the nonrational or empirical aspect of the sociocultural manifold; the truth of reason must give mainly cognition of the rational aspect; while the truth of intuition, as a direct, momentary, and axiomatic grasp of reality, must give knowledge of all that is supersensory and superlogical in the manifold.

Sociology and the social sciences of the twentieth century were altogether wrong in assuming that the truth of natural science is purely empirical and sensory. They forgot that syllogistic and mathematical logic, which are largely independent of any sensory observation, yield propositions that are more valid than those based upon sensory observation. They forgot also that without mathematics and logic none of the natural sciences could discover and prove any law. The main principles and conceptions, the main methods of verification in natural science, are derived from logic.

Since the truth of reason plays such an important part in natural science, it is not surprising that its role in social science must be even greater. Only complete ignorance of the real systems of truth employed in natural science could account for the suicidal attempt of the social sciences and sociology to exclude the truth of reason from their own principles of inquiry. From now on, this fatal error must be avoided. Social scientists must realize that the great social thinkers from Confucius, Plato, Aristotle, St. Augustine, St. Thomas Aquinas up to Ibn Khaldūn, Vico, Montesquieu, Locke, Hobbes, Hegel, K. Marx, Comte, and Spencer, to mention but a few names, made their most important discoveries through logical, epistemological, and mathematical analysis. There is need to open wide the gates of science to reason, in all its qualitative and quantitative forms.

The social sciences of the first part of the twentieth century committed a still greater blunder in dispensing entirely with intuition as a source of knowledge. Here again they wrongly assumed that intuition does not play a role in natural science, especially in connection with discoveries and technological inventions. They fancied that intuition could give only superstition and error. Thoughtful observation will disclose the paramount role of intuitional knowledge in discoveries and technological inventions and in the fine arts, ethics, law, religion, and philosophy. Any careful empirical study will show that intuitional truths lie at the base of all science. From mathematics and physics up to the social sciences, there are ultimate postulates and axioms which are not based upon, and cannot be proved by, either logic or sensory observation, and which, nevertheless, determine the most important developments in the science. These intuitional verities are unavoidable in any science and are the conditions of the validity of all deductive and inductive propositions of which the science is made up.

Social science might observe that the source and starter of most of the important discoveries recorded in history—from those of Archimedes and Plato through Galileo, Newton, and R. Mayer up to the mathematical insight of H. Poincaré—was intuition: momentary, certain, and adequate revelation. The same is true in regard to technological inventions, as has been revealed in the testimony of the inventors themselves. Still greater is the role of intuition in the creation of the great values in the fine arts and religion, in law and ethics, as again we know from the recorded experiences of the great masters. Any creation is a discovery, as is also any discovery a creation. The great artist opens up to us the potentiality which exists but which lies concealed from our view until discovered by creative genius. Likewise, scientific discovery is creation, in the sense of making actual a potential uniformity or law which had hitherto been unnoticed.

In view of this paramount role of intuition in any cognition or creation, one can but wonder at the folly of the social sciences and sociology. By denying intuition, they were deprived of basic sources of cognition and of creativeness. Thus crippled, they naturally could not soar above the flat level of platitudes, nor penetrate beyond the most superficial sensory aspect of sociocultural reality; therefore, they were doomed to become progressively arid, unenlightening, uninspired, and uncreative.

In their own interest, from now on, the social sciences must avoid this blunder. They must utilize all three sources of human cognition. Taken separately, each of these sources may equally mislead—and the history of human thought is a graveyard filled with wrong sensory observations, wrong syllogistic conclusions, fallacious pseudointuitions. Taken together, they check and supplement one another, and give more valid knowledge than that given by any one of these sources taken separately. An integral system of truth instead of the one-sided truth of senses—such is the first requirement for the social sciences if they want to become real and immortal values.

B. The system of truth changed; the framework of the referential principles and methods of the social sciences must change also. Here again they must abandon in large part the framework of principles and methods of the natural sciences. These are fit to catch purely inorganic or organic fish; they are unfit to catch sociocultural fish. They are not constructed for that purpose. More concretely, this means that the natural science concepts of time, space, connection, causality, chance, equilibrium, motion, change, force, mass, identity, and difference cannot fruitfully be used in a study of sociocultural phenomena. Their place must be taken by a set of concepts and referential principles and methods designed for reality differing in important respects from the purely inorganic or organic. These may run somewhat parallel to those of the natural sciences, but each will differ from the corresponding natural science concept, principle, or method. The astronomical, physical, and biological concepts of time and space will be superseded in social science by the quite different concepts of sociocultural time and sociocultural space; the concept of physicochemical or biological system, by the sociocultural system, with very different component structures and properties; the concept of natural science causality, which is especially inapplicable to sociocultural phenomena, by a concept of meaningful-causal relationship peculiar to sociocultural phenomena; the concept of natural science chance, by that of incidental congeries, devoid of any meaningful-causal cohesion, determinacy, and unity. Similarly, the natural science concepts of force, mass, factor, equilibrium, and others will be replaced by social science concepts somewhat homologous but different.

As with the concepts, so also with methods. Social science observation will be something fundamentally different from the externalistic observation of the natural sciences. The natural scientist may experiment with certain phenomena without observing uniformities, while the social scientist, paying attention to the meaning component in the same variables, may find connections highly important for social science. And, vice versa, variables which from a natural science point of view are connected may be from a social science point of view wholly unconnected. These considerations suffice to indicate the second fundamental reformation the social sciences must achieve.

C. When the system of truth is changed and the framework of referential principles and methods is transformed, the content and character of the social sciences will be fundamentally modified from top to bottom. The problems they will study, the facts they will observe, the conclusions they will draw—all will differ profoundly from those in the period discussed. As a result, there will be more adequate cognition, not merely of the fleeting, ever-changing, and uncertain sensory appearance of sociocultural phenomena, but more especially of the deeper layers of sociocultural reality. Through this knowledge will come an understanding of the nature of sociocultural phenomena and of the uniformities to be observed in its static and dynamic forms. The formulas of uniformities that can then be derived will be more valid and more accurate than the misleading formulas of the spurious uniformities of the period discussed.

D. The importance of such knowledge for applied social science is obvious. Some important future trends can be roughly predicted; efficient means of correcting social evils can be devised; the creative enrichment of human experience can be inspired; and in all fields of culture there can be created magnificent and lasting values.

When this revolutionary transformation has been made, then, and only then, will the social sciences be real, autonomous scientific disciplines, truly equal to the natural sciences. Then, and only then, will they embody real knowledge and true wisdom. Then, and only then, will they be a perennial value as immortal as any real value. Therefore, this Declaration of Independence of the Social Sciences is also their Magna Charta. It aims to elevate them from the status of serfdom to the natural sciences and to politicians up to a status of equal membership with other sciences and with philosophy, religion, art, and ethics in the great union of the cardinal sociocultural values.

6

Referential Principles
of Integralist Sociology

A Brief Summary

The foregoing analysis of the principles of sociocultural causality, space, and time reveals the fundamental difference between these principles and the corresponding concepts of the natural sciences. It clarifies also what we mean by the homology of referential principles in the two fields. What is said of these principles applies equally to all the other basic methodological concepts of the sociocultural and natural sciences, such as that of equilibrium. This principle, as it is used in the natural sciences, is either entirely inapplicable to the study of sociocultural phenomena or else has to be drastically transformed into something that bears only a remote resemblance to the concept of equilibrium in the natural sciences.[1] The same is true of practically any corresponding referential principles in the two fields. They run parallel and are homological but are nevertheless profoundly different. This means that adequate cognition of sociocultural phenomena requires its own set of basic principles, especially adapted to the peculiar nature of sociocultural phenomena, and therefore distinct from the referential notions of the natural sciences. The substitution of such a set for the present framework of one-sided, pseudoempirical sociology and social science means a profound revolution in the field of these disciplines.[2]

A tentative sketch of the principles of such a set follows. For the sake of brevity, let us denote such a school of sociology and social science by the term *integralist,* in contradistinction to the one-sided,

Originally published in *Sociocultural Causality, Space, Time* (Durham, N.C.: Duke University Press, 1943): 226–37. Reprinted by permission of the publisher.

1. Cf. P. Sorokin, *Social and Cultural Dynamics* (New York: American Book Company, 1941), 4: 670–93.

2. Like any political revolution, it is opposed by the powers of the old regime in sociology and social science. When they cannot cope with it through creative measures, they attempt to suppress it by censorship and other mechanical means. So it was in the past, and so it still is.

pseudoempirical school. The exposition should begin with the system of truth, as the basic referential principle of any scientific discipline.

The Integralist System of Truth, Cognition, and Sociocultural Reality

Instead of being built primarily upon the empirical system of truth and sensory sociocultural reality, the integralist sociology rests upon the integralist conception of sociocultural reality and the integralist system of truth as developed in *Dynamics*.[3] The integralist school claims that sociocultural reality, including man as its creator, bearer, and agent, is a complex manifold. It has its empirical aspect, to be cognized and studied through sensory perception and the methods of the truth of the senses: sensory-empirical observation in all its forms—experimental, statistical, clinical, and otherwise. The *logico-rational aspect* of sociocultural phenomena, represented by all consistent systems of thought—scientific, philosophical, religious, ethical, artistic, and so forth—is to be apprehended through the discursive logic of human reason, including mathematical, deductive, and inductive logic and analysis in all their valid forms.[4] The integralists go even further. Logical thought, they say, is indispensable for cognition of even the empirical aspects, since without human logic and dialectic, no empirical cognition, no collection and analysis of relevant facts, no adequate observation, no valid experiment is possible. Without mathematical and so-called "symbolic" logic, deductive and inductive logic, no sound empirical judgment, theory, concept, or generalization is conceivable. Hence the indispensability of the truth of reason in social science and sociology. Even the most empirical, most behavioristic, most mechanistic theories in this field have always employed rational truth (though generally in an imperfect or perverted form). The incoherent jibbering of idiots may perhaps dispense with this type of cognition, but such a phenomenon has no relation to real knowledge.

Finally, sociocultural reality has its supersensory, superrational, and metalogical aspect. It is represented by the great religions, absolutistic ethics, and the truly great fine arts. We must not forget again that these

3. Ibid., vol. 4, chap. 16.
4. The sociologist must not forget that science, philosophy, and other systems of thought are also sociocultural phenomena. So far as they embody a logical, consistent, rational idea, they constitute logical, consistent, rational compartments of sociocultural reality. Comprehension of this aspect is possible chiefly through logical thought, because only thus can one understand the meaning of a scientific or other theory. It takes mind and thought to understand mind and thought. Sensory perception, for instance, may give us the image of a book but not the systems of meanings objectified in this vehicle.

have composed one of the vastest and most important segments of sociocultural reality. We must also keep in mind that these great religions, ethical norms, and fine arts are irreducible either to the mere complex of sensations or to a set of purely rational and logical propositions. In this sense they are superrational and supersensory. This *supersensory, superrational, metalogical* phase of sociocultural reality, including man himself, must be apprehended through the truth of faith—that is, through a supersensory, superrational, metalogical act of "intuition" or "mystic experience," representing a type of cognition *sui generis*, profoundly different from sensory perception and the logical activity of reason.[5]

The sociocultural world, including man, certainly exhibits such supersensory, superrational, and superlogical aspects, of which we get a glimpse partly through our own intuition and particularly through the intuition of a small, select group endowed with charismatic grace and represented by the "geniuses," "seers," "mystics," and certain "visionaries," the founders and creators of religious and moral codes; by the truly great thinkers; and also by eminent poets, composers, artists, and the like. Normal intuition respecting the comparatively familiar phases of sociocultural reality is vouchsafed to almost all human beings; exceptional intuition concerning the complex verities of sociocultural and cosmic reality is possessed only by the élite, such as Buddha or Lao-tse, Plato or St. Augustine, St. Paul or Master Eckhart, Phidias, Bach or Beethoven, Dante or Shakespeare, or Sir Isaac Newton. In chapter 16 of volume 4 of *Dynamics,* it is shown that intuitions, often untranslatable into words or concepts (like a profound mystic experience, a great symphony, a Parthenon, and other creative processes of human genius also inexpressible in words), are the foundation of the ultimate postulates and axioms of science, religion, ethics, and the arts. It is likewise demonstrated that they are the creative sparks which stimulate our sense organs and our logical faculties to erect an empirico-logical superstructure of valid propositions upon this intuitional basis. Attention is also drawn to the fact that the creators of science, philosophy, religion, and moral codes, as well as the foremost artists and poets, are at the same time discoverers of an aspect of reality hitherto unknown.[6]

Through the creative discoveries of these select few, we obtain some cognizance of this, the most mysterious and profound aspect of sociocultural and cosmic reality. To many a downright empiricist, such an

5. For a discussion of this, see ibid., vol. 4, chap 16, and vol. 2, chaps. 1–3.
6. See ibid., chap 16.

admission of the truth of faith *(horribile dictu!)* may appear equivalent to the injection of ignorance, superstition, and the like into the social sciences. Yet if they are real empirical observers of themselves, of their fellow men, of the structure and development of science, philosophy, religion, ethics, and the fine arts, they cannot deny either this source of cognition or the existence of the aspect of reality discovered through it. It is as much an empirical datum or fact as any other datum or fact and equally unquestionable.

We know also that many an eminent sociocultural explorer discovered many an essential truth about sociocultural reality primarily through intuition—not through any mechanical tabulating machinery, empirical experiment, juggling with statistical data, or application of the "technique of the case study in fieldwork." Neither Chinese nor Hindu sages, neither Plato nor Aristotle, grasped the fundamental verities concerning man, society, and culture by means of these "scientific techniques." They grasped them principally through intuition and the logic of human reason, assisted by observation.

To dispense with one of these sources of cognition of sociocultural phenomena means deliberately to forfeit one of the channels through which we obtain our knowledge and thus to blind ourselves to the most important aspect of sociocultural reality. Those who desire such mutilation and distortion of their knowledge are naturally free to follow this path. The integralist social scientist welcomes any contribution to his understanding of the sociocultural manifold through all three possible sources of knowledge. Science is enriched by any creativeness—employing empiricism, logic, or intuition—because any act of creation, as has been said, is a discovery of the unknown, of what is merely latent or potential until a great genius displays to us the hidden verity, now as the mystic Godhead, now as Plato's *Republic,* now as the Parthenon, now as Bach's *Mass in B Minor,* now as Newton's *Principia.* These aspects of sociocultural reality—often inexpressible in words—were its hidden potentialities; otherwise they could not have been actualized or discovered by a genius. Once they are actualized and embodied in empirical systems, they enrich our knowledge of sociocultural reality fully as much as all the "mechanical research of mediocre clerical manipulators" put together.

These three systems of truth and reality, with their three sources of cognition, though distinguishable from one another, are essentially one and inseparable. The distinction is but a division of labor of the cognizing mind. Specializing in the field of its own competence, each of the systems is dependent upon the others, not only for a fuller knowledge of reality, but also for the sake of verifying the validity of its results by comparison with those of the others.[7] In this sense, the three systems of truth represent a single integralist system of cognition and truth, and the three aspects of the sociocultural world are but aspects of one integral sociocultural reality.

In stressing this cardinal point, we obviously diverge from the beaten path of one-sided empirical truth, returning to the integralist system propounded by Plato and Aristotle, and by Erigena, St. Thomas Aquinas, and Nicholas of Cusa—a system congenial in several respects to many contemporary currents of philosophical, scientific, and religious thought whose representatives are mentioned in chapter 16 of *Dynamics*.

Such a conception does not call for any rupture with empiricism and sensory truth. On the contrary, it rigorously insists that the sensory aspects of sociocultural reality should be studied chiefly by means of empirical methods and techniques. Merely to speculate about this and that empirical phenomenon, and the relationship between them, is a fruitless and precarious activity. The same is true of a purely "intuitive" perception. In these respects, the integralist school is no less empirical than the most rigorously empirical school. But in contradistinction to one-sided empiricism, it denies that empiricism is the only system, giving us the whole truth and nothing but the truth. Besides it there are other, no less important systems of truth which reveal aspects of the sociocultural manifold that are inaccessible to empirical knowledge. Thus, instead of dispensing with anything valuable, in the cognitive sense, in any of the systems of truth, the integralist method contains them all and is hence fuller and more adequate than any of them taken separately.[8]

7. As mentioned in ibid., chap. 16, taken separately each of these three sources of cognition is often misleading. Therefore the best procedure is to use all of them and, whenever possible, to check the results of one source by the testimony of the others. Hence the necessity of their cooperation and "mutual aid" and the advisability of not accepting the findings of one source of knowledge until they are corroborated by other sources.

8. These considerations refute those critics who characterize my theory of the systems of truth as a variety of skepticism. They derive such a conclusion from the fact that, according to my theory, there is not one but three systems of truth, which alternately rise and decline. Contrary to the tenets of skepticism or agnosticism, each of the systems of truth, within its legitimate field of competency, gives us genuine cognition of the respective aspect of reality. Taken all together, they furnish still fuller and more adequate knowledge than each taken separately. This cognition is not a fictitious preoccupation with artificial constructs of pseudoreality, manufactured by the mind itself, as predicated by skepticism, agnosticism, and a priori Kantian philosophy of the *als ob*, or "as if," but is a cognition of genuine reality, in its authentic aspects, a true *adequatio rei et intellectus*. We are never out of touch with true reality, though we never grasp it in all its infinite manifoldness, in its "infinitude of infinitudes." Such a system of truth, cognition, and reality is the very antithesis of skepticism!

The Integralist Conception of the Properties of Sociocultural Reality

From this basic postulate of the integralist theory, its other principles follow. First of all, there is the integralist conception of sociocultural reality, which manifests itself in several forms.

1. It conceives sociocultural reality as a complex of so-called "material" and "immaterial" aspects. In contrast to one-sided empirical social science or philosophical pure meaning, it does not regard or define sociocultural reality as simply a sensory or material or perceptional complex of singularistic individuals and material objects, as empiricists do (or should do if they are consistent); nor does it reduce an empirically given sociocultural phenomenon to a mere immaterial complex of ideas, values, and meanings, as pure "meaningologists" do. As we have seen, it defines sociocultural phenomena as a synthesis of "immaterial," "nonsensory," "timeless and spaceless meanings," objectified in "material," "sensory," "perceptional" vehicles and agents.[9] The fact that none of the so-called "strict" empiricists in the field of social science has been able to avoid the meaning aspect, and that no idealist has been able to avoid the material aspect, is a particularly instructive demonstration of the fallacy of the purely empirical or purely intuitive or exclusive rational approach.

2. The integralist conception of reality, moreover, recognizes the "givenness" (the datum) in this reality of three different aspects: the empirical or sensory, the rational or logical, and the supersensory, metalogical, or transcendental aspects. Such an integral conception is reached through the avenue of meanings. In our definition of sociocultural reality, meanings together with their vehicles are one of the most important components, without which no sociocultural phenomenon is possible. In analyzing the meanings, we find that some of them concern the purely empirical, perceptional aspect—be it a business firm, a person, or an event (such as a murder, a play, or a wedding). Other meanings represent exclusively logical and rational phases, such as the phenomena of logic, mathematics, scientific or philosophic theory, and so on. All these rational phenomena are a "sector," or aspect, of this reality. Finally, a large portion of the meanings concern supersensory, metalogical, or transcendental subjects: "God," "the soul," "the ultimate reality," "sin," "salvation," and the like. They constitute a substantial portion of sociocultural reality in the form of revealed religions, mystic values, magical beliefs, transcendental philosophical systems, and the like.

One may like or dislike any of these aspects, but no sane person

9. Cf. chap. 1 of this book; and Sorokin, *Dynamics*, vol. 4, chaps 1–2.

and no sound empirical observer can fail to perceive that all these aspects are given as *data* in sociocultural reality. A one-sided empiricist
may dismiss the transcendental aspect as prejudice, superstition, or
illusion. But if he is a good observer, he must admit that such transcendental meanings and values as those relating to saints, devils, the soul,
salvation, and sin have occupied a very large place in the empirically
given sociocultural reality—in the form of religious, mystic, magical,
ethical, philosophical, aesthetic, and even scientific beliefs, systems,
and congeries, objectified in millions of vehicles and agents.

   3. Through its distinction between sociocultural systems and congeries, the integralist conception unifies the valid parts of the concepts of
the empirical "sociocultural atomists" and "rational and totalitarian
integralists"; of the partisans of totalitarian or rational unity, order,
and uniformity of sociocultural phenomena; and of the proponents
of their complete casualness, contingency, and nonuniformity. Since
sociocultural systems are, by definition and in fact, consistent unities—
logical, rational, and orderly—and since they are given in the total
culture of any area, sociocultural reality possesses rational, orderly,
consistent aspects, or sectors. Insofar as this is true, the rationalists
and uniformists are right. Since the total culture of any area reveals
also congeries, which, by definition and in fact, are casual, devoid of
any unity, order, and uniformity, sociocultural reality has also an aspect, or sector, where contingency, nonuniformity, and accident reign
supreme. Insofar as this is true, the "atomists" and "casualists" are
right. When, however, either of these factions extends its claims beyond the legitimate limit, and views the sum total of sociocultural reality as either entirely rational, uniform, and orderly, or entirely contingent, incoherent, and accidental, it is emphatically mistaken.[10]

   Thus in one consistent conception, the integralist school of sociology embraces the valid parts of the purely empirical, singularistic, atomistic, and sense-perceptional conceptions; of the purely rational,
logical conceptions emphasizing rationality, logic, orderliness, and
uniformity; and, finally, of the purely intuitive, mystic, metalogical
conceptions of reality as the transcendental "City of God," as stressed
by the "sociologies" of the truth of faith. The integral sociocultural
reality is obviously richer than any one of these partial concepts.[11] It

   10. Cf. ibid., vol. 4, chaps. 3–5 et passium.
   11. The integralist sociology not only embraces the valid parts of each of these conceptions but explains how each of these one-sided theories has come about. The integralist *Wissensoziologie* offers the following fundamental explanatory principle: The
essential character of the sociological system of each prominent thinker is largely a function of two variables: of the system of truth and reality assumed by the thinker; and of

is a coexistence of rational, nonrational, and superrational elements; of the sensory and the supersensory; of uniformity and nonuniformity; of order and chaos; of the "immanently necessary" and of the causal and contingent.

Similarly, the integralist sociology organically reconciles sociological nominalism with realism, stating that sociocultural systems are realities *sui generis,* whereas congeries are singularistic and nominalistic and possess no structural or functional reality as a whole. It reconciles sociological determinism and indeterminism, giving *suum cuique.* Immanent self-regulation and self-determination of the systems is indeterministic, because it is their own self-determination; whereas their external determination, and especially the external determination of the congeries, is imposed from outside and is therefore deterministic.

---

the totality of his existential, especially sociocultural, conditions. If the system of truth of the thinkers of the most diverse cultures and periods is similar (say, the system of sensory truth), their theories will exhibit many essential similarities, in spite of the profound difference of their existential conditions. If the existential conditions are similar, the theories will display a series of similarities, at least in secondary points, in spite of the dissimilarity of their major premise—the system of truth assumed. Finally, if both the system of truth and the existential conditions of the thinkers are similar, their theories will be similar in all important characteristics.

The reasons for the proposition are as follows: (1) Since the sociological system of the thinker is, for the most part, notably consistent, the system of truth and reality he assumes is the major premise that "defines the rest of the system." Otherwise, it would not be a consistent system but a congeries. (2) Insofar as any thought is a reaction of the mind to the phenomena it is confronted with, the totality of the existential conditions under which the thinker is born, lives, and thinks cannot fail to stamp his thought generally. The proposition demands a drastic modification of such *Wissensoziologie* as that represented by K. Mannheim, who, as I understand him, attempts to account for any "ideology" and "utopia" in terms of certain existential conditions such as class position and mobility, hardly mentioning the major premise—the system of truth—assumed by the thinker. See K. Mannheim, *Ideology and Utopia* (New York: Harcourt, Brace, 1936).

Inductive verification of the proposition bears it out very well. The conditions of existence of the thinkers of Brahmanic-Buddhist India and Taoist China, of Hesiod and Homer, of the Mohammedan Sufist mystics (such as al Hosayn Mansour al-Hallaj), of the Christian Church Fathers (Hippolytus, Origen, Tertullian, St. Augustine, and others), were certainly as different as they could be. Their system of truth, however, was similar, as the system of truth of faith. Hence the essential similarities of their respective "sociologies." They all pay scant attention to the empirical "City of Man" and to empirical man as such; they all concentrate on the supersensory and superrational, transcendental aspect of sociocultural phenomena, on the supersensory "City of God"; they all view empirical sociocultural objects and phenomena as illusions, as pseudovalues: they all solve the problem of causation by ascribing the cause to a superempirical "Brahma," "Destiny," "God" or "gods," "Providence," and so on.

The same is true of the empirical thinkers who assume the truth of the senses. How-

The same is done by integralist sociology with regard to idealism and materialism; for an empirical sociocultural phenomenon is made up partly of the component of meanings, which are immaterial, timeless, and spaceless, and devoid of any properties of material phenomena, and partly of the components of vehicles and agents (viewed as material bodies and biological organisms), which are material and posses all the important properties of matter (both inorganic and organic).

Likewise, the integralist theory reconciles sociological singularism (individualism) and universalism, temporalism and eternalism. Ontologically, the individuals exist either as isolated Robinson Crusoes (though an absolutely isolated individual is not a sociocultural phenomenon) or as parts of a sociocultural system; likewise, a sociocultural system exists, but as a system, as a whole. The sociocultural world of pure validities and values is eternal, timeless, and spaceless—

---

ever different were the conditions of life of the ancient Hindu "positivists" and empiricists, such as Kautaliya (cf. B. K. Sarkar, *The Positive Backgrounds of Hindu Sociology*) (Allahabad, 1937); of the ancient Chinese empiricists, such as Mo-Tze and his school, called the "Chinese Sophists" (cf. esp. A. Forke, "The Chinese Sophists," *Journal of Royal Asiatic Society* 39: 1ff; and M. Granet, *La Pensée chinoise* (Pari's: A. Michel, 1934), quoted 432ff); of the Sophists and positivists of ancient Greece and Rome; of Thrasymachus, Protagoras, Gorgias, Lucretius, and the Epicureans; of the empiricists of the West, from Machiavelli to Karl Marx, and of most of the contemporary empirical social scientists—their theories, nevertheless, exhibit a series of basic similarities. They all reduce sociocultural reality to its purely empirical aspect; perceive it as a singularistic and "atomistic" complex; deal with concrete material topics; and give an empirical tabloid interpretation of the origin and development of social life, culture, and man, viewing them in the light of an economic, materialistic, and mechanistic interpretation of history.

Finally, the same is true of the idealistic integralists, such as Plato, Aristotle, Erigena, St. Thomas Aquinas, Ibn Khaldūn, G. B. Vico, and the more modern representatives of this school of thought.

In brief, the assumed system of truth of the thinkers defines the situation for the superstructure of the theory they build upon it. It makes comprehensible also why their superstructure is what it is—why, for instance, the sociologies of the partisans of the truth of faith are mainly those of the transcendental "City of God," whereas those of the empiricists are of the empirical "City of Man," with all the paraphernalia of the type to which each belongs. In my course on the history of social thought, this proposition is systematically verified for the principal sociological systems of India, China, Greece, Rome, Europe, and America. It explains virtually all the important characteristics of the theories of each prominent social thinker. (For a corroboration of the proposition in a different setting, cf. H. Leisegang, *Denkformen* [Berlin, 1928]; also Sorokin, *Dynamics*, vols. 1 and 2, where the same proposition is demonstrated in respect to forms of the fine arts, concepts of time and space, and other "first principles," and the systems of ethics and law.) Their character is equally conditioned by the system of truth of the respective culture.

an eternalistic being; their vehicles and agents are temporal and belong to the world of becoming.

Finally, the integralist school embraces and assigns to its proper place sociological absolutism and relativism. True reality is the "infinitude of infinitude"; as such, it is absolute, metalogical, and metasensory, and as Reginald the Dominican said, is defined by itself (*absoluta specificantur a se, relativa ab alio*). It is the source of absolute values as the measure, principle, and criterion of empirically given values of whatever kind—empirical knowledge, religion, ethics, law, art, and so forth. They all are measured by the absolute; they all are mere "approximations" of it, relative in time and space, ever changing, valid today and outmoded tomorrow. Even the famous dictum "Everything is relative in this empirical world" is likewise relative, since the dictum itself is included in the "everything" and is a part of the empirical world.

This relativity, however, presents gradations in all the principal meaning values accessible to us; a more adequate knowledge or value is nearer to the absolute than a less perfect knowledge or value. The nearer it is to the absolute, the more it is an "end"; the farther it is from it, the more it is a "means."[12]

A similar reconciliation is effected by the integralist theory in regard to other important principles, such as the ideational (metalogical and metasensory), sensate (sensory), and idealistic (rational and integralist) conceptions of time, space, causality, number, vitalism, mechanism, and so on.[13] Each of these different conceptions of the several categories is valid when applied to its own proper sphere. The integralist concept of time, space, causality, and other categories organically embraces all three supersystems and thus reconciles them, assigning to each its appropriate sphere and precluding the invasion by any one of them of fields to which it is unsuited.

Finally, the integralist sociology organically reconciles the linear, the cyclical, and other conceptions of the direction of sociocultural processes, giving *suum cuique* in its interpretation of creatively recurrent sociocultural processes: they are unique at any given moment if all their characteristics are considered; they are age-old if only the dominant patterns are taken into account. Some links of the creatively recurrent processes are linear, others are cyclical; but on the whole, they are ever new variations of age-old themes.[14]

12. For these principles and their fluctuations, cf. Sorokin, *Dynamics*, vol. 2, chaps. 4–9 et passim, and vol. 4, chaps. 2, 3, 12, 13, 18, and 19.
    13. Cf. Chaps. 1–4 of this book; also Sorokin, *Dynamics*, vol. 2, chaps. 11–12.
    14. Cf. ibid., vol. 1, chap. 4; vol. 2, chap. 10; and vol. 4, chaps. 14–15.

Conclusion

The preceding chapters, supplemented by the four volumes of *Dynamics* give a sufficiently clear idea of what the integralist theory is and what it should be. Though the referential framework of sociology runs somewhat parallel to that of the natural sciences and consists of the same categories of truth, connection, system and congeries, causality and chance, change, time, space, and the like, these principles are substantially different, as regards content and meaning, in the social sciences from those of the natural sciences. Mere mechanical borrowing and importation of principles from the natural sciences cannot serve the purpose of the scientific study of sociocultural phenomena; for when literally transposed from the one field to the other, they prove to be inadequate. The invariable result is the distortion of these principles as they are given in the natural sciences; the creation of an amateurish and superfluous pseudophysics, pseudomechanics, pseudomathematics, and pseudobiology, running parallel with the real natural sciences; and, finally, a virtual failure to grasp the essence of sociocultural phenomena in their static and dynamic aspects.

This means no disrespect, however, to the natural sciences. On the contrary, it preserves the real spirit of science in general and of the natural sciences in particular. After all, the most highly developed natural sciences have become what they are, not through blind imitation of a physicist by a chemist, or of a chemist by a biologist, or of a biologist by an astrophysicist, but through the discovery and application of the theory and technique adequate to the nature of the phenomena studied. In the last analysis, the specific principles and methods of the several natural sciences are far from being identical; indeed, they are notably different from one another. The same is true of the social sciences.

Together with the factual study pursued, in the light of the referential principles of social science in general and of sociology in particular, throughout my *Dynamics,* this outline should afford a sufficiently clear idea of what is the precise nature of sociocultural phenomena, why a strictly imitative application of natural science principles is inadequate for their investigation, and what are the specific principles and methods of a scientific examination of these phenomena. In order to be truly scientific, such a study must conform to the canons of the integralist school.

7

Sociology of Yesterday, Today, and Tomorrow

The "Preparatory" Character of Today's Sociology

Spencer, Tarde, Bernard, Whitehead, Berr, and Joël noted a recurrent alternation of analytical, fact-finding periods and generalizing or synthesizing periods in the history of science and philosophical thought.[1]

In the terms of this theory, the general sociology of the last forty-five years or so (1920–65) appears to be more analytical and fact-finding than the general sociology of the preceding period (1875–1920). Compared with the recent period, general sociology at the end

Presidential address delivered at the annual meeting of the American Sociological Association, Chicago, September 1965. Originally published in the *American Sociological Review* 30 (December 1965): 833–43. Reprinted by permission of the publisher.

1. "Each science has its eras of deductive reasoning, and its eras when attention is chiefly directed to collecting and collating facts." Herbert Spencer, *First Principles* (New York: Appleton, 1888), 269. "It is safe to predict that a century of adjustment . . . will follow the century of discovery. . . . Civilization requires that an afflux of discovery and an effort to harmonize discoveries shall coincide or follow one another." Gabriel Tarde, *The Laws of Imitation*, trans. Elsie Clews Parsons (New York: Henry Holt, 1903), 151ff.

"Thus we observe experimentation and systematic theorizing alternatively succeeding one another since Galienus up to the present time." C. Bernard, quoted by François Mentré, *Les générations sociales* (Paris: Editions Bossard, 1920), 37. H. Berr contends that such an alternation recurs in social and humanistic disciplines every thirty to forty years (quoted by Mentré, op. cit., 36–38).

"New directions of thought arise from the flashes of intuition bringing new material within the scope of scholarly learning. . . . One aspect of the adventures of ideas is this story of the interplay of speculation and scholarship, a strike sustained through the ages of progress." Between the alternating periods of creative intuitional synthesis and scholarly elaboration and analysis, there are periods of "happy balance," the periods of "culminating greatness." Alfred N. Whitehead, *Adventures of Ideas* (New York: Macmillan, 1933), 138 and chap. 7. Karl Jöel similarly refers to the alternation of periods of "binding and loosening" (*Bindung und Lösung*), integration and differentiation in the history of philosophical thought, in *Wandlungen der Weltanschauung: Eine Philosophigeschichte als Geschichtsphilosophie*, 2 vols. (Tübingen: J. C. B. Mohr, 1928–31), 1:22–26.

About various two-phase rhythms, see Pitirim Sorokin, *Social and Cultural Dynamics* (New York: American Book Co., 1941), 4:398ff.

of the nineteenth and the beginning of the twentieth century was more productive in formulating vast sociological syntheses, in discovering broad uniformities and trends, and in building grand systems of sociology. Exemplified by the systems of Spencer, Marx, Durkheim, Tarde, Weber, Scheler, Simmel, Spengler, Tönnies, Ward, Sumner, Pareto, Ross, and others, this period established and developed sociology as a generalizing science, boldly delineated its essential character, its subject matter, tasks, and methods. Their synthesizing theories are still the basic framework and referential systems for today's sociology.

The diagnosis of contemporary sociology as predominantly analytical, elaborative, and fact-finding is derived from several of its essential characteristics.

1. In comparison with research done during the preceding period, recent sociological research has been directed more toward the techniques of investigation and somewhat less toward the discovery and formulation of substantive, broad theories concerning basic sociocultural problems.

2. The bulk of recent sociological research has dealt mainly with the comparatively specific "microsociological" problems and only a minor part of it has investigated such "macrosociological" fundamental problems of sociocultural reality as "civilizations," "cultural systems and supersystems," or "global societies" and the social systems of history. This preoccupation with narrow, concrete phenomena has led many sociologists to take a negative attitude toward broad investigations of the basic sociocultural forms and processes, toward "grand systems of sociology," and toward philosophical analysis of the presuppositions and assumptions of empirical research.

3. The main body of current research represents mainly a reiteration, variation, refinement, and verification of the methods and theories developed by sociologists of the preceding period, beginning with the mechanistic and ending with the sociologistic schools.[2] Almost all the technical refinements and the reformulations of previous theories and uniformities concern the secondary features. Few of these improvements represent anything revolutionary or basically new.[3] They supply us with larger statistical samples and collections of "facts"; they suggest some refinements of the techniques of interviewing or questioning, statistical sampling, data processing and content analysis,

2. Analyzed in my *Contemporary Sociological Theories* (New York: Harper and Row, 1928).

3. See a corroboration of this in my *Fads and Foibles in Modern Sociology and Related Sciences* (Chicago: Henry Regnery, 1956) and in my *Sociological Theories of Today* [New York: Harper and Row, 1966].

some elaboration of sociometric, psychometric, psychodramatic, "scalogrammatic," "group dynamic," "operational," "projective," "cybernetic," "semantic," "experimental," "functional-structural," and "analytical" research; they furnish us with a number of formulae of uniformities, indexes, and tests, allegedly more "precise" than before; and once in a while they offer an improved variation of a previous sociological theory. But when these refinements, improvements, and reformulations are viewed in the light of the preceding currents of sociological thought, they turn out to be, at best, improvements of details only and sometimes no improvements at all. In spite of an enormous amount of sociological research done in this period, with a few exceptions it has been a "pedestrian," "epigonic," and "Alexandrian" rather than a truly creative period. No new Platos and Aristotles, Newtons and Galileos of sociology have emerged during the period, nor even many leaders of the caliber of the eminent sociologists of the end of the nineteenth and the beginning of the twentieth century—Spencer, Tarde, Durkheim, Weber, Pareto, Scheler, Spengler, Ward, Sumner, W. I. Thomas, and the like. It remains "epigonic" also in its accentuation of "negative" social phenomena like crime, insanity, conflicts, and other forms of "sociocultural pathology" instead of a concentrating on such positive phenomena as genius, creativity, altruism, and so on.

4. Sociological research has increasingly assumed the form of collective research. Thanks to the participation of a large army of researchers in collective research projects, "the steam shovels" of numerous investigating crews have dug up an enormous mass of "facts." In this mass of facts now and then some grains of cognitive "gold" have naturally been found; but the excavations have turned up only a few gold nuggets and have failed to strike a rich vein of a new sociological knowledge.[4] The few such nuggets that have been discovered have been found mainly by the "individual prospectors," both sociological and nonsociological.

4. Of 1045 "findings" (empirical scientific discoveries) Berelson and Steiner claim for the recent "behavioral sciences," at least 90 percent are really truisms, platitudes, discoveries made long ago by philosophers, biologists, and other scientists rather than by "behavioral sciences"; a large portion of these "findings" represent disguised methodological, philosophical, and speculative propositions which can hardly be called "scientific empirical discoveries." Only 5 to 10 percent of these 1045 "findings" can be accepted as minor scientific discoveries in recent psychology, biology, anthropology, and sociology. Although their "inventory" of scientific discoveries is enormously inflated, it omits several "middle-range" uniformities discovered by recent sociology which are much more significant cognitively than most of the "minor findings" listed in the "inventory." See Bernard Berelson and Gary A. Steiner, *Human Behavior: An Inventory of Scientific Findings* (New York: Harcourt, Brace and World, 1964).

5. Despite the preoccupation with narrow problems, research techniques, and fact finding, recent sociologists have also displayed a strong proclivity to formulate the most heterogeneous "analytical" theories and to construct generalized "conceptual schemas" and models of sociocultural phenomena claimed to be applicable either to all social systems, groups, and cultures or to many of them ("middle-range theories"). This activity has become so popular that one of our colleagues ironically called it "Look, Ma! I'm theorizing."

One of the consequences of this proclivity has been an astounding proliferation of most heterogeneous, often discordant, sociological theories, paradigms, and systems.[5] This is a natural result of the preva-

5. Current classifications of the main types of today's sociological theory reflect this multitude and discordance. Don Martindale lists as the main types "positive organicism," "conflict theory," the "formal school," "social behaviorism," and "sociological functionalism" in *The Nature and Types of Sociological Theory* (Boston: Houghton Mifflin, 1960). Charles and Zona Loomis describe the seven sociologists they studied as "typological analyst," "generalizing and specializing analyst," "interaction theorist," "structural analyst," "historical and systematic analyst," "analyst of social institutions and systems," and "theorist of general social action and social system" in *Modern Social Theories* (Princeton, N.J.: Van Nostrand, 1961). Armand Cuvillier enumerates the following sociologies: biological, psychological, Durkheimian school, metaphysical, systematic, phenomenological, relational, historical, behavioral, sociopsychological, instinctivist, personalistic, and others. See his *Manuel de sociologie*, 2d ed. (Paris: Presses universitaires de France, 1962), 2. Nicholas S. Timasheff distinguishes neopositivistic, ecological, functional, analytical, philosophical, and historical currents of sociological thought in *Sociological Theory* (New York: Random House, 1957). Paulo Dourado de Gusmão, in *Teorias sociológicas* (Rio de Janeiro: Fundo de cultura, 1962), differentiates the following types of sociological theory: encyclopedic, evolutionary-organic, economic, psychosociological, realistic-sociologistic, relational, mechanistic, *verstehende*, cultural, fluctuational, cyclical, phenomenological, sociometric, epistemological, and socioactional. A still more complex and detailed classification is given by Helmut R. Wagner in "Types of Sociological Theory: Toward a System of Classification," *American Sociological Review* 28 (1963): 735–42. He divides all sociological theories into three main classes: *(a)* "positive sociological theories," subdivided into neopositivism, human ecology, structure-functionalism, social behaviorism, and biopsychological theory of culture; *(b)* "interpretive sociology," subclassified as theory of cultural understanding, interpretive sociology of action and interaction, interpretive social psychology, and social phenomenology; *(c)* "nonscientific or evaluative theory" with its subclasses: social-philosophical theory, ideological social theory, and humanitarian reform theory. Each of the subclasses is subdivided in turn into several subdivisions. See also Roberto Agramonte, *Estudios de sociologia contemporaneas* (Mexico: Universidad Nacional Autónoma, 1963), and Alfredo Povina, *La sociologia contemporanea* (Cordoba: Assandri, 1954).

In my *Sociological Theories of Today*, I classify the main currents of recent sociological thought as follows. (Each subdivision of each main current is in turn divided into several subclasses.)

1. Singularistic-atomistic theories

lent analytical and fact-finding methods of studying multidimensional sociocultural realities. By their very nature, these approaches consist of concentrating on a selected aspect or set of facts, abstracted and detached from complex, multidimensional phenomena.

Being analytical or fact-finding, each of such theories isolates from the total, multidimensional reality of the human universe one of its dimensions, elements, parts, or relationships, studies it in detail, and then presents the results of the study in the form of a fully developed "ecological," "functional," "structural," "psychological," "behavioral," "formal," "dialectic," "phenomenological," "cybernetic," "sociometric," "psychoanalytical," or some other type of sociological theory. Exactly in this way a vast number of strikingly different and often discordant currents of sociological thought have emerged and proliferated in modern sociology.

This overabundance of heterogeneous analytical and fact-finding theories in modern sociology is simultaneously its dialectical advantage and disadvantage, its strong and weak point, its important contribution to the further growth of scientific sociology and a potential factor in its stagnation and sterility.

Detailed study of specific elements or dimensions or parts or relationships, abstracted from the total sociocultural reality, permits each sound analytical and fact-finding theory to give us more adequate knowledge. All sound analytical and fact-finding theories, taken together, enrich our knowledge of many important aspects of the total sociocultural reality. Such is the advantage and contribution of the various analytical and fact-finding theories in modern sociology.

Their disadvantage, fallacy, and danger consists in imperialistic extension of the main propositions of each analytical or fact-finding the-

---

     A. Physicalistic-mechanistic
     B. Quantitative-atomistic
  2. Systemic theories: Macrosociologies of cultural systems or civilizations
     A. "Totalitarian"
     B. "Nontotalitarian"
     C. "Dichotomic"
     D. "Typological"
  3. Systemic theories of social systems
     A. "Social action" and "analytical"
     B. "Functional-structural" and "nomenclature"
     C. "Dialectic"
     D. "Pseudobehavioral" (mixed)
     E. Mixed taxonomies of social systems (groups)
     F. Mixed theories of social change
  4. An integral system of structural and dynamic sociology

ory over different realities or over the total sociocultural reality and
in a lack of integration, reconciliation, and mutual complementation
of the heterogeneous and discordant analytical and fact-finding theories into one integral theory that gives a sound knowledge of not one
but of all the basic aspects of the total sociocultural universe, and thus
a fuller knowledge of the whole sociocultural reality.

The danger of an unwarranted extension of the conclusions of each
analytical and fact-finding theory over the whole sociocultural universe or over different realities is quite real. As a matter of fact, most
such theories are so extended, and thereby commit the errors of identifying or equating the total, multidimensional reality with one of its
dimensions or element or relationship, the whole with its part, different sociocultural realities with the specific, selected reality investigated
by a given theory.[6] These errors often outweigh the knowledge given
by analytical and fact-finding theories. For this reason they frequently
foster pseudoscientific ignorance rather than scientific truth. As long
as any science consists largely of this sort of theory, it remains a semiscience, giving not only the truth but also half-truth, sham-truth,
and plain error. So far as the modern, predominantly analytical, and
fact-finding sociology depends on theories of this kind, it remains a
semiscience.

Lack of integration, reconciliation, and mutual complementation
of numerous analytical and fact-finding theories in today's sociology
is also an important danger seriously threatening a further creative
growth. Each such theory gives a knowledge of only one "speck" (element, relationship, dimension, or uniformity) of the immense multidimensional total sociocultural reality; moreover, the "speck" is studied
in a state of isolation, torn out of the "whole configuration" of which
it is a part. All the existing theories of this sort yield, at best, knowledge
of several scattered "specks" of the total sociocultural universe, without enlightening us much about their mutual relationships, their place
in the total universe, or about the universe itself as a whole. Such
knowledge is obviously meager and quite limited. It resembles the
knowledge of a few pieces of an unassembled jigsaw puzzle. The puzzle
remains unsolved despite knowledge of its pieces. Like several pin-
points of light in the darkness of night, the knowledge supplied by
theories in question illuminates a few "specks" in the darkness but it

6. All such theories violate the principle of limits beyond which they become fallacious or faulty. See on this principle my *Society, Culture, and Personality* (New York:
Harper and Brothers, 1947), chap. 46, and *Social and Cultural Dynamics*, vol. 4,
chap. 14.

does not make visible the total reality hidden in darkness, so that we often misinterpret even the lighted-up "specks." Misinterpreting the "specks" pinpointed by analytical and fact-finding theories is unavoidable. When we forget the truths, well established in the physical, biological, and psychological sciences, that whether "the speck" is "an elementary particle," "atom," "cell," "tissue," "organ," "organism," "human being," "group," or an isolated cultural phenomenon (in art, science, philosophy, ethics, politics, and economics), the same "speck" or "unit" has different properties when it is in a state of isolation and when it is constituent part of a unified (holistic) system. For instance, a neutron after its entrance into the nucleus of an atom becomes more stable, while in its "free" state it exists only a short time and dissociates into proton, electron, and neutrino. The properties of atoms, ions, and radicals tangibly change when they enter a molecule. The same is true of cell, tissue, organ, organism, man, social group, and cultural phenomenon.[7]

As a result of the unwarranted extension of the knowledge of "specks" supplied by analytical and fact-finding theories, and of the meagerness and uncertainty of such knowledge, the recent predominantly analytical and fact-finding theories have increased our knowledge of the total sociocultural reality only slightly, especially in the field of the multidimensional, macrosociological systems of "civilizations," cultural supersystems, and great historical social systems. In some cases they have even yielded more pseudoscientific sham-truth, half-truth, and plain error than valid truth.

This explains why further production of analytical and fact-finding theories cannot greatly enrich our knowledge of the total sociocultural reality and why sociology (or other science) has to pass—for its further growth—from the phase of predominantly analytical theory and fact-finding research into one syntheses, reconciliation, and integration of all sound analytical and fact-finding theories and their narrow uniformities into much broader, generalized, multidimensional theory and uniformities. These considerations explain also why analytical and synthesizing periods alternate in the development of sciences and philosophy. If sociology, or any science, cannot pass from one of these states into the other, it is bound to become stagnant and increasingly sterile because a mere increase of the known "specks" of the total

---

7. This verity is unquestionably proved by the recent upsurge of systemic theories in all sciences: physical, biological, psychological, and sociocultural. On this recent upsurge of systemic theories, on the proofs of this verity, and the respective literature, see my *Sociological Theories of Today*, chap. 5 et passim.

sociocultural reality cannot give us an adequate knowledge of the whole. On the other hand, without increasing knowledge of these specks and their empirical realities, few if any fruitful syntheses, broad generalizations, and valid uniformities can be formulated; without new and relevant empirical material, the synthesizing and generalizing theories are bound to turn increasingly into empty abstractions, ascetically detached from empirical realities and adding little to our understanding of their what, how, and why.

To sum up: Today's predominantly analytical and fact-finding sociology is at a crossroads. If it chooses to stay for an indefinitely long time in that state, it condemns itself to the sterile state of knowing more and more about less and less; if it chooses the way of growth, it must pass eventually into the phase of synthesizing, generalizing, and integrating sociology.

Now questions arise: What are the chances of such a passage? Are there symptoms or signs that sociology is already making such a transition, and if there are such signs, what is likely to be the shape of sociology to come?

Prognosis of the Shape of Sociology to Come

Any prediction of the future course of science or creative activity can be but conjectural because the very notion of creativity implies something new, unforeseen, and unpredictable.

With this stipulation, and assuming there will be no global, suicidal war, I am inclined to believe, first, that sociology will continue to grow not only externally, as it has done successfully in the recent period, but internally, as a generalizing science of the superorganic or sociocultural reality; second, that to accomplish this growth it will increasingly pass from the present, predominantly analytical and fact-finding character to the predominantly integrating, synthesizing, and generalizing one; third, that there are already some signs of such a passage and transformation; fourth, that this coming sociology, through its integration, reconciliation, and mutual complementation of the existing, largely discordant, analytical and fact-finding theories will greatly increase the knowledge of the whole superorganic, human universe as well as of its basic empirical dimensions, relationships, and uniformities; fifth, that it will investigate the positive, creative, sociocultural phenomena no less than the negative, pathological, and destructive; sixth, that after realizing all the syntheses, generalizations, and uniformities possible at this stage, sociology will pass into a new analytical

and fact-finding phase, to collect relevant new facts and to study analytically important new "specks" of sociocultural reality. This alternation of the two phases will continue in the future if and as long as
sociology matures and grows.

Such are my guesses. Now what are the reasons and empirical signs
that today's analytical and fact-finding sociology is going to pass eventually into the phase of a synthesizing, generalizing, integrating sociology that unifies all the sound parts of analytical and fact-finding theories into a logically and empirically valid multidimensional system?

My first reason for that prognosis has already been given: no growing science can eternally remain in the analytical and fact-finding
phase. Sooner or later it has to pass into the phase of great synthesis;
otherwise, it is doomed to be stagnant and sterile. The same is true of
the synthesizing-generalizing phase. I have also mentioned my second
reason: the empirical fact that these phases frequently alternate in the
history of growing sciences and systems of philosophical thought. If
logically and empirically such an alternation were unnecessary, it
would not have recurred many times in the lives of growing sciences.
On the other hand, the stagnant periods in the development of science,
philosophy, fine arts, religion, ethics, politics, and economics show a
long, conservative adherence to the prevalent, established, routine patterns of thought, style, or activity. The longer such patterns persist,
the more frequently repeated and practiced, the more hackneyed, sterile, and uncreative the respective sciences become. My third reason is
the important empirical fact of a growing concordance among the existing analytical and fact-finding theories, their progressive convergence toward an expanding set of principles and propositions consistent with all or most of them. Here is a brief enumeration of some of
these principles and propositions.[8]

1. Explicitly or implicitly, all currents of sociological thought now
accept sociocultural phenomena as a meaningful, "normative,"
"value-laden," "superorganic" realm of reality, different from the inorganic and organic realities.

2. Whether recent currents of sociology clearly specify the internal
structure of sociocultural phenomena, they all admit (directly or circu-
itously) three distinct components of these phenomena: interacting
individuals who create, realize, and exchange, through meaningful
actions and reactions (interactions), meanings, values, and norms;

---

8. This thesis of convergence is developed and demonstrated in my *Sociological Theories of Today*, chap. 18 et passim; in my *Society, Culture, and Personality*; and in my
Dynamics.

"immaterial" meanings, values, and norms (often called "symbols" or "images"), superimposed on inorganic and organic phenomena and thus transforming these into the superorganic reality of *sui generis;* and the biophysical media in which and through which the interacting individuals "objectify," "materialize," and exchange their "symbolic," "immaterial" meanings, values, and norms. These biophysical media are the "vehicles" of meaningful interaction and "the solidified conserves" of the meanings, values, and norms accumulated in the countless meaningful interactions during the course of human history. This third component is often called "material culture" or the "material substratum" of society.

3. Sociocultural phenomena have three different levels of realization: ideological, given in the minds of persons; behavioral, realized in overt, meaningful interaction; and "material," objectified by and solidified into the biophysical "vehicles" and "conserves." Under different terms—"material culture," "material basis of society," "symbols," "ideologies" or "ideological superstructure," "ego" and "alter," "social behavior," "social roles," and so on, these three levels are recognized—clearly or vaguely—in practically all sociological theories of our time.

4. Viewed from a different standpoint, all sociocultural phenomena have cultural, social, and personal aspects. Though in their empirical forms these aspects are distinctly different from one another, nevertheless, they all represent three main concrete forms of multidimensional superorganic phenomena. For this reason, the empirical forms of the cultural, social, and personal aspects of sociocultural reality are closely interdependent and none can be adequately understood without consideration of the other two. This theory in diverse independent formulations appears in most of the recent sociologies, psychologies, and psychiatries.

5. The same can be said of the distinction between cultural systems (with their subsystems and supersystem) and congeries, between social systems (organized groups) and social congeries (unorganized and disorganized aggregates of individuals), and between integrated personality systems and unintegrated and disintegrated personalities. The objective ground for this distinction between system and congeries is the undeniable fact that in the sociocultural universe causal or causal-meaningful unities (systems) exist, as well as singularistic aggregates whose parts are adjacent in space or time but devoid of any causal bonds. This distinction is confirmed by and explains the fact that sociocultural systems are studied by the recently emerging systemic theories while sociocultural congeries are investigated by the singularistic-

atomistic theories. As long as systemic theories study sociocultural systems and atomistic-singularistic theories investigate sociocultural congeries, both approaches and their methods are fully warranted, and they complement each other.

6. From this distinction between system and congeries three other principles follow. They are also increasingly recognized by most currents of contemporary sociological thought. The first of these principles consists in distinguishing *cultural* systems and congeries from *social* systems and congeries. This distinction warrants a study of cultural and social phenomena as separate dimensions of the total superorganic reality (with a subsequent unification of the results in a higher synthesis, clarifying the relations of the cultural and the social dimensions to each other and to the personal dimension of the total superorganic reality). This distinction and a subsequent synthesis are already largely accomplished. They manifest themselves in the establishment of the theories of "culturology" contrasted to those of "sociology"; in the macro- and microsociological theories of cultural systems (civilizations," *Hochkulturen*, and "supersystems") differentiated from those of social systems; in two kinds of the theories of *Wissensoziologie*—one taking as independent variable the category of social groups to explain cultural systems and congeries, the other taking the cultural category as independent variable and the social as dependent variable. The same is true with regard to the personality dimension in its relations with the cultural and social dimensions of the total sociocultural reality. Few psychologists now endeavor to understand or explain any individual—his "mind" and behavior—without considering social and cultural factors; few sociologists ignore the accumulated knowledge of psychology concerning the mental and behavioral properties of a human being. Psychological and sociological studies of this dimension are complementary, not mutually discordant or exclusive, as a few voices still contend.

7. The second principle following from the distinction between system and congeries is a growing effort to classify cultural as well as social systems in a logical order, in which each system is a subsystem of a larger system, beginning with the smallest units and ending with vast cultural and social supersystems. In the field of cultural systems this trend is exemplified by Spengler's, Toynbee's, Northrop's, Kroeber's, and my own theories of "civilization" and cultural supersystems, with their subdivisions of these supersystems into their main systems, these into smaller systems, and so on down to the smallest cultural systems.

In the field of social systems this trend manifests itself in similar attempted gradations of social systems beginning with the smallest "social units"—dyads, triads, and "small groups"—as subsystems of larger social groups and ending with such social supersystems as self-sufficient "society," self-sufficient "community," "nationstate," "global society," and vastest "social systems" of other sociologists.

8. The third principle resulting from the distinction concerns the proper methods of studying systems and congeries. Since congeries include a single unique phenomenon *or* a mass of singularistic-atomistic phenomena, the problem of proper methods (and also the kinds of cognitive results expected from each method) can be briefly summed up in terms of the proper method for, and the kind of cognitive results expected from, studies of unique, unrepeated sociocultural phenomena, of singularistic-atomistic mass phenomena repeated in time or space, and of social and cultural systems. Unique sociocultural phenomena can only be *described,* as in an ideographic history. They do not provide a firm basis for generalized conclusions or for formulating uniformities. The unique sociocultural realities correspond to the single atom or particle in the microphysical world. The physicists call this world "the microcosm of lawlessness," "the realm of discontinuity and uncertainty." This characterization of the physical "microcosm of lawfulness" fits well the unique sociocultural phenomena. They are poor ground for hunting uniformities, generalized propositions, or scientific predictions.

Congeries of singularistic psychosocial phenomena, frequently repeated in time and space (e.g., births, deaths, marriages, divorces, repeated fluctuations of prices, etc.) lend themselves to statistical observations and once in a while to inductive or experimental tests. They correspond to the ever-repeated macrophysical phenomena of large aggregates of atoms susceptible to mass observation by statistical and inductive methods. In physical as well as in psychosocial sciences, these methods often discover chance uniformities in the relations among such phenomena. On the basis of the discovered uniformities, their future states can often be predicted with varying degrees of accuracy within specified conditions and time–space limits.

Finally, the modern biophysical sciences sharply separate the class of biological and psychosocial systems from "the lawless physical microcosm" of single atoms or particles and from the large aggregates of atoms or particles of macrophysics with their probabilistic relationships and uniformities. Biological and sociocultural systems, no matter how small the number of atoms they represent, display orderly relationships and, now and then, uniformities quite different from the above two classes. Physicists designate these relationships and uniformities by terms ranging from "the inner law of direction" (Eddington), to order determined by a "free will" (Planck), "conscious mind" or Athman (Schrödinger), or "conscious, voluntaristic decision" (Margenau). Schrödinger's analysis of genes and biological organisms illustrates the difference between a biological system and microphysical and macrophysical phenomena. Representing a small aggregate of atoms, genes belong to the microphysical world and, as such, should display the discontinuity, uncertainty, unpredictability, and "lawlessness" of microphysical phenomena. Instead, genes appear to be highly integrated systems. They contain in themselves a "plenitude pattern" or "the plenotype" of the respective organism—the totality of its hereditary characteristics. Even more, genes preserve their specific individuality unimpaired from generation to generation. Amidst ever-changing environmental conditions, they carry on their integrity and plenotype and, through it, they predetermine the essential characteristics of an organism and the stages of its life course. Thus "incredibly small groups of atoms, too small to display exact statistical laws, do play a domineering role in the very orderly and lawful events within a living organism" (Schrödinger).

These properties of an organism as a system that bears in itself the basis of its individuality and perpetuation, of self-directing change and passage through the immanently predetermined phases in its life career are applicable, with a slight variation, to sociocultural systems. From the moment of their emergence they also bear in themselves the main phases of their life career, and this life career consists largely of an unfolding or realization of their potentialities. Like genes and organism, they have a tangible margin of autonomy from external forces. External forces can hinder or facilitate a full realization of a system's potentialities (its inherent "plenotype"); now and then they can even destroy a system; but they cannot radically change its inherent properties and the succession of states or phases in its life history, if such a succession is an inherent part of its life career. Change of a "univariant" sociocultural system differs from that of "bivariant" or "multivariant" systems; the forms, phases, rhythms, periodicities, and directions of quantitative and qualitative changes differ in each personal or sociocultural system largely according to its nature. In this sense any system molds its own destiny.

These properties of systems require the following modifications in the methods of their study.

A. Throughout its study, a system must be treated as a unified meaningful-causal whole with its triple interdependence among the components of a system, between the whole system and its components, and between all components and the whole system.

B. A study of a system has to proceed not only "from parts to the whole" and "from each part to the other parts" but still more so "from the whole to the parts" (along the lines of the triple interdependence).

C. An explanation of the important structural properties of the whole system, as well as those of its essential parts, and explanation of its "physiological" (repeated) processes as well as of the phases through which system passes in its life course—its rhythms, periodicities, and other changes—must be sought, first of all, in the system itself, in its life functions; in the nature of its component meanings, values, norms, and "vehicles and material conserves"; in its human members and their relations with each other; second, in the relations of the system to other systems of which it is a subsystem or with which it shares a larger system; third, in its total sociocultural environment. Residual problems may be "explained," sometimes, by the biophysical milieu of the system or by interference of some extraordinary—unforeseen and unpredictable—"factors," forces, and events.

This means that the system's structural and dynamic properties, and its life course, cannot be "explained" by merely environmental factors, or by the system's part taken for "the factor" of the whole system (i.e., by the system's "economic" or "ideological" or "technological" or other part), nor along the line of such formulae as "stimulus–response," "challenge–reaction," and other procedures that largely neglect the system as a unified whole.

The methods for studying sociocultural congeries and systems just outlined are essentially in agreement with the corresponding conclusions of the biophysical sciences. With some variations, these conclusions are also supported by most of the sociologists competent in the problems of epistemology, methodology, and logic.

9. An essential agreement also exists concerning the abstract-empirical character of the important "substantive" sociological theories. No significant theory can be purely abstract, devoid of relevant empirical content, nor can it consist of a mere collection of empirical facts without an adequate explanatory theory. The recent "fact-finding" research in sociology has accumulated a mountain of empirical data, but only a modest part of it has resulted in significant conclusions or has discovered uniformities of a "middle-range" generality. The bulk of this research has produced purely local, temporary, "informational" material devoid of general cognitive value. The main reason for these meager results has been the lack of adequate theory.

In contrast to this shortcoming of empirical studies, many of the recent abstract theories suffer from an "ascetic detachment" from empirical sociocultural realities. Representing a peculiar mixture of "ghostly" social system models, devoid of empirical content, mechanistic analogies of "equilibrium," "inertia," "thermodynamic laws," "cybernetic feedback" or "homeostasis," and speculative "prerequisites" for systems' self-preservation,[9] these abstract schemas of social systems form abstract networks with mesh so large that practically all "empirical fish" slip through, leaving nothing in the hands of the fisherman-researcher.

Besides, these schemas are constructed in such a "static" way that they fail to register most of the changes in the fished sociocultural "waters." As a result of their "ascetic detachment" from empirical sociocultural facts, they do not enhance our grasp of the empirical realities of the superorganic world. At present, the inadequacy of one-sided theories is generally acknowledged, and sociologists of all "denominations" increasingly try to avoid it.

In short, the growing convergence among different currents of sociological thought appears to represent a trend likely to continue in the future.

Finally, the fourth reason for my prognosis is that despite their apparent discordance and contradiction, existing theories are mutually exclusive or contradictory only where they are wrong, while in a number of essential points they are mutually complementary rather than exclusive. Each contains, side by side with its defective and questionable points, a body of correct propositions which are quite reconcilable with or complementary to the valid propositions of other theories. Considering the multidimensionality of the total sociocultural reality, it is only natural that each current of sociological thought attend to, and stress different aspects of, this multifarious reality. So far as these aspects are real, and accurately depicted by different theories, each theory is sound and reconcilable with the sound parts of other theories. Even more, these sound parts can be unified and incorporated into a more "multidimensional" and more adequate *integral* theory yielding a fuller and more accurate knowledge of the superorganic universe than each of the existing theories. Some imperfect attempts to build such integral theories are already being made; my integral system is one such imperfect endeavor. No doubt better, more adequate integral systems of sociology will be built in the future.

In their sound parts the singularistic-atomistic theories of social, cultural, and personal congeries are reconcilable and complement the sound body of the systemic theories, for each class of these theories

9. These mechanistic analogies are cognitively much more misleading than the "organismic analogies" of the preceding period.

gives a real knowledge of singularistic and systemic forms of the total superorganic reality. The sound part of macrosociological theories of vast sociocultural systems and supersystems complements the micro-sociological studies of small groups and small cultural unities. Sociologies of cultural systems and congeries complement sociologies of social systems and congeries. Valid contributions from the analytical, structural-functional, dialectic, empirical, integral, and other currents of sociological thought are quite reconcilable with one another. The same can be said of dualistic, trichotomous, and other typologies: each of these "opens" a particular dimension of sociocultural reality and thereby enriches our knowledge of it. The *Gemeinschaft–Gesellschaft* dimension, the "militant–industrial," the "sacred–secular," the "fami-listic–contractual–compulsory," the "primary–secondary" dimension, and other typologies do not contradict but complement one another; in their totality they deliver to us a fuller knowledge of more dimensions of the human universe than each does alone. If all these typologies are logically and empirically integrated into a unified system, our knowledge of the total superorganic reality becomes richer and more adequate.

Similar considerations apply to almost all other differences among seemingly discordant sociological theories of social change, among the classifications of social groups, cultural systems, repeated "physiological processes" within systems, and "evolutionary trends," and among many other basic theories. Almost all of them contain part of the truth—some a larger, some a smaller part—and these sound parts can be, and will be increasingly, integrated into scientifically more adequate theories in the future sociology.

Such, in brief, are the reasons for my prognosis of the shape of integral sociology to come. Of the two roads, sociology will choose the road of creative growth and will eventually enter its new period of great syntheses. I hope that in this conjectural prognosis I may be as lucky as in my previous prognostications of the wars, revolutions, liberation in man of "the worst of the beasts," dictatorships, and other changes in sociocultural life, which I did at the end of the 1920s and reiterated in considerable detail in my *Dynamics*.[10] Despite severe criticism of my "forecastings," almost all of them have come to pass. I hope that my guess of "the shape of sociology to come" will also be confirmed by its objective development in the future.

10. See *Dynamics*, vol. 3, chap. 16, and vol. 4, chap. 17; and *The Crisis of Our Age* (New York: E. P. Dutton, 1941).

II

EARLY WORK

Reflections from the Russian Period

8

L. N. Tolstoy as a Philosopher

> The Absolute may be given only in intuition, while everything else
> emerges from analysis. Metaphysics is a science which lays claim
> to a cognition without symbols.
>
> Bergson, *Introduction to Metaphysics,* 198

I

That L. N. Tolstoy is a great artist no one will dispute; but that Tolstoy
is a great thinker and, specifically, a philosopher remains a matter of
doubt. Evidence of the existence of such doubt is provided by Professor
A. A. Isayev's book, *Count L. N. Tolstoy as a Thinker,* and this certainly is not an isolated example, since there is a series of other articles
that treat Tolstoy as a thinker in a similarly skeptical manner. "One
experiences disillusionment," says Professor Isayev, "when one attentively follows the philosophy and publicism of Tolstoy. First and foremost, the eye is struck by numerous contradictions. These concern not
only details, but fundamental positions as well." "The numerous contradictions can be explained only by the fact that Tolstoy in his works
often adheres to the methods of a journalist. No doubt he glanced
through and looked over a large number of books. But it is not apparent that he attentively studied and considered from all sides the questions upon which he hastens to express his opinion." "The reader gets
an unpleasant impression from Tolstoy's urge to be eccentric, his irre-
pressible inclination for paradox," and so on.[1] From the foregoing citations, it is clear that Professor Isayev's verdict is rather severe. One is
forced to this conclusion because the author makes use of a whole
array of evidence in indicting Tolstoy: figures, facts, observations, and
so forth. In spite of this, however, we consider his verdict to be inaccu-

Originally published, in Russian, in booklet form (Moscow: Mediator Press, 1914).
Translated by Lawrence T. Nichols. A version of this chapter first appeared in Palmer
Talbutt, *Rough Dialectics: Sorokin's Philosophy of Value* (Amsterdam: Rodopi Press,
1998). Reprinted by permission of the publisher.
    1. A. A. Isayev, *Count L. N. Tolstoy as a Thinker,* 228–30.

rate and advance the opposite thesis, contending that in reality Tolstoy is a great philosopher.

II

In our opinion, the negative attitude toward the philosophy of Tolstoy is based, to a significant degree, upon a misunderstanding, namely, that the demands made of Tolstoy are not those that ought to be made of a philosopher. For this reason, it becomes necessary to say a few words about what philosophy is, and what its problems of study are.

It is well known that up to now philosophy has been seeking a definition of itself. At one time, it was the alma mater of all the sciences, but in the course of cultural development, the sciences have little by little distinguished themselves from philosophy. Until recent times, an eclectic *summa* was understood as belonging to philosophy—logic, epistemology, ethics, aesthetics—but now even these sciences are gradually differentiating themselves from philosophy and becoming independent of it.

It becomes necessary to seek a new definition of philosophy [*definitio artis philosophandi*]. Some define it as the generalization and systematization of the facts given by the particular sciences (Spencer), others as "the science concerned with principles" (Iberveg), and still others as the science of thought and values (Rickert and Windelband),[2] and so on.

Without entering into any substantial criticism of all these definitions, which would lead us astray, let us note that they are all either without a grounding in logic, or else present only words instead of conceptions (the school of value), or else do not accord with the essence of the matter. But along with this they contain some kernel of truth—insofar as they consider philosophy as embracing the world in its entirety.

It has already been some time since a definition of philosophy was proposed by E. V. de Roberty, one that has been reiterated in his most recent works and particularly in his article "*Le problème sociologique et le problème philosophique.*" "Philosophical thought is profoundly different from scientific thought," writes de Roberty. "The philosopher (the metaphysician as well as the theologian) utilizes the most

---

2. H. Rickert, "On the Concept of Philosophy," *Logos* 1 (1910). See also his *Zwei Wege der Erkenntistheorie, Kantstudien* 14, no. 4, and his other works; W. Windelband, *Preludes* (Tubingen: J. Mohr Publishers, 1911), 23.

mature ideas of his environment and his times (or the 'partial syntheses' of the different sciences) in order with their help to erect a new
edifice: *a general synthesis of the world.*"[3] Science is always analytic
and hypothetical, philosophy always synthetic and apodictic. The criteria of scientific "truth" and of philosophic "truth" are entirely distinct, as are the criteria of "truth" in the sciences and in works of art.
Just as aesthetic phenomena, along with science, constitute a distinct
species of social thought, so philosophy, along with these species, constitutes a self-sufficient *modus* of social thought. Similar to this understanding is Professor Petrazhitsky's definition of philosophy as "the
theory *of the real in general.*"[4]

In his latest work, G. Simmel approaches the same definition of
philosophy. The most characteristic feature of philosophy, he says, is
the desire "to think without premises."[5] From this feature, it follows
that neither the methods nor the truths of the particular sciences are
mandatory for philosophy. Since all the sciences begin with premises,
and since no premises are mandatory for philosophy, philosophy has
the right to consider any proposition dictated to it by its system. This
explains why various philosophies proceed from various premises.
*"Das Recht und die Pflicht der Philosophie, sich mit grosserer Unab-
hangigkeit von dem Gegebenen, als sie in andern Erkenntnisprovinzen
bestehet, ihr Objekt selbst zu fixieren, bringen es mit sich, dass die
verschiednen philosophischen Lehren auch von grundsatzlich vershie-
denen Problemstellungen ausgehen"* [The right and duty of philosophy—to fix its object for itself with a greater independence from what
is given than is exercised in all the other provinces of knowledge—
entail that different philosophical doctrines start from problems which
are also posed in fundamentally different ways].[6]

Whatever their differences in composition, all philosophical systems
have something in common, namely, a comprehension of the world
in its entirety and unity. *"Mann kann den Philosophen vielleicht als
denjenigen bezeichnen, der das aufnehmende und reagierende Organ
für die Ganzheit des Seins hat,"* says Simmel [one can perhaps desig-

3. E. V. de Roberty, *"Le problème sociologique et le problème philosophique,"* Re-
vue philosophique 11 (1911). See there also "A New Statement of the Fundamental
Questions of Sociology."

4. L. Petrazhitsky, *Introduction to the Study of Law and Morality* (St. Petersburg:
Erlikh Publishers, 1907).

5. G. Simmel, *Hauptprobleme der Philosophie* (Leipzig, 1911), 8.

6. Ibid., 10. [English translation is by Rudolph H. Weingartner in *Georg Simmel,
1858–1918: A Collection of Essays, with Translations and a Bibliography,* ed. Kurt H.
Wolff (Columbus, Ohio: Ohio State University Press, 1959), 283–84.]

nate the philosopher as the man who has an organ which is receptive and reactive to the totality of being]. (Can one then grant the title of philosopher to anyone having a faculty for apprehending and responding to being in its entirety?) Every person is always striving for one thing or another: for the guarantee of bread, for the teaching of the church, and so forth; whatever he may be studying, the philosopher—as philosopher—always desires to grasp the entirety of the world, to construct a synthesis. For this reason, he "has a special sense for perceiving the *integrity* of things and of life, and for the possibility of transplanting this inner contemplation, or this feeling, of integrity into concepts and their combinations."[7] The history of philosophy gives complete support to this definition. Every philosopher, as philosopher, strives for just this comprehension of the unity and entirety of things. Philosophers have seen this unity now in matter (Democritus), now in ideas (Plato), now in the spirit (Hegel), now in the will (Schopenhauer), and so forth.

This comprehension of the entirety of the world, of its unity in diversity, is possible in two ways: either, proceeding from an indivisible external absolute, we bring the whole world to the absolute and lead it into the soul; or else, proceeding from the depths of our "I," we construct the whole world out of it. The first way is the way of mysticism;[8] the second way is that of solipsism and Kantianism ("The whole world is my representation of it," or "The whole world is the content of my consciousness").

From these characteristics of philosophy, it follows that the criteria of value and "truth" for philosophy and for science are not one and the same. Science always begins with premises and, during the study of a phenomenon, analyzes it. Its syntheses are always partial syntheses. Philosophy, on the other hand, desires to "think without premises." It is essentially a synthesis of the world and, as such, has its own criterion of "truth," distinct from that of science, just as aesthetic phenomena have their own criterion of "truth" that does not resemble scientific truth.

The "truth" of philosophy, in Simmel's opinion, is the *typicality* of the reaction of the human spirit to the unity and entirety of the world, or—to put it another way—philosophy is a temperament considered

7. Ibid., 12.
8. The essence of things is God. Every individual thing is a manifestation of God. My "I" is also the divinity realizing itself in me. Therefore knowledge of God and of the world is possible, because the world, God, and "I" are one and the same.

through a picture of the world.[9] Philosophy, says Simmel, "does not mark out the objectivity of things—the 'sciences,' in the narrow sense do this—but the types of human 'spirituality' as they are manifested in a definite understanding of things" [*Zeichnet nicht die Objektivität der Dinge nach—das tun die 'Wissenschaften' ins engeren Sinne— sondern die Typen menchlichen Geistigkeit, wie sie sich je an einer bestimmten Auffassung der Dinge offenbaren*]. Therefore it is entirely possible that "truth in general is a concept that is completely immeasurable and useless for expressing the wholeness of philosophy" [*ist Wahrheit überhaupt nicht der ganz angemessene Begriff, um den Wert einer Philosophie auszudrucken*].[10] The teachings of Schelling, Schopenhauer, Plato, and others have long since been refuted from the scientific point of view, because they "contradict the facts." They do, however, possess their own value and truth, on whose account they are as necessary as the sciences.[11]

From what has been said, it becomes completely clear why philosophy has always studied certain problems: "the essence of things," the "I" and the reciprocal relations between the "I" and the "not-I," the meaning and value of the world and of its development, and the meaning of our life. These four problems constitute the substratum of every philosophy and follow immediately from the definition of philosophy given above.

Having with these few strokes defined the characteristics of philosophy and of the philosopher (the strokes are a digression, but in view of the unclear conception of "philosophy," they are indispensable for what follows), let us return to our theme.

---

9. Ibid., 23–24. See the analogous views of James: "The history of philosophy, to a significant degree, appears as the history of the peculiar clash of human temperaments" and so on. W. James, *Pragmatism* (Eglantine Publishing Co. [New York: Longmans Green, 1907]), 11 and elsewhere.

10. Simmel, 27–30. Every philosopher therefore has the right to contend as Hegel did (in reply to the accusation that his position contradicted the facts), "Then so much the worse for the facts." This means that the "truth" of philosophy is not defined in terms of its agreement or disagreement with facts that are mandatory for the particular sciences but that it carries within itself, in its own self-enclosure and logical unity, the criterion of its own philosophical "truth." In this sense it is impossible not to recognize a deep truth in the saying of Augustine, "Credo quia absurdum." Not everything that is absurd from the point of view of science will be seen as such from the point of view of philosophy.

11. See the similar views of H. Bergson (*Time and the Freedom of the Will* [New York, 1910], *Introduction to Metaphysics* [London: Macmillan, 1913]) and L. Nelson (*Introduction to Metaphysics* [Gottingen: Vanderhoeck and Rupert, 1908]).

III

"All who turn to the science of our day not for the purpose of satisfying idle curiosity, nor in order to play a role in science, nor to make a living at science, but simply in order to answer direct, simple, vital questions find that science answers for them thousands of complex and learned questions—but not that one question to which every intelligent person seeks an answer: 'What am I, and how am I to live?'" So writes L. N. Tolstoy in *The False Sciences*. In saying this, Tolstoy immediately advances two of the fundamental problems of philosophy and marks out the border between science and philosophy. That this distinction between science and philosophy, or "knowledge and wisdom" (understanding) is not accidental, is evident from the whole character of the worldview of Lev Nikolayevich.

"The wise are not always the learned, and the learned are not always the wise," he says, citing Lao-tse. "Experimental sciences, when pursued for their own sake and cultivated without any *guiding philosophical idea,* are like a face without eyes," he adds.[12] In the same work, in section 7, he distinguishes two types of ignorance: "natural ignorance" and the "ignorance" of "the truly wise," by which he understands a mass of knowledge not essential to life, not answering the basic questions of "What am I?" and "How am I to live?"

I will not extend these citations further. From what has been said, it is already evident that Tolstoy clearly and sharply distinguishes two species of science: the true and the false sciences. For the moment, this is quite sufficient. (Whether or not Tolstoy contradicts this position we shall see further on.)

And thus Tolstoy distinguishes false knowledge and true wisdom, or philosophy. This gives us the right, and provides the basis, to study Tolstoy as a philosopher.

Above we noted that the fundamental problems of philosophy, following from its essence as a world-embracing system, appear to be: (1) the problem of the essence of the world; (2) of the "I"; (3) of the relationship or knowledge of the "I" and "not-I"; and (4) of the value and meaning of being. These problems always constitute the essence of every philosophy, and every philosophy, once it has assumed something for its basic premise, answers all these questions in a deductive manner in agreement with its premise. In this agreement with its foundation is contained also the criterion of its "truth," of its typical response to the unity of the world.

12. L. N. Tolstoy, *The False Sciences* (Moscow: Mediator Press, 1911), 15, 11.

Did Tolstoy occupy himself with these questions? The answer is clear: the entire activity of Tolstoy the nonartist consists in nothing other than the resolution of these questions, a resolution not by means of scientific analysis but by means of a philosophic, world-embracing synthesis. Having assumed a definite premise, Tolstoy constructs upon it, in a consistent manner, an entire system of philosophy, in which each part follows with logical inevitability from the preceding premises and appears as an indispensable link in this well-proportioned edifice of philosophic creativity. In its turn, this edifice conditions the smallest details of the worldview and conduct of Lev Nikolayevich. Therefore, to remove isolated parts of this system, as Professor Isayev does, and then to criticize them from the point of view of "the facts" and the particular sciences is to not understand the essence of philosophy. Tolstoy, like Hegel, could reply to such criticism, "Then so much the worse for the facts."

It is true that Tolstoy does not employ sophisticated philosophical terminology—"the transcendent," "the immanent," "the phenomenal," "the noumenal," etc.—whose presence often relates a man to "philosophers." But it is hardly necessary to point out that the essence of the matter is not altered by whether one employs sophisticated words in the resolution of problems or speaks in simple, comprehensible words. (Why Tolstoy is "simple," moreover, has reasons of its own; see below.)

IV

What is Tolstoy's response to the fundamental question of philosophy: What is the essence of the world (things *an und für sich*)? Wherein lies its oneness in the appearance of diverse, multifaceted forms? Above we noted two types of world-embracing philosophic syntheses: the way proceeding from the absolute found outside the "I" and that proceeding from our "I." Tolstoy unquestionably takes the first path. Let us try briefly to outline his response.

"I know that there is within me *that without which nothing would exist. And that thing is what I call God.*" So responds Tolstoy to the first question of philosophy. "Every man who thinks about what he is cannot help but see that he is not everything but is a particular, separate part of *something*," he continues. "And having realized this, a man ordinarily thinks that this *something* from which he is separated is the material world that he sees. But as soon as a man thinks about this a bit more deeply, or learns what the wise have thought about the

matter, he realizes that this *something* from which people feel themselves separated is not the material world, but something else. If a man
thinks about it more deeply he will realize that the *material world* that
never ends and that has no limit *is not something genuine, but only
our fantasy* [last part my italics], and that for this reason that *something* from which we feel ourselves separated is something having no
beginning and no end, neither in time nor in space, and is something
immaterial, spiritual, that man acknowledges as his source of life, and
is that which the wise have called and call God."[13]

And so the condition of every being, the basis of the entire world,
is God. God is that logically prior being without whom nothing is
comprehensible and nothing is possible. "Prove that God exists!" ex-
claims Tolstoy. "Could there be a more foolish notion than to prove
God? To prove the existence of God is the same as proving the existence of one's own life. Prove it to whom? How? Why? *If there is
not God, then there is nothing.* How can He be proven? God is. It is
unnecessary for us to prove His existence."[14]

Since the essence of things, the foundation of being, is God, and
the physical world is only something that seems to be, "our fantasy,"
one might ask: What are the characteristics of God? What is He with
respect to ourselves, and what is He Himself, *an und für sich*, Do we
apprehend Him or not? If we apprehend, then how and why is such
apprehension of Him possible?

Analyzing Tolstoy's understanding of God, we meet a whole series
of negative definitions. First of all, God is something immaterial and
spiritual. Since God is the basis of every being and life, and the corporeal is only something that seems to be, it follows that God cannot be
physical.

The second characteristic sign of the divinity is manifested in His
infinitude and inexhaustibility, which result in our inability to exhaust
Him by means of our mind. God is not completely comprehensible to
the intellect. "God cannot be known through reason," says Tolstoy.
"It is impossible to understand rationally that God exists and that
there is a soul within man; in the same way, it is impossible to understand that there is not God, and that there is no soul within man,"
he repeats insistently. The first inference—that God is unknowable
through reason—brings Tolstoy close to criticism and agnosticism.
But does this signify that God is completely unknowable? No, it does

13. L. N. Tolstoy, *The Way of Life* (Moscow: Mediator Press, 1911), "God,"
2–3.
14. Ibid., 16. Cf. also sec. 5, p. 15.

not. Although he approaches agnosticism in the unknowability of God through reason, Tolstoy departs from it completely by making *feeling* the instrument of understanding. In this he agrees with the mystics generally and with the most recent philosophers (for example, Bergson) who make so-called "intuition" the instrument for understanding the absolute. "*To feel God within oneself is possible and not difficult. To apprehend God, however,* to apprehend what He is, *is impossible and unnecessary.*" "Everyone can *feel* God, but no one can apprehend Him. And so don't try to apprehend Him, but try, while fulfilling His will, to develop an ever more lively *feeling* of Him within yourself."[15]

God cannot be expressed in words and concepts, for if He were expressible, then it would no longer be possible for us to strive for Him, there would be no life, and He would not be infinitue. For this reason, "even the pronoun 'He,'" says Tolstoy, "as this is applied to God, already violates in my mind the whole idea of Him. The word 'He' somehow belittles Him." If one wished, one could construct a very close analogy between the role of the intellect in Tolstoy and the so-called "cinematographic mode of thought" of Bergson on the one hand, and between the "feeling" of Tolstoy and the "intuition" of Bergson on the other.[16] And so we do not know God fully, but we do "feel" God fully. We are not able to express Him, but we are fully able to experience Him in feeling (see below).

What, then, are His characteristics that we do know, and which we can express in words? They are love, intelligence, absolute perfection, truth, and an absolutely wise will. "Love and intelligence," says Tolstoy, "are those characteristics of God which we recognize in ourselves, but that which He is in Himself we cannot know." "Man needs to love, but it is possible to really love only that in which there is no evil. And for this reason there must exist that which contains no evil: God." Further on he says: "A man cannot help but feel that something is happening in his life, that he is someone's instrument. But if he is someone's instrument, then there is someone who is working the instrument. *And that someone who is working it is God.*" "The supreme will is that which we understand as and name God." "Every truth comes from God."[17]

Such, in short, are the known characteristics of God, and such is Tolstoy's answer to the first question of philosophy. And so the essence

15. Ibid., 12.

16. See H. Bergson, *Creative Evolution* (Paris: F. Alcan, 1907) and *Introduction to Metaphysics.*

17. Tolstoy, *The Way of Life,* "God," 5, 6, 11, 10.

of things is God. We do not completely know Him through the mind, but we do know Him completely through feeling (intuition). The known characteristics of God are love, intelligence, absolute perfection, and absolute will. With this answer, Tolstoy has already determined all his answers to the remaining problems of philosophy.

V

If the essence of things (the logically prior being) is God, then it is clear that our "I" or "soul," as part of everything, is nothing other than a part of God. "The intangible, invisible, immaterial thing that gives life to all that exists we call God. *That intangible, invisible, immaterial source, separated by a body from all else and known to ourselves, we call the soul.*" Since the physical "My" is something that appears to be, it follows that the soul is spiritual. God is an infinite ocean, while the soul is part of that ocean, imprisoned in a material shell. The entire physical "My" is constantly changing, in eternal "flux," while the soul alone is indivisible and unchanging, just as God is indivisible and identical to Himself. "A man who has lived a long life has experienced many changes: in the beginning he was an infant, then a child, then an adult, and then an old man. But no matter how much a man changes, he always speaks of himself as 'I.' *And this 'I' within him has always been one and the same.* The very same 'I' was in the infant, and in the adult, and in the old man. *Thus this changeless 'I' is that which we call the soul.*"[18]

As a part of God, the soul possesses all of His characteristics. Thus, like God, it is inexpressible. ("We cannot say with words what sort of thing this 'I' is, but we know this 'I' better than anything else which we know.") Just as God presents Himself as the condition and foundation of every being, so for us the soul presents itself as the condition of all knowledge and being. "We know," says Tolstoy, "that if it were not for this 'I' within us, we would know nothing, nothing in the world would exist for us, and we ourselves would not be."[19] And since, like God, the soul is wise and perfect, it is also, like God, love and will.

Such is Tolstoy's answer to the second question of philosophy, an answer that follows with logical inevitability from his first position on the essence and condition of all being.

From these two positions there naturally follows the resolution of

---

18. Ibid., "The Soul," 3.
19. Ibid., 3–4.

the third problem of philosophy: How is knowledge of the essence of things possible *an und für sich?* How is knowledge of God possible?

Since God is the essence of things, the foundation of being, and since the soul is a part of that being, it follows that the soul and God are one and the same. And if the soul and God are one and the same, then our "I" (the soul) can know God absolutely, because "God lives in me" and "I in Him." We can express neither God nor the soul in words, but we *know* God, immediately feel or experience God. "When I reflect, it is more difficult for me to understand what sort of thing my body is, than what sort of thing my soul is. No matter how near my body may be, it always remains *foreign,* and only the soul is *my own.*"

"For God, I am another He. In me He finds that which will always be like Himself." "It is possible to know God only in yourself. If you do not find God in yourself, you will not find Him anywhere."[20]

Because God and the soul are identical, absolute knowledge of God is possible. This conclusion, as the reader can see, is completely correct logically and inescapable. Such is the resolution of the third problem of philosophy. From this last conclusion immediately results what appears at a glance to be a paradoxical relation of Tolstoy to science, against which Professor Isayev particularly protests.

Science studies that which is given to us by the sensory organs— that is, the external world, the world of substantial-material things— and not the foundation of being. The external world, however, as has already been indicated above, is, in Tolstoy's opinion, merely something that seems to be—"our fantasy"—and not something authentically real. (Compare this with the Kantian "appearance.") From this, it is clear that the sciences that study this "something that seems to be" cannot be true sciences but only sciences of "the imaginary," whose value is therefore not great.[21]

"If a man thinks that everything he sees around him is an infinite world of just the same sort as he sees, then he is badly mistaken. All that is physical a man knows only because he has one type of sight, hearing, and sense of touch rather than another. *Were these senses different, the whole world would be different.* So it is that we do not know, and cannot know, what sort of thing is the physical world in

20. Ibid., 11; "God," 4.
21. Compare this with Bergson's concept of intellectual knowledge as symbolic knowledge and intuitive knowledge as absolute knowledge. See his *Introduction to Metaphysics, The Perception of Changeability* (Oxford: Clarendon Press, 1911), and *Philosophical Intuition* (Paris: Librarie Armand Colin, 1911).

which we live. The only thing that we truly and fully know is our soul," he says. *"All that is material in this world we cannot know as it really is. We know only that which is spiritual within ourselves."*[22]

From these words, it is evident that Tolstoy places truth—absolute and certain truth—above knowledge. All that is relative and uncertain (as, in his opinion, knowledge of facts and of the external world seem to be) Tolstoy does not value highly. This opinion of his, Professor Isayev notwithstanding, is neither paradox nor eccentricity but the inescapable conclusion of his whole philosophical construction. Ordinary science, according to Tolstoy, knows many trifles but does not know that which is important: God, the soul, and the meaning of life. Inasmuch as only the latter are known by us with certainty (feeling), while the former constitute a relative knowledge of the imaginary, it is understandable that the value of the former is quite low. On this point, as on several others, Tolstoy closely approaches Kant and his dualism of the phenomenal and the noumenal.

VI

It remains for us now to characterize Tolstoy's resolution of the fourth problem of philosophy: the meaning and value of life. This problem occupies a dominant position in Tolstoy's philosophy—so dominant, in fact, that it is easy to take him for a pragmatist advancing the principles of utility and suitability for life as the criteria of truth. More attentive study, however, indicates that one cannot speak of Tolstoyan pragmatism, that the question "How should I live?" as well as its resolution are the logically inescapable conclusions of the principles of his philosophy previously indicated. Inasmuch as God is the source of every life, life is nothing other than a manifestation of God or a part of God striving for unification with Him. "The life and happiness of a man consist in the ever greater unification of the soul—separated by a body from other souls and from God—with those things from which it is separated."[23]

If life is a manifestation of God and a striving for God, and God is happiness, then life also is happiness. Such is Tolstoy's syllogism. "According to false teaching," says Tolstoy, "life in this world is evil, and happiness is attained only in a future life."

"According to true Christian teaching, the goal of life is happiness

22. Tolstoy, *The Way of Life*, "God," 3, 5.
23. Ibid., "Life Is Happiness," 3.

and this happiness is found here. True happiness is in our hands. Like a shadow, it follows a good life." Since a part of God is contained in man (the soul), and God is happiness, therefore happiness is within us. Such is the new conclusion of Tolstoy. "God has come into me and through me He is seeking His own happiness," he says. "And what can the happiness of God be like? Only this, to be Himself." "What greater happiness can there be for you, when you have God and the whole world within you?" he asks.[24] "If happiness is not within you yourself, then you will never encounter it," he says, citing Augustine.

From what has been said, it is evident as well that the thesis "The kingdom of God is within us" is not a paradox but an inescapable conclusion from fundamental premises. And so life is value and the supreme blessing. Its meaning consists in an ever greater unification with its first foundation—God. "Human life is a never-ending process of unification of a spiritual being separated by a body with that to which it knows itself to be united. Whether a man realizes this or not, whether he wishes it or not, such unification is irresistibly accomplished in that condition which we call human life. The difference between those persons who do not understand their vocation and do not wish to fulfill it, and those who do understand their vocation and wish to live in conformity with it, consists in this—that the life of those who do not understand is unending suffering, while the life of those who understand and who fulfill their vocation is unending, ever-increasing happiness." "All suffering is only the 'My,' born of the fact that a man does not recognize his oneness with God, but sees in himself only a physical personality: Ivan, Mavra, and so on. From this it follows also that while he does not recognize God within himself he becomes weak and unhappy, but when conscious of Him in himself he becomes 'free, all-powerful, and knows no evil.'" And the more he is aware of Him in himself, the more strongly he strives for Him, the more filled with meaning his life becomes. This is the highest and ultimate purpose, in relation to which every other purpose becomes relative. Every other purpose, when fulfilled, ceases to be a purpose, says Tolstoy, whereas striving for God never loses its significance, because God is the highest, the ultimate perfection. "One thing alone does not lose its joyous meaning: the consciousness of our movement toward perfection."[25] In other words, the striving for God is the highest governing principle.

24. Ibid., 3–4, 5–7.
25. Ibid., 9, 10.

From this principle, in turn, come the following theses:

A. If the meaning of life consists in unification with God, then unification with other people is unavoidable, because God is contained within them. Hence the general meaning of happiness. "True blessings are few. Only that is genuinely a blessing and a good which is a blessing and a good for all. Therefore one ought to desire only that which is in accordance with general happiness. The person whose activity is directed toward that end will find happiness."[26] This thesis is nothing but the famous principle "Do unto others as you would have them do unto you."

B. From this it follows that unification with God requires unification not only with other people but also with all living things, because these also are a part of God. "In our hearts we feel that what we live and call our 'I' is the very same not only in every person, but also in a dog, a horse, a mouse, and even in a plant." Hence the imperative, "Recognize yourself not only in mankind, but in every living being; don't kill and do not cause suffering and death."[27]

C. Since God is happiness and love, unification with Him is love. "This unification occurs as the soul, manifesting itself in love, frees itself more and more from the body." Hence the thesis, "In order to be truly happy only one thing is necessary: love, love all—the good and the evil alike. Love without ceasing, and you will be unceasingly happy." "My life is not my own," writes Tolstoy, "and therefore its purpose cannot be only my own happiness. Its purpose can only be that which is the will of the One who sent me into life. And He wills that all should love one another, the very thing in which my general happiness consists."[28]

D. From what has been said comes Tolstoy's rejection of physical life—a thesis that at first glance is paradoxical. The body and matter are the boundaries that set us apart from our soul, a part of God, who is our first principle. They hinder our unification with Him and so must be confined and restricted. Hence the thesis, "The more a man lives for the body, the more he is deprived of true happiness." "Some people seek happiness in power, others in love of learning, in science, while others seek it in pleasure." "Those who have more closely approached true philosophy, however, have understood that general happiness—the object of the striving of all people—must not consist in one of those particular things that can be mastered only by some. On the contrary, true happiness must be that which we can all possess at once, without diminishing it and without jealousy, and must be that

26. Ibid., 11.
27. Ibid., "One Soul in All," 7.
28. Ibid., "Life Is Happiness," 12–13.

which no one can lose through his own will. And happiness is this: happiness is in love."[29]

E. Equality. Since "the basis of human life is the Spirit of God living within people—one and the same for all—people cannot possibly be not equal among themselves." "No matter who people may be in themselves, and no matter who their fathers or grandfathers may be, all people are still as equal as two drops of water, because one and the same Spirit of God dwells in them all." "Only those who do not know that God dwells in them can consider some people more important than others."[30]

Here we see a complete parallel between Tolstoy and Kant. For Kant, every man is an end in himself and all are equal, not because, as people, they are ends in themselves, but rather because every man is an embodiment of intelligent will—the absolute good—and, as such, equal to any other. And the majority of philosophical theories support the principle of equality in the very same way. Only recently has there been an attempt to support this principle otherwise.[31]

But as has already been shown above, from this it follows that not only people but all living things are equal to one another.[32] From this the motive for *Is This Really So Necessary?* and related publications becomes understandable—as do even such details of Tolstoy's worldview as his vegetarianism.

From the very same principle come the motives that Tolstoy brings to *What Is Art?* Every art that is understood by only certain persons and not by all is a false art because it differentiates humanity and increases inequality. Therefore it must be rejected. This also explains why Tolstoy sets up as his criterion of artistry the contagiousness of moral experience, whose other side is universality and comprehensibility.[33]

29. Ibid., 14, 15.
30. Ibid., "Inequality," 3, 11.
31. See Kant, *The Foundations of the Metaphysics of Morals* (Riga: J. F. Hartknoch, 1785). On the latter point, also see G. Simmel, *Die Probleme der Geschichtphilosophie* (Leipzig: Duncker and Humblot, 1907), 73–83.
32. See Tolstoy, *The Way of Life,* "One Spirit in All."
33. And the conception of art of Lev Nikolayevich is itself a simple conclusion from his entire system. The highest value is God, happiness. Beauty and truth are subordinate values. They are only the means that make possible the realization of happiness. Therefore the best art is only that art which promotes the attainment of happiness—that is, which propagates and expresses feelings of love, forgiveness, and so on. (See *What Is Art?* [Moscow: Mediator Press, 1898], 68, 52, 202–3, and elsewhere.) Those works that express other feelings—that is, those that do not lead to happiness—are "harlots," "debauchery," and so forth. See also his appraisal of the story of Joseph.

By means of the principle pointed out above, and in no lesser degree by means of the same principle of equality, the reason becomes clear for Tolstoy's rejection of "wisdom" and of the false science that studies a thousand "empty things," discusses them in poorly understood language, and at the same time differentiates among people. From this same principle (derived in turn from other, higher principles) results also his demand for a change to "plain living." In the same way, one can understand his irreconcilability with teachings such as Nietzsche's "superman," the morality of masters and slaves, and so forth. These are polar positions that cannot be combined.

And the entire activity of Tolstoy the nonartist was a great fulfillment of his own principles, a great equalization of the rich and poor of this world, of the learned and "the ignorant," of masters and slaves. Reflecting the best of what human thought has attained, he converted it into his own philosophical creativity, brought it into union with his entire system, and as a result put these thoughts into a clear and simple statement, equally well understood by the educated and the illiterate.

I will not draw out further details of the worldview and conduct of Tolstoy from his fundamental principles. (If one wished, it could be shown.) From what has already been said, it is clear that Tolstoy's philosophy constitutes a single whole in which each part is united with every other and flows logically from what has gone before. And this is seen not only in the fundamental principles but also in the details of his philosophy and life. Taking as his fundamental position the thesis that the essence and the foundation of being and life is God, Tolstoy step by step, in a full and systematic way, develops his system. Since the essence of the world is God, then my "I" is also God because I am part of the world. Since God and I are one and the same, I can know Him. If I can know Him, then the significance and value of my life is to strive for Him. Since He is happiness and love, my striving for Him is manifested in love. Since He is contained in the "I" of others and in all living things, then while striving for Him I should strive for others and for all living things. And from this thesis all the principles, the most important of which we have enumerated above, flow of themselves.

From this it is clear that the criticism of Professor Isayev can hardly be considered successful. It is possible to disagree with Tolstoy's system, or to reject it, but to deny its beauty and logic is hardly permissible.[34] Of course, this can be done, but such an attempt of its very nature must be unsuccessful.

34. There are undoubtedly vague points in Tolstoy (primarily on the mutual relations between God and the material world), but we leave the analysis of these aside in view of the importance for us here of the general system of his philosophy.

VII

In concluding this brief characterization of Tolstoy's philosophical system, I would like to dwell on one further point of his philosophy and its significance for us.

In the realm of artistic creativity, as is well known, there is a distinction between national and general human types. And this distinction concerns not only the types themselves, as products of the artistic creativity of a particular artist, but along with this it applies to the artists themselves and to the whole character of their creativity as manifestations of nationality or expressions of the psychosocial tenor of life of the social group or the people.

To a certain degree this phenomenon seems possible also in the realm of philosophy. Above we have shown that the philosophical is a typical temperament observable through the worldview, in contrast to artistic creativity, in which the worldview is observable through the temperament. If this is really so, then the very typicality of temperament already presupposes to a certain degree that it cannot be the temperament of an individual but rather the temperament of a group, class, or nation. The history of philosophy gives partial support to this phenomenon. Thus, for the Greeks, national philosophy appears in Plato, with his firm, "hard" kingdom of ideas, and not in Heraclitus, with his "all is flux," because even the "becoming" of Heraclitus speaks of something firm. His "becoming" is not an uninterrupted process but is nothing other than a synthesis of two "firm" concepts: being and nonbeing. Only by combining them was he able to obtain "becoming." Uninterrupted change is not known to the Greeks as a distinctive method. The very attempt to construct "becoming" speaks of the same "firm" being. (Recall, following Heraclitus, Zeno and his motionless arrow.)

The same sort of typical philosophies appear for the Germans in Kant and Hegel, with their most abstract and strictly logical systems and their complete renunciation of all empiricism. For the English, on the other hand, the great empiricists Mill and Spencer are characteristic. As the typical French philosopher, everyone would probably cite Comte. Of course, to some degree this division is relative, but nonetheless it appears that there is some truth in it.

Approaching Tolstoy from this point of view, we shall perhaps not be mistaken if we designate him and his philosophy as typical of the Russians. Glancing at our past history—and, in particular, at the history of the intelligentsia in Russia—we see that it is one of continuous self-sacrifice, a constant and incessant "devotion of the soul to its

other," a constant, bright love not stopping short of any sort of sacrifice. Along with this, it seems that one could hardly find anywhere a
greater rejection of all class and national boundaries than in Russia.
Not in vain did Dostoyevsky speak of this or V. Solovyov accept it
with certain reservations. And so it is not without reason that the entire
history of Russian literature appears as one of continuous heroism, an
unending sermon on the ideals of love and truth, a constant "appeal
for heroic deeds," as S. A. Vengerov quite rightly maintains.[35]

From another vantage point, this love is not rational or artificial
but spontaneous and purely mystical. In addition, this mysticism does
not appear to be accidental for us. The endless snowy plains, the songs
of the blizzard, the long twilight and endless forests, together with the
sorrow of our life even in ancient times were constructing the soul of
the Russian man in a mystical harmony. Consider our popular sayings,
our epic stories, and especially our songs—can one not feel in them,
together with grief, a deep secret?

In this connection, could anyone possibly represent Dostoyevsky
not as a Russian but as a German or a Frenchman? Hardly. The Kara-
mazovs and the Raskolnikovs could only have been created by Dostoyevsky, and not by anyone else. We remember also that the major
criticism directed at Western science by Solovyov (and others before
him) was precisely the criticism of excessive rationalism and neglect
of "feeling"—that is, of mysticism. If we keep in mind other similar
examples, then perhaps it will not seem strange that these same two
features dominate the philosophy of Tolstoy: mysticism and love.

The history of philosophy has known many "essences of the
world." Such "essences" have taken the form now of matter, now of
spirit, now of will, now of logic, and so forth. But there has hardly
been any philosophical system that so sharply and clearly declares the
"essence of things" to be God, whose fundamental attribute is a love
that knows no boundaries or limits, a love that is not "intellectual"
but immediately alive.

35. See S. A. Vengerov, *The Heroic Character of Russian Literature* (St. Petersburg:
Prometei Publishers, 1911). Also, his *In What Does the Charm of Russian Literature
Consist?* [Petrograd, 1919].

9

Notes from a Sociologist:
At the Crossroads

Russia is at a parting of the ways. Within her there is a battle between centripetal and centrifugal forces. Will the centripetal forces triumph, strengthening the social group and binding it together as an intact unity? Such is the question that lies before each of us.

It is difficult at present to give a definite answer to this question. The situation is too complex; there are too many conditions on whose interplay depends one or another aspect of the battle. The old ties that bound the state together have fallen to the ground. The old "mechanical solidarity" held together only by coercion, by the powerful fist of despotism, has fallen. Its song is over.

What has brought this change about? Many things. Enthusiasm has been born in a people that have just cast off the ancient way of slavery. A burst of creativity, so long suppressed by the old regime, has arisen. There has been born that great inspiration, that joy, that "madness of the brave" when the impossible becomes possible, the unattainable attainable, the invincible vanquished. At such moments, a person dares to do heroic deeds, and the people dare to do the greatest acts.

Briefly, in place of the mechanical tie of despotic coercion, in place of the clamps of prison walls, a new bond of free, conscious unity has appeared, of workers' hands sincerely extended to one another and prepared to preserve and support social unity.

All this is so. All this is beyond doubt.

But along with this has arisen a whole series of doubts, a whole series of "*buts*" that involuntarily raises an alarm in each of us and involuntarily inspires apprehension about the safety and happiness of the people, the fate of the revolution, and the fate of the state.

There is a desire for a free union. But is this desire sufficiently realized by the broad masses? Are the dangers that arose from the moment of the fall of the old regime sufficiently recognized? If they are recog-

Originally published in *Volya Naroda*, 30 April 1917, p. 1. Translated by Lawrence T. Nichols.

nized, then is the will for the creation of new social ties sufficiently strong? Shall it, moreover, maintain among all the necessary attitude and the necessary knowledge for the realization of its desire?

The answer is difficult. . . .

Meanwhile this local fire has been put out. However, now in one, now in another place, former units of Russia, like fires, have broken out and flared up, then died down, but have not entirely disappeared.

Will they vanish? Or will they, on the contrary, flare up into a general fire, into the reign of total anarchy?

It is difficult to decide. The battle between centripetal and centrifugal forces continues. The battle of revolutionary order with elemental disorder goes on. It is not finished. Which of these shall triumph cannot be seen. The revolution generates wonders; it creates heroes. We think it shall be that way for us in the future. Hope springs eternal. But the way out is not clear.

Each needs to know what every self-consciously responsible person is required to do. The doctrine of critical-thinking personalities, more than at other times, is fitting now. More than at other times, the situation calls to mind the theory of the role of personality in history. Personality is not everything, but it is not nothing. It is a unit of force. Let each of these units raise up what it wishes: the black banner of anarchy, with its skull and crossbones, igniting the flame of the conflagration of the state—or genuine revolutionary order.

Having raised up and having resolved, personality alone shall see what to do and how to do it.[1]

1. The daily political newspaper, *Volya Naroda* "(the will of the people") was published in 1917 by the Social Revolutionary Party, of which Sorokin was a prominent member. Sorokin was one of five editors (the others being A. A. Argunov, A. I. Gykovska, V. S. Mirolyubov, and E. A. Stalinska), and his name appeared fourth on the masthead of each issue.

According to a 1995 study by Yuri Doykov, director of the Emigration History Research Center in Archangelsk, Russia, Sorokin wrote 132 articles and editorials for *Volya Naroda* (including some under such pen names as "V. Vygov" and "P.S."). Among these were fifteen columns under the heading "Notes from a Sociologist" that analyzed the unfolding revolutionary process. This and the next piece are excerpts from two such columns, demonstrating the intensity of Sorokin's political involvement at the time and thereby also illumining the dramatic nature of his subsequent decision to abandon politics entirely and devote his life to science.

10

Notes from a Sociologist: Delay

The proverb says, "A Russian is slow on the uptake." According to another, "Better late than never." I do not know if these sayings are true for other moments of Russian history. In relation to the present moment, however, they are entirely correct.

If one looks at the events of the revolutionary days—in particular, at the conduct of the organizational leaders of Russian democracy and at the slogans guiding the movement—an unbiased observer cannot but notice one characteristic feature that strikes the eye in all the actions of these leading organizations. This feature is systematic delay.

We delay terribly. The government is behind schedule with laws of every sort. The parties lag in not having taken from the very first days of the revolution the positions they take now.

Let us look further, at the actions of the Soviet of Workers' and Soldiers' Deputies. Does the soviet move in front of life, or is it dragged along behind like a prisoner? Alas! Neither the government, nor the parties, nor individual organizers who offer themselves to the working people have been in front of life or been its leaders. Rather, they have accommodated themselves to events and have barely caught up with them.

Do you require proofs? They are plentiful. The government has been tardy with the law prohibiting sales and other transactions involving land. It has also tarried in passing an act guaranteeing the right of working people to the land. The parties have delayed in taking the correct position in relation to the war and to problems of the moment.

And the Soviet of Workers' and Soldiers' Deputies? In its activity one can see this delay especially clearly. Only now has it understood and resolved upon the necessity of imposing discipline in the army. . . .

And in place of the triumphant hymn of the Revolution, there begins the plaintive panegyric, " 'Ay, ukhnem!' Once again, yes, once again, 'ay, ukhnem!' "

"How long, O Lord!" one wants to say in these circumstances. Did

Originally published in *Volya Naroda*, 4 May 1917, p. 1. Translated by Lawrence T. Nichols.

the Revolution really leave us with our old "interior"? Shall we really in the future, as before, repeat limply and half-hopelessly, "Maybe— yes, very likely," and instead of directing events with a firm hand, lag behind them like prisoners relying only on the old "wherever the winding way leads"? It is sad. "How long, O Lord!"

Early Empirical Studies

11

An Experimental Study of Efficiency of Work under Various Specified Conditions

In 1921 and 1922, while in Russia, I tried to apply the experimental method for the clarification of the problem whether the communistic or individualistic organization of labor is the more efficient. My banishment interrupted the study.[1] In 1926–28 in Minnesota I decided to resume the experimental study of a similar problem. The problem which I decided to study experimentally was: providing that all other conditions remain constant, and only the investigated condition varies, does the efficiency of work depend on, and vary with, different systems of remuneration, such as "individual" and "collective"; "equal" and "unequal"; remuneration of the worker himself and that of his good friend; finally, is the overt pure competition, not remunerated by any material value, a factor of efficiency? If each of these factors influences the efficiency of the work, in what way and how?[2] Such were the problems of the experimental study. You can easily see their theoretical and practical—even purely economic—significance, especially for our age of a reconstruction of the capitalistic system, rationalization of labor organization, and communist, socialist, and equalitarian tendencies.

The Technique of the Experimentation and the Human Material

Experimentation was first made with a group of preschool children from three to four years of age, in the Child Welfare Institute of the

Coauthored with Mamie Tanquist, Mildred Parten, and Mrs. C. C. Zimmerman. Originally published in the *American Journal of Sociology* (March 1930): 765–82. © 1930 University of Chicago. All rights reserved. Reprinted by permission of the publisher.

1. See P. Sorokin, "Die Russische Soziologie der Gegenwart," *Jahrbuch für Soziologie* 2: 474–75.

2. Preliminary results of the first series of these experiments were published in my paper "Arbeitsleistung und Entlohnung," *Kölner Vierteljahrshefte für Soziologie*, 7, heft 2 (1928), 186–98. This paper gives the results of the several series of experiments made after the above paper was written.

University of Minnesota; later on with three high-school boys from
thirteen to fourteen years of age; and still later on with the group of
kindergarten children (in cooperation with Miss M. Tanquist). The
preschool children were taken because, being young, they were not
imbued with either socialist or capitalist bias like the grown-up persons. The objective of the experimentation was unknown to them and
therefore did not influence their behavior. The whole series of experiments was for them mere "play," somewhat hard, sometimes tiresome,
but "play." As to the high-school boys, I took them in order to find
to what extent the results obtained from the preschool children were
valid for grown-up boys. The objective of the experimentation was
also unknown to them. They simply were "hired" to do some work
for which they were paid. Possibly after the first two or three experiments, the boys guessed that there was some experimentation. But
what it was they were not told, and, on the basis of the boys' talk to
their parents, they seemed not to have guessed the objective of the
work which they did.

The first series of experiments was made during April, May, and
June of 1927. The work which was done by the preschool children
was running and carrying marbles from one corner of the yard of the
Child Welfare Institute and the hall of the kindergarten to another;
picking up small wooden balls or pegs of a definite color from a box
filled with balls, squares, and triangular objects, or with pegs of various colors; filling cups with sand, carrying them a certain distance,
and emptying them there. The work of the high-school boys consisted
in carrying water pails from one place to another; in filling a pail with
sand and carrying it to a certain place; and finally, in computing a
list of points on paper and in performing the operations of addition,
subtraction, multiplication, and division of a series of arithmetical
problems given in a specially prepared list.

In choosing these types of work I took into account the following
considerations. First, the work had to require some exertion; it was
not to be done merely for the pleasure of doing it. Contrariwise, the
effect of each type of remuneration and competition could not be noticed. We ascertained that this requirement was fulfilled by the chosen
types of work. The second condition which had to be satisfied by the
types of work chosen was that they could be easily measured without
any subjective rating and grading by the investigator.[3] From this standpoint, all the above types of work were quite satisfactory. All that we

3. Such a rating introduces a subjective element and is always very questionable in
its validity.

had to do in the measurement of the efficiency of the work was to compute the number of sand cups or pails filled and carried to a certain place, or the number of marbles carried, or the number of balls or pegs picked from the box.

The next point to establish was "the equality of all other conditions" except those which were studied. This was easily done through the identity of the kind of work done, of the children working, of the time of work, of cups, of distance, of boxes, and so forth.

More difficult was an elimination of the effects of fatigue and practice. Their elimination was reached through a series of repetitions of the same work and alteration or reversal of the order of the work under each pair of conditions studied. One day the children started the work with an "equal" or "collective" remuneration and passed to the work with an "unequal" or "individual" remuneration, while the next day the sequence of the work under these conditions was the reverse. Under such circumstances the effects of fatigue, practice, and similar factors are likely to be eliminated, and the total amount of work done in a series of the experiments under each of the conditions studied may be reasonably ascribed to the difference in the method of remuneration.

Finally, I wanted to be quite certain that the difference in remuneration was well understood by the children. The first experiments, where we were not certain that the children well understood the point, were excluded from the results. After the first two or three experiments, the difference became quite clear for the children and was conspicuously expressed in their "speech reactions."

As a "remuneration" to the children for the work I used various kinds of children's toys and, later on, pennies. Professor Tanquist used pennies entirely. It goes without saying that the amount of remuneration for the whole group of child workers of each day was the same when they worked for the "group" and for "themselves," under "equal" and "unequal" remuneration. If, for instance, one day's remuneration for collective playing house of the children consisted of an airplane, automobile, and moving mouse, as identical as possible an airplane, automobile, and mouse was given to them when they worked for individual remuneration, he who did most could choose the one of these things which he preferred, the next one in efficiency could take his choice of the remaining toys, and so on. In total, the whole group received the same amount of toys as in the case of group remuneration. The same was true in regard to pennies. As to the remuneration of the high-school boys, they were paid by money only: fifteen cents each for ten minutes of work under equal remuneration (a total

TABLE 1. Relative Efficiency of Work of Preschool Children under "Group" and "Individual" Remuneration

Type of Work	No. of Experiment	No. of Children Working in Each Pair of Experiments	Time of Work under Each Type of Remuneration		No. of Marbles or Sand Cups Carried	
			Min.	Sec.	"Group" Remuneration	"Individual" Remuneration
Carrying marbles	1	2	2	45	10	11
	2	4	2	45	22	23
	3	3	5		$17\frac{1}{2}$*	18
	4	2	5		$7\frac{2}{6}$*	$9\frac{5}{6}$*
Total			15	30	$56\frac{5}{6}$*	$61\frac{5}{6}$*
Filling sand cups and carrying	5	4	3		11	17
	6	3	3		14	14
	7	2	6		19	18
	8	2	6		15	21
Total			18		59	70
Grand total of experiments			33	30	115	$131\frac{5}{6}$*

* The fraction indicates the proportion of the distance over which the last marble or sand cup had been carried when time was called.

of forty-five cents for the three boys) and twenty, fifteen, and ten cents, according to efficiency of the work for ten minutes of work, under unequal remuneration (a total of forty-five cents, also).

Not entering here into a description of other, less important technical points, the above gives an idea about the character and the technique of the experiments and shows to some extent that on our part we did all that was humanly possible in the way of equalization of "all the other conditions" and keeping all the relevant circumstances under our control. Let us turn now to the results of the experiments.

Efficiency of Work of the Preschool Children under the "Collective or Group" and under the "Individual" Remuneration

This is shown by table 1. By the "collective or group" remuneration is meant that the toys were not allowed to be "taken home" as an individual possession of the children but were given to their collective "playhouse," where every one of them could enjoy them as a "collective possession." By "individual" remuneration is meant that the child who earned his toy could "take it home" and do with it whatever he would like to do: he had a full right of property over it. The results of the table are clear. They sum up as follows: in all the experiments, with the exception of that of number 7, individual remuneration stimulated a greater efficiency in the work of the same children than collective remuneration. The exception, experiment number 7, was in fact fictitious. On this day the work continued six minutes and was commenced with collective remuneration; after six minutes of the work of filling relatively heavy cups with sand and carrying them, the children were tired; therefore the incentive of individual remuneration was not able to completely overcome the effects of this fatigue. But the next day, when the same work was started with individual remuneration, it resulted in twenty-one cups instead of nineteen during the previous day and only fifteen instead of eighteen during the previous day. The difference for the first four experiments in the efficiency under both systems of remuneration was that between fifty-six and sixty-one units of work for a total period of work time fifteen minutes, thirty seconds; for the next four experiments, the difference was fifty-nine and seventy units of work for a period of time equal to thirty-three minutes, thirty seconds. Taking into consideration the shortness of time, the difference in efficiency was rather remarkable. If we imagine instead of thirty-three minutes 333 days and instead of four or two workers forty thousand of them, then the above difference would grow to an enormous amount, quite important from the economic standpoint.

Efficiency of Work under the Remuneration for "A Worker Himself" and That for "His Friend": Experimental Test of Individual's Sociality and Its Decrease with an Increase of Social Distance

The next problem, related to the above, was to find out whether there was a difference in the efficiency of work when remuneration for it was given to the working child himself and when he worked for another child in the working group while the other child worked for him. If there had been no "egotism," the amount of work of the same child or the same group of children would have been equal in both cases. If there was "egotism," then there had to appear a difference and it had to be greater the less "social" or the more "egotistic" an individual

TABLE 2. Relative Efficiency of Work for "Himself" and for "Friend"

No. of Experiment	No. of Children Working in Each Pair of Experiments	Time of Work (Min.)	No. of Marbles Carried	
			For "Himself"	For "Friend" "Co-worker"
1	4	2	35½	32½
2	4	2	32	28½
3	4	4	33	33
4	4	4	68½	62½
5	4	2	30	29½
6	4	2	33	26
Total of six experiments		16	232	212

was. Such a test could be regarded as one of the most valid criteria of "sociality" or "altruism" of an individual. In this sense, the test is a real test of the altruism or egotism of an individual, maybe even more adequate than the existing forms of "mental tests." The results of the experiments of this type are given in table 2.

The table shows that the efficiency of work for "himself" was greater than for a fellow co-worker. The difference between 232 and 212 units of work indicates the stimulating role of "egotism" in work. It is necessary to keep in mind that in the remuneration for a fellow co-worker, the children worked for their best friend in the same team, one he himself chose, and that the interests of each child in each pair or "working team" were mutual. In spite of this, the efficiency of work was different even in such an "egotistic–altruistic" situation. If we suppose that in the remuneration for "somebody" else, this "somebody" would be a total stranger to the child, and not his best friend co-worker, the difference would be incomparably greater. A couple of experiments made with the children for the elucidation of this problem partly showed this.

Later on, in 1928, in a different form, I made an experimental study of the same problem with the students of the University of Minnesota, and the results of the study seem to corroborate this expectation. In this case the study was carried out in the following forms.[4]

Unfortunately, in this study, the above test of sociality, where the amount of work was made a thermometer of sociality, could not be applied. This was the reason why I had to apply another test to find

4. See P. Sorokin, *Experimente zur Soziologie, Zeitschrift für Völkerpsychologie und Soziologie* (March 1928) 1–10.

out how sociality changes with an increase of social distance or "strangeness" of various groups. In this case, as "the thermometer of relative sociality," the amount of money which the students were ready to give for the three "causes" indicated below was taken. To be sure, this thermometer is absolutely inadequate to measure the comparative sociality of various individuals; a rich man may give more than a poor man and yet be less social than the second one. But the amount of money, given by the same individual, at the same time, for the benefit of various groups, seems to be a pretty good indication of the individual's sociality in regard to these various groups. Starting with this premise, the author and, according to his request, H. R. Hosea and O. D. Duncan, instructors of sociology in the University of Minnesota, one day addressed six classes of sociology in our university with the request to contribute as much as every student could for the following three purposes: first, for diagrams and a computing machine for the class itself; second, for "three brilliant students in the sociology department who were financially ruined by the Mississippi inundations and who would be forced to leave the university unless we would help them"; third, in the name of "the International Students' Relief" for the students of the Chinese and Russian universities who were dying from starvation. The students were told that the diagrams or computing machine would be exceedingly helpful for them in their examinations. We took care to describe most realistically the pitiful situation of the brilliant students whose families were ruined by the Mississippi inundation, which happened shortly before. In a similar way, quite realistically was depicted the terrible situation of the Chinese and Russian students. In brief, each of us played "an actor's role" to make the students believe that we were sincere and were really collecting the money for these groups. We took pains to ascertain that the students believed in our sincerity and did not have the slightest idea that all this was done only for experimental purposes. After this each of the students was given a slip of paper and instructed to write how much he could give—and give immediately—for each of these purposes. Slips were collected and their results will now be given.

From the character of the three groups for whose benefits the contributions were solicited, it will be seen that the first group was the class itself; the second, the students of the same department and the same university, but not of the same class. Thus the second group was more remote socially than the first. The third group was still remoter socially; it was also composed of students, but of students in Chinese and Russian universities. Thus the social distance increases as we go from the first to the third group. On the other hand, the importance

TABLE 3. Contributions and Contributors for Three Causes

	Class	I For Class Diagrams, Etc.	II For Impoverished Students of University of Minnesota	III For Chinese and Russian Students
Amount of money contributed	A	$ 7.30	$ 6.00	$ 3.55
	B	6.25	3.90	2.65
	C	5.30	6.60	5.00
	D	6.75	5.75	2.25
	E	11.10	6.05	5.75
	F	11.55	4.70	3.25
Total		$48.25	$33.00	$22.45
Number of persons contributing	A	43	33	23
	B	27	16	11
	C	40	36	29
	D	23	22	10
	E	20	15	14
	F	32	16	12
Total		185	138	99
Comparative for money con- tributed (cause I = 100)		100.0	68.4	46.5
Comparative indices for num- ber of persons contribut- ing (cause I = 100)		100.0	74.6	53.5

of the cause decreases as we go from the third to the first group; while the Russian and the Chinese students needed help to keep from dying of starvation (danger for life), the second group risked only to be forced to drop the university education, and the third cause was mere convenience in preparing for the examination. If the social distance had not played any part in conditioning the intensity of the sociality, we would have had to expect that the amount of the contributions for the second and the third cause would have been, at least, no less than for the first cause, and the number of the students who would contribute for these causes would have been at least not less than for the first cause. The factual situation, however, was very different. It is shown by table 3.

The table shows, first, that in spite of the least importance of cause I, the same students contributed for it a greater amount of money than for causes II and III, "self-altruism" here happened also to be stronger than the altruism for others; second, that in spite of the greatest need of help in the cause III, the contribution for it was the least; third, similar is the picture shown by the number of students who contributed for one or all of these causes. Out of the total of 202 students who responded to the appeal (those who did not make any contribution are excluded from the table), the greatest number, 185, contributed for the least important cause, and the least number, 99, for the third cause. Of course, there were individuals who contributed more for the second or the third cause than for the first; there also were, individuals who contributed only for the third or for the second cause, not giving anything for the first cause; we see even that in class C the amount of the contribution for the second cause, $6.60, is greater than for the first cause. And yet, when the total results are taken, they show clearly that intensity of sociality decreases parallel as the social distance of the groups increases. This conclusion corroborates K. Pearson's similar generalization and tentatively shows that it seems to be possible to be a "cosmopolitan" or "internationalist" in sociality equally social toward all human beings only in speech reactions. In factual or actional sociality, such a situation seems to be little probable.[5]

Efficiency of Work under "Equal" and "Unequal" Remuneration

The next problem was to find out whether the efficiency of work was the same when the members of the working group were remunerated "equally" and "unequally" in proportion to the work done by each member, the total amount of the remuneration for the whole working group being the same in both cases. The results of the experiments along that line are shown in table 4.

The data below clearly show that an "unequal" remuneration stimulated more efficient work than an "equal" one. Practically all the experiments, not to mention their total series, show this. Thus, though total remuneration for the whole group in each of the cases of the equal and unequal remuneration was the same and all the other conditions remained equal, a remuneration according to effort and work done or an unequal distribution of the remuneration within the group stimulated greater exertion in work's efficiency than an equal distribution of it. This is true in regard to the children as well as the boys. In con-

5. The same study has shown that in their "speech reactional sociality" these students were "internationalists." But only 27.4 percent of them showed a consistency between their "actional" and "speech reactional" altruism. See the quoted paper.

TABLE 4. Relative Efficiency of Work under "Equal" and "Unequal" Remuneration

Type of Work	No. of Experiment	No. of Children Working in Each Pair of Experiments	Time of Work Min.	Sec.	"Equal" Remuneration	"Unequal" Remuneration
Preschool Children						
Picking balls from box	1	3	3		201	219
	2	3	3	45	246	265
	3	2	3	55	172	195
	4	3	2	45	142	187
	5	3	5		302	349
Total			18	55	1,063	1,215
Carrying marbles	6	3	3	50	20	22
	7	3	3	15	31	34
	8	2	3		19	20
	9	3	3		26	29
	10	5	2		25	31
	11	3	2		24	25
	12	3	2		27	27
	13	3	2		27	29
Total			21	5	199	221
Filling sand cups and carrying	14	4	4	30	14	18
	15	4	4	30	18	18¹/₂
	16	2	3		6	7¹/₂
Total			12		38	44
Grand total of experiments			52		1,300	1,480
High-School Boys						
Filling pails with water or sand and carrying	1	3	10		170	227
	2	3	10		108	138
	3	3	5		17	23
Total			25		295	388

trast with the results where the work was physical, in a purely intellectual work (computation of the points and solving of arithmetical problems), the difference in efficiency of the work under equal and unequal remuneration was practically insignificant. In thirteen minutes, three boys computed 4,963 points with nineteen mistakes under equal and 4,965 points with twenty-six mistakes under unequal remuneration. The same number of arithmetical problems was solved in fifteen minutes, thirteen seconds, in the case of equal and in thirteen minutes, fifty seconds, in the case of unequal remuneration. This probably was due to the fact that efficiency, accuracy, and rapidity of the mental work could be controlled voluntarily in a less degree than the muscles of feet or arms or body machinery.

TABLE 5. Relative Efficiency of Mental and Manual Work of Kindergarten Children under "Equal" and "Unequal" Remuneration

Type of Work	No. of Experiment	No. of Experiments with Each Group	Length of Time in Each Experiment (Min.)	Length of Time in Six Experiments (Min.)	No. of Marbles Carried or Pegs Picked Up	
					"Equal" Remuneration	"Unequal" Remuneration
Manual work (carrying marbles)	1	6	3	18	408	413
	2	6	3	18	447	454$1/4$
	3	6	3	18	401	418$3/4$
Total		18		54	1,256	1,286
Mental work (picking up pegs)	1	6	3	18	936 (11)*	923 (5)*
	2	6	3	18	1,125 (37)*	1,125 (35)*
	3	6	3	18	811 (137)*	910 (111)*
Total		18		54	2,872 (185)*	2,958 (151)*
Grand total of experiments		36		108	4,128	4,244

* Figures in parentheses represent the number of errors made by picking up pegs of a wrong color.

In order to find out to what extent these results were typical, in 1928 similar experiments with the same technique were carried on, under my direction, by Mamie Tanquist, a graduate student then, now a professor. This time we took three groups of kindergarten children, each group consisting of four children. The work was of two kinds: carrying marbles (physical work) and picking up pegs of a definite color out of a box filled with pegs of different colors (half-physical, half-mental work). With each of these three groups in each kind of work, six pairs of experiments were made, a total of eighteen pairs of experiments of carrying marbles and eighteen pairs of experiments of picking up pegs, which gives a grand total of thirty-six experiments. The duration of the work was in all experiments the same, namely three minutes under equal and three minutes also under unequal remu-neration, which gives for each of the pairs of work six minutes. This shows that this time the experimental series were much longer and were carried with three different groups. The results obtained were in essential agreement with the results given above. In an abbreviated form, the total "output of work" of each of the three groups of the children in each of the six pairs of work are shown by table 5.

The table is in conspicuous agreement with the data given above. It shows also that in the mental or half-mental work of picking pegs, the difference in the efficiency under equal and unequal remuneration is much less consistent than in the efficiency of the manual work—the result strikingly similar to that given by the physical and mental work of the high-school boys. The number of mistakes made in picking up pegs of a wrong color here, however, happened to be consistently less under unequal than under equal remuneration. Thus the totality of the experimental data indicates clearly that work under the unequal remuneration is more efficient than under the equal remuneration and the difference in the efficiency is much greater in purely manual work than in mental or half-mental work. If, instead of these kinds of work, we suppose other—and much more unpleasant—kinds, and if, instead of the three or six minutes of work, we suppose a much longer time, then we have every reason to expect a still greater contrast in the efficiency of work under these two systems of remuneration. Imagine further that instead of four working children we have hundreds of thousands of laborers working many hours a day with the same difference in their efficiency as is given in the table; then it will be comprehensible what an enormous difference there would be in an output of the produce of labor of two identical countries, in one of which the remuneration of the laborers is equal, in another unequal. From the standpoint of the efficiency of work, the experiments testify in favor of the system of the unequal remuneration.

Strikes

This preference of the system of "unequal" remuneration has, however, its own drawback. While in all the cases of the "equal remuneration" we did not have any single case of "a strike" among the working children, we had them several times in the cases of the unequal remuneration. Among the working children of the Child Welfare Institute, two of the children who were the least efficient and therefore got the least prizes, several times after their failure, said, "I won't work more," and twice stopped work in the process of the experiment and twice refused to work in the experiments of the next day. Similar cases happened also with the kindergarten children. By ceasing to work, these strikers at the same time spread a disorganizing influence among other working children to such an extent that several times they made the continuation of the experiments impossible. In order to prevent this, we had to "lie" and to give occasionally to these failures the first or the second prize (to encourage them) while they should have received the least prizes. These phenomena I styled "strikes," and one can see that they indeed represented a kind of behavior identical with what is usually styled by the term of strike. Thus, though the system of unequal remuneration stimulates a greater efficiency of work than the system of equal remuneration, the latter is followed in a less degree by "labor disturbances" and "strikes" than the former.

Influence of "Pure Competition" on Efficiency of Work

The greater efficiency of work under unequal remuneration in the above tables was probably due to two different factors: first, the incentive of the first prize in remuneration ("pecuniary incentive"); second, the factor of competition inherent in such a stimulation (to desire to "beat other competitors"). Even in the work under equal remuneration there was interstimulation and factual competition, but in the work under unequal remuneration, to this form of interstimulation an additional factor of an overt competition for a better prize and for a victory was added. Guided by this hypothesis, I wished to determine more exactly the stimulating role of a pure competition not followed by any pecuniary remuneration. For this purpose, a series of experiments was made with the children of the Child Welfare Institute and with those of the kindergarten. This series of experiments consisted in a study of the comparative efficiency of work under equal and unequal remuneration in which the children were not told "who beat" and no speech stimulation in form "try to beat" was used. Each experiment of such work was paralleled by the same kind of work, but before it the children were told that they would receive no remuneration for their work but "we would like to see who can beat and we will tell you who beat." In this way, three different situations were created: in two of them, there was a stimulus of a pecuniary character but no special speech stimulation ("try to beat" and no particular stressing of "who beat"); in the third situation, there was a stimulus of an overt competition with these speech reactions but there was no pecuniary incentive and remuneration. Such a situation is styled "nonpecuniary or pure competition." The results of the experiments are shown by tables 6 and 7.

Table 6 shows that as far as manual work is concerned, the work under the pure competition was more efficient in all five working teams of children than the work under the equal remuneration. The manual work under the pure competition was more efficient in two out of the three working groups than even the work under the unequal remuneration [table 7]. Only in the half-mental work of picking pegs was the work under the pure competition less efficient than that under equal

TABLE 6. Relative Efficiency of Work with Equal Remuneration and without Remuneration

Group	Type of Work	No. of Experiment	No. Working in Each Experimental Trial	Time of Work (Min.)	No. of Marbles Carried or Pails Filled with Sand and Carried	
					"Equal" Remuneration	"Pure Competition" (No Remuneration)
Child Welfare Institute	Carrying marbles	1	3	2	26$\frac{1}{2}$	28
		2	3	2	26	128
		3	3	2	24	27
		4	3	2	25	30
Total		—		8	104$\frac{1}{2}$	108
High-school boys	Filling pails with sand and carrying	1	2	8	16$\frac{1}{2}$	18

or unequal remuneration. I am not prepared to explain this last result at present. But the results in their total are rather remarkable in their witnessing to a great incentive power of the nonpecuniary-competitive situation. They testify that human efficiency may indeed be stimulated through pure competition—in this case, through a mere speech reactional incentive: "We want to see who can beat and we will tell it"—no less than through pecuniary stimuli. Replace the above very modest form of the used stimuli of the pure competition by a large audience in a theater or on a political stage or in the newspaper, and the above modest speech reactional stimulation by deafening and sonorous eu-

TABLE 7. Relative Efficiency of Work of Kindergarten Children with "Equal" and "Unequal" Remuneration and without Remuneration

Type of Work	Group	No. of Children Working in Each Experimental Trial	Time of Work* (Min.)	No. of Marbles Carried or Pegs Picked Up		
				"Equal" Remuneration	"Unequal" Remuneration	"Pure Competition" (No Remuneration)
Carrying marbles	A	4	18	408	413	433
	B	4	18	447	454$\frac{1}{4}$	445
	C	4	18	401	418$\frac{3}{4}$	442$\frac{1}{4}$
Total			54	1,256	1,286	1,321$\frac{1}{4}$
Picking up pegs	A	4	18	936	923	892
	B	4	18	1,125	1,125	994
	C	4	18	811	910	782
Total			54	2,872	2,958	2,668

* The 18 minutes spent by each group represents the total time spent in 6 experiments of 3 minutes each.

logy of the men praised or blamed by poets, papers, magazines, public speeches, by "glory," "fame," "popularity," and other noisy forms of competitive, nonpecuniary stimulation, and then the actions of the greatest heroism, exertion, and sacrifice and the actions of the greatest madness, folly, and crime, performed many times in the history of various groups from the motives free from any pecuniary interests, would be to some extent comprehensible. The experiments really show the role of pure competition to be much more effective than it is usually thought to be. They also suggest that the factor of nonpecuniary competition may be used with some effectiveness in a society for stimulation of the desirable forms of behavior, and its utilization would not cost the society anything. These statements require, however, the following reservation: the pecuniary incentive used in the experiments was rather modest (a few pennies or a toy). It is probable that when it is considerably greater, its weight would increase and the pecuniary greediness in such cases might greatly outdistance the incentive of pure competition. This is, however, merely a guess, one which should be studied separately.

Individual Differences

The above results are the totals of the work done in each, or a series of, experiments by the whole group of children or boys who worked in it. These results do not mean that each child or each boy worked in an identical way in the experiments. The "individual profile" of the work of each worker varied strongly. The difference in the efficiency of work for "themselves" and for a "friend"; for "pure competition," for "equal" and "unequal" remuneration; for "individual" and "group" remuneration, varied from child to child. Some of the "workers" worked with almost the same efficiency under all these conditions, while others worked very efficiently "for themselves" or for an "unequal" remuneration and very lazily for a "friend" or for "equal" and "group" remuneration. Few of the children happened to be most efficient under "equal" and most inefficient under "unequal" remuneration.

In brief, the experiments disclosed a conspicuous contrast in the variability of the children's "individual labor profile." They opened to our eyes a variability of human personality in regard to "labor actions" and the difference in the children's responsive exertion to the above different types of stimulation. We tried to correlate the main types of the individual labor profiles with a series of possible variables, such

as nationality, I.Q., age, sex, "good or poor" worker generally, occupation of the father, economic standing of the family, school success.
But on account of the limited number of the cases, or on account of
the real lack of correlation, the attempts did not yield any definite
results. For instance, the unequal remuneration happened to be the
most effective for the four out of six children with the highest I.Q.;
and the same remuneration happened to be the most effective for four
out of six children with the lowest I.Q. Somewhat similar were the
results of the correlations of other possible variables with the type of
the individual labor profile. But whatever may be the factors causally
correlated with the type of the profile, a conspicuous difference of the
types of human personality in this respect is beyond doubt. For practical purposes, this suggests the possibility of a scientific diagnosing of
the labor profile of a man and corresponding selection of employees
and workers for various enterprises. When, for instance, we need a
group of hard, efficient, and honest workers in various public institutions where pecuniary or competitive incentives are limited, the type
of a laborer who works as efficiently under "equal" or "group" or
"nonpecuniary" remuneration would be obviously more suitable.
And, vice versa, the persons who exert themselves in a work for their
own enrichment and aggrandizement evidently are more fit for the positions which require great effort, exertion, and some risk to be performed successfully.

Summary

Other conditions being equal, individual remuneration stimulates a
greater efficiency of work than group remuneration; the work of an
individual for himself is more efficient than his work for a friend or
for other men; the efficiency of work or the amount of help to other
individuals decreases with an increase of social distance between the
helper and the helped; unequal remuneration stimulates a greater efficiency of work in a group than equal remuneration on the other hand,
an unequal distribution of remuneration facilitates the phenomena of
strikes and revolts on the part of those who are "failures"; pure competition is likely to be an incentive to work not less efficient than an
equal remuneration without competition. These regularities manifest
themselves more clearly in manual than in mental kinds of work. In
all these respects, there are noticeable differences in the profile of the
work of separate individuals.
    There are some serious reasons to think that these results are appli-

cable to a great many individuals and social groups. However, before they are extended, it is necessary to test them through a series of similar experiments with other groups of individuals. If this paper can stimulate other social investigators to such experimentation, its purpose will be achieved, regardless of whether these results are similar to or dissimilar from the above. An organization of similar experimental studies on a large scale promises to yield a series of important practical results which can be profitably applied in public and private corporations for an appropriate selection of employees and the most appropriate system of their remuneration and stimulation to efficient work.

12

Social Mobility

Conception of Social Mobility and Its Forms

By social mobility I understand any transition of an individual or social object of value-anything that has been created or modified by human activity—from one social position to another. There are two principal types of social mobility, *horizontal* and *vertical*. By horizontal social mobility, or shifting, I mean the transition of an individual or social object from one social group to another situated on the same level. Transitions of individuals, as from the Baptist to the Methodist religious group, from one citizenship to another, from one family (as a husband or wife) to another by divorce and remarriage, from one factory to another in the same occupational status, are all instances of social mobility. So too are transitions of social objects—the radio, automobile, fashion, communism, Darwin's theory—within the same social stratum, as from Iowa to California, or from any one place to another. In all these cases, shifting may take place without any noticeable change of the social position of an individual or social object in the vertical direction. By the vertical social mobility, I mean the relations involved in a transition of an individual (or a social object) from one social stratum to another. According to the direction of the transition, there are two types of vertical social mobility: *ascending* and *descending*, or *social climbing* and *social sinking*. According to the nature of the stratification, there are ascending and descending currents of economic, political, and occupational mobility, not to mention other, less important types. The ascending current exists in two principal forms: as an infiltration of the individuals of a lower stratum into an existing higher one; and as a creation of a new group by such individuals and the insertion of such a group into a higher stratum instead of, or side by side with, the existing groups of this stratum. Correspondingly, the descending current has also two principal forms: the first consists in a dropping of the individuals from a higher social position

Originally published in the *Journal of Applied Sociology* 11 (1922): 21–32.

into an existing lower one, without a degradation or disintegration of the higher group to which they belonged; the second is manifested in a degradation of a social group as a whole, in an abasement of its rank among other groups, or in its disintegration as a social unit. The first case of "sinking" reminds one of an individual falling from a ship; the second of the sinking of the ship itself with all on board, or of the ship as a wreck breaking itself to pieces.

The cases of individual infiltration into an existing higher stratum or of individuals dropping from a higher social layer into a lower one are relatively common and comprehensible. They need no explanation. We must dwell a little more, however, on the second form of social ascending and descending, the rise and fall of groups.

The following historical examples may serve to illustrate. The historians of India's caste society tell us that the caste of the Brahmins did not always have the position of indisputable superiority which it has held during the last two thousand years. In the remote past, the caste of the warriors and rulers, or the caste of the Kshatriyas, seems to have been not inferior to the caste of the Brahmins; and it appears that only after a long struggle did the latter become the highest caste. If this hypothesis be true, then this elevation of the rank of the Brahmin caste as a whole through the ranks of other castes is an example of the second type of social ascent. The group as a whole being elevated, all its members, *in corpore,* through this very fact, are elevated also. Before the recognition of the Christian religion by Constantine the Great, the position of a Christian bishop, or the Christian clergy, was not a high one among other social ranks of the Roman society. In the next few centuries the Christian church, as a whole, experienced an enormous elevation of social position and rank. Through this wholesale elevation of the Christian church, the members of the clergy, and especially the high church dignitaries, were elevated to the highest ranks of medieval society. And, contrariwise, a decrease in the authority of the Christian church during the last two centuries has led to a relative abasement of the social ranks of the high church dignitaries within the ranks of the present society. The position of the pope or a cardinal is still high, but undoubtedly it is lower than it was in the Middle Ages. The group of the legists in France is another example. In the twelfth century, this group appeared in France, as a group, and began to grow rapidly in significance and rank. Very soon, in the form of the judicial aristocracy, it asserted itself into the place of the previously existing nobility. In this way, its members were raised to a much higher social position. During the seventeenth, and especially the eighteenth centuries, the group, as a whole, began to "sink," and finally disappeared in the conflagration of the Revolution. A similar process took place in the elevation of the communal bourgeoisie in the Middle Ages, in the privileged Six Corps or the *Guilda Mercatoria,* and in the aristocracy of many royal courts.

To have a high position at the court of the Romanovs, Habsburgs, or Hohenzollerns before the revolutions meant to have one of the highest social ranks in the corresponding countries. The "sinking" of the dynasties led to a "social sinking" of all ranks connected with them. The group of the communists in Russia, before the Revolution, did not have any high rank socially recognized. During the Revolution the group climbed an enormous social distance and occupied the highest strata in Russian society. As a result, all its members have been elevated *en masse* to the place occupied by the Czarist aristocracy. Similar cases are given in a purely economic stratification. Before the oil and automobile era, to be a prominent manufacturer in this field did not mean to be a captain of industry and finance. A great expansion of these industries has transformed them into some of the most important kinds of industry. Correspondingly, to be a leading manufacturer in these fields now means to be one of the most important leaders of industry and finance. These examples illustrate the second, collective form of ascending and descending currents of social mobility.

The situation is summed up in the following scheme:

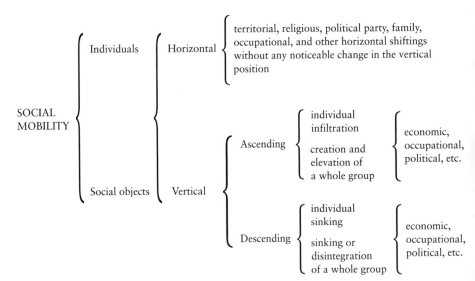

Intensiveness or Velocity and Generality
of Vertical Social Mobility

From the quantitative point of view, we must further distinguish the intensiveness and the generality of the vertical mobility. By its *intensiveness*, I mean the vertical social distance, or the number of strata—economic, or occupational, or political—crossed by the individual in his upward or downward movement in a definite period of time. If, for instance, one individual in one year climbed from the position with an income of $500 to a position with an income of $50,000, while another man in the same period succeeded in increasing his income only from $500 to $1000, in the first case the intensiveness of the economic climbing would be fifty times greater than in the second case.

For a corresponding change, the intensiveness of the vertical mobility may be measured in the same way in the field of the political and occupational stratifications. By the *generality* of the vertical mobility, I mean the number of individuals who have changed their social position in the vertical direction in a definite period of time. The absolute number of such individuals gives the *absolute generality* of the vertical mobility in a given population; the proportion of such individuals to the total number of a given population gives the *relative generality* of the vertical mobility.

Finally, combining the data of intensiveness and relative generality of the vertical mobility in a definite field (e.g., in the economic), we may obtain the *aggregate index* of the vertical economic mobility of a given society. In this way we may compare one society with another, or the same society at different periods, to find in which of them, or at what period, the aggregate mobility is greater. The same may be said about the aggregate index of the political and occupational vertical mobility.

Immobile and Mobile Types of Stratified Societies

On the basis of the above, it is easy to see that a social stratification of the same height and profile may have a different inner structure caused by the difference in the intensiveness and generality of the (horizontal and) vertical social mobility. Theoretically, there may be a stratified society in which the vertical social mobility is nil. This means that within it there is no ascending or descending, no circulation of its members; that every individual is forever attached to the social stratum in which he was born; that the membranes or hymens which separate one stratum from another are absolutely impenetrable, and do not have any "holes" through which, or any stairs and elevators with which, the dwellers of the different strata may pass from one floor to another. Such a type of stratification may be styled as absolutely closed, rigid, impenetrable, or immobile. The opposite theoretical type of the inner structure of the stratification of the same height and profile is that in which the vertical mobility is very intensive and general; here the membranes between the strata are very thin and have the largest holes to pass from one floor to another. Therefore, though the social building is as stratified as the immobile one, nevertheless, the dwellers of its different strata are permanently changing; they do not stay a very long time in the same "social story," and with the help of the largest staircases and elevators are *en masse* moving "up and down." Such a type of social stratification may be styled open, plastic, penetrable, or mobile. Between these two extreme types there may be many middle or intermediary types of stratification.

Some Results of a Study of the Vertical Mobility

I have undertaken a study of the vertical mobility from the standpoint of its factors, its forms, its fluctuation in time and space, the channels through which it goes on, and the social mechanism which controls it; from the standpoint of the characteristics of the people who are placed at the upper and the lower social strata, and, finally, from that of the effects of social mobility. This study is to be published soon in the form of a book. Here I will lay down some of the tentative conclusions to which I have come in the process of the study. For the sake of brevity I put these conclusions quite dogmatically. Necessary corroborations are given in the book.

Propositions Concerning the Fluctuation of the Velocity and Generality of the Vertical Mobility in Space and Time

1. There has scarcely been any society whose strata were absolutely closed, or in which vertical mobility in its economic, political, occupational, and other forms was not present.

2. There has never existed a society in which its vertical mobility has been absolutely free and in which the transition from one social stratum to another has had no resistance.

3. The intensiveness and generality of the vertical mobility varies from society to society (fluctuation in space) and within the same society from time to time.

4. In the fluctuation of the vertical mobility in time, there seems to be no definite perpetual trend toward either an increase or a decrease of the intensiveness and generality of the mobility. All trends seem to have been only temporary, being superseded by the opposite ones in a longer period of time. This is proposed as valid for the history of a country, for that of a large social body, and, finally, for the history of mankind.

5. The nineteenth and the twentieth centuries in the history of the Western societies have been the periods of highest mobility in its occupational, economic, and political forms. However, in the past there have been periods of an equal and, perhaps, even that of a greater mobility.

6. The occupational vertical mobility of the present Western societies has the following characteristics. First, percent of transmission of occupational status from the father to the sons fluctuates from 90 to 3 percent according to occupation and country. The most common or typical index of the transmission varies from 20 to 50 percent. Second, within the last three or four generations in many occupations, there seems to have been a tendency toward a decrease of the transmission of occupation from the father to the sons. In some other occupations, however, the tendency seems to have been reversed. Third, the number of inter- and intraoccupational vertical shiftings within the life of the last generation seems to be somewhat greater than within the life of the preceding generation. Fourth, within the same occupation, the more qualified and better paid strata shift less intensively than the less qualified and more poorly paid strata. Members of an occupation which disappears shift more intensively than the members of an occupation which develops and prospers. Fifth, the sons of the fathers who belong to the same occupation are dispersed throughout different occupations, and the members of the same occupation are recruited from different social groups and strata. However, the closer affinities are the occupations, the more intensive among them is mutual interchange of their members; and, vice versa, the greater is the difference between occupations, the less is the number of individuals who shift from one group to another. Sixth, under normal conditions, these "ups" and "downs" go on gradually and orderly and are selective, being controlled by the machinery of social selection. In time of revolution they are sudden and nonselective. Seventh, different individuals move in the

vertical (occupational) direction at different velocities. The greater is the number of the occupational strata to be crossed, the less is the number of the "jumpers."

7. Shifting on the economic ladder within the present Western societies is characterized by somewhat similar traits. It increases in the period of social upheavals (war, revolution, industrial transformation, and so on). Like the occupational strata, among the richest people of a country there are climbers who were born in a poor family, and among the poor population there are the people who were born in a rich family. However, in difference from the occupational mobility, there seems not to have existed the tendency toward a decrease of the transmission of economic status from the father to the sons during the last few generations. Many characteristics of the present occupational and economic mobility are applied to the present political mobility.

Propositions Concerning the Channels and the Machinery Which Control the Vertical Mobility of Individuals

1. The most common channels through which vertical shifting of individuals goes on are the series of social institutions like army, church, school, political parties, and different occupational institutions. They play the role of "elevators" through which people go "up" and "down."

2. With the exception of the periods of anarchy, the vertical mobility of individuals and their placement at different social strata is controlled by a complex machinery of social testing, selection, and distribution of individuals within the society. This machinery is composed out of social institutions of family, church, and school, which test general intelligence and character of individuals, and out of different occupational institutions, which retest the results of the family, church, and school testing and especially test the specific ability of individuals necessary for a successful performance of a definite occupational function. This "testing and selective" role of these institutions is no less important than their "educational and training" role. From this it follows that the population of different social strata is selective.

Propositions Concerning the Characteristics of the Population of Different Social Strata of a Society

Being selective in a considerable degree, the population of different social strata exhibits several bodily, mental, and moral differences. Part of them is the result of selection and heredity, another part is that of environmental differences. As a general rule, the population of the upper strata has a taller stature, a greater weight, a greater cranial capacity or greater size of head, better proportions of body, and is more handsome than the population of the lower strata. The contention that the upper classes of the same society are more dolichocephalic and more blond than the lower classes is not warranted by the facts.

Concerning the vitality and health, the upper strata have a greater duration of life, lower mortality, and are healthier than the population of the lower strata. Birthrate of the upper classes at the present moment and in many periods in the past has been lower than that of the lower classes. However, the rule cannot be applied to all times and countries.

Population of the upper strata has a higher intelligence and is richer with the ambitious, bold, and adventurous characters, with inventive minds, with harsh and nonsentimental natures, and with the cynical persons, than the population of the lower classes. The above means that social stratification and distribution of individuals according to physical and mental qualities are positively correlated. The correlation is, however, not perfect, and it not constant. There are overlappings. The correlation decreases in the period of degeneration of the upper classes or of a whole society and may even disappear.

Propositions Concerning the Effects of Mobility

1. *In the field of racial composition of a society.* Under the condition of lower procreation of the upper strata, an intensive vertical mobility leads to wasting of the best population of society. It is probable that in the long period of time this wasting may lead to a racial depletion of the population. This is the price paid by a mobile society for its rapid progress.

2. *In the field of human behavior and psychology.* An intensive vertical mobility facilitates an increase of the plasticity and versatility of behavior, open-mindedness, mental strain, intellectual progress, and progress of discoveries and inventions. On the other hand, it facilitates an increase of mental diseases, superficiality, insensitiveness of nervous system, skepticism, cynicism, and idiosyncrasies; it also diminishes intimacy in interrelations of individuals, increases their social isolation and loneliness, favors an increase of suicide, hunting for sensual pleasure, and restlessness; finally, mobility facilitates disintegration of morals.

3. *In the field of social processes and organization.* Mobility, under some conditions, facilitates a better and more adequate social distribution of individuals among different social strata, economic prosperity, and social progress.

The effects of mobility on social stability are very complex, partly positive, partly negative; all in all, rather negative. Its influence upon longevity and continuity of culture-complex is negative also. It facilitates atomization and diffusion of solidarity and antagonisms, increase of individualism, followed by a vague cosmopolitanism and collectivism.

Diagnosis Concerning the Future Trend of the Mobility

At the present moment there are several symptoms of a decrease of the vertical mobility within the present Western societies. They are, however, opposed by the symptoms of the opposite character. Therefore, it is difficult to say certainly whether these societies continue to drift toward a greater mobility or toward an immobility.

13

The Future of the Rural
and Urban Worlds

At this point we may raise some questions about the future of rural and urban societies. Will the present division of labor continue? Will rural–urban differences increase in the future? What are the future prospects of each society? What is going to happen to the agricultural population and to mankind as a whole? It is needless to stress the fact that answers to these questions must be tentative. With this reservation always in mind, let us briefly discuss the chief possibilities for the future. These may be divided into three classes: First, the rural world may grow at the expense of the urban world. Secondly, the urban world may grow at the expense of the rural, until the latter—and the farmer-peasant class—disappear from the scene of history. Thirdly, both societies may continue in the future, irrespective of whether the existing division of functions and the existing differences between city and country increase, decrease, or remain constant. This third possibility seemingly contains within itself three subhypotheses. Let us turn now to a brief analysis of each of the main hypotheses.

1. *Hypothesis of the future growth of the rural world at the expense of the urban.* The first hypothesis can scarcely be maintained, for it is contradicted by the facts of recent history, as well as by other convincing evidence. The last few centuries, as we have already shown, have been characterized by a very marked growth of the urban population—a growth far greater than that of the population as a whole. The number of European cities with populations above 100,000 was 23 in 1800, 146 in 1900, and 202 in 1920.[1] A similar development took place among cities on other continents. Moreover, the proportion of the agricultural population in the total employed population has been

Originally published in *A Systematic Source Book in Rural Sociology* with Carle C. Zimmerman and Charles J. Galpin (Minneapolis: University of Minnesota Press, 1932), 3:635–42. Reprinted by permission of the publisher.
   1. See the detailed figures in Henri Bunle, "Superficie et population des contrées de la terre vers 1920," *Bulletin de l'Institut international de statistique*, 20 (1927). See also the *Annuaire statistique des grandes villes* (1927).

decreasing from year to year. The following figures sum up the situation in the last few decades. The percentage of the population engaged in agriculture decreased in the United States from 44.1 in 1880 to 32.5 in 1910 and 26.3 in 1920; in Belgium from 44.0 in 1846 to 16.01 in 1910; in England and Wales from 12.0 in 1881 to 6.5 in 1921; in Germany from 42.5 in 1882 to 28.6 in 1907; in Sweden from 51.6 in 1870 to 38.4 in 1920; in Switzerland from 31.2 in 1900 to 25.5 in 1920; in Finland from 74.8 in 1880 to 65.1 in 1920; in Canada from 34.28 in 1911 to 32.82 in 1921; in Australia from 44.0 in 1871 to 25.8 in 1921; in New Zealand from 29.0 in 1881 to 24.5 in 1911; in Austria from 62.6 in 1870 to 59.1 in 1900; in Hungary from 70.5 in 1890 to 69.1 in 1900; in Denmark from 46.2 in 1901 to 40.3 in 1911; and in Scotland from 16.2 in 1871 to 10.3 in 1901.

Thus the percentage of the population engaged in agriculture has been decreasing regularly in a great many countries. In others, such as Norway, the Netherlands, Italy, France, Cuba, Bulgaria, and British India, there has been no conspicuous decrease, but neither has there been a definite increase. These countries do not compensate for the decrease of the agricultural population in other countries. On the whole, the last few decades have been characterized by a decrease in the proportion of the world's population engaged in agricultural pursuits.[2]

A universal return to rural conditions would necessitate a great decrease in the population of many countries, the decay of machine civilization and mechanical industries, and the abandonment of present agricultural methods, based on the use of machinery, which enable a few persons to perform tasks that required the labor of many under the earlier agricultural system with its less efficient technique. It would mean also the decay of modern means of transportation and communication. In brief, it would mean the annihilation of the principal results of the industrial revolution and of the fundamental characteristics of machine civilization, and a return to production techniques of an earlier period. Such an abandonment of urban forms of civilization as a world movement is extremely improbable. It may, of course, occur

2. The following are the sources of the data: *Statistical Abstract of the United States* (1925), 47; *Annuaire statistique de la Belgique* (1920), xxiv; *Census of England and Wales, General Report* (1921), 143; *Statistisches Jahrbuch für das Deutsche Reich* (1926), 14; *Statistisk Årsbok för Sverige* (1926), 20; *Statistisches Jahrbuch der Schweiz* (1926), 61; *Annuaire statistique de Finlande* (1927), 48; the *Canada Year Book* (1926), 674; *Official Yearbook of the Commonwealth of Australia* (1926), 889; Eugene Merritt, "The Agricultural Element in the Population," *Journal of the American Statistical Association* 15 (March 1916): 58ff. See also some of the yearbooks of other countries.

temporarily and in some degree in a particular country, as it did in the past in Greece and Rome, in India and in Arabia, and as it did in the years from 1917 to 1922 in Soviet Russia. It may happen again, but it will be a temporary and local phenomenon, by no means typical of the general trend. The considerations we have presented enable us to reject as improbable the hypothesis that the rural world will grow at the expense of the urban.

2. *Hypothesis of complete urbanization in the future.* Although cities may continue to grow at the expense of the country in the near future, the hypothesis of the complete urbanization of mankind and the disappearance of rural life and of the agricultural classes is untenable. For in the first place a completely urbanized society could not survive. Like any other society it would need food, and therefore it would have to have a class of people, whether large or small, delegated to produce it. But with the establishment of such a class the society would cease to be wholly urban. Industry under such a regime would be unable to obtain raw materials and so would cease. Moreover, without a rural hinterland, the market for industrial products would not be large enough to enable the factories to operate successfully. Finally, it is highly doubtful whether such a society could maintain its biological balance. If it were not recruited by migrants from agricultural countries, and if it suffered from the low birthrate associated with urbanization, it is likely that the population would either remain stationary or, more probably, decrease. Such a society would certainly be engulfed by degrees by more prolific societies.

These self-evident facts show that a wholly urban society is an impossibility. Furthermore, it is extremely doubtful whether a very highly—though not completely—urbanized society with a very small rural hinterland, either in its own or in a foreign country, could endure very long. If its rural hinterland were too small (not in the territorial sense, necessarily, but too small to furnish the urban society with its necessary food products and to consume the industrial products), and if the rural area had become considerably urbanized, the stability of the society would be jeopardized. The insufficiency of agricultural products, both food and raw materials, would be a permanent menace. Any crisis would convert this menace from a potential to an active one; disturbances would occur, especially if the population were actually suffering, and undermine the stability of a society already precariously balanced. Insufficiency of raw materials, impeding the operation and development of industries, would result in an increase of unemployment. Unemployment would result also from the inability of a small rural population to consume large quantities of industrial products. A condition of overproduction, presumably, would follow, and in turn would lead to business depression and further increase in unemployment. Unemployment usually augments social disturbances—riots, disorders, and revolutions—and these, under such circumstances, would aggravate the situation still more.

Another difficulty in an almost wholly urban society would be that of obtaining a sufficient supply of human material. The small rural hinterland could not yield many migrants to the urbanized region, which would be likely to have a very low birthrate and to be incapable of increasing its population by means of propagation. The small rural hinterland, according to the supposition, is already considerably urbanized; hence it, too, would be likely to have a low birthrate. The urban society would be likely therefore to have either a static or, more probably, a decreasing population, and to die out eventually, by fast or slow degrees, as circumstances determined. It would be doomed to gradual obliteration, to replacement by more fertile and better balanced societies, or to disorganization and chronic anarchy.[3] Ancient Rome and Greece during the later periods of their history and contemporary Austria are actual examples that approach fairly closely the hypothetical case discussed. These considerations are sufficient to show why urbanization cannot be complete and why it cannot proceed too far without endangering the well-being and continued existence of the societies in which it prevails. Complete urbanization is impossible and nearly complete urbanization is very improbable.

3. *Hypothesis of the continued coexistence of the rural and urban worlds.* This hypothesis is more likely to be fulfilled than either of the preceding ones. Both the rural and the urban worlds will perhaps continue to exist to some degree and in some form. But how and in what form? Will rural–urban differences be accentuated more and more and the differentiation between the two societies be increased? Will they remain as they are now? Or will the differences decrease? The third possibility appears to be the most probable. The differences between urban and rural societies will probably decrease in the future, for both seem to be approaching a middle type that we may call "rurban."

We will present briefly the main reasons for our conclusion. We have seen that one of the chief differences between the city and the country has been in means and extent of communication and contact. . . . Railroads, automobiles, telephones, telegraphs, radios, movies, and

---

3. For a similar but more detailed analysis of the situation, see Corrado Gini, *I fattori demografici dell' evoluzione delle nazioni* (Turin, 1912).

newspapers, however, which are now very widely diffused, have decreased the mutual isolation of city and country in a very high degree. Formerly a village or farm was isolated from the rest of the world; now it is included in the world network created by modern systems of communication. The rural class, therefore, has begun to have the same contacts and sources of information as the urban population.

This "social telephone system" between the city and the country bridges the gulf between these worlds and tends to obliterate differences between their cultures. The urban cultural patterns spread more and more over the rural world, while the rural cultural patterns make their way into the urban world. Thus the candle of rural–urban differences is being burned at both ends. . . . In part 3 of this work it was shown that such has been the tendency in all fields of rural–urban culture; the cities and the country have constantly approached a mean cultural type.

The second important difference between the rural and urban worlds has been the greater mobility of the urban as compared with the rural population. The invention of modern means of communication and transportation has tended to decrease this difference by increasing the mobility of the rural population, stimulating greatly the migration from country to city, and vice versa. Immobility, especially the territorial immobility of the rural population, belongs to the past. Cultivators, formerly immobile, have found themselves plunged into the stream, and like the urbanites they have moved from place to place and from position to position, swept on by strong horizontal and vertical currents. This result has in its turn tended to decrease further the mutual isolation of country and city. The two societies have tended to merge as differences in mobility have decreased.

The effects of the modern technical revolution have been similar. At first machinery and mechanical devices were used only in urban industries, a fact that increased greatly the differences in occupation between city and the country. The situation, however, has changed greatly. Agricultural work has been mechanized increasingly by the introduction of electricity, gas, oil, tractors, combines, steam engines, and a great many other types of agricultural machinery. The nonmechanical character of agriculture as contrasted with the mechanized industries has become less and less marked. Hence even the occupational differences between the two societies have decreased.

This difference will doubtless be decreased still further by the increased use of electric power, which is beginning to play a revolutionary role. The first stage of the industrial revolution was the use of steam power. This power could not be transmitted over great distances, however; consequently all industries using machinery were concentrated in the cities, where great factories were built. The countryside was comparatively free from this invasion; its principal occupation continued to be agriculture, while the urban world became predominantly industrial. Thus from the occupational standpoint the invention of steam power widened the gap between city and country. The replacement of steam power by electricity and the development of the natural gas industry, however, tend to produce a very different condition, for electricity and natural gas can be transmitted easily and cheaply over vast distances, and consequently factories and other industrial establishments can be spread out over a large territory in places convenient for particular industries. As a result, in America as well as in several other countries we are witnessing the removal in increasing numbers of factories and industrial establishments from cities to rural districts. . . .

Agricultural purity is thus becoming increasingly contaminated by encroaching industrialism. The country as an occupational milieu is becoming more like the city. In addition there is a growing agricultural industry in and around the city. Vegetables, fruit, dairy products, and poultry are being produced near the city, and farmers are settling in the city itself. Sometimes they are induced to come by the fact that their farms are nearby and the change is a small one in point of distance; sometimes they may intend to retire; sometimes they are attracted by better health conditions or better educational facilities. In this way, once more, differences are being reduced.

Differences in the total sizes of the rural and urban populations and in their densities are also fundamental. Although we cannot say with certainty that these differences, too, tend to decrease, we can at least assert that they cannot increase much and that probably they will become less conspicuous in the future. The unprecedented development of cities today, both in size and in density of population, is due largely to steam power. Among other factors, the existence in the cities of large industrial establishments employing tens of thousands of persons has forced the commercial, clerical, and professional classes to stay in the cities. The result has been the growth of large cities, some having populations of several millions, concentrated in a comparatively small area. The size of the cities and the density of their population have become so great that the cities have already begun to be biologically unhealthful, psychologically uncomfortable, economically expensive and wasteful, and morally and socially dangerous. . . . The same conveniences cost considerably more, quantitatively and qualitatively, in large cities today than in middle-sized or small ones.

As large cities grow larger, there is a progressive and disproportionate rise of the expenses necessary to maintain them. This condition must have an adverse effect on their further growth, retarding or even stopping it. If it were not for electric power and natural gas, the present system would perhaps have to take its course. But electricity and natural gas make it possible for many institutions and industrial establishments to function successfully elsewhere than in large cities and for many people to live more comfortably outside large cities without foregoing the advantages of the city. As the process continues whereby industrial establishments move from the cities, an increasing percentage of the population previously engaged in the large cities will naturally be employed in these extraurban industries.

In these and other ways the growth of the large cities in total population and in density is likely to be retarded, while that of the small towns and villages develops. Thus in another respect the contrast between city and country seems to be decreasing.

Our general conclusion must be that all the principal differences between rural and urban societies—differences in means of communication, in mobility, occupation, total population, and density—are tending to diminish. Rural and urban societies, as we have already indicated, are approaching a type of rurban society in which they will draw closer together and will resemble each other more than they have in the recent past. If this tentative conclusion is correct, the climax of rural–urban differentiation has been reached and passed. Society was not, of course, divided into city and country at the beginning of human history, and when this differentiation first appeared it was slight. But the cleavage gradually widened, although there were fluctuations. Finally, under the influence of steam-power civilization, the two societies became radically different. The use of electricity, however, and such recent inventions as the radio and the automobile have begun to produce a *rapprochement* that in all probability will develop.

III

THEORETICAL FRAMEWORKS

Social Space and Time

14

Social Time: A Methodological and Functional Analysis

No concept of motion is possible without the category of time. In mechanics, for example, time is considered the independent variable which is a continuous function of the three coordinates which determine the position of a particle. Time is likewise a necessary variable in social change. The adequacy of the concepts of astronomical or calendrical time in the study of the motion or change of social phenomena thus represents a problem of basic importance. Are periods of years, months, weeks, days the only, or even the most readily applicable, temporal measures in a system of social dynamics? Most social scientists have proceeded on the tacit assumption that no system of time other than those of astronomy or the imperfectly related calendar is possible or, if possible, useful. They have assumed a time, the parts of which are comparable, which is quantitative and possessed of no qualitative aspects, which is continuous and permits of no lacunae. It is the object of this paper to demonstrate that in the field of social dynamics such restriction to a single conception of time involves several fundamental shortcomings.

Newton's formulation of the concept of a time which is uniform, infinitely divisible, and continuous probably constitutes the most definite assertion of the objectivity of time. In the realm of astronomy the modern doctrines of relativity have shown, from one point of view, the contingent nature of Newtonian time. From another angle such philosophers as Bradley, Berkeley, and Kant and, more recently, Spencer, Guyau, James, and Bergson have leveled criticism against the universal applicability of such a concept. In the field of sociology, with the exception of certain members of the Durkheim school, very little attention has been devoted to this fundamental category.

That the astronomical is not the only possible concept of time is

Coauthored with Robert K. Merton. Originally published in the *American Journal of Sociology* 42 (March 1937): 615–29. © 1937 University of Chicago. All rights reserved. Reprinted by permission of the publisher.

evident after a brief consideration. In philosophy there exists what may be called an "ontological time." Aristotle and Zeno, to choose at random, both conceived of a time which is nonmaterial, completely subjective. For Kant, time is the formal a priori condition of all perceived phenomena.[1] Berkeley and Bradley condemn time as a mere appearance having no objective reality. James, on the other hand, sees the concept of an "objective" time as a useful fiction. Bergson holds that "imaginary homogeneous time is an idol of language, a fiction."[2]

Concepts of time in the field of psychology are also quite different from that of astronomy. Time is here conceived not as "flowing at a constant rate, unaffected by the speed or slowness of the motion of material things,"[3] but as definitely influenced by the number and importance of concrete events occurring in the particular period under observation. As James pointed out: "In general, a time filled with varied and interesting experiences seems short in passing, but long as we look back. On the other hand, a tract of time empty of experiences seems long in passing, but in retrospect short."[4]

Thus, in actual perception, we are far from experiencing the ideally conceived time which *aequabiliter fluit*. Experiments in the field of psychology have found a difference between the individual's estimate of duration and the actual duration of astronomical time elapsed.[5] In the experience of the individual, time is far from being "infinitely divisible," Zeno's age-honored paradox of Achilles and the tortoise notwithstanding. Various experiments have shown that individuals cannot distinguish time differences of less than one-hundredth of a second.[6]

The very introduction of the concept "mental age" in psychology is evidence of the methodological inadequacy of astronomical chronol-

---

1. It should be stated at the outset that we are not concerned with the controversy of the a-prioristic or empiristic derivation of time as a category. Much of Durkheim's analysis of this problem is vitiated by his efforts to insert it within this controversial context, so that he tends to raise issues not amenable to scientific treatment. The present discussion has some bearing on contemporary problems of *Wissenssoziologie,* particularly those which Scheler has designated as "formal problems" of the sociology of knowledge.

2. Henri Bergson, *Matter and Memory* (London, 1919), 274.

3. J. Clerk Maxwell, *Matter and Motion* (New York, 1878), 28.

4. William James, *Principles of Psychology* (New York, 1922), 1:624; cf. H. Hubert and M. Mauss, *Mélanges d'histoire des religions* (Paris, 1909), 207.

5. Mary Sturt, *Psychology of Time* (London, 1925), chapter on "Duration." This has long been realized. See the experimental analyses by Lotze, Münsterberg, Hemholtz, Bolton, Woodworth, etc.

6. Ibid., chap. 1.

ogy in this field. It is found empirically that there is no constant relation between chronological and mental age, so that many psychological considerations of human behavior in relation to "age" demand a temporal frame of reference different from that ordinarily employed. As we shall see, this indictment is even more telling in the social field.

In the field of economics it has likewise been recognized that astronomical or clock time is not always applicable. For example, Marshall, in his famous analysis of economic equilibrium as dependent upon "long" and "short" periods over which the market is taken to extend, early perceived this inapplicability of astronomical time.[7] As Opie puts it:[8]

> When he [Marshall] distinguished long and short periods he was not using clock-time as his criterion, but "operational" time, in terms of economic forces at work. Supply forces were given the major attention, and a time was long or short according as it involved modifiability or fixity in some chosen forces on the supply side. The greater the modifiability of the supply forces, the longer the period of time under discussion, *irrespective of clock-time* [italics ours].

The concept of economic time has been expressly singled out for treatment by Erich Voegelin and, somewhat less analytically, by Streller, but it is also tacitly assumed in much of the analysis of Böhm-Bawerk, W. S. Jevons, Otto Effertz, Knut Wicksell, and many other economists.[9]

These various concepts of time and, above all, the revolutionary changes in the astronomical field itself engendered by Einstein's analysis of the notion of simultaneity illustrate the essentially operational criteria of time. If we seek the operations which enable us to determine the time at which social events occur, it becomes manifest that even today all such time determinations are by no means referred to astronomical or even calendrical frameworks. Bridgman has generalized this class of facts, saying that "the methods which we adopt for assigning a time to events change *when the character of the events changes,* so that time may appear in various guises."[10] Thus, social

7. Alfred Marshall, *Principles of Economics* (London, 1925), 330.

8. Redvers Opie, "Marshall's Time Analysis," *Economic Journal* 41 (June 1931): 198–99.

9. Erich Voegelin, "Die Zeit in der Wirtschaft," *Archiv für Sozialwissenschaft und Sozialpolitik* 153 (1924): esp. 204; Rudolph Streller, *Statik und Dynamik in der theoretischen Nationalökonomie* (Leipzig, 1926), 126ff; also his *Die Dynamik der theoretischen Nationalökonomie* (Tübingen, 1928), passim.

10. Percy W. Bridgman, "The Concept of Time," *Scientific Monthly* 135 (August 1932): 97. Cf. the entire symposium on "The Time Scale" in the same number of this journal.

time expresses the change or movement of social phenomena in terms of other social phenomena taken as points of reference. In the course of our daily activities we often make use of this means of indicating points of time. "Shortly after the World War," "I'll meet you after the concert," and "when President Hoover came into office" are all related to social rather than astronomical frames of reference, for the purpose of indicating specific points of time—"time when." Moreover, such references express far more than the nominally equivalent astronomical or calendrical referrents ("ca. 1918–19," "11 P.M.," "March 1929"), for they usually establish an added significant relation between the event and the temporal frame of reference. For example, the very choice of President Hoover's assumption of office as an indication of the time at which, say, two thousand postmasters were replaced by others tells us far more than the statement that such replacements occurred in March of 1929. In other words, the calendrical reference itself becomes significant only when it is transformed into social time. The methodological importance of this will be discussed later.

In a similar fashion we indicate durations of time by such references as "for a semester," "for a working day," "for the duration of Lent." These are references to generally comprehensible time durations without any mention of astronomical phenomena. Moreover, there is no fixed relationship between the first two of these durations and astronomical phenomena, since these social intervals may vary independently. Such designations, if they are not survivals of a very common means of indicating a tract of time among primitive peoples, at least perform the same function.

> To indicate the duration of time, primitive peoples make use of other means, *derived from their daily business,* which have nothing to do with time reckoning; in Madagascar, "rice-cooking" often means half an hour, "the frying of a locust," a moment. The Cross River natives say: "The man died in less than the time in which maize is not yet completely roasted," i.e. less than about fifteen minutes; "the time in which one can cook a handful of vegetables."[11]

The time expressions, both of duration and indication, are in reference to social activities or group achievements. Those periods which are devoid of any significant social activity are passed over without

11. Martin P. Nilsson, *Primitive Time Reckoning* (Lund, 1920), 42. Numerous examples of social designations of time duration and indication appear in the ethnographic literature. See, e.g., the monographs of J. H. Hutton, J. P. Mills, W. Hough, J. Roscoe, A. C. Hollis, R. Firth, W. H. I. Bleek, and L. C. Lloyd.

any term to denote them.[12] Time here is not continuous—the hiatus is found whenever a specific period is lacking in social interest or importance. The social life of the group is reflected in the time expressions. The names of days, months, seasons, and even of years are fixed by the rhythm of collective life. A homogeneity of social beats and pulsations of activity makes unnecessary astronomical frames of reference. Each group, with its intimate nexus of a common and mutually understood rhythm of social activities, sets its time to fit the round of its behavior.[13] No highly complex calculations based on mathematical precision and nicety of astronomical observation are necessary to synchronize and coordinate the societal behavior.

Thus, the Khasis name their months according to the activities which take place in each: "the month for weeding the ground," "the month when cultivators fry the produce of their fields," etc.[14] In the Meitheis tribe all time reckonings are in accordance with the *chahitaba*: each year is named after an important personage.[15] Codrington says of the Melanesian system that "it is impossible to fix the native succession of months into a solar year; months have their names from what is done."[16] Among the Navajos, "the names of the calendar months are vividly descriptive of the life of the family, as well as of the life-round of the sheep controlled by them."[17]

We see, then, that systems of time reckoning reflect the social activities of the group. Their springs of initiation are collective; their continued observance is demanded by social necessity. They arise from the round of group life, are largely determined by the routine of religious activity and the occupational order of the day, are perpetuated by the need for social coordination, and are essentially a product of social interaction. Durkheim lucidly observed in this connection that a "calendar expresses the rhythm of collective activities, while at the same time its function is to assure their regularity."[18]

Agricultural peoples with a social rhythm different from that of

12. Cf. Elsdon Best, *The Maori Division of Time* (Dominion Museum Monograph No. 4, 1922), 19.

13. Sturt, op. cit., 141. "Time is a concept, and this concept is constructed by each individual under the influence of the society in which he lives."

14. P. R. T. Gurdon, *The Khasis* (London, 1914), 193.

15. T. C. Hodson, *The Meitheis* (London, 1908), 105.

16. R. H. Codrington, *The Melanesians* (Oxford, 1891), 349.

17. D. and M. R. Coolidge, *The Navajo Indians* (Boston and New York, 1930), 60. The previously mentioned ethnographers, among others, describe further instances (see n. 11).

18. Emile Durkheim, *Elementary Forms of Religious Life* (New York and London, 1926), 11.

hunting or of pastoral peoples differentiate time intervals in a fashion quite unlike the latter. Periodic rest days seem to be unknown among migratory hunting and fishing peoples or among nomadic pastoral tribes, although they are frequently observed by primitive agriculturists.[19] Likewise, a metropolis demands a frame of temporal reference entirely different from that of a small village. This is to say, time reckoning is basically dependent upon the organization and functions of the group. The mode of life determines which phenomena shall represent the beginning and close of seasons, months, or other time units.[20] Even in those instances where natural phenomena are used to fix the limits of time periods, the choice of them is dependent upon the interest and utility which they have for the group. Thus, the year among the Hebrews, "as naturally it would with an agricultural people," depended upon the annual course of the crops.[21] The system of time varies with the social structure.

Astronomical time is uniform, homogeneous; it is purely quantitative, shorn of qualitative variations. Can we so characterize social time? Obviously not—there are holidays, days devoted to the observance of particular civil functions, "lucky" and "unlucky" days, market days, etc. Periods of time acquire specific qualities by virtue of association with the activities peculiar to them. We find this equally true of primitive and more complex societies. Thus, says James:

> An ingenious friend of mine was long puzzled to know why each day of the week had such a characteristic physiognomy for him. That of Sunday was soon noticed to be due to the cessation of the city's rumbling, and the sound of people's feet shuffling on the sidewalk; of Monday, to come from the clothes drying in the yard and casting a white reflection on the ceiling; of Tuesday, etc. . . . Probably each hour in the day has for most of us some outer or inner sign associated with it as closely as these signs with the day of the week.[22]

19. Hutton Webster, *Rest Days* (New York, 1916), 101ff.
20. Nilsson, op. cit., 58ff; cf. Hubert and Mauss, op. cit., 119ff.
21. F. H. Woods, "Calendar (Hebrew)," in *Encyclopedia of Religion and Ethics*, 3:108.
22. James, op. cit., 1:623. F. H. Colson summarizes the functional importance of social definitions of time intervals: "How do we ourselves remember the days of the week? The obvious answer is that something happens on one or more of them. If by some means or other we lose count in the course of the week, Sunday is unmistakable, even if personally we have no religious feeling about the day. So, too, school half-holidays or early-closing days force themselves on the notice of those who are not directly affected by them. But if nothing happens it is very doubtful whether a week-sequence could maintain, much less establish, itself" (The Week [*Cambridge*, 1926], 63).

Taoism prescribes, according to the "magical universistic" book of chronomancy, "the propitious days on which to contract marriages, or remove to another house, or cut clothes; days on which one may begin works of repair of houses, temples, ships."[23] The Mohammedans consider Monday, Wednesday, Thursday, and Friday to be fortunate days; Tuesday, Saturday, and Sunday to be evil and unfortunate days. Friday is observed as a holy day, a day of rest, by the Mohammedans, in the same way as Saturday by the Jews and Sunday by the Christians. Among the Greeks the calendar had a definitely sacral character with a complete designation of lucky and unlucky days. Thus, the fourth and twenty-fourth were considered as dangerous days for some enterprises; the fifth as utterly unlucky; the sixteenth as an unlucky birth- or marriage-day for a girl; the fourteenth as a good day to break in cattle.[24]

We need hardly remark that we are here not concerned with the validity of what is expressed by these beliefs. They are, in any case, social facts; they reveal the various qualities actually attributed to definite units of time; they serve to indicate that a merely quantitative measure of time will not account for the qualities with which the various time units are endowed by members of a group. Quantitative approaches ignore the fact that "the human mind does tend to attach an unusual value to any day in the calendar that is in any way outstanding."[25] From this it does not necessarily follow that social time has no quantitative aspects, but it does appear that it is not a pure quantity, homogeneous in all its parts, always comparable to itself and exactly measurable. In judgments of time there enter considerations of aptitude, opportunity, continuity, constancy, and similarity, and the equal values which are attributed to time intervals are not necessarily equal measures.[26]

These differences in quality lead to the dependence of relative values of time durations not only on their absolute length but also on the nature and intensity of their qualities. Quantitatively equal periods of time are rendered socially unequal, and unequal periods are socially equalized. For example, "the numerically equivalent parts of the Hindu *kalpas* are not conceived as being of equal dura-

23. J. J. M. de Groot, *Religion in China* (New York, 1912), 245ff.
24. Cf. Hesiod, *Book of Days* (London, 1858): "A perpetuall Calendar of Good and Bad Daies; Not superstitious, but necessarie (as farre as naturall Causes compell) for all Men to observe."
25. A. L. Kroeber, *Anthropology* (New York, 1923), 262.
26. Hubert and Mauss, op. cit., 208. See especially the able discussion of the qualitative aspects of time in the chapter on "La representation du temps."

tion."[27] Or, similarly, the Chongli measure long periods of time by generations (the term of office of each set of elders), which may be quantitatively unequal but which are nevertheless regarded as equal by virtue of their identical qualitative aspects.[28]

Summing up, we may say that thus far our investigation has disclosed the facts that social time, in contrast to the time of astronomy, is qualitative and not purely quantitative; that these qualities derive from the beliefs and customs common to the group; and that they serve further to reveal the rhythms, pulsations, and beats of the societies in which they are found.

Mathematical time is "empty." It has no marks, no lacunae, to serve as points of origin or end. Yet the calendar maker requires some sort of starting point or fixed datum. Some beginning, arbitrary or not, must be set in order to initiate any system of time reckoning which purports to be continuous. For this purpose, "recourse has generally been had to the date of some civil historical occurrence conventionally selected."[29] In all cases the point of departure is social or imbued with profound social implications; it is always an event which is regarded as one of peculiar social significance.[30]

Thus, there have been introduced such social frames of reference as the death of Alexander or the Battle of Geza among the Babylonians, the Olympiads among the Greeks, the founding of Rome (*anno urbis conditae*) and the Battle of Actium among the Romans, the persecution of Diocletian and the birth of Christ among the Christians, the mythological founding of the Japanese empire by Jimmu Tenno and the discovery of copper (Wado era) in Japan, the Hegira among the Mohammedans, the event of the white pheasant having been presented to the Japanese emperor (Hakuchi era).[31] "Egypt never had any idea of dating the annals except by the years of rule of the reigning Pharaoh."[32] The Armenians likewise reckoned by the number of years of the kings or of the patriarchs. From these few examples, culled from an almost

27. Ibid., 207.
28. Mills, *The Ao Nagas*, 400.
29. Alexander Philip, *The Calendar* (Cambridge, 1921), 48.
30. Cf. Maurice Halbwachs, *Les Cadres sociaux de la mémoire* (Paris, 1925), 71ff. See also Durkheim, op. cit., 10–11; E. Durkheim and M. Mauss, "De quelques formes primitives de classification," *L'Année sociologique* (1901–2): 1–71.
31. F. K. Ginzel, *Handbuch der matematischen und technischen Chronologie* (Leipzig, 1906), 1:136, 222, 238, passim. Ginsel's monumental three volumes contain a wealth of historical data pertaining to this subject.
32. George Foucart, "Calendar (Egyptian)," in *Encyclopaedia of Religion and Ethics*, 3:92.

inexhaustible store, we see some justification of the proposition that nations form their eras in terms of some remarkable event which has social implications.

Thus, we cannot carry over into social time the characteristic of continuity which is postulated in the Newtonian conception of astronomical time.[33] Critical dates disrupt this continuity. Nilsson, whose study of primitive time reckoning is perhaps the most thorough, is insistent on this point. The *pars pro toto* principle of time reckoning (i.e., the counting, not of units as a whole, but of a concrete phenomenon occurring but once within this unit) suggests that calculations of time are essentially discontinuous. The natural year may be continuous, but that of the calendar has both a beginning and an end, which are frequently marked by a temporal hiatus and are usually observed with some sort of social ceremony.

The common belief which holds that divisions of time are determined by astronomical phenomena is far from accurate.[34] Our system of weekly division into quantitatively equal periods is a perfect type of conventionally determined time reckoning. The Khasi week almost universally consists of eight days because the markets are usually held every eighth day. A reflection of the fact that the Khasi week had a social, rather than a "natural," origin is found in the names of the days of the week, which are not those of planets (a late and arbitrary development) but of places where the principal markets are held. In a similar fashion, the Roman week was marked by *nundinae* which recurred every eighth day and upon which the agriculturists came into the city to sell their produce. The Muysca in Bogotá had a three-day week; many West African tribes, a four-day week; in Central America, the East Indian archipelago, old Assyria (and now in Soviet Russia), there is found a five-day week; the population of Togo had a six-day week; the ancient Hebrews and most contemporary civilized societies, a seven-day week; examples of the eight-day week may be had among the Romans, Khasis, and many African tribes; and the Incas had a ten-day week. The constant feature of virtually all these weeks of varying lengths is that they were always found to have been originally in association with the market.[35] Colson indicates quite clearly that the earliest forms of the continuous week of which we have any knowledge were

33. Marshall had likewise conceived of the possibility that the assumption of continuity is not justified in the case of economic phenomena (see n. 7).

34. Nilsson, op. cit., 281: "It should not be forgotten that astronomy and the calendar are not identical. In matters of the calendar, practical utility is welcomed more than refined astronomical calculations."

35. Ibid., 363.

justified by the groups which used them on grounds which have nothing to do with the moon.[36] The appearance and spread of this time
unit was always in conjunction with some periodically observed social
event and did not come about through observation of the heavenly
bodies. Moreover, as Hutton Webster perspicuously suggests, some
phase of the social structure usually accounts for the variations in the
length of the week.

> The shorter intervals of three, four, and five days reflect the simple
> economy of primitive life, since the market must recur with sufficient
> frequency to permit neighboring communities, who keep on hand no
> large stocks of food and other necessaries, to obtain them from one an-
> other. The longer cycles of six, eight, and ten days, much less common,
> apparently arise by doubling the earlier period, whenever it is desired
> to hold a great market for the produce of a wide area.[37]

In like manner the duration of the month is not necessarily fixed
by the phases of the moon. Mommsen states, for example, that among
the Romans there was a calendar system "which practically was quite
irrespective of the lunar course" and which led to the adoption of
"months of arbitrary length."[38] This same disregard of the moon's
course in the determination of month durations has continued to the
present. Unequal periods of astronomical time are socially equated, as
is evidenced by the practice of paying monthly salaries. The equality
of months is conventional, not astronomical; social duration does not
equal astronomical duration, since the former is a symbolic, the latter
an empirical, duration.

Even today the pervasive "coloration" of astronomical time by social considerations is manifest—witness the new convention of "daylight saving time." The desired result, an increased number of daylight
hours for recreation and leisure, could have been attained simply
by shifting working hours to 8:00 A.M.—4:00 P.M. But the "9:00 to
5:00" designation has become so deeply rooted in our economy that
the presumably less violent innovation of changing the numerical designations of units within the twenty-four-hour cycle was deemed preferable. The conventional nature of time designation is thus clearly emphasized.

All calendrical systems have one characteristic in common. They
arise from, and are perpetuated by, social requirements. All social

36. Colson, op. cit., 3, 112–13.
37. Ibid., 117–18.
38. Theodor Mommsen, *History of Rome* (New York, 1885), 1:279. See, in connection with this subject, the whole of chap. 15.

events which are periodical, which demand, at a certain time, the presence of a number of individuals (particularly when they come from different social groupings or from some one large social group), necessitate some common means of time designation which will be mutually understood by those concerned. Religious ceremonies, rites, seasonal festivals, hunts, military expeditions, markets, intertribal conferences, and the like—all of which demand the complex cooperation of many persons at a fixed time—are the origins of a strictly defined system of time indication. Those systems of time which are common among small, closely interwoven groups participating in the same social rhythm are no longer adequate as the field of interaction expands. Individuals coming together from varied social and cultural backgrounds require some temporal scheme which will be equally intelligible to all if they are to synchronize and coordinate their activities.

In ancient cities there first arose the significantly large congregation of individuals with different backgrounds. Then it was that there became manifest the necessity of creating a frame of reference which would be mutually comprehensible. Thus, among the Latins:

> When city life began it was naturally found necessary to have a more exact measure of the annus and the religious events included in it. Agriculture was still the economic basis of the life of the people; and in keeping up the agricultural religious rites within the city it was convenient, if not absolutely necessary, to fix them to particular days. This was, beyond doubt, the origin of the earliest(?) calendar of which we know anything.[39]

Similarly, it was the necessity for regulating the religious cult that "first created the calendar in Greece."[40] And, according to Spinden, even the apparently strictly astronomical calendar of the Mayas was fundamentally for religious purposes.[41]

39. W. Ward Fowler, "Calendar," in *Encyclopaedia of Religion and Ethics,* 3: 133. Cf. the observation by Georg Simmel, who notes that the conditions of the metropolis are such that "the relationships of the typical urban resident are so manifold and so complicated and, above all, are so interwoven into an organism of so many parts through the agglomeration of so many persons with such differentiated interests, that the whole would break down into an inextricable chaos without the most exact punctuality in promises and performances . . . [without] an unambiguity in appointments and agreements, similar to that which is mediated externally through the general diffusion of watches" (P. A. Sorokin, C. C. Zimmerman, and C. J. Galpin, "Large Cities and Mental Life," *A Systematic Source Book in Rural Sociology* [Minneapolis, 1930], 1: 244).

40. Nilsson, op. cit., 366.

41. H. J. Spinden, "Maya Inscriptions Dealing with Venus and the Moon," *Bulletin of the Buffalo Society of Natural Sciences,* vol. 14, no. 1 (1928); cf. Philip, op. cit., 7: "It is found that luni-solar calendars have a preeminently sacral or religious origin."

* *

The foregoing argument may be summarized by a number of basic propositions. Time systems are numerous and varied, differing also in their effective applicability to events of different character. It is a gratuitous assumption that astronomical or even calendrical time systems are best fitted for designating and measuring simultaneity, sequence, and duration of social phenomena. All time systems may be reduced to the need of providing means for synchronizing and coordinating the activities and observations of the constituents of groups. The local time system varies in accordance with differences in the extent, functions, and activities of different groups. With the spread of interaction between groups, a common or extended time system must be evolved to supersede or at least to augment the local time systems. Since the rhythm of social activities differs in different groups or within the same highly differentiated society, local systems of time reckoning are no longer adequate. Even bionatural events (e.g., maturation of crops) no longer suffice as a common framework of temporal reference as the area of interaction is enlarged, since these phenomena do not occur simultaneously in different areas. The final common basis was found in astronomical phenomena and in the more or less widespread diffusion of conventionalized time continuities. Thus, the social function of time reckoning and designation as a necessary means of coordinating social activity was the very stimulus to astronomical time systems, the introduction of which was made imperative by the inadequacy of local systems with the spread of contact and organized interaction and the resulting lack of uniformity in the rhythms of social activities. Astronomical time, as a "time esperanto," is a social emergent. This process was more rapidly induced by urbanization and social differentiation which involved, with the extension of multidimensional social space, the organization of otherwise chaotic, individually varying activities.

Local time systems are qualitative, impressed with distinctly localized meanings. A time system aimed to subsume these qualitatively different local systems must necessarily abstract from the individual qualities of these several systems. Hence, we see the important social element in the determination of the conception of a purely quantitative, uniform, homogeneous time; one-dimensional astronomical time was largely substituted for multidimensional social time.

For facilitating and enriching research in the field of social dynamics, the concept of social time must be reintroduced as an auxiliary, if not as a successor, of astronomical time. The search for social periodicities based upon the unquestioned adoption of astronomical criterions of time may have been largely unsuccessful precisely because social phenomena involve "symbolic" rather than "empirical" equalities and inequalities; social processes which at present seem to lack periodicities in terms of astronomical measures may be found to be quite periodic in character in terms of social time. It is at least worthy of trial. The possible objection that such efforts would simply resolve themselves into correlations between different sets of social phenomena is tenable only if one ignores the fact that the usual procedures simply involve correlations between astronomical (or calendrical) and social phenomena. Moreover, what are the theoretical grounds, tacit or expressed, for expecting correlations between astronomical and social sequences?[42] And, finally, what is the possible significance of such correlations when they are found? The fact is—and to the best of our knowledge its implications have been persistently overlooked—that when social and astronomical ("time") phenomena are related, other social correlates of the same astronomical phenomena must be ascertained before these relations take on any scientific significance. Otherwise, these constitute but empirical uniformities which remain theoretically sterile. If we are to enhance our knowledge of the temporal aspects of social change and processes, we must enlarge our category of time to include the concept of social time.

42. Were it not for the fact that many social scientists still ignore this elementary rule of procedure, one need hardly emphasize the principle that statistical correlations should be employed only to test conclusions arrived at on other grounds (cf. John M. Keynes, *A Treatise on Probability* [London, 1921], 426).

15

Social Space, Social Distance, and Social Position

Geometrical and Social Space

Expressions like "upper and lower classes," "social promotion," "N. N. is a climber," "his social position is very high," "they are very near socially," "right and left party," "there is a great social distance," and so on are quite commonly used in conversation, as well as in economic, political, and sociological works. All these expressions indicate that there is something which could be styled "social space." And yet there are very few attempts to define social space and to deal with corresponding conceptions systematically. As far as I know, after Descartes, Thomas Hobbes, Leibniz, E. Weigel, and other great thinkers of the seventeenth century, only F. Ratzel, G. Simmel, and recently E. Durkheim, Robert E. Park, Emory S. Bogardus, Leopold von Wiese, and the writer have tried to give greater attention to the problem of social space and to some others connected with it.[1]

As the subject of this book is social mobility—that is, the phenomenon of the shifting of individuals within social space—it is necessary to outline very concisely what I mean by social space and its derivatives. In the first place, social space is something quite different from geometrical space. Persons near each other in geometrical space—e.g., a king and his servant, a master and his slave—are often separated by

Originally published in *Social and Cultural Mobility* (New York: The Free Press, 1959): 3–10. Reprinted by permission of the publisher.

1. See E. Spektorsky, *The Problem of Social Physics in the Seventeenth Century*, 2 vols. (Warsaw, 1910; Kiev, 1917); F. Ratzel, *Politische Geographie* (Berlin: B. Oldenbourg, 1923), chaps. 12–15; G. Simmel, *Soziologie* (Leipzig: Dencker and Humblot, 1908), chap. 9; Robert E. Park, "The Concept of Social Distance," *Journal of Applied Sociology* 8, no. 6; Emory S. Bogardus, several papers on social distance in the *Journal of Applied Sociology* (1925–26); P. Sorokin, *Sistema Sotsiologii* (St. Petersburg: Kolos Publications, 1920), vol. 2, chap. 1 et passim; Leopold von Wiese, *Allgemeine Soziologie* (1924), 104, 154, 178ff; E. Durkheim, *Les formes élémentaires de la vie religieuse* (Paris: Alcan, 1912), introduction and conclusion.

the greatest distance in social space. And, vice versa, persons who are very far from each other in geometrical space—e.g., two brothers, or bishops of the same religion, or generals of the same rank in the same army, some staying in America, others being in China—may be very near each other in social space. Their social position is often identical, in spite of the great geometrical distance which separates them from each other. A man may cross thousands of miles of geometrical space without changing his position in social space; and, vice versa, a man may stay at the same geometrical place, and yet his social position may change enormously. President Harding's position in geometrical space was changed greatly when he went from Washington to Alaska; and yet his social position remained the same as it was in Washington. Louis XVI and the Czar Nicholas II remained in the same geometrical space, in Versailles and in Czarskoie Selo, when their social positions were changed enormously.

These considerations show that social and geometrical space are quite different things. The same may be said of the derivatives from these conceptions, such as "geometrical and social distance," "climbing in geometrical and in social space," "shifting from position to position in geometrical and in social space," and so on.[2]

In order to define social space positively, let us remind ourselves that geometrical space is usually thought of as a kind of "universe,"

---

2. From this it follows that the so-called "ecological approach" to the study of social phenomena may have only a limited value and is not suitable for a study of the greater part of social changes. The ecological approach may grasp the phenomena and changes as far as they are located and reflected on the geometrical territory, e.g., different territorial zones on the city (loop, residential zone, and so on) and shifting of the population from one geometrical place to another. But it cannot grasp all "zones" of social groups dispersed and not located at a definite geometrical territory (e.g., a Masonic society); it cannot grasp all nonterritorial shiftings in social space; it is helpless in regard to vertical circulation within a society; and so on. The greater part of social phenomena belong to this type and are not reflected properly on the geometrical territory. Hence, the limited possibilities of the ecological approach in the study of social phenomena. Within its appropriate limits it is useful and may be welcomed. The approach is not new. Without the term "ecological," it has been excellently used by many statisticians for a long time. See G. von Mayr, *Statistik und Gesellschaftslehre* (1897), 2:45–65, 109–26, 329ff. Similar good "ecological" chapters may be found in many other statistical works dealing with the problem of migration and demography. The same approach styled "ecological" is given by the works of R. D. McKenzie, *The Neighborhood* (Chicago: University of Chicago Press, 1923); Robert E. Park and Ernest W. Burgess, *The City* (Chicago: University of Chicago Press, 1925); Charles T. Galpin, *Rural Life* (New York: The Century Co., 1918), chap. 4; J. H. Kolb, *Rural Primary Groups* (Madison, 1921). E. Waxweiler's "ecology" (*Esquisse d'une Sociologie* [1906], 39ff) is quite different from the ecology of the above-mentioned authors.

in which physical phenomena are located. The location in this universe is obtained through definition of the position of a thing in relation to other things chosen as "the points of reference." As soon as such points are established (be it the sun, the moon, Greenwich, the axes of abscissas and ordinates), we can locate the spatial position of all physical phenomena with relation to them, and then, through that, with relation to each other.

In a similar way we may say that social space is a kind of universe composed of the human population of the earth. As far as there are no human beings, or there is only one human creature, there is no human social space or universe. One man in the world cannot have any relation to other men; he may be only in geometrical but not in social space. Accordingly, to find the position of a man or a social phenomenon in social space means to define his or its relations to other men or other social phenomena chosen as the "points of reference." What are taken as the "points of reference" depends upon us. It is possible to take a man, or a group of men, or several groups. When we say that "Mr. N., Jr., is a son of Mr. N., Sr.," we take a step toward the location of Mr. N. in the human universe. It is clear, however, that such location is very indefinite and imperfect; it gives us only one of the coordinates of location (the family relation) in a complex social universe. It is as imperfect as a geometrical location which says: "The tree is two miles from the hill." If such a location is to be satisfactory, we must know whether the hill is in Europe or in some other continent of the earth, and in what part of the continent, and under what degree, and if the tree is two miles to the north or south, east or west, from the hill. In brief, more or less sufficient geometrical location demands an indication of the located thing to the whole system of spatial coordinates of the geometrical universe. The same is true in regard to the "social location" of an individual.

An indication of a man's relation to another man gives something, but very little. An indication of his relation to ten or to one hundred men gives somewhat more but cannot locate the man's position in the whole social universe. It is similar to the location of a thing in geometrical space through a detailed indication of the different things around it, without indication of the latitude and longitude of the things. On this planet there are more than one and a half billion human beings. To indicate a man's relations to several dozen men, especially when they are not prominent, may mean nothing. Besides, the method is very complex and wasteful. In place of it, social practice has already invented another method, which is more satisfactory and simple, and which reminds one somewhat of the system of coordinates used for the location of a thing in geometrical space. This method consists in (1) the indication of a man's relations to specific groups, (2) the relation of these groups to each other within a population, and (3) the relation of this population to other populations included in the human universe.

In order to know a man's social position, his family status, the state of which he is a citizen, his nationality, his religious group, his occupational group, his political party, his economic status, his race, and so on must be known. Only when a man is located in all these respects is his social position definitely located. But even this is not all. As within the same group there are quite different positions, e.g., that of the king and a common citizen within a state group, the man's position within each of the fundamental groups of a population must also be known. When, finally, the position of the population itself, e.g., the population of North America, is defined in the whole human universe (mankind), then the social position of an individual may be thought to be quite sufficiently defined. Paraphrasing the old proverb, one may say: "Tell me to what social groups you belong and what function you perform within each of those groups, and I will tell you what is your social position in the human universe, and who you are as a socius." When two people are introduced this method is usually applied: "Mr. A. (family group) is a German professor (occupational group), a staunch Democrat, a prominent Protestant, formerly he was an ambassador to," and so on. This and similar introductions are complete or incomplete indications of the groups with which a man has been affiliated. The biography of a man in its essence is largely a description of the groups to which the man has had a relation, and the man's place within each of them. Such a method may not always inform us whether the man is tall or not, whether blond or dark, "introvert or extrovert"; but all this, though it may have a great significance for a biologist or a psychologist, is of relatively small value for a sociologist. Such information does not have any direct importance in the defining of a man's social position.

To sum up: (1) social space is the universe of the human population; (2) man's social position is the totality of his relations toward all groups of a population and, within each of them, toward its members; (3) location of a man's position in this social universe is obtained by ascertaining these relations; (4) the totality of such groups and the totality of the positions within each of them compose a system of social coordinates which permits us to define the social position of any man.

From this it follows that human beings, who are members of the same social groups and who within each of these groups have the same function, are in an identical social position. Men who differ in these respects from each other have different social positions. The greater the resemblance of the positions of the different men, the nearer they are toward each other in social space. The greater and the more numerous are their differences in these respects, the greater is the social distance between them.[3]

The Horizontal and the Vertical Dimensions of Social Space

Euclid's geometrical space is space of the three dimensions. The social space is space of many dimensions because there are more than three different social groupings which do not coincide with each other (the groupings of the population into state groups, into those of religion, nationality, occupation, economic status, political party, race, sex and age groups, and so on). The lines of differentiation of a population among each of these groups are specific or *sui generis* and do not coincide with each other. Since relations of all these kinds are substantial

---

3. This conception of social distance is quite different from that offered by Robert Park and Emory Bogardus. Their conception is purely psychological and not sociological. From their standpoint, persons who psychologically like each other are socially near; the persons who dislike each other are socially far from each other. There is no doubt that the study of such psychology of sympathy and antipathy is very valuable. But it seems to me it is not a study of social distance in the sociological sense of the word. A master and a slave, a king and a beggar, may like each other very much. But to conclude from this that their social positions are similar, or that there is no great social distance between them, would be utterly fallacious. The Orsini and the Colonna in Italy of the fifteenth century hated each other. Their social positions, however, were very similar. This clearly shows that my conception of social space and social distance is objective (because the groups exist objectively) and sociological, while Dr. Park's and Dr. Bogardus's conception is purely psychological and subjective (as far as it measures the social distance by the subjective feelings of liking and disliking). Even in regard to the *psychology of solidarity,* the above sociological conception may be very helpful. Similarity of social position of individuals results usually in a "likemindedness" because it means the similarity of habits, interests, customs, mores, traditions inculcated in the individuals by similar social groups to which they belong. Being "likeminded" they are likely to be more solidary than the people who belong to the different social groups. See the details in P. Sorokin, *Sistema Sotsiologii,* vol. 2 passim. See the quoted works of Robert E. Park and Emory S. Bogardus. As a concrete example of the use of a sociological system of social coordinates for the definition of leadership see the paper of F. Stuart Chapin, "Leadership and Group Activity," *Journal of Applied Sociology,* no. 3. In essence his method is identical with that above outlined and quite different from the psychological approach of Robert E. Park and Emory S. Bogardus. Another example is given by the study of E. Hoag, *The National Influence of a Single Farm Community* (1921).

components of the system of social coordinates, it is evident that the social space is a universe of many dimensions; and the more differentiated is the population, the more numerous are the dimensions. In order to locate an individual in the universe of the population of the United States, which is more differentiated than that of the natives of Australia, a more complex system of social coordinates must be used to indicate the more numerous groups with which one is connected.

For the sake of a simplification of the task it is possible, however, to reduce the plurality of the dimensions into two principal classes, provided that each is to be subdivided into several subclasses. These two principal classes may be styled the vertical and the horizontal dimensions of the social universe. The reasons for this are as follows: several individuals who belong to the same social groups are easily found, e.g., all may be Roman Catholics; Republicans; engaged in the automobile industry; Italians, according to native language; American citizens, according to citizenship; and so on. And yet, their social position may be quite different from the vertical standpoint. One of them may be a bishop, within the Roman Catholic group, while others may be only common parishioners; one of them may be a boss, within the Republican party, while others are only common voters; one may be the president of an automobile corporation, while others are only the common laborers; and so on. While their social position from the horizontal standpoint seems to be identical, from a vertical standpoint it is quite different. The horizontal dimension and its coordinates are not sufficient for a description of these differences. The same may be said about the positions of a commander-in-chief and a soldier in an army; and of those of a president and a clerk in a university. One cannot help thinking of their interrelations in terms of vertical dimensions. Our common representations of social position are very closely associated with it. Such expressions as "he is a social climber," "he goes socially down," "the upper and the lower classes," "he is at the top of a social pyramid," "the bottom of a society," "social ranks and hierarchies," "social stratification," "horizontal and the vertical differentiation," "the superposition of social groups," and so on are commonly used. The interrelations of individuals, as well as those of groups, are thought of either as situated on the same horizontal level or as hierarchically superimposed upon each other. Shifting from group to group sometimes does not involve any social rise or descent; at other times it is thought of as inseparable from the vertical dimensions. A social promotion is thought of as a social ascent; a degradation, as a social sinking. This common manner of thinking may be conveniently used for scientific description. On account of its familiarity, it helps to obtain a proper orientation in the complex social universe. The discrimination between the vertical and the horizontal dimensions expresses something which really exists in the social universe: the phenomena of hierarchy, ranks, domination and subordination, authority and obedience, promotion and degradation. All these phenomena and corresponding interrelations are thought of in the form of stratification and superposition. For a description of such relations the vertical dimension is very helpful and convenient. On the other hand, interrelations free from such elements may be conveniently described in terms of the horizontal dimension. In brief, from the technical standpoint, as well as from that of the nature of the social universe, there is no reason to avoid the above rather common discrimination of the two principal dimensions of the social universe.

This book deals with social phenomena in their vertical dimension. It studies the height and the profile of the "social structures"; their differentiation into social strata; the people who live within each stratum; the shifting of the population along the lines of the vertical dimension. In short, it deals with social stratification and the vertical social mobility. Horizontal structure of the social bodies is omitted and is touched only by the way, incidentally.[4] Such being the object of the book, it is necessary to make a constant use of such terms as "the upper and the lower social strata," "people socially inferior and superior," and so on. In order to avoid any misunderstanding, I must emphatically stress, that such terminology does not signify any evaluation on my part, and means only some formal location of the people within the different social strata. Maybe the inhabitants of the upper strata are really better than those of the lower ones; maybe they are worse. It is up to the reader to make such judgments. For me these terms are no more than convenient tools for analysis and description of the corresponding phenomena and their factual interrelations. The task of any scientific study is to define the interrelations of the studied phenomena as they exist. The task of the evaluation is entirely out of the field of such a study. This should be constantly kept in mind in order to avoid misunderstanding.

So much for the general conceptions of social space and its dimensions. The details and development will be given in the course of the book.

4. Two volumes of my *Sistema Sotsiologii* are devoted to an analysis of the horizontal differentiation of human population. There is also given a classification of social groups into (a) simple and (b) cumulative, and it analyzes the structure of a population from the standpoint of this classification.

Social and Cultural Systems

16

Ideational, Sensate, Idealistic, and Mixed Systems of Culture

Internal and External Aspects of Culture and Methods of Reading Them

The elements of thought and meaning which lie at the base of any logically integrated system of culture may be considered under two aspects: the *internal* and the *external*. The first belongs to the realm of inner experience, either in its unorganized form of unintegrated images, ideas, volitions, feelings, and emotions; or in its organized form of systems of thought woven out of these elements of the inner experience. This is the realm of mind, value, meaning. For the sake of brevity, we shall refer to it by the term "mentality of culture" (or "culture mentality"). The second is composed of inorganic and organic phenomena: objects, events, and processes which incarnate, or incorporate, or realize, or externalize, the internal experience. These external phenomena belong to a system of culture only as they are the manifestations of its internal aspect. Beyond this they cease to be a part of integrated culture. This means that for the investigator of an integrated system of culture the internal aspect is paramount. It determines which of the externally existing phenomena—and in what sense and to what extent—become a part of the system. In other words, it controls the external aspect of the culture.

Deprived of its inner meaning, the Venus of Milo becomes a mere piece of marble identical in its physicochemical qualities with the same variety of marble in the state of nature. A Beethoven symphony turns into a mere combination of sounds, or even into a vibration of air waves of certain lengths to be studied by the laws of physics. Aristotle's *Metaphysics* becomes a material paper object—a book similar to millions of other books. Deprived of this internal aspect, many phenom-

Originally published in *Social and Cultural Dynamics* [1937] (reprint, New Brunswick, N.J.: Transaction Books, 1985), 20–39. Reprinted by permission of Sergei Sorokin and Peter Sorokin.

ena fundamentally different in their cultural nature become similar. The action of a surgeon plunging his knife into the body of his patient and that of a murderer knifing his victim become indistinguishable, on account of the likeness of their external forms.

Several questions now arise: Can we grasp the internal aspect of a given culture adequately? Since it is somewhat elusive, and often inferential—in the sense that in order to grasp it, one has to "read" it in external vehicles which differ from the internal meaning—how can we be sure that our reading is correct, that we do not superimpose on a given configuration of external cultural phenomena meanings which are not there?

The answer to the above questions depends upon what is meant by the true, or *real*, mentality incorporated in a given complex of external vehicles. Out of several possible kinds of real meanings the following may be mentioned.

The term *real meaning* can refer to the state of mind of the person or group of persons creating or using given external vehicles—for instance, the meanings which Beethoven had in mind in the composition of his music, or which Dante kept before him in writing the *Divine Comedy*, or which are intended by any other creator or modifier of a complex containing cultural value. Here we have the *psychological* interpretation of what is the *real* meaning of a given phenomenon. According to this point of view, the correct reading of the internal aspect of culture is that which regards it exactly in the same way as it was regarded by its creators or modifiers.

But can this be done with any certainty? Can the reading of the creators, the modifiers, of any individual or group be correctly restored and restated? In many cases, yes. And for a simple reason: the meaning or purpose is often clearly and explicitly announced by the creator. We can grasp the essential meaning of Aristotle's *Politics* or Dante's *Divine Comedy* or Newton's *Principia* or Lincoln's "Gettysburg Address" because it is there in their works, expressed explicitly.

The character of the cultural objects in themselves—inscriptions, letters, chronicles, books, memoirs, and other "evidences"—often furnishes a sufficient basis for the restoration of the original meanings intended by the creators. If this were not so, the whole science of history would have to be discarded because such a psychological reading of culture is one of the main procedures of history.

This, then, is one way of reading the real mentality of cultural phenomena. It will be used to some extent in the present work.

It is not, however, the only form of reading possible. There may also be a *sociologico-phenomenological reading* of the inner aspect of cultural phenomena. This form of interpretation is perhaps more important for my purposes, and for sociologists in general, than that which is purely psychological.

What are the essentials of the sociologico-phenomenological reading?

First there is a causal-functional reading of culture which aims to discover the causal-functional relationships between the component parts of a cultural value or complex. Many persons may not be aware of the real causes of their actions and that there is a causal relationship between their activities and those of their contemporaries; they may not be aware of the causal connection between many of the variables in their cultural scheme; yet such causal relationships may exist. It is the privilege of the scientist to discover and to demonstrate their existence. As soon as this is done, the details of a cultural configuration, independently of any psychological meaning which may be given to them, become at once comprehensible as the elements of a causally bound unity. In other words, the first form of the sociologico-phenomenological interpretation of the mentality of cultural phenomena is the causal-functional reading. Theoretically at least it may be quite independent of the psychological reading. The significance of the relationship between density of population and crime, business cycles and the mortality rate, modes of production and forms of property, religion and the divorce rate, are examples of the sort of phenomena to which the causal reading may be applied.

A second form of the sociologico-phenomenological interpretation of the internal aspect of culture is the *logical reading*. We may know nothing about the psychological meaning of cultural values or about their causal relationships; yet in regard to many cultural complexes we can legitimately put the following questions and expect to find satisfactory answers: Are the elements of a given culture logically united, or are they logically contradictory? Do they make a comprehensible and consistent system, or do they not? If they do, what is the nature of the system? Are there unifying principles that permeate all the components of a given configuration, or not? These and similar problems may arise and be answered regardless of any psychological reading of the cultural configuration in question. In many cases the psychological interpretation helps to discover the logical meaning; often they go together; sometimes we cannot say anything about the psychological meaning; sometimes it clashes with the logical reading. Whatever the situation is, the logical reading stands upon its own feet, theoretically independent of the psychological significance.

The necessity for the logical interpretation follows also from the limitations of the psychological reading. The point is, in other words, that most of the cultural phenomena represent the results of the activities of many individuals and groups, whose purposes and meanings may be different from one another, often opposite. They all mix together, partly reinforcing, partly inhibiting, partly modifying one another, to such an extent that there is little likelihood of our distinguishing one from another. Whether we take the Parthenon or one of the great Christian cathedrals or a set of mores or laws or beliefs or any other cultural creations, they all are the manifestations of the activities, efforts, aims, volitions, ideas, feelings of large masses of individuals and combinations of groups. It would be next to impossible to decipher or separate what in these complex cultural values manifests the aims and meanings of each of the participants in their creation, or what is the "psychological reading" of each.

The assumption of the present work is that any cultural complex may be logically interpreted, an assumption made by any scientific study.

One special aspect of this assumption deserves, however, to be mentioned specifically. It is as follows: Euclid's and Lobachevsky's systems of geometry are both logically unimpeachable; both follow the canons of the same mathematical logic in the most perfect way; yet their theorems and deductions differ. How are we to explain such a discrepancy? The answer is simple. Both are logically correct, both follow the same canons of mathematical logic, but they start with different major premises: one with the axiom that the straight line is the shortest distance between two points, the other with a different assumption. This discrepancy at the roots of each system leads to a whole series of differences in subsequent deductions, despite the identity of the logico-mathematical canon being applied in both cases. The major premise of each system once accepted, each is logically valid within its own limits. This principle is particularly important in the field of the logical readings of culture.

We may sum up this discussion with the statement that a proper logical reading of cultural phenomena requires, first, the application of the canon of deductive and inductive logic; second, the realization of the possibility that the major premises of various cultures may differ; third, the assumption of an impartial position in regard to the validity or invalidity of the major premises. If the investigator grasps the characteristic premises of a culture accurately, his main task then is to show to what extent the culture is integrated from the standpoint of these premises, judged by the inflexible canons of logical validity. If he succeeds in solving this problem, his main task is ended. In defining the major premises of a given culture, he illuminates its soul, body, and its sociocultural physiognomy; by indicating the extent and the character of its logical integration, he answers the question as to its integration or nonintegration.

In the logical interpretation of culture complexes this rigorously scientific and impartial attitude is preserved throughout the present work. The canon of logical norms remains the same in the study of all the different cultures, but the logicality or nonlogicality of each is judged always from the standpoint of its major premises (if it has any).

A further point in regard to method suggests itself. If the nature of the major premises of a culture plays such an important part in the qualification of its logical integration, it follows that the key principle by which the character of an integrated culture may be understood should be sought, first of all, in these premises. In any chain of logical judgments, whether in regard to culture or otherwise, the entire series of deductions, and especially the conclusion, are conditioned by the statement with which the chain begins. Thus in the syllogism "All human beings are mortal; Socrates is human; therefore Socrates is mortal," the choice of Socrates, the statement that he is human, and the conclusion as to his mortality all were controlled in advance by the original premise, which therefore embodies the key by which the nature of the entire unity, i.e., the syllogism, is characterized. Thus, if we wish to discover the key to such a unity aside from the logic by which it is shaped, we must turn not to second premise or conclusion but to the major premise itself. A similar method must be employed in dealing with a logically integrated culture unity. It is for this reason that in the subsequent pages, which are devoted to preliminary classification of the main types of integrated culture, I shall follow the rule of arranging the types of culture not upon the basis of their secondary characteristics but according to their major premises.

Ideational, Sensate, and Mixed Systems of Integrated Culture: Preliminary Definitions

Many systems of logically integrated culture are conceivable, each with a different set of major premises but consistent within itself. Not all those, however, are likely to be found in those cultural complexes which have been in actual existence; and still fewer will serve as fruitful instruments for ordering the chaos of the cultural worlds which we can perceive into a limited number of completely comprehensible unities.

We can begin by distinguishing two profoundly different types of the integrated culture. Each has its own mentality; its own system of truth and knowledge; its own philosophy and *Weltanschauung;* its own type of religion and standards of "holiness"; its own system of right and wrong; its own forms of art and literature; its own mores, laws, code of conduct; its own predominant forms of social relationships; its own economic and political organization; and, finally, its own type of human personality, with a peculiar mentality and conduct. The values which correspond to one another throughout these cultures are irreconcilably at variance in their nature; but within each culture all the values fit closely together, belong to one another logically, often functionally.

Of these two systems, one may be termed *ideational* culture, the other *sensate.* And as these names characterize the cultures as a whole, so do they indicate the nature of each of the component parts.

The probability is that neither the ideational nor the sensate type has ever existed in its pure form; but all integrated cultures have in fact been composed of diverse combinations of these two pure logico-meaningful forms. In some the first type predominates; in others, the second; in still others both mingle in equal proportions and on an equal basis. Accordingly, some cultures have been nearer to the ideational, others to the sensate type; and some have contained a balanced synthesis of both pure types. This last I term the *idealistic* type of culture. (It should not be confused with the ideational.)

Let us now turn to a closer scrutiny of the culture types we have named. What specifically is meant by the ideational, the sensate, the idealistic, and other intermediary categories? What are their major characteristics? How are these characteristics combined and how do they operate to give united or integrated systems of culture? And, finally, why should these types of culture be regarded as fundamental and capable of providing the best possible means of understanding how the millions of fragments of the perceptual sociocultural world have been integrated into ordered systems? Such are the problems with which we shall start our study.

Since the character of any culture is determined by its internal aspect—by its *mentality,* as we agreed to call it—the portraiture of the ideational, sensate, and mixed types of culture begins properly with the delineation of the major premises of their mentality. As a starting point let us assume that these major premises concern the following four items: (1) the nature of reality; (2) the nature of the needs and ends to be satisfied; (3) the extent to which these needs and ends are to be satisfied; (4) the methods of satisfaction.

A. *The nature of reality.* The same complex of material objects which compose one's milieu is not perceived and interpreted identically by various human individuals. Without entering here into the psychological, biological, and other reasons for this, let us simply state the fact that the heterogeneity of individual experiences, together with other factors, leads to a multiplicity of the modes of perception of the same phenomenon by different persons. On one extreme is a mentality for which reality is that which can be perceived by the organs of sense; it does not see anything beyond the sensate being of the milieu (cosmic and social). Those who possess this sort of mentality try to adapt themselves to those conditions which appear to the sense organs, or more exactly to the exterior receptors of the nervous system. On the other extreme are persons who perceive and apprehend the same sensate phenomena in a very different way. For them they are mere appearance, a dream, or an illusion. True reality is not to be found here; it is something beyond, hidden by the appearance, different from this material and sensate veil which conceals it. Such persons do not try to adapt themselves to what now seems superficial, illusory, unreal. They strive to adapt themselves to the true reality which is beyond appearances. Whether it be styled God, Nirvana, Brahma, Om, Self, Tao, Eternal Spirit, *l'élan vital,* Unnamed, the City of God, Ultimate Reality, *Ding für und an sich,* or what not, is of little importance. What is important is that such mentality exists; that here the ultimate or true reality is usually considered supersensate, immaterial, spiritual.

It is evident that the mentality which accepts the milieu in its sensate and material reality will stress the satisfaction of the sensual bodily needs. Those who see it as a mere appearance will seek the satisfaction mainly of spiritual needs through an interaction with the ultimate reality. Those who occupy an intermediate position will be sensitive to needs partly sensate and partly spiritual.

B. *The nature of the needs and ends to be satisfied.* Needs may be viewed as purely carnal or sensual, like hunger and thirst, sex, shelter, and comforts of the body generally; as purely spiritual, like salvation of one's soul, the performance of sacred duty, service to God, categoric moral obligations, and other spiritual demands which exist for their own sake, regardless of any social approval or disapproval; or as mixed or carnal-spiritual, like the striving for superiority in scientific, artistic, moral, social, and other creative achievements, partly for their own sake and partly for the sake of human fame, glory, popularity, money, physical security and comfort, and other "earthy values" of an empirical character.

C. *The extent to which these needs and ends are to be satisfied.*

Each need may be regarded as requiring satisfaction to a different extent or on a different level, from the widest and most luxurious maximum to the narrowest and poorest minimum. One's need for food may range from a small amount of coarse bread and water, barely sufficient to maintain the physiological expenditures of the body, to the most extravagant gluttony, where all means are employed not only to supply luxurious and fine foods but also to stimulate the satiated appetite by various devices. The same is to be said of clothing, shelter, sex, self-protection, recreation, and amusement. This also holds true for the purely spiritual and for the mixed or carnal-spiritual needs.

D. *The methods of satisfaction of needs.* These may be, or appear to be, different with various individuals. We can divide them roughly into three main classes:

1. Modification of one's milieu in that manner which will yield the means of satisfying a given need; for instance, one suffering from cold can start a furnace, build a fire, put on a warm fur coat, etc.

2. Modification of self, one's body and mind, and their parts—organs, wishes, convictions, or the whole personality—in such a way as to become virtually free from a given need, or to sublimate it through this "readjustment of self." In the above illustration of suffering from cold, one can train oneself to become less sensitive to cold or to endure it within considerably broad limits. The same can be said of other needs.

3. Modification partly of milieu and partly of self. In the case of cold, to return to our example, we often resort to both methods—we may light a fire but also engage in vigorous physical activity to warm ourselves.

Ideational Culture

In the terms of the above four items, its major premises are these: (1) Reality is perceived as nonsensate and nonmaterial, everlasting being (*Sein*); (2) the needs and ends are mainly spiritual; (3) the extent of their satisfaction is the largest, and the level, highest; (4) the method of their fulfillment or realization is self-imposed minimization or elimination of most of the physical needs and to the greatest possible extent. These major premises are common to all branches of the ideational culture mentality. But, on the basis of variations under (4), it is possible to distinguish two fundamental subclasses of the ideational culture mentality and the related culture system:

A. *Ascetic ideationalism.* This seeks the consummation of the needs and ends through an excessive elimination and minimization of the carnal needs, supplemented by a complete detachment from the sensate world and even from oneself, viewing both as mere illusion, non-real, nonexisting. The whole sensate milieu, and even the individual "self," are dissolved in the supersensate, ultimate reality.

B. *Active ideationalism.* Identical with general ideationalism in its major premises, it seeks the realization of the needs and ends, not only through minimization of the carnal needs of individuals, but also through the transformation of the sensate world, and especially of the sociocultural world, in such a way as to reform it along the lines of the spiritual reality and of the ends chosen as the main value. Its bearers do not "flee from the world of illusion" and do not entirely dissolve it and their own souls in the ultimate reality but strive to bring it nearer to God, to save not only their own souls but the souls of all other human beings. The great spiritual reformers, like the early Christian Apostles and such popes as Gregory the Great and Leo the Great, may serve as examples of the active ideational mentality.

Sensate Culture

The sensate mentality views reality as only that which is presented to the sense organs. It does not seek or believe in any supersensory reality; at the most, in its diluted form, it assumes an agnostic attitude toward the entire world beyond the senses. The sensate reality is thought of as a becoming, process, change, flux, evolution, progress, transforma-tion. Its needs and aims are mainly physical, and maximum satisfaction is sought of these needs. The method of realizing them is not that of a modification within the human individuals composing the culture, but of a modification or exploitation of the external world. In brief, the sensate culture is the opposite of the ideational in its major premises.

These traits are common to all varieties of the sensate culture men-tality. But on the basis of the variation in the fourth item (i.e., method of adjustment) it is possible to distinguish three main varieties of this type.

A. *Active sensate culture mentality (active "Epicureans").* Sharing with other forms of sensate mentality all the above four premises, it seeks the consummation of its needs and ends mainly through the most "efficient" modification, adjustment, readjustment, reconstruction of the external milieu. The transformation of the inorganic, organic (tech-nology, medicine, and the applied disciplines), and the sociocultural world, viewed mainly externally, is the method of this variety. The great executives of history, the great conquerors, builders of empire, are its incarnation.

B. *Passive sensate mentality (passive "Epicureans").* This is charac-terized by the attempt to fulfill physical needs and aims, neither

through the inner modification of "self" nor through efficient reconstruction of the external world but through a parasitic exploitation
and utilization of the external reality as it is, viewed as the mere means
for enjoying sensual pleasures. "Life is short"; "*Carpe diem*"; "Wine,
women, and song"; "Eat, drink, and be merry"—these are the mottoes
of this mentality.

   C. *Cynical sensate mentality (cynical "Epicureans")*. The civilization dominated by this type of mentality, in seeking to achieve the
satisfaction of its needs, uses a specific technique of donning and
doffing those ideational masks which promise the greatest returns in
physical profit. This mentality is exemplified by all the Tartuffes of the
world, those who are accustomed to change their psychosocial "colors" and to readjust their values in order to run along with the stream.

The Mixed Types of Mentality and Culture

All the other culture mentalities represent in their major premises a
mixture of the ideational and sensate forms in various combinations
and proportions. With one conspicuous exception they are, therefore,
eclectic, self-contradictory, poorly integrated logically.

   A. *Idealistic culture mentality*. This is the only form of the mixed
class which is—or at least appears to be—logically integrated. Quantitatively it represents a more or less balanced unification of ideational
and sensate, with, however, a predominance of the ideational elements. Qualitatively it synthesizes the premises of both types into one
inwardly consistent and harmonious unity. For it reality is many-sided,
with the aspects of everlasting being and ever-changing becoming of
the spiritual and the material. Its needs and ends are both spiritual and
material, with the material, however, subordinated to the spiritual.
The methods of their realization involve both the modification of self
and the transformation of the external sensate world: in other words,
it gives *suum cuique* to the ideational and the sensate.

   B. *Pseudoideational culture mentality*. Another specific form of the
mixed type is the unintegrated, pseudoideational mentality. One might
style it "subcultural" if the term culture were used to designate only
a logically integrated system.

   The nature of reality is not clearly defined but is felt largely as sensate. Here needs and ends are predominantly of a physical nature. They
are only moderately satisfied, and the method of satisfaction is neither
an active modification of the milieu to any appreciable degree, nor
a free modification of self, nor a search for pleasure, nor successful
hypocrisy. It is a dull and passive endurance of blows and privations,
coming from the outside, as long as these can be borne physically. This

minimization of spiritual and carnal needs is not freely sought; it is imposed by some external agency (*vis absoluta*). It is the result of help-lessness to resist. The oppressive power is so overwhelming that, after several unsuccessful attempts to oppose it, there remains to those op-pressed no energy to try to free themselves and to adapt themselves physically and spiritually to a better order. Given an opportunity, a pseudoideationalist may easily plunge into passive, cynical, or even active "Epicureanism." The life processes of slaves under dire and cruel conditions, of many prisoners, of subjects under the cruel regime of their rulers, of some primitive people who live in a condition of misery and privation, of groups stricken by a great catastrophe bringing with it utter ruin, of sensate persons stricken by an incurable malady—these offer examples of this type of mentality.

* *

It is obvious that an examination of the characteristics of the ideational and sensate culture types is a different problem from that of how these mentalities and their characteristics are distributed in various actual culture complexes and in the actual behavior of individuals and groups. Our investigation thus falls into two parts or has two aspects: (1) the elucidation of the meaning and content of each culture type, as these follow from the major premises; and (2) the discovery of the actual distribution of the characteristics of all types in time and space.

In concrete social reality none of the types which are designated above is often found in pure form, unmixed with others, either in an individual or in a group or culture. On the other hand, these types and their characteristics are not distributed identically among individuals, groups, or cultures. In some the ascetic ideational, in some the active ideational, in some the passive or active sensate, in some the idealistic predominates. A close examination of the life history of an individual or group would reveal the major current of the flow of its culture pat-terns.

Each of the seven forms described above and the combination of elements of which it is composed are associated, logically and function-ally, with several additional characteristics.

1. Since the ascetic ideational mentality strives toward the ultimate, supersensory reality, lasting, eternal, unchangeable, and not toward the ever-changing and ephemeral sensate reality, it associates itself ei-ther with indifference to, and a detachment from, the physical environ-ment ("What is the use of trying to adapt oneself to that which is merely illusory!"), or a reluctance to change it ("Only fools try to write on waves"), or with a contempt for it. Hence ataraxia, self-sufficiency,

apathy, imperturbability, indifference, Nirvana, and insensibility to temporal existence, to its pains and pleasures, sorrows and joys, life and death, are traits common to all shades of such a mentality—from the Hindu, Buddhist, Taoist, Sufist, Jainist, Zoroastrian, Greek, Roman ascetic "primitive" ideationalism, cynicism, skepticism, and, in part at least, stoicism, to ascetic Christianity, and to all other varieties of the ascetic ideational culture mentalities.

2. The above attitude leads logically either to a repression of bodily needs or to a detached indifference to them as if nonexistent.

3. The attention is turned to the principle of being, views reality as everlasting and unchangeable being (*Sein*), in contradistinction to ever-changing becoming (*Werden*); the ultimate reality remains eternally the same, unchangeable even in its manifold modifications. Only illusions and appearances change. Empirically viewed, this mentality is thus static in its essence: static in its philosophy, in its *Weltanschauung*, in its choice of values and behavior. Time, in the sense of "before and after," "past, present, and future," "long and short," measured by empirical units, either does not play any role in such a mentality, or it becomes identical with the eternal, ultimate reality and, as such, is "punctuated" only by the changes in the distance of the ascetic ideational mind from total engulfment by, or union with, this everlasting being.

Quite contrary are the standpoint and satellites of the active sensate mentality. It sees only the empirical reality. Full of appetites and vigor, it wants to change the surrounding sensate environment to meet its needs. The empirical reality is ever changing, is ever in a flux; consequently, the adaptive activities must also vary incessantly.

Therefore, this mentality is inseparable from a dynamic, evolutionary, progressive principle. From the earlier representatives of this mentality, from Heraclitus and Lucretius to the modern evolutionists, devotees of transformation, progress, dynamism, movement, mobility, revolution, incessant change, and adjustment, the dynamic principle has regularly been an integral part of the theories and practices of the followers of the active sensate mentality. Here the time category plays a most conspicuous part, and time perspective is an indispensable trait of a mentality which is historical par excellence.

Likewise, in their practical activity, when it is integrated consistently with the active sensate mentality, the eternal panacea of such theorists is "readjustment"—readjustment by all means, at all times, at all cost.

Active ideationalism and the idealistic mentalities occupy an intermediate position between the two extreme standpoints. Active ideationalism, side by side with the philosophy of being and eternal value, of eternalism, admits some, though subordinated, becoming; some interest in the affairs of this world; some empirical activities; and some temporal values, subordinate to, and, as it were, a shadowy reflection of, the eternal. Similar is the position of the idealistic mentality, but it puts more emphasis on becoming, on the empirical, temporal aspects of things and values.

Passive sensate mentality is imbued with a still more pointed, extreme philosophy of becoming ("The past is no more; the future may never be; the present is all that we can be certain of"), with its *carpe diem*, with decisive preference for the values of the given moment rather than any lasting, future values.

Cynical sensate mentality is somewhat similar to the passive sensate. But, being obliged to exert themselves to get what passive "Epicureans" receive as gifts, the devotees of this type of mentality have to resort to hypocrisy as their technique, and in this lies their principal difference from passive "Epicureans."

Finally, an enslaved pseudoideationalist is here, as in other points, a creature of the circumstances rather than their master.

4. The ascetic ideational mentality facilitates man's control of himself, especially of his bodily senses, of his emotions, feelings, wishes, lusts. The active sensate mentality leads to man's control of the external world, so far as its material and sensate aspects are concerned (since any externality is apprehended mainly as a material and sensate phenomenon or process). The reasons for this are evident and follow directly from the nature of each mentality. Historically, the character of the first type has been frequently demonstrated by the almost miraculous repression of vital needs in the asceticism of Hindus, Buddhists, Taoists, Christians, Jainists, Sufists, not to mention the numberless ascetics affiliated with smaller sects. On the other hand, full-blooded, energetic "Epicureans" always have been the main transformers of the external milieu, whether it involved pioneering in the wilderness, or the organization of business empires, metropolitan centers, political or other organizations.

As to the other forms of mentality, the active ideational and the idealistic, each of these types logically combines in itself satellites of both opposite sorts. Each implies the development of self-control, as well as control of environments. The first is stressed more in the active ideational, the second in the idealistic mentality, though in neither is there stress to such an extent as in each of the extreme types of sensate and ideational.

The passive sensate mentality does not imply either of these controls; it seeks only an uninhibited satisfaction of individual lusts from the given milieu.

5. The ascetic ideational mentality is mainly of an "introvert" nature (directed upon self and its analysis and modification). The active sensate mentality and its adaptational activities by definition are of an "extrovert" nature (pointed toward the transformation of the sensate milieu).

6. The ascetic ideational mentality, on the one hand, opens wide the mental eyes and ears to grasp, register, and understand the essence of soul, mind, ultimate reality, God, the devil, good, evil, salvation, eternal value, consciousness, conscience, justice, and so on. One is plunged into this intangible realm. However, an active sensate mentality, on the contrary, dissolves the inner life and inner world into external. In contrast to ideationalists, "Epicureans" view the whole inner life, its processes, and all spiritual and immaterial phenomena as either ignorant delusion or aberration or a peculiar by-product ("function," "effect," "resultant") of purely physiological processes in the nervous system or in any other part of the body.

An ideationalist spiritualizes the external, even the inorganic, world; an "Epicurean" mechanizes and materializes even the spiritual, immaterial self.

The position of the active ideational and idealistic mentalities in this respect is intermediary. Both imply internal and external worlds, the active ideationalist paying more attention to internal and immaterial reality than the idealist. The passive sensate mentality implies a generally narrow tendency to view everything in terms of sensual pleasure and its opposite. With such a view much of the content of reality is missed.

7. Each of the types of adaptation discussed implies logically a different conception of self, or the "ego," and its relationship to other forces and agencies. The ascetic ideational mentality tends to dissolve the self in the universe of impersonal and immaterial reality.

The active sensate mentality implies a corporeal conception of self which makes it inseparable from the body; a skeptical or irreligious or disrespectful attitude toward nonmaterial forces and agencies; individual pride and self-reliance and a care of the body and its well-being, because it is looked upon as identical with self and personality.

8. The above being true, it is logically inevitable that the ascetic ideational mentality will require and stimulate cognition of inner, psychical, and mental processes (not, however, in terms of physiology or chemistry) from the most elementary psychological processes of sensation, perception, recollection, representation, thinking, emo-

tions, wishes, volitions, etc., to the most sublime and subtle experiences of ecstasy, trance, mysticism, suggestion, and hypnosis, and others like "reunion with the absolute," "revelation," "divine inspiration," etc.; from the simplest ideas about immaterial phenomena to the most difficult conceptions of ultimate reality, the human soul, immortality, God, truth, justice, value, and others which are the concern of the humanitarian sciences, i.e., ethical systems, religions, law, aesthetics, philosophy, and education. Since an ideationalist is, so to speak, everlastingly brooding over such matters, since the knowledge and the understanding of them are essential for him in his attempt to modify, control, or dissolve his inner self, it is obvious that all this should lead to an increase of the ideationalist's direct experience in these fields of immaterial phenomena. Hence it will not be surprising later when we discover inductively that the periods of predominance of ideational mentality always have led to a domination, in human knowledge, of theological, ethical, and other systems of thought which deal with these immaterial and sublime problems. On the other hand, such cultures and periods have regularly been marked by a stagnation and regress of the natural sciences and other disciplines dealing with the external, sensate, material phenomena.

For the same reasons, the active sensate mentality is naturally associated with, logically requires, and stimulates man's knowledge of the external, material world. Thus, in a society or culture which at a given period is predominantly sensate, we must expect a successful development of natural sciences and a blossoming of man's knowledge of the material, external world and of the technical inventions for its control.

9. For similar reasons the whole intellectual, moral, and psychosocial gestalt of the ideational mentality is profoundly different from the active sensate.

(a) Ideational truth and its criteria cannot be identical with sensate. What is truth or science for one is often prejudice, ignorance, error, heresy, blasphemy, for the other.

(i) Ideational mentality implies the acceptance of the validity of the inner experience—divine inspiration, mystical union, revelation, pure meditation, ecstasy, trance—as the ultimate basis and source of truth. The sensate mentality implies the validity of perception, rests entirely, or mainly, on man's external sense organs.

(ii) The ideational wisdom, knowledge, mentality, seems to be marked by idealism, spiritualism, quietism, religiosity, organicism, mysticism, indeterminism, qualitativism. The sensate mentality, knowledge, science, is characterized by materialism, empiricism, mechanisticism, determinism, quantitativism.

(iii) An ideationalist is prone to interpret the whole external world according to the patterns and traits of his inner experience. As a result, he spiritualizes the material world, even in its inorganic part; he dissolves it in the inner experience.

An "Epicurean," on the contrary, materializes and externalizes the inner experience.

(*b*) Similarly, and for similar reasons, the moral, social, and other values should be different in these mentalities. Since an ideationalist is indifferent to the external world and is centered at the inner, always "immaterial," or supersensate world, and since his ideal is to repress his sensual and material needs as much as possible, the external values of material character which can give but a transient satisfaction of sensual needs have no, or little, value for him. He seeks to be independent of them and self-sufficient. He wants to live in the eternal, imperishable world. His values are of an inner and immaterial character. The reverse is the situation for the sensate mentality. Its criteria of value are the fitness of a given external object, of the way of handling it, and of specific forms of extrovert activity to satisfy mainly sensual needs. He does not want to seek imperishable, everlasting values. Such values are nonvalues to him, being almost useless for the satisfaction of his manifold needs. Life is short, and in this short life the sensual needs are transient—a good meal has its value only when one has an appetite and can enjoy it. Love and sex again are of value only when they can be enjoyed; for an old or impotent man, they are of no value at all. Therefore, why miss a chance when it comes and can be enjoyed, why seek for something eternally lasting, since such a thing either does not exist, or, if it exists at all, provides a much smaller measure of enjoyment than the incessant series of pleasures which follow from the satisfaction of all wishes at the moment of their greatest intensity?

In regard to *all values,* as has been pointed out, an ideationalist places more emphasis on the long-time, permanent values than on those that are immediate, transient, short-lived. His standpoint gravitates to the philosophy of being, everlasting, unchangeable, enduring.

After these considerations, the following typical traits implied in ideational and sensate mentalities will be comprehensible.

(*c*) In the field of moral values the ideational mentality tends to be associated with the values which are absolute, eternal, and everlasting. Ideational moral systems, whatever their secondary traits, are marked first by indifference to, or contempt of, or a low evaluation of, the external empirical world and its material values ("My kingdom is not of this world").

The sensate mentality implies and is associated with an opposite type of moral code. It chooses and emphasizes predominantly the sensate, empirical, material values. Eudaemonism, hedonism, utilitarianism, sensualism; the morals of "*Carpe diem,*" of "Wine, women, and song"—these are forms established by the sensate mentality. Man should seek pleasure and avoid pain; utility is positive, disutility is negative. The maximum pleasure for the greatest number of beings: this is in essence the motto of sensate moralists.

The second characteristic of the moral systems of a sensate culture type is that they are never absolute but are always relativistic, varying "according to circumstances and situations." They can be modified, have no sacred, unalterable, eternal imperatives.

The third quality of the sensate code is that it has little to do with any transcendental or supersensory values and either mocks at such values, ignores them, or mentions them only to repudiate them and to bolster up its own principles.

(*d*) Logically, aesthetic value, art, likewise cannot be identical in the ideational and sensate culture mentalities. They should be as profoundly different as are the other values. So far as the *style* of art is concerned—whether it be in painting, sculpture, music, literature, drama, architecture—in the ideational mentality it is symbolic, its physical exemplars being merely the visible signs of the invisible world and inner values. But in the sensate culture, art must be sensate in form; "naturalistic," in the sense that its intention is to reproduce objects in a shape which imitates closely that in which they appear to our organs of sense. As to the *subjects* and the *aims* and *purposes* of art, they show analogous divergences in the two culture types. In general, sensate art deals with those materials which serve and help to increase the sensate happiness of man; ideational is the handmaid of religion, absolutistic ethics, eternal values.

(*e*) The same difference appears in regard to social and practical values. A regime professing sensate ideals will approve anything that increases the sum total of sensate enjoyment; and that leads to man's control over nature and over other men, as the means of satisfying ever-expanding needs. Of a special importance in such a state of society is the search for material objects which under the circumstances are particularly efficient in bringing satisfaction. As one of the most efficient means has always been material wealth, in a sensate society it is the *alpha* and *omega* of comfort, of the satisfaction of all desires, of power, prestige, fame, happiness. With it everything can be bought, everything can be sold, and everything can be gratified. Therefore, it is quite comprehensible that the striving for wealth is inevitably one of the main activities of such a culture, that wealth is the standard by

TABLE 1. Summary of the Main Traits and Satellites of the Discussed Types of Adaptation

Types of Culture Mentality

Main Elements	Ascetic Ideational	Active Sensate	Active Ideational	Idealistic	Passive Sensate	Cynical Sensate	Pseudo-ideational
1. Reality	ultimate reality, eternal, nonsensate, transcendental	sensate, empirical, material	both, with emphasis on the eternal and nonsensate	both approximately equally represented	sensate, narrow, shallow	sensate, but with spiritual mask	painfully sensate; spiritual, but indifferentiated; felt and sensed but not thought through (unintegrated)
2. Main needs and ends	spiritual	manifold and richly sensate	both, with predominance of spiritual	both approximately equally represented	narrow sensate	sensate, with a spiritual mask	mainly sensate, with elements of spiritual not differentiated
3. Extent of satisfaction	maximum	maximum	great, but moderated	great, but balanced	maximum for narrow sensate needs	according to circumstances	very limited
4. Method of satisfaction	mainly self-modification	mainly modification of external milieu	both ways, with prevalence of self-modification	both ways	utilization of external milieu	milieu's utilization through superficial and purely external change of the psychosocial traits of the person, without change of itself	mere enforced endurance of the milieu

Logical Satellites							
5. *Weltanschauung*	being (*Sein*): lasting value; indifference to transient values; imperturbability; statism	becoming (*Werden*): transient values; full-blooded sense of life, joy, and grief; dynamism and endless readjustment (progress, evolution)	both, with emphasis on being	both equally represented	narrow and extreme becoming ("*Carpe diem*")	narrow becoming, with a mask of being	undifferentiated and not thought through, vague and fragmentary ideas (lack of integration)
6. Power and object of control	self-control, repression of the sensual man and of "self"	control of the sensate reality	both, with emphasis on self-control	both equally represented	no real control of either self or milieu	control of assuming and putting off masks	no control; mere endurance of the effects of other forces acted on by external power
7. Activity	introvert	extrovert	both, with emphasis on introvert	both equally represented	parasitism of introvert–extrovert type	specific introvert–extrovert	enforced extrovert–introvert; fatalistic
8. Self	highly integrated, spiritual, dissolved in the ultimate reality, aware of the sensual world as illusion or content of self; antimaterialistic	highly integrated, sensate, dissolved in immediate physical reality; materializes self and all the spiritual phenomena; materialistic, caring for integrity of body and its sensual interest; sensual liberty, sensual egotism	both, with emphasis on spiritual, etc.	both equally represented	no real integration of self; mere flux of unintegrated physical sensations; self almost identical with stomach, sex organs, etc.	no real integration; similar to the passive sensate, but scheming and manipulating	no integrated self, except as a vague center of sensations; with some fanciful, animistic, or other ideas and images; remains on a half-animal level (unintegrated)

TABLE 1. *continued*

Types of Culture Mentality

	Ascetic Ideational	Active Ideational	Idealistic	Active Sensate	Passive Sensate	Cynical Sensate	Pseudo-ideational
9. Knowledge	develops insight into and cognition of the spiritual, psychical, immaterial phenomena and experiences; concentrates upon these exclusively; leads to arts of education and modification of man's inner life	both, but more moderately, with emphasis on the spiritual	both equally represented	develops science of natural phenomena and technical inventions; concentrates on these; leads to arts of technology, medicine, hygiene, sanitation, and modification of man's physical actions	develops only the "culinary" and "bedroom" techniques of sensual enjoyment	same as in passive sensate plus the technique of deception and hypocrisy	does not give any real opportunity to develop any form of integrated knowledge and cognition except some fragments acquired through imposed "trial and error"
10. Truth; its categories, criteria, and methods (of arriving at)	based on inner experience, "mystic way," concentrated meditation; intuition and "revelation"; prophecy	both, with the "inner way" emphasized	both equally emphasized (scholasticism)	based on observation of, measurement of, experimentation with the exterior phenomena through exterior organs of senses, inductive logic	nothing coherent; no truth except sensations	nothing coherent	nothing, differentiated and thought through clearly

11. Moral values and systems	absolute transcendental, categoric, imperative, everlasting, unchangeable	relativistic and sensate: hedonistic, eudaemonistic, utilitarian; seeking maximum sensate happiness for largest number of human beings; "morals of rightly understood egotism"	both, with emphasis on the absolute and the external	both equally emphasized	no real moral values except sensual, "Wine, women, and song"; amoralism; nihilism	no real moral values, except sensate masked by spiritual; cynicism, nihilism	no differentiated moral system, except apathetic and dull submission to fate, and sensual disapproval of hard blows and approval of easier times followed by vague ideas about the other world's justice
12. Aesthetic values	"ideational" subservient to the main inner values, religious, nonsensate	sensate, secular, created to increase joys and beauties of a rich sensate life	both, with emphasis on the nonsensate	both equally emphasized	narrow sensual; refinedly pathologic	sensate, masked with spiritual	undifferentiated and vague
13. Social and practical values	those which are lasting and lead to the ultimate reality: only such persons are leaders, only such things and events are positive, all others are valueless, or of negative value, particularly wealth, earthly comfort, etc.; principle of sacrifice	everything that gives joy of life to self and partly to others: particularly wealth, comfort, etc.; prestige is based on the above; wealth, money, physical might become "rights" and basis of all values; principle of sound egotism	both, with emphasis on spiritual	both equally emphasized; live and let live	narrow and extremely sensual; "après moi le déluge"	narrow and extremely sensual with a mask of spiritual values; Tartuffeism	no choice given; undifferentiated; as God or boss decides

which almost all other values are judged, that it is, in fact, the supreme value of values. Pecuniary value thus becomes the measuring stick of scientific, artistic, moral, and other values. Those who are excellent moneymakers are the leaders of such a society. Those who are wealthy are its aristocracy. They are simultaneously public leaders, high priests, moral examples, kings who ennoble others, the Four Hundred which is envied, if not deeply esteemed. Under these conditions, writers, artists, scientists, ministers, public officials, and men of the professional classes hope and act mainly to write a "bestseller," to obtain the best-paying position, to have the highest scale of remuneration, and so on. If arms and force, not money, are the means to maximum happiness, then these instruments are the supreme arbiters of value, instead of money.

* *

In this respect, the ideational mentality differs from the sensate once again. An ideationalist is either quite indifferent to all these illusory and transient values or is even inimical to them as the sources of the disturbances of the peace of mind and of the perdition of the human soul. In a thoroughgoing ideational society, wealth or any other sensate value cannot become dominant but at best will be tolerated only as turpitudinous. The most successful dealers in wealth do not have much chance to become the bearers of prestige, the leaders, the evaluators, the assessors of men, objects, and values, in such a society.

Enough of contrasts for the present. Table 1 will make plain at a glance by its arrangement in tabular form the results of this examination of the several types of culture mentalities.

17

Principle of Immanent Change of Sociocultural Systems and Congeries

> Since we never reckon that we understand a thing till we can give an account of its "how and why," it is clear that we must look into the "how and why" of things coming into existence and passing out of it.
>
> Aristotle, *The Physics*, 194*b*

Three Hypotheses on the "Why" of Sociocultural Change

We know that viewed in their empirical aspect, all sociocultural phenomena change incessantly, without any exception whatsoever. The question arises: Why do they change but do not remain unchangeable? Why this relentless becoming instead of everlasting permanency?

The general answer to this question is easy: not only sociocultural phenomena but all empirical phenomena—inorganic, organic, and sociocultural—are subject to change in the course of their empirical existence. To be in an incessant flux, as Heraclitus said, is their destiny. Therefore a mere reference to this universal uniformity of empirical reality is sufficient to answer the above question in its general form.

Granting this, the question arises: Where shall we look for the roots of change of sociocultural phenomena, and how shall we interpret it? Shall we look for the "causes" of the change of a given sociocultural phenomenon in the phenomenon itself, or in some "forces" or "factors" external to it?

The question may sound "metaphysical," and yet it is not. We shall see that it is of primary methodological and scientific importance. The

Originally published in *Social and Cultural Dynamics* [1937] (reprint, New Brunswick, N.J.: Transaction Books, 1985), 630–46. Reprinted by permission of Sergei Sorokin and Peter Sorokin.

character of the answer to it determines the very character of almost all "causal," "factorial," and many other analyses of the social science.

Logically, three answers are possible to the question, and all three have been used in social science. The first solution of it is the *externalistic theory of change*. Such a theory looks for the reasons ("causes," "factors," or "forces") of change of any sociocultural system in some "variables" that lie outside of the sociocultural system itself. Explicitly or implicitly, this standpoint is the predominant theory at the present time.

Take almost any historical, sociological, economic, or other work dealing with a study of the change of any social and cultural phenomenon. When the investigators set forth the problem of what are the "factors," "reasons," "variables" responsible for the change, they almost invariably take variables or factors external to the phenomenon studied, and through the change of this external factor(s) explain the change of the phenomenon under investigation. If an author sets forth a problem of why the family has changed during, say, the last hundred years, he turns for the explanation to such variables as the change of industrial conditions, or density of the population, or the state laws, or the biological factors, up to sunspots and climatic conditions. The family itself is assumed to be something purely passive, devoid of any capacity of change by itself, and pushed by this or that external force along the line of change. Without such a "factor" it seemingly is destined to remain changeless and "stationary." The same method is followed when an investigator deals with the factors of change of the state, of economic, political, and social institutions, of art, science, philosophy, law, and ethics, and of practically any social and cultural phenomenon. The predominant mode of explanation of change is externalistic. In quantitative and statistical studies, the factor, "the independent variable," is in most cases a variable external to the dependent variable. Exceptions certainly exist, and we shall see them, but the dominant procedure is externalistic. This concerns practically all the social, and, in a considerable degree, the biological sciences. Its general manifestation is the triumph of the so-called "environmental" theory, especially in explanation and interpretation of human affairs.

Broadly viewed, "environmentalism" is a theory and method of externalistic explanations of any change through "environmental forces" that lie outside, but not within, the unit studied. These external—environmental—forces are assumed to be shaping, controlling, modifying, changing, pushing, pulling, creating, and destroying the phenomenon studied. The unit itself is assumed to be a merely passive focal point of the application of these forces and factors. It is supposed to have no forces of change of its own. This externalistic environmentalism now pervades social sciences. Almost everything and every change is explained environmentally, from crime and religion up to the business cycle and pure genius.

Another variety of this externalism is given in widely spread mechanistic and behavioristic interpretations of mental and sociocultural phenomena. The very nature of the mechanistic theory of sociocultural change consists in an extreme form of the externalistic interpretation. What is curious—but typical of the contemporary mentality—is that the second part of the Descartian and Newtonian law of inertia, namely, that if a material body is in the state of motion it has to move rectilinearly and uniformly (just because it *is* in the state of motion), has been neglected: the mechanistic interpretation of sociocultural change usually assumes that any sociocultural phenomenon is in a state of rest or static equilibrium and remains in the state of rest until some "external force" thrusts it out of its place and keeps it moving and changing. Otherwise, the phenomenon is assumed to have no *proprium motum* and must be in a state of inertia, or "being at rest." Somewhat similar is the externalism of the behavioristic theories of any psychosociocultural change, and not only of the behavioristic but also of the predominant psychological theories of the present time. Their fundamental principle is *stimulus–response*. Without a stimulus—and the stimulus is almost invariably something external to man or organism or any sociocultural phenomenon—man or any sociocultural system is assumed to be incapable of giving any "response," exerting any activity, or experiencing any change or transformation. Implicitly, this formula of stimulus–response is to a considerable degree externalistic, and in the work of many a psychologist and social scientist it is such explicitly.

A further variety of this externalism is a wide current of "reform" and "reconstructive" movements, which look for the "roots of evil" and for "the patented cure" of any social and cultural phenomenon in "the environment and factors" external to the person or social institution or cultural unit under consideration. The wrongdoing and cure of a criminal are widely regarded as due to his milieu and not inherent in the criminal himself. A root of defectiveness in a social institution— be it the family, the political or economic organization—is again looked for not in the institution itself but in its environmental forces. A modification of these conditions is expected to produce automatically the desirable change of the system itself.

This concise characterization shows the nature of the externalistic theory of change, its varieties, and its contemporary popularity. It

demonstrates also that the question raised is not merely "academic."
We see how the externalistic postulate determines the essential character of all the "causal and factorial" research in all the fields of the
social sciences; how it shapes the "techniques and procedures" of
the research; how it pervades the practical policies and activities in
the field of reformistic and reconstructive social movements; how it
influences the theoretical and practical mentality and activity of its
partisans in their daily affairs, as well as in special sociocultural conditions.

The second solution of the problem is opposite: it may be styled
the *immanent theory of sociocultural change.* In regard to any sociocultural system, it claims that it changes by virtue of its own forces
and properties. It cannot help changing, even if all its external conditions are constant. The change is thus immanent in any sociocultural
system, inherent in it, and inalienable from it. It bears in itself the
seeds of its change. If the external conditions of family, state, economic
organization, political party, or any social system are assumed to be
constant; if the same is assumed for any integrated system of art or
science, philosophy, religion, or law, each of these social and cultural
systems does not remain the same but is immanently destined to
change by virtue of its own existence and functioning. Some of its
properties will disappear, some new ones will emerge; certain traits
will be growing, certain others decreasing. Rapidly or slowly, the system will undergo a transformation. Such, in brief, is the essential nature of this theory.

One can easily see that it is opposite to the externalistic hypothesis.
Once assumed, it leads (for a consistent mind) to a series of conclusions
in the study of almost all social and cultural problems quite different
from those of the externalistic postulate. In a study of a transformation
of any sociocultural system, the partisan of the immanent theory of
change will look for the reasons or factors of the change first of all in
the internal properties (actual and potential) of the system itself and
not in merely its external conditions. He will not try to find some external factor through whose "pushing," "pulling," or "pressing" he could
explain the change. He may consider any such factor as subsidiary;
but in most cases he will not ascribe to it the whole of the change and
its essential forms. In reformistic and reconstructive schemes for the
"improvement" of this or that sociocultural evil, he would not rely
exclusively or even mainly upon a mere rearrangement of the external
conditions. Like a doctor, he would study first of all the system itself
and its immanent properties, and this study would give him a real basis
for his diagnosis. If he sees that the system is, speaking figuratively,

similar to the organism of an eighty-year-old man, he will declare all the attempts to turn it into an organism of a twenty-year-old youth futile, no matter what rearrangement of external conditions is made. His reason will be that, on the basis of valid experience, an eighty-year-old organism cannot be changed into a youthful system. If the immanent properties of the system have potentialities of a more cheerful nature, he will expect that, in some way, when the time comes, they will be manifested. And his prescription—which does not neglect the external conditions—will, as a rule, put an emphasis on the inner potentiality and efforts of the system itself. He would not invest much hope in a purely mechanical rearrangement of the external circumstances. To sum up, once assumed, the principle of immanent change of sociocultural systems leads to an immense amount of research and practical activity in procedures, techniques, and policies profoundly different from the principle of the externalistic theory of change. Such is the second theory in the field.

Finally, there has been the third—*intermediary* or *integral*—answer to the problem. It attempts to view a change of any sociocultural phenomenon as the result of the combined external and internal forces. Often it assumes an eclectic character, putting both factors side by side without any serious attempts to indicate what is the specific role of the immanent and of the external forces. In few instances, however, is the synthetic or integral character of the principle carried through and put into actual operation. In such cases—and only in these—the integral character of the principle is realized and its nature is not disfigured. Such are the three main answers to the problem put. Which of these is most valid?

My answer is in favor of the principle of immanent change of each sociocultural system supported by the externalistic principle, within certain conditions and limits. The main reasons for such a standpoint are as follows.

First, the principle of immanent change of a sociocultural system is supported by empirical observation. We do not know any empirical sociocultural system or phenomenon which does not change in the course of its existence or in the course of time. In the whole empirical sociocultural world there has existed hardly any system which has remained unchanged. This observation is incontestable. The objection possible is that though change is unquestionable, it remains unknown to what it is due: to purely immanent forces of the system, or to an incessant influencing of it by a set of external factors. The objection is valid. Therefore, for the solution of the problem, we must turn to other empirical and logical evidences.

Such a combined—logico-empirical—evidence can be formulated in the following proposition: Any system which is, during its existence, a going concern, which works and acts and does not remain in a state of rest, in the literary sense of the word, cannot help changing just because it performs some activity, some work, as long as it exists. Only a system which is in an absolute vacuum at the state of rest and is not functioning can escape change under these conditions. One can take the best automobile engine, put in it the best oil, and keep other conditions constant; and yet, if it runs and works, sooner or later it will change, and after a due time it would be worn out. In our case, we agreed to keep it in the constant but best possible external milieu. Its change, therefore, is due to the fact that it runs, works, operates, acts.

The change is an immanent consequence of the system's being a going concern. Its functioning makes change inevitable. The same can be said of any other mechanical system, if it is a going concern. Still more valid is the proposition for organic systems. One of the most fundamental properties of a living organism is its activity—external or internal—its motility, its work, its dynamic nature. In other words, an organic system is a going concern by its very nature. As such, as long as it lives, it works, acts, operates. As long as it does that, it cannot help changing. "Life can never be in equilibrium." "Complete equilibrium is never attained (by an organism) and would be fatal if it were attained, as it would mean stagnation, atrophy, and death." Regardless of any milieu, man cannot help undergoing an incessant change during his existence, in passing from childhood to maturity and then to old age and death. Only perhaps freezing or putting man into semidead anabiotic conditions can greatly slow up the tempo of change. But such conditions mean turning the man from a living and going concern into a kind of mummy. Such a possibility corroborates and does not disprove the proposition.

Since any sociocultural system is composed of human beings as one of its components, and since any organism, so long as it exists, cannot help changing, the sociocultural system is a "going concern" and cannot help changing so long as it exists, regardless of its external conditions, even when they are absolutely constant. The very performance of any activity, any reaction or response, to a given environment *a*, changes the system and makes it react differently a second time, and then a third time, and subsequent times. Other components of any sociocultural system are meanings and vehicles. These also bear in themselves the seeds of their, and of the system's, change. All the meanings that contain in themselves some potential contradiction—and according to Hegel, all meanings have it (see further)—sooner or later make it explicit and germinate their own change for elimination of it. In this sense, they also change immanently, as meanings grounded in empirical reality, as thought of by empirical human beings. All the vehicles *qua* vehicles are also going concerns: functioning as vehicles, they work, are used, operated with, often worn out in their functioning. Therefore, they cannot help changing too.

These logico-experiential considerations are sufficient in order to make the principle of immanent change of the sociocultural phenomena valid. If a partisan of an externalistic principle protests that any such system or organism does not exist in a vacuum, but in a certain environment to which it incessantly reacts, and through which, therefore, it is changed, the answer is that the existence of the environment of a given system is one thing, and imputation to that environment of the whole or the main part of the change of the system is quite another thing. If of two variables—no matter what they are—one is changing while the other remains constant, no logician or statistician would ascribe the change of the first variable to the other—the constant one. If *a* varies while *b* remains constant (except if *b* is God or Prime Mover), elementary inductive logic forbids us to see in *b* the cause of the variation of *a*. If the milieu of any system that is a going concern remains constant while the system changes, the milieu cannot be regarded as the cause or the source of the change of the system. If the simplest microorganism (for instance, *Paramecium caudalum*) in Metalnikov's and Jenning's experiments reacts to a stimulus *a* in a certain way for the first time, and if it reacts to the same stimulus in the same conditions differently the second time, the change evidently is due neither exclusively nor mainly to the environment nor to *a* but to the immanent property of the organism to change by virtue of its very existence and therefore its activity. Even the very capacity to react or respond to the stimulus is a capacity immanent in the organism.

All this means that the problem of why a sociocultural system changes is falsely set forth. Its change is neither a mystery nor a problem difficult to explain. Much more difficult would it be to understand a case of unchangeableness of any sociocultural system—if such a case had ever occurred.

In view of a wide popularity of the externalistic theories nowadays, it is advisable to go deeper in the examination of their shortcomings. Their first defect is that they are useless, because, at the best, any consistent externalistic theory of change does not solve the problem but merely postpones the solution, and then comes either to a mystery, in a bad sense of this term, or to the logical absurdity of pulling the proverbial rabbit out of mere nothing. Suppose we assume that change is not immanent in sociocultural systems. For an example, let us take the family (*a*). According to the externalistic theory for an explanation of why the American family has changed during the last fifty years, we have to take some factor external to it: say, change of industrial conditions (*b*). When such an explanation is given, we may ask: But why have the industrial conditions changed? According to the consistent externalism, we have to take some external factor to explain the change of *b*. Let it be (*c*), say, a change in the density and mass of the population, or in the climatic conditions, or in the sunspots, or whatnot. Being given *c*, we can put the same question in regard to it: why has *c* changed? And so on, *ad infinitum*. This is what I mean by the postponement of the solution.

Second, if a consistent externalist continues to claim that in the process of this regression he somehow can find a solution, we shall drive him into one of the four blind alleys. (*a*) Either to the endless regression, from *a* to *b*, *b* to *c*, *c* to *n* and so on endlessly, none of which can change itself or can be a source of change for the others. The whole regression is endless and fruitless and cannot give either change or an end in this hopeless hunt for a self-starting agent in the endless regressive movement from factor to factor. Or, (*b*), to the ultimate Prime Mover, be it God, or any other ultimate principle, itself either unmoved (as in Plato-Aristotle's theory) or self-moving (as in some other theories). If, in the search for the ultimate source of change in metaphysics, such a solution may or may not be adequate, in the study of the empirical and sociocultural phenomena such a solution does not solve the problem at all. For the externalistic theories of change do not invoke here the ultimate Prime Mover, which itself is not and cannot be empirical, but take one of the empirical "variables" as the factor of change.

Or, (*c*), to an ascription of immanent change to some of the sociocultural or generally empirical systems; for instance, to climate, to "means and modes of production" of Marxism, to a "demographic factor," and so on. But such a solution means an abandonment of the externalistic theory and self-contradiction, for it signifies that, contrary to the externalistic thesis, some of the sociocultural or empirical systems bear in themselves the reason of their change and can be self-starters and movers of other systems or variables. Such a thesis is but a variety of an immanent principle of change. In addition, such an escape is burdened with several other sins. It has to demonstrate why some of the sociocultural systems (for instance, the family, religion, or science) cannot change themselves, while some others (for instance, means and instruments of production, density of the population, mores, art, or sunspots) can do that. Farther on, most of the externalistic factorial theories in their "explanations" of the why of change usually move from the sociocultural to the biological (demographic and other biological) factors, and from these to the inorganic (climatic, geographic, atomic, etc.) factors. They regard such a regression as particularly scientific because it "explains" sociocultural phenomena by biological, and the biological phenomena by the physicochemical. Whatever is the validity of such an assumption in the study of other problems, in this problem the procedure and respective dogma are certainly wrong. The reason is that observationally and logically, the most dynamic or changeable phenomena are exactly the sociocultural; then come the biological; then the physicochemical.

The criticized procedure thus amounts to an "explanation" of the most "self-moving" sociocultural phenomena by the less dynamic biological and by the least "self-moving" physicochemical variables.

Finally, (d), the fourth blind alley into which such an externalist may try to run for salvation, is the logical absurdity of producing something (change) out of nothing (from the systems which are devoid of immanent change, according to the externalistic theories). If the sociocultural systems are devoid of change; if the same is true of the biological and inorganic phenomena; if neither the line of infinite regression, nor a postulating of the ultimate Prime Mover, nor an arbitrary ascription of immanent change to something is assumed, then the only source of change that is left to the externalist is "nothing." But a long time ago Melissus said: "For if it [change] comes into being, before it came into being, it must have been nothing; if, then, it was nothing, nothing could ever come out of nothing."

Such, then, are the four blind alleys into which the consistent externalistic principle leads. None of them solves or can solve the problem.

For all these reasons, the principle of an exclusive and consistent externalism is untenable. In contrast to it, the principle of immanent change of a sociocultural system is free from these logical and factual errors. Therefore, with an adequate limitation and subsidiary admission of the externalistic principle, it is much more valid than the externalistic hypothesis.

The endorsement of the immanent principle of change does not hinder a recognition of the role of the external forces in the change of the sociocultural system. Any sociocultural system lives and functions amidst other sociocultural systems. If each of these bears in itself the seeds of its own change, their interaction leads to this change still more. If a system a contains in itself the reason for its change and so do the systems b and c and n, then the interaction of a with b or c or many of these systems facilitates the change of *a* and *b* and of each interacting system still more.

The above is sufficient to answer the problem of *dynamics:* why a whole integrated culture as a constellation of many cultural subsystems changes and passes from one state to another. The answer is: it and its subsystems—be they painting, sculpture, architecture, music, science, philosophy, law, religion, mores, forms of social, political, and economic organizations—change because each of these is a going concern and bears in itself the reason of its change.

Some Implications of the Principle of Immanent Change

A. *Principle of immanent generation of consequences.* The first implication of the principle of immanent change may be formulated as follows: As long as it exists and functions, any sociocultural system incessantly generates consequences which are not the results of the external factors to the system but the consequences of the existence of the system and of its activities. As such, they must be imputed to it, regardless of whether they are good or bad, desirable or not, intended or not by the system. One of the specific forms of this immanent generation of consequences is an incessant change of the system itself, due to its existence and activity.

B. *Principle of immanent self-determination of the system's destiny (Existence Career).* The second fundamental implication of the principle of immanent change is the principle of immanent self-determination of the potentially given course of the existence of a sociocultural system. It may be formulated as follows: As soon as a sociocultural system emerges, its essential and "normal" course of existence, the forms, the phases, the activities of its life career or destiny are determined mainly by the system itself, by its potential nature and the totality of its properties. The totality of the external circumstances is relevant, but mainly in the way of retarding or accelerating the unfolding of the immanent destiny; weakening or reinforcing some of the traits of the system; hindering or facilitating a realization of the immanent potentialities of the system; finally, in catastrophic changes, destroying the system; but these external circumstances cannot force the system to manifest what it potentially does not have; to become what it immanently cannot become; to do what it immanently is incapable of doing. Likewise, the external conditions can crush the system or terminate an unfolding of its immanent destiny at one of the earliest phases of its development (its immanent life career), depriving it of a realization of its complete life career; but they cannot fundamentally change the character and the quality of each phase of the development; nor can they, in many cases, reverse or fundamentally change the sequence of the phases of the immanent destiny of the system.

This proposition is a mere result of the principle of immanent change and immanent generation of the consequences. With all the traits at a given moment (t^1), the system acts in the form of a; a introduces changes in the milieu and in the system itself. Therefore, for the next moment, t^1, the system's total situation is determined by the external and internal consequences of the act a. This situation at t^1 is thus determined by the system's properties and activities at the moment t^1. The same is true for the moment t^2, t^3, . . . t^n, up to the end of the existence of the system. This means that any sociocultural system, as soon as it emerges as a system, bears in itself its future destiny. To use Aristotle's example, an acorn as soon as it emerges bears in itself its destiny, namely the unfolding destiny of an oak and of nothing else. So with the initial system of any plant or animal organism. The same is still truer of a sociocultural system: a moronic family cannot unfold itself into the great Christian church or develop the properties of the Royal Scientific Society; from an emerged contractual business concern one cannot expect the properties, functions, and life career of the early Christian monastery; from a sensate "Society of Connoisseurs of Wines and Women," the characteristics and destiny of an ascetic society; from the state, the functions and destiny of a sentimental philanthropic society; from a real university, the functions, behavior, and life career of a criminal gang; and so on. As soon as a sociocultural system emerges, with all its properties and *modus vivendi* and *modus agendi,* it contains in itself its "normal" future. At any moment of its existence and activity, it creates it, controls it, determines it, and molds it. In this sense, to use the proverb, any sociocultural system is the molder of its own future.

This does not deny the role of the external circumstances. But as mentioned, it specifies their functions. The external agencies may crush the system and in this way prevent it from a realization of its immanent destiny. Earthquake, fire, plague, inundation, war, and other agencies external to a given system—the family, the artistic society, the religious or political sect—can kill all or a part of its members; can destroy its property and other instrumentalities of its activities; can disperse the members; and in hundreds of forms may put an end to the existence of the system. Still more frequently, the external circumstances may accelerate or retard, facilitate or hinder, reinforce or weaken a realization of the immanent potentialities of the system and therefore of its destiny. All this is granted as self-evident. And yet, all this does not determine fundamentally the "normal" career and phases of the development of the system. All this does not and cannot force the system *a* (oak, man, criminal gang), destined to have a life career *b* to have a life career fundamentally different, for which *a* does not have any potentiality.

C. *Immanent self-determinism as synthesis of determinism and indeterminism.* The preceding analysis raises the question: What is the relationship of the immanent principle to the problem of determinism–indeterminism? Is the immanent principle of change a variety of determinism, or is it that of indeterminism? The answer is: neither or both. So far as the immanent principle implies that the normal course and the essential traits of the system are greatly determined by the potentialities of the system at the moment of emergence, it is self-deterministic. It is also deterministic so far as the influence of external factors is concerned, when it reaches beyond the margin of the system's autonomy. Considering, however, that the determining potentialities of the system are the system itself and are its immanent properties, the determinism of the system turns into self-determinism. Self-determinism is the equivalent of freedom. When we ourselves determine something, we feel ourselves free; and especially when this self-determination flows spontaneously from us as something quite natural to us and emanating from our very nature. The self-determination of a system is exactly this: it is rooted in the system; it expresses its very nature and its most essential potentialities; it flows spontaneously from the system and cannot do otherwise. For all these reasons the principle of immanent self-determination is equivalent to the principle of *sui generis,* different from determinism and indeterminism. It is different from both also in the sense that the very notion of the potentialities of the system, as we shall see in the next paragraph, contains an element of indeterminacy on its fringes and in no way means a rigid necessity, as has been shown above. In all these aspects, the principle of immanent change of a system implies a considerable margin of autonomy from all the agencies that are external to the system; and also some amount of indeterminacy within the system itself, so far as realization of its potentialities is concerned.

Such is the definite and precise answer to the question raised. The answer appears to be more adequate and sound than the half-truths of pure determinism and indeterminism. The stated principle organically and logically unites in itself the valid parts of either of these principles and is free from the fallacies of either. It clearly indicates in what sense and to what degree the sociocultural system is free and in what respects it is deterministic. In application to man and man's sociocultural world it synthesizes the doctrine of "free will" with the doctrine of determinism and "predestination." The next paragraph will specify still more fully the conclusion reached.

D. *Principle of differential degrees of self-determination and dependence for various sociocultural systems.* If any sociocultural system bears in itself the reason of its change and determination of its destiny, three questions arise: (1) In the unfolding of the potentialities of the system in its life career, is there only one quite rigid and definite course for the system, or are there several possibilities or routes to be traveled? (2) Is the margin of self-determination of the system and its dependence upon the external conditions the same for all sociocultural systems, or is it different for different systems? (3) If so, upon what conditions does the relative portion of self-determination and dependence upon external agencies in the systems depend?

The answer to the first question is as follows: The role of the external milieu and the nature of the immanent potentialities of any sociocultural system force us to admit a margin of indetermined possibilities in the development of the life career of the system. I say a "margin," not the complete indeterminacy. Such a margin means the rejection of a fatalistic and absolutely determined course of development of the system. Put in symbolic form, this thesis means that a given system a has an immanent potentiality b, which has to be unfolded in the course of its existence. Due to environmental factors and to potentiality containing a margin of variations at its fringes, this b in one case will actualize into ba, in another into bb, in the third into bc, and so on, up to bn. In different external milieus, the difference between the actualizations of this b will be still greater.

Turn now to the second question: Is the margin of self-determination of the future career of the system the same for all sociocultural systems? Are all the social and cultural systems equally dependent or independent of the external conditions in shaping their own destiny?

This destiny is shaped, as we have seen, by the immanent forces of the system itself and by the milieu in which it exists. Are the shares of both "molders" constant for any system?

The amount of self-determination of a system's destiny depends first upon the kind of social or cultural system and, second, upon the kind of milieu.

Third, we must distinguish farther between the total and the specific immunity of the system from its environment in the molding of its own destiny.

Let us assume, first, that we have social and cultural systems of the same kind: say, the family, or the state, or the business firm; or a philosophical school or an art system.

E. Other conditions being equal (including the milieu), in the social and cultural systems of the same kind, the greater and better is their integration, the greater is their self-determination (and autonomy from the environment) in molding their own destiny.

Unfolded, the proposition implies:

1. Other conditions being equal, of the social and cultural complexes, the least amount of self-determination is found in unorganized social groups and in cultural congeries.

2. Other conditions being equal, the highest amount of self-determination belongs to those social and cultural systems which are most perfectly integrated, causally and meaningfully, where the causal interdependence of the components and elements of the system is the greatest and their relationship is the most solidary (among human agents) and most consistent among the components, where, neither actually nor potentially, is there any contradiction, any *Spannung*, any inner tension, antagonism, or conflict.

Finally, between these types stand the intermediate systems, which are neither congeries nor perfectly integrated systems. Such are the social systems where only the causal interdependence is found but where relationships are not quite solidary; or the cultural systems where relationships of the elements of the system are somewhat eclectic, not quite consistent, and actually or latently conflicting between and in each of its components. In such systems there always is found what Max Weber, M. Scheler, and E. Barthel style *Spannung*, a kind of tension or latent antagonism; a hidden split or crack, which flares into an open split of the system as soon as the respective adverse interference of the external conditions takes place.

One word of caution: integration and lack of it should not be mixed with fashionable terms like "plasticity," "capacity of adjustment to environment," "progressiveness," and the like. These terms are not equivalent to good or poor integration.

Well-integrated systems may be both elastic and rigid in their structure and tactics, according to the conditions; the same is true of the poorly integrated systems.

Of other conditions relevant to the amount of self-direction of a system in molding its own destiny, the following ones can be mentioned:

3. Other conditions being equal (including the identical environment and the perfection of integration), the greater the power of the

system, the greater its autonomy from the social, biological, and cosmic environment and the greater its self-control and self-direction. The proposition seems almost axiomatic. But the weakness of the proposition consists in the indeterminacy of the term "power." Left at that, it is valid, but fairly indefinite. What is the power of a sociocultural system? How can it be measured? And measured it must be, in order that we can say which system is more powerful.

I do not know any satisfactory device for a measurement as well as for a clear definition of the power of a social or cultural system. All that one can do is to indicate a few rough criteria which are somewhat measurable and which can give at least a very rough, but nevertheless hardly misleading, "index" of the power of the system.

Other conditions being equal, (a) the greater the membership of a social system; (b) the better their biological and mental and social qualities; (c) the greater the sum total of real knowledge, experience, and wisdom at its disposal; (d) the more efficient its organization in the sense of the distribution of rights-duties-functions among its members (including the distribution to everybody according to his talent and ability); (e) the greater the sum total of the means and instruments of influencing human conduct as well as of modifying biological and cosmic nature; and, finally, (f) the better its solidary integration (discussed above); the greater is the power of the group—the more independent it is from the external conditions in the realization of its potentialities.

With a slight modification, the same criteria are applicable to the comparative power of cultural systems. The greater the number of the human agents of the system (of art, religion, philosophy, science, etc.); the better their biological, mental, moral, and social qualities; the greater the wisdom, knowledge, and value it incorporates (value or system of meanings: religious, scientific, artistic, ethical, etc.); the better it fits the social organization of its followers; the greater is its logico-causal integration (within the system of meanings and between all its components); the greater the sum total of means or vehicles for its unfolding, broadcasting, and maintenance at its disposal; the greater the power of the cultural system—the more independent it is from its environmental forces.

Here, however, a greater emphasis is to be put upon the value (the system of meanings) the system incorporates and the consistency of the integration of its elements and components than in the social system.

Each of these conditions is unquestionably a basic constituent of the power of a social or cultural system. Taken separately, each condition cannot be an index of the power of the system. Taken together, they give a very approximate, but hardly misleading, indicator of that power.

This proposition then sums up, if not all, then probably the most essential uniform conditions of the comparative autonomy of the system (in building its destiny) from the external conditions, and explain the relative share of the system's self-control and self-regulation in molding its own destiny.

Summary

1. The reason or cause of a change of any sociocultural system is in the system itself, and need not be looked for anywhere else.

2. Additional reason for change of a system is its milieu, which is again composed mostly of the immanently changing systems.

3. Any sociocultural system changing immanently incessantly generates a series of immanent consequences, which change not only the milieu of the system but also the system itself.

4. Bearing the seeds of its change in itself, any sociocultural system bears also in itself the power of molding its own destiny or life career. Beginning with the moment of emergence, each sociocultural system is the main factor of its own destiny. This destiny, or the system's subsequent life career, represents mainly an unfolding of the immanent potentialities of the system in the course of its existence.

5. The environmental forces are not negligible, but their role consists essentially in retardation or acceleration, facilitation or hindrance, reinforcement or weakening of the realization of the immanent potentialities of the system. Sometimes they can crush the system and put an end to its existence or stop the process of unfolding the immanent potentialities at one of the early phases. They cannot, however, change fundamentally the immanent potentialities of the system and its normal destiny in the sense of making the life career of an unfolding acorn that of a cow, or vice versa.

6. So far as the system, since the moment of its emergence, bears in itself its future career, it is a self-determining system. So far as the future of the system is determined mainly by the system itself, such self-determination is free, as flowing spontaneously, in accordance with nature, from the system itself. This self-determination is different from determinism and indeterminism. It is a principle *sui generis*.

7. The process of unfolding the immanent potentialities of the emerged system is somewhat predetermined by the system, but this

predetermination leaves a considerable margin for variations. In this sense it is not absolutely and narrowly preconditioned. Only the main direction and the main phases of the unfolding are predetermined; the rest, including most of the details, are "free" and become an unforeseen and unpredictable matter of chance, environment, and free choice of the system.

8. Since the destiny or life career of any system is the result of the system's self-control and of the influence of the environmental forces, the relative share of each of these two factors in molding the system's career is not constant for all sociocultural systems. The share of the self-control of the system is the greater, the more perfectly the system is integrated and the more powerful it is.

9. As a rough indicator of the elusive concept of the power of a sociocultural system, the following less elusive combination of the criteria is offered: the greater the membership of the system; the better the members biologically, mentally, morally, and socially; the greater the actual wisdom, knowledge, and experience the system has at its disposal; the better it is organized; the greater the total sum of means of influencing human behavior and forces of nature at its disposal; the more solidarily (or consistently) the system is integrated; the more powerful it is; the more independent from the forces of the environment—the greater is the share of its own control in molding its destiny.

IV

GLOBAL CONFLICT AND SOCIAL RESOLUTION

War and Revolution

18

The Perversion of Human Behavior
in Revolution

After many years of peaceful "organic" evolution, the history of mankind has entered again into a "critical" period. Revolution, hated by some people and welcomed by others, has come at last. Some societies are burning in its fire already; toward others this danger is approaching. Who can predict how wide this conflagration of revolution will spread? Who can be quite sure that this hurricane will not sooner or later destroy his own house? No one. But if we cannot predict that, we can at least know what revolution is. We live amidst it. Like a naturalist, we can observe, analyze, and study it.

For five years the author of this book has lived in the circle of the Russian Revolution. Day after day during this time he has watched it. This book is a result of this observation. It represents not an ideographic description of the Russian Revolution but an essay in sociological analysis of the phenomena typical of all serious and great revolutions. The task of a historian is to portray a strict description of a concrete historical event in all its individuality and unrepeated singularity. The task of a sociologist is considerably different: in all social phenomena, only those traits are interesting for him which are general for all facts of the same type whenever and wherever they may have happened. Sombart says quite rightly: "The battle *at Tannenberg* is the object of historical investigation; "*the battle* at Tannenberg is the object of sociology. The University *of Berlin* belongs to the sphere of History; *the University* of Berlin to the department of sociology."[1] Similarly the *Russian* Revolution with all its details is the object of a historian. The Russian *Revolution,* as a type of revolution, is the object of the sociologist.

It is true that we are very often told: "The history of mankind does not repeat itself." But is the history of the earth repeated and that of the

Originally published in *The Sociology of Revolution* (Philadelphia: J. B. Lippincott, 1925), 3–16. Reprinted by permission of Dr. Sergei Sorokin.
    1. W. Sombart, *Soziologie* (1923), sec. 7.

solar system and of the accessible part of the world? With all identity organisms, cells, and their elements are not repeated either. Does this fact prevent the repetition, in this unrepeated process, of many phenomena which are described in the laws of physics, chemistry, and biology? Is it not true that on the earth H_2 and O have given water innumerable times in spite of the unrepeated history of the earth? Have not the phenomena and causal relations described in the laws of Newton, Mendel, Avogadro, and Gerard been repeated countless times? By this I want to say that the historical process, though unrepeated as a whole, is woven out of repeated elements. This is as true of the history of mankind as it is of the history of organic and inorganic nature. Here also "similar causes under similar conditions produce similar results." War and peace, famine and prosperity, conquest and liberation, growth and decay of religion, government of minority and government of majority, etc.—all these phenomena taken as causes have repeated frequently in different relations of space and time. In spite of all the different conditions in which these processes have taken place, the fundamental similarity of the phenomena of the same type—for example, of war wherever and whenever it has taken place—could not be annihilated absolutely by these different accompanying conditions. Therefore the results of these similar causes had to be repeated in a more or less complete degree. The theory of the Book of Ecclesiastes was not far from the truth. The fundamental fault of the many theorists of the philosophy of History has consisted only in that they have looked for "repetition" not where repetitions ought to be sought. The latter are seen not in the complicated and great events of History but in the elementary, usual, and daily facts from which the former are composed and into which they can be analyzed.[2]

From this point of view it seems that the uninterrupted creation of history is not so endlessly new and inexhaustible as they imagine. History is like an author who without interruption is writing ever new dramas, tragedies, and comedies with new characters and heroes, with new scenery and environment, but . . . with the old subjects which many times in the previous works of this indefatigable author have been repeated before. Like the writer who has written himself out, history, in spite of all its creative forces, has to be repeated.

All of the above may be said of the great tragedy called "revolu-

---

2. See about this principle of repetition my *A System of Sociology.* See also Tarde, *Social Laws,* chap. 1; A. Bauer, *Essai sur la Revolution,* 1–8; corresponding pages in E. Hayes, *Introduction to the Study of Sociology* (New York: Appleton, 1922); and E. Ross, *Foundations of Sociology* (New York: Macmillan, 1919).

tion." It has been given on the historical scene rather often. Every staging of it is new. The conditions of time and space, scenery and actors, their costumes, monologues, dialogues, and the chorus of the crowd, the quantity of the acts and of "striking scenes"—all these are variated. But, nevertheless, in all this dissimilarity a great many similarities are repeated. All these different actors amidst the different scenery act the same play called "revolution."

Let us now ask ourselves: What is revolution?

We have a great many definitions of the latter. The most numerous amongst them represent very incorrect conceptions. To these belong the "sweet" definitions, on the one hand, and the "bitter," on the other. I mean by this the definitions which deal with imaginative but not with real revolutions as they have been given in history.

E. Bernstein says, "At the present time it is possible to name as revolutions only those periods in which the amount of liberty is increased." Another writer asserts, "The October *coup d'état* is usually described as revolution; but torture and revolution are incompatible. As in Soviet Russia, where tortures are usual phenomena, there is only reaction but not revolution."

These conceptions of revolution may be taken as examples of the fictitious—"sweet"—definitions for, as the reader will see further, almost all revolutions during revolutionary and postrevolutionary periods have not only augmented the sum of the freedom of the population but have regularly reduced it. May it be inferred from this that many ancient and medieval revolutions, as well as the great French Revolution, are not revolutions? Revolution and torture not only do not represent incompatible phenomena but, on the contrary, in fact every revolutionary time has always been stamped with a great increase of murders, sadism, cruelty, bestiality, and tortures. Does it follow from their cruelties that the Russian or French, English or Hussite revolutions are not revolutions?

These examples show the incorrectness and subjectivity of such conceptions of revolution. Their authors are Don Quixotes of revolution, who do not want to see the real prosaic girl of Toboso or the barber's basin, and see in them the beautiful Dulzinea or wonderful knight's helmet. Some of these "illusionists" try to get out of these contradictions by pointing out that all these negative traits of revolution do not belong to its essence and represent only "occasional elements" in it or are the expression of "reaction" but not of "revolution." In this argument is hidden the same illusionism. If almost all revolutions are regularly accompanied with such negative traits (torture, diminution of liberty, pauperization, growth of bestiality, and so on), then what objective reason have we to call these traits "occasional accompaniments"? To consider them as "occasional accompaniments" of revolution is no more possible than to consider the abatement of mercury in the thermometer as an "occasional accompaniment" of abatement of temperature. The "illusionists" like to appeal to "the reaction" as a source of all negative phenomena connected with revolution. Alas! They scarcely give themselves an adequate account of the great significance of this reference.

It is possible that they may be surprised at the statement that every revolutionary period as a whole inevitably consists of two stages indissolubly connected with one another. "Reaction" is not a phenomenon beyond the limits of revolution but is an unavoidable part of the revolutionary process itself, its second half. The dictatorship of Robespierre or Lenin, Cromwell or Žižka, signified not the end but the flare of revolution. The former was only the mark of its transition into the second stage—the stage of "reaction" or "restraint"—but not its end. Only when "reaction" is finished, when society enters the period of its normal evolution—only then revolution may be considered as finished. These "illusionists" condemning "reaction" do not understand that by this they blame nothing but revolution itself in its second stage.

This idea is illustrated in the following scheme:

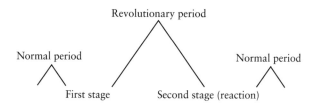

What is said above of the "sweet" illusionists may be likewise applied to the "bitter" ones.

Regarding revolution as a "creation of Satan," they are as far from understanding real revolution as the former. By praising "reaction," they are not aware that in spite of their hating revolution they laud it, only not in its first but in its second stage. . . .

There is nothing to be said against this sort of definitions save that they are too formal and do not give quite a complete representation of revolution. It is not my intention to add to all these definitions one more. Social sciences abuse definitions too much, often giving nothing in essence but only a formal conception. I will act in another way, as naturalists usually do. I will make a study of a series of revolutions of different times and peoples: the Russian revolutions of 1905, 1917–

24, and that of the seventeenth century; the French revolutions of 1789, 1848, 1870–71; the German Revolution of 1848; the English Revolution of the seventeenth century; some medieval and antique revolutionary periods; the Egyptian, Persian, and other great revolutions. This study should give the fundamental traits of what is styled as revolution.

Only such revolutions as the Czecho-Slovak of 1918 and the American of the eighteenth century, which do not represent the struggle of one part of the same society with another but rather the struggle of a society with another quite different from the former, I exclude from my study. Revolutions of this sort are rather the processes of war and differ considerably from revolutions proceeding within the confines of the same society.

Of the latter revolutions, my attention is fixed principally on the great and deep ones because they show us the typical characteristics of them most clearly. Among them I analyze with the greatest attention the Russian Revolution proceeding before our eyes. It is worthy of this attention: it is one of the greatest revolutions; I have had the opportunity to study it directly; and, finally, it pours light upon many sides of other revolutions.

The two latter conditions, from my point of view, are particularly important. In spite of the popular opinion about "the judgment of history" expressed in the statements that "it is better seen from the distance"; that "after many generations a better valuation of historical events is possible"; that "not through the present must the past be explained, but on the contrary"—in spite of this, I think the opposite opinion is more true.

Not the descendants, but the contemporaries, are the better observers and judges of historical events. The experience of the former, founded only on certain documents, is very unsatisfactory, while the experience of the latter is direct; the acquaintance of contemporaries with events is adequate, as they perceive them daily and personally, while the knowledge of the descendants is indirect, occasional, fragmentary, and disfigured. This statement is at any rate true in the case of those contemporaries who enlarge the circle of their personal experience by the experience of other people, by statistical observations, and other scientific methods of supplementing and correcting the individual experience. Utilizing these aids, the contemporary generation is better guaranteed against mistakes than a historian who studies these events some generations after and against the errors of a foreigner observing from a distance the rare and occasional facts that reach his notice.

In natural sciences the direct experience has long been preferred to the indirect. Here usually the past is explained by the present observations or experiment. In social sciences the full value is not yet sufficiently understood of explaining the past by the present, of trying to understand many outlived historical events by the direct observation and investigation of the processes proceeding around us.

The above explains why I give the greatest attention to the Russian Revolution. Its direct observation helps to understand other revolutions and makes their many sides comprehensible. A series of revolutions studied in this manner provide us indeed with many similarities and regularities of which in their total is composed the typical phenomenon styled as revolution. What these traits are the reader will see later. Here I will say only that the definitions criticized above not only fail to point out all the characteristics of revolution but scarcely indicate the characteristics that are most fundamental. . . .

The real nature of revolution is very different from these romantic representations of it which are usual among its apologists. Many of its traits pointed out in this book may appear to them as offensive, as disfiguring "the beautiful face of revolution." Therefore they may find "a reactionary mind" in my book.

What, then? I willingly agree to this accusation and am ready to accept the name of "reactionary" but a reactionary of a very unusual type.

The reader will gather from the book that revolution is a bad method for the improvement of the material and spiritual conditions of the masses. Verbally promising the realization of many of the greatest values, in fact it leads as often and as much to opposite results. Revolution does not tend to socialize so much as it tends to biologize the people; does not only increase but also reduces the sum of liberties; does not improve alone but also impairs the economic and spiritual state of the working classes. Whatever gains it yields are purchased at a prodigious and disproportionate cost. It punishes not only and not so much those aristocratic classes which, thanks to their parasitism, licentiousness, incapacity, and oblivion of social duties deserve, if not punishment, then at least degradation from great position, as it punishes millions of the poor and working classes who in the paroxysm of despair think to find the end of their misery in revolution. If such are the objective results of revolution, then in the name of man, his prosperity, his rights, his freedom, and for the sake of the material and spiritual progress of the working classes, it is not only my right but it is my duty to abstain from the idolatry of revolution. Amongst many "idols" of Bacon there is also "the Idol of Revolution." Amongst numerous idolators and dogmatists who sacrifice man to different idols there are many idolators of revolution. In spite of many millions of men sacrificed to this "god," its worshippers continue to demand new and ever new hecatombs. Is it not time to abstain from this demand and finish this sacrificing? Like every dangerous illness, revolution represents the results of many causes. But the inevitability of disease does not oblige me to welcome and laud it. If this ideology is "reaction," I willingly accept the epithet of "reactionary."

The history of social progress teaches us that all fundamental and really progressive acquisitions have been the results of knowledge, peace, solidarity, cooperation, and love; but not the results of hate, bestiality, and mad struggle which are inevitably connected with every great revolution. This explains why in answer to the calls of revolution I should like to say: "My Father, let this cup pass from them." It is true that all these apprehensions are considerably diminished in connection with "little" revolutions not followed by great civil war. At first it seems very commendable to overthrow without blood-struggle incapable government and degenerated aristocracy which hinder social progress. If the real situation were such, I should not have objected at all to revolution. I am not a defender of any parasitic, talentless, and corrupt aristocracy. But, alas, revolutions, spoken of in the terms of medicine, represent *maladie a-typique*, the development of which it is impossible to foresee. Sometimes, beginning with a slightly dangerous symptom, it suddenly becomes worse and ends with death. The same may be said of revolution. Who can be quite sure that by setting fire to a little pile of revolution, he does not start the beginning of a great conflagration which will burn not only the tyrants but the incendiaries themselves with many thousands of innocent people as well. Therefore in this problem it is absolutely necessary to "consider seven times before cutting once."

This is necessary to bear in mind, especially now when the air is full of combustible material, when order—a necessary condition of every progress—is troubled, and the storm of the horrible revolution threatens to spread over many societies.

At the present time mankind more than at any time needs order. Even imperfect order is now better than disorder, as "a bad peace is better than a good quarrel."

Instead of revolutionary experiments, there are other methods of improvement and reconstruction of social organization. The principal canons of the latter are the following:

1. A reform must not violate human nature and contradict its fundamental instincts. The Russian revolutionary experiment, as well as many other revolutions, give us examples of the opposite.

2. An attentive scientific study of concrete social conditions has to precede every practical realization of reform in them. A great part of revolutionary reconstruction breaks this rule.

3. Every reconstructive experiment at first must be tested on a small scale. Only when it gives a positive result is it possible to realize it on a greater scale. Revolutions neglect this canon.

4. Reforms have to be realized only by legal and constitutional means. Revolutions disdain these restrictions.[3]

A violation of these canons renders every endeavor at social reconstruction unsuccessful. Similar canons are understood and applied, for example, . . . [to] improving a breed of cows. But, alas, these canons very often are considered unnecessary in the reconstruction of human society. An ignorant man here often becomes a leader of revolutionary reforms; a consideration of real conditions is not seldom condemned as "bourgeois prejudice"; demand for prudence as cowardice or civil dishonesty; the demands of peaceful and legal methods as "reaction." "The spirit of destruction" here *eo ipso* is recognized as the "spirit of creation." These "revolutionary methods" make the failure of revolutionary reconstructions and their sacrifices quite comprehensible. An inhabitant of some other planet watching these facts might conclude that on the earth cows . . . are more valued than human creatures: the former are often treated with more consideration than the latter; they are not sacrificed so willingly and in so numerous quantity as men are sacrificed *ad majorem gloriam* of revolution.

It is difficult to decide whether everyone observing these facts ought to weep or smile.

At any rate it will not be unjust to equalize the rights of man in this respect to the privileges of a . . . cow. This demand is rather modest and easier of realization than the demands of many "Declarations of the Rights of Man and Citizen."

---

3. See about this Hayes, *Introduction to the Study of Sociology,* chap. on social control, and his *Sociology and Ethics* (New York: Appleton & Co., 1921). See also Ross, *The Principles of Sociology* (New York: The Century Co., 1920), chap. 45.

19

The Cause and Factors of War and Peace

Main Cause versus Multiple Causation

In order that a diagnosis of the preconditions of peace may be precise and fruitful, we must distinguish between the main or necessary cause of peace and its supplementary factors, both positive and negative. By the main or necessary condition is meant the factor without which peace cannot prevail. By the supplementary factors are meant the numerous and diverse conditions that either facilitate the realization of the effects of the necessary cause or neutralize them. Thus, in diphtheria, the necessary cause is infection. Positive supplementary factors are those conditions favoring the spread of germs and decreasing the immunity of the human organism to infection; negative supplementary factors are inoculation and similar influences that neutralize or inhibit the effects of infection, thereby turning the necessary cause into an *insufficient* cause. The necessary cause of birth is conception. The positive supplementary factors are all the conditions that favor the growth of the fetus into a child. Negative supplementary conditions are those which, like abortion and disease, inhibit this development of the fetus. The main cause of a given phenomenon is always the same, but the supplementary factors are diverse, variable, and shifting in their nature as well as in their combinations.

I am perfectly aware of the many objections against distinguishing between the necessary cause and the supplementary factors. These objections can be found in almost all the serious treatises on inductive logic, such as those by J. S. Mill, A. A. Tshuproff, J. Venn, C. Sigwart, and others, as well as in a number of special monographs on causality. However, the logical and investigational advantages of such a distinction are so great, and its disadvantages so comparatively small, that the objections can be disregarded. They are really far from decisive. The principle of the main cause and supplementary factors is generally used in causal analysis throughout the natural sciences. Their experi-

Originally published in *The Annual Report of the American Historical Association* 3 (1942): 83–95. Reprinted by permission of the publisher.

ence confirms its validity and fruitfulness. Nearly all the advances in the natural sciences have involved the discovery of the main or necessary cause of a given phenomenon and some of its supplementary factors.

Without such a procedure we are hopelessly lost in almost any causal analysis of sociocultural phenomena in general, and of war and peace in particular. The "multiple-factor" theory of war (or peace) looks nice on paper, especially when it is given a mathematical appearance: "War is a function of the variable a, b, c, . . . m [$w = f(a, b, c, . . .)$]." But as soon as the formula is applied to real variables, it becomes either meaningless nonsense or a denial of causation. It results in an infinite regression leading either to a "Prime Mover" or to the proposition that the whole world is the cause of everything. First, it is impossible to describe the countless antecedent conditions of a particular war or of war in general. Second, if such a description were possible, it would not clarify the causes of war at all because it would remain but an incomplete catalogue of millions of conditions without any distinction as to which of these are causal and which are incidental. Third, if the theory of multiple causation means a selection of a few of the myriad circumstances amidst which war occurs, the choice is bound to be perfectly arbitrary. The selected variables would be so heterogeneous, incommensurable, and noncomparable that no one could combine them into a meaningful unity. Still less could one measure their relative causative power.

Suppose from the countless antecedent conditions of World War I we select the vicissitudes of the Czarist regime in Russia, the shot at Sarajevo, the visit of Poincaré to Russia in the summer of 1914, heterogeneous composition of the Hapsburg empire, the peculiarities of the psychology of Viscount Gray or of Wilhelm Hohenzollern, the rainy season in some part of central Europe, Germany's expansionist policy, the state of the sunspots, and the Franco–English–Russian alliance. Anyone who puts these or other heterogeneous variables into one formula produces nothing but a meaningless collection of words without sense or unity. We cannot measure the relative causal role of any of these in commensurable factors. Hence, the theory of multiple causation is not applicable to sociocultural phenomena generally, or to the study of war and peace in particular.[1] It is far more inadequate than the theory of a main cause and supplementary factors. This explains why I use the latter in preference to the former.

1. See a development of this criticism of multiple causation and of other pseudo-mathematical procedures in my *Sociocultural Causality, Space, Time* (Durham, 1943).

Main Cause of Internal and International Peace

1. The main cause of internal social peace is the presence in the given society of a well-integrated system of basic values, with their corresponding norms of conduct.[2] The fundamental values of the various factions and members of the society must be essentially in harmony with this system and with one another.

2. The main cause of international peace is the presence in each of the interacting societies of a well-integrated system of ultimate values and their norms, all of which are compatible with one another.

3. In a given universe of societies or within a particular society, the probability of peace varies directly with the integration of the systems of the basic values and their mutual compatibility. When their integration and harmoniousness decline, especially suddenly and sharply, the chances for international or civil war increase.

Before elaborating these propositions, a few clarifying comments are in order.

A. Our attention is focused on the main values and not on the minor values of the given societies. What exactly are the major values of any society must be found by factual investigation. In general they are composed of the basic ethicojuridical, religious, scientific, economic, political, and aesthetic values and those of self-respect and independence. This does not prevent different societies from stressing now religious, now economic, now political values as *primus inter pares*. In spite of such concrete differences from society to society and from period to period, these values are generally fundamental ones.

B. We speak not of this or that specific value but of a system of all the primary values. Where the main values are integrated, they make one unified system in which they are all meaningfully interconnected and causally interdependent. When one of the basic values of a society becomes incompatible with certain main values of another society, the whole system of one becomes irreconcilable with the system of the other. In the causation of either peace or war, this or that isolated value does not operate alone, but the whole system of major values as a whole is the effective unit.

C. By integration of the main values is meant their meaningful-causal interdependence—meaningful in the sense that they are logically or aesthetically consistent, articulating the same values, princi-

---

2. Every basic value has its set norms of conduct, with their "thou shalt" and "thou shalt not." Religious, ethicojuridical, scientific, economic, political, aesthetic values—each has its code conduct.

ples, and norms in different ways; causal in the sense that when one of them changes notably, the rest also change. When the whole system experiences a transmutation, each of the main values undergoes a corresponding transformation. Values that do not have this meaningful-causal interdependence remain unintegrated; those losing their previous integration become disintegrated.[3]

D. Finally, we are concerned with the compatibility of the systems of values but not with their similarity, homogeneity, or identity. The point is that two systems of values may be heterogeneous and yet not incompatible with one another. In a society like ours, the citizens have different religions, aesthetic tastes, and political ideas. Yet they are compatible with one another, and their heterogeneity does not lead to civil war.

Having clarified these propositions, we may ask what are the evidences of their validity.

Evidence of the Validity of the Propositions

The following negative and positive corroborations can be mentioned. Each of these sets of evidence sums up in a fairly regularly repeated uniformity and therefore is a more adequate proof than a mere collection of singularistic facts. Let us begin with the series of negative corroborations.[4]

Negative Evidence

By negative proofs are meant those uniformities that exhibit either an explosion or increase of war whenever the integration of the main values of their compatibility decreases. If this decrease occurs among the factions and members of a given society, the result is civil war or severe and bloody punishment. If the decrease of integration and harmony occurs among the value systems of different societies, the result is international war.

A. The first set of negative corroborations consists of the countless outbreaks of war when two hitherto isolated societies, with different systems of values, come for the first time into direct and durable con-

3. See on this my *Social and Cultural Dynamics* (New York, 1937–41), 4: chaps. 1, 2, 3.
4. Factual data for corroboration cannot be given in this short paper but they can be found in ibid., vol. 3, chaps. 9–14; and in Quincy Wright, *A Study of War*, 2 vols. (Chicago, 1942).

tact. The contact makes real the potential irreconcilability of their contrasting main values. According to the proposition, such a situation must lead to war, and it has done so fairly uniformly, in ancient as well as in more recent times. Quincy Wright's study shows that the warfare of comparatively isolated peoples has the lowest mean index (2.03); next come peoples with moderate intercultural contacts (index: 2.59); finally the peoples with wide and close cultural contacts (index: 2.91).[5] Early history and anthropology give us hundreds of cases of wars occasioned by the meeting of two formerly isolated tribes. If their basic values were different, such a contact has almost invariably been followed by warfare. The same is true of historical societies. A notable portion of the wars of these societies occurred precisely when, in the process of migration or expansion or colonization, one society met another for the first time. The contact was almost invariably followed by wars, whether of defense, offense, misunderstanding, subjugation, or colonization, even when the societies had no conscious military objectives. So it was in the history of Egypt, Babylonia, China and Persia, Greece and Rome, Europe and the Americas. When Egyptians met Nubians or Palestinians or Hyksos or any other group with different values, war followed. When in the process of peaceful colonization the Greeks met other peoples and societies, war took place. The same is true of the Macedonians and the Romans throughout their history. The expansion of these empires meant contact with other societies having different systems of values. The resultant wars lasted until one part was destroyed or subjugated, or their values became compatible. The same is true when West met East; when the Spaniards met the aboriginal Americans; and so on through the chronic colonial wars that have been going on continually.

B. This partly explains why the rapid expansion of contact and communication after the thirteenth century has been followed by an increase of war on this planet. New technical means of communication and transportation have brought face to face an ever increasing number of tribes, societies, nations, and empires. The irreconcilability of their value systems was thus systematically intensified. Consequently wars, especially colonial conflicts, increased until, in the nineteenth century, the truly isolated groups had almost disappeared. They all were subjugated by force and then divided between the great powers.

In all these wars the real cause is not the fact of contact and expansion of intersocietal interaction. By themselves contact and interaction are neither war-making nor peace-making factors. Contact and inter-

5. Wright, *A Study of War*, 559. See also table 12 on p. 557.

action as such are not the cause of diphtheria: a person can have thousands of contacts with other persons and still be free from diphtheria. He may be in touch with a sick person and yet remain healthy as long as he does not get the infection. The cause is infection by the germs; contact is a facilitating circumstance. Similarly, intersocietal contact and interaction do not lead to war, if the value systems of the respective societies are not incompatible. The cause is the incompatibility. Social contact and interaction are facilitating factors.

C. The third set of corroborations is given by civil wars arising from a rapid and fundamental change in the ultimate values of one part of a given society while the other part either does not undergo it or moves in the opposite direction. This means a rapid increase in the incompatibility of the main values of the two parts of the society. According to the present thesis, some sort of civil strife should follow such a transformation. And this has uniformly been the case. Practically all the civil wars of the past have emerged from a sudden increase of the contrast in the major values of revolutionaries and counterrevolutionaries. From the civil wars of Egypt and Persia to the recent upheavals of Russia and Spain, history consistently offers evidence of the validity of our proposition.

D. The fourth set of proofs consists of the cases where in the universe of interacting societies a profound transformation of the value systems occurs only in one or a few without occurring simultaneously in the other interacting societies. Such a situation means again a greater incompatibility of the values of these societies. The result of such an increase has uniformly been an outbreak of war between the societies involved. Take, for instance, the historical cases of profound religious transformation. When Akhenaton's religious revolution occurred in ancient Egypt, the result was civil and then international war. When the Buddhist religious transformation occurred in India, a similar series of conflicts followed. The emergence of Christianity, the Byzantian iconoclastic reformation, and the Protestant Reformation each resulted in a long series of wars. The same is true of such religious variations of Christianity as the Hussite movement and the Albigensian "heresy." The story has been repeated many times in human history with monotonous uniformity.

If the transformation occurs in the realm of political or politico-economic values, it assumes the form of a political or politico-economic revolution. If the changes in one society are sufficiently radical, they are generally followed by a series of "revolutionaries wars" with the unrevolutionized neighbors. The wars of the Cromwellian, French, Russian, and Nazi revolutions are typical illustrations of the uniformity. There are few profound political or economico-political revolutions in history without their aftermaths of war.

E. A fifth group of proofs is epitomized by the fact of the increase of war attendant upon an acceleration of sociocultural change in a given universe of interacting societies. This is especially true in the West and throughout the world during the last five centuries. The real cause of an increase of war in such periods is not acceleration. If it proceeds at an orderly and uniform pace in all societies, no intensified irreconcilability of the value systems occurs, and therefore no internal or external war follows. This is witnessed, for instance, by the rapid rate of change in Europe and America during the second part of the nineteenth century. Variation in the tempo of change per se is neither a war-making nor a peace-making factor. It is neutral. If it has made for war in certain cases, the reason is that not all the societies changed at the same rate. This made for greater incompatibility in their value systems; hence the increase of bloody conflicts. During rapid change, the main values are in a state of flux and do not have time to "settle" and become universal; they become somewhat disintegrated, thereby further facilitating war.

F. The sixth category of evidence includes the following facts. Empires composed of highly heterogeneous and conflicting populations and cultures often initiate wars in order to prevent a development of internal movements threatening their unity. In cases of this kind, the incompatibility first manifests itself internally, in the form of struggle and civil war. This eventually provokes international war.

G. We next consider the opposite instance, where the nation is perfectly integrated internally. In other words, it is highly nationalistic. But being thus unified, it differs fundamentally from other societies with respect to its system of values. Its norms are incompatible with theirs. An ultranationalistic state does not respect or tolerate its neighbors' ways. The uniform result of such arrogance and intolerance has been war.

In both of these cases the cause of the wars is not heterogeneity or homogeneity per se. In different situations they could lead to other results. In the situations described, they lead to war because they produce a clash of the values of the given societies.

H. The eighth series of corroborations involves the major movements in the magnitude of war in the history of Greece, Rome, and European countries from the sixth century B.C. to the present time.[6] Two recently computed "curves" of the movement of war in these

---

6. For the facts and details, see the four volumes of my *Dynamics*.

countries—my own and Quincy Wright's—agree in practically all essential points. The major fluctuations of these curves cannot be accounted for by any hypothesis except the one proposed herein. According to our hypothesis, we should expect the greatest magnitude of war, measured by the casualties per million of the population, in the periods of radical transformation of the main values of the societies. That is exactly what these curves show.

In Greece the most belligerent centuries are the fourth and fifth B.C. We know that these centuries saw a most profound and rapid transformation of the value system of Greek society. The old religious or ideational system was crumbling; the new sensate system was not yet built. All Greece was in a state of immense flux. No value or norm remained universally binding for all states, groups, or individuals. Complete sociocultural anomie became supreme. In these conditions, the incompatibility of the common values enormously increased.

When values cease to be universally binding, their controlling power evaporates. Human beings and groups become dominated mainly by blind, egotistic, biological impulses. Brute force supplemented by fraud becomes supreme. It would be a miracle if under these circumstances wars and civil strife did not enormously increase. Indeed, war reached its highest level in Greek history during these centuries.

The most belligerent centuries in the history of Rome were the third and first B.C. and the third A.D. Why? The third century witnessed the long and bloody conflict between irreconcilable value systems of Rome and Carthage. The first century B.C. saw the great transmutation of the formerly semi-ideational values of Rome to an overripe sensate form. The transformation was enormously accelerated by the impact of the sensate Hellenic culture upon the Roman society. At the end of the second and during the first century B.C., as in Greece, it led to anomie. In this situation, as we would expect, an increase of civil and international wars occurred. Finally, a rise of the "curve" in the third century A.D. is again quite comprehensible. In the third century A.D., Christianity, with its ideational system of values sharply opposed to the dominant sensate system, came to the surface as a tangible power. The struggle between the pagan (sensate) and Christian (ideational) systems assumed public form. Hence, according to the proposition, war had to increase. (For the next few centuries, no reliable data are available).

If we take eight main European countries and study the most belligerent periods of their history, the results are similar. Their war-maxima fall in the periods of increasing incompatibility and disintegration of the value systems. Without going into details for each country, we can summarize the movement of war in Europe as a whole, from the twelfth century to 1925.

From its initial low point, the curve begins to rise very slowly in the thirteenth and fourteenth centuries, and then faster during the fifteenth and sixteenth centuries, until it reaches its first peak in the seventeenth. Then it declines slightly in the eighteenth and much more in the nineteenth century, although there is a minor rise at the close of the eighteenth and at the beginning of the nineteenth. In the twentieth century it soars to a point unprecedented in all the 2500 years of Western society.

Our hypothesis well accounts for these three maxima of war. The period from the end of the twelfth to the seventeenth century saw the profound transformation of the European system of values from the medieval ideational to the modern sensate. The ideational values were disintegrating and the modern sensate system was not matured. The atomization and relativization of values resulted in the collapse of their stabilizing power. Their incompatibility—interindividual, intergroup, and interstate—became much greater than before. Hence, an increase of international as well as civil wars throughout Europe. But by the seventeenth century Europe had attained a new integrated system of ultimate values. Disintegration gave way to integration. Consequently there occurred the decline of the curve of war-magnitude during the eighteenth and the nineteenth centuries.

Its temporary rise at the end of the eighteenth and at the beginning of the nineteenth centuries is easily explained. It was due to the clash between those who wanted to liquidate the last remnants of the feudal order and the ideational culture and those who wanted to preserve them. After this short-lived clash, the curve of war markedly declined throughout the nineteenth century. These decades were the zenith of a well-integrated sensate culture and social order. The clash of values within the European universe was at its minimum. Hence the peaceful character of these decades.

With the beginning of the twentieth century we witness a rapid disintegration of sensate culture.[7] All its values were relativized and atomized to such an extent that none of them remained universally valid. Marriage, private property, God—all these values were undermined, criticized, and ground to dust. Social anarchy became supreme. No single value was recognized as binding equally the Hitlerites and anti-

7. See the evidences in ibid., all volumes, and in my *Crisis of Our Age* (New York, 1941).

Hitlerites, communists and capitalists, rich and poor, religious believers and atheists. As a result, the values lost a great deal of their restraining power. An ever-increasing part of the population was guided by sensual, egotistic, and biological impulses. Force and fraud became again the chief norms of conduct.

This incompatibility of values, together with a tremendous growth of interindividual, intergroup, and inter-societal relationships, made inevitable an unprecedented explosion of civil and international wars. Thus we find ourselves in the bloodiest century of the last 2500 years of human history.

In this manner the actual maxima of war-magnitude in the history of at least ten countries (Greece, Rome, and eight European countries) unequivocally support our hypothesis.

I. Murder is individual war. What is the cause of murder, and how does it increase and decrease in the course of time? We know that murders are committed for many different reasons. In spite of this variety, all murders have one and the same cause, although their supplementary factors vary. The cause is the same as that of war. This is true of murders committed for material advantage, murders by fanaticists, murders of revenge, feud, passion, or insanity, and of murders for self-preservation. In all these cases, the cause is either the irreconcilable nature of the parties' basic values (murders of fanaticism, altruism, revenge, feud, passion) or an extreme atomization thereof (killings committed for material gain, self-preservation, or insanity). In the latter instance, these murderers are governed primarily by blind and disorganizing biological impulses. Both types reproduce in miniature the aforementioned condition of social anomie.

This theory of murder causation is supported by the fact that persons with strongly integrated values do not commit murders of the second type, no matter how dire the emergency or how tempting the profit. My study shows that the percent of persons taking the lives of their fellows during famine or other great emergencies is no more than one percent. The rest may perish, but they will not slay.[8] Similarly, murders of the first type (feud, revenge, passion, fanaticism) are committed only by persons whose norms are diametrically and uncompromisingly opposed to those of their victims.

J. Further evidence is offered by changes in the severity and extensity of punishment for crimes, especially capital punishment. Severe punishment is an index of irreconciliable conflict between those who

8. See my *Man and Society in Calamity* (New York, 1942), 81–82 et passim.

punish and those who are punished. In this sense it is also a form of
interindividual and group war. We know that the severity of punishment for crimes is not constant but fluctuates, in penal codes as well as
in concrete practice, from period to period and from society to society.
Elsewhere the criminal codes of Greece, Rome, and of the main European countries have been studied in considerable detail.[9] Changes in
the severity of punishment both in the penal codes and in actual practice in these countries were systematically investigated. When the periods of increase and decrease of the severity of punishment were defined, the problem of the cause of these fluctuations was studied. The
solution was as follows: "Each time, when in a given group, the ethicojuridical heterogeneity and antagonism of its members increase, the
amount as well as the severity of punishment imposed by one part of
the society upon the other tends to increase; and, other conditions being equal, the greater the incompatibility, the greater is the increase."[10]
A sufficient body of evidence was given in *Dynamics* to demonstrate
the validity of the proposition.

K. Finally, our proposition is supported by the inadequacy of all
the other theories of the causes of war and peace. These take the form
of either a theory of multiple causation or of some exclusive specific-
factor hypothesis. The latter emphasizes some particular variable such
as economic or political elements, sunspots, density and size of population, climate, etc. None of these, however, can stand even an elementary test. One can take either mine or Professor Wright's war curves
and try to explain their "ups and downs" in terms of any of these
theories. The result is failure. These theories simply do not fit the data,
and the data do not fit the theories.

The inadequacy of the multiple-causation type of theory has been
set forth above. We may add one more point to that discussion. When
multiple causation assumes the form of some kind of equilibrium theory, stating that a change of any variable of the equilibrium system is
one of the causes of war or peace, it does not get us anywhere. Since the
variables are numerous, they are arbitrarily chosen from the countless
antecedent conditions amidst which war or peace occurs. They remain
incommensurable and incessantly varying in each case. The concept
of equilibrium is inapplicable to social systems.[11] This conclusion is
reinforced strongly by Wright's attempt to use such a theory of multi-

9. See my *Dynamics*, 2:515–627.
10. Ibid., 595. See there the factual corroboration.
11. See ibid., vol. 4.

ple causation. In spite of the enormous material collected, and the many valuable contributions made, his attempt is unsuccessful. He leaves unsolved the problem of the causation of war and peace.[12]

Positive Evidence

Since I have presented most of the evidence under the heading "negative evidence," here I need mention only three of the more important corroborations.

A. The first concerns the minima of war in the history of Greece, Rome, and Europe. In all these countries, the minima of war or the maxima of peace fall exactly in the periods when the integration of their systems of values was high and the universe of the interacting states or nations was harmonious.

In Greece before the sixth century B.C., the system of basic values was highly integrated. It was an ideational or religious-patriotic system permeating all compartments of Greek society and culture, unchallenged and unquestioned. It was essentially the same in practically all the Greek states. For this reason we should expect a low level of war during that period. The facts show that such was the case. Wars did not disappear, of course, because the integration was not perfect, nor were incompatibilities in the secondary aspects of the system lacking as in the communities of Ionia, Sparta, and Athens. From time to time, the Greek states came into contact with quite different cultures, like the Persian, the values of which were far from compatible with their own. In these conditions wars broke out once in a while, but their magnitude was far below the level of the fifth and fourth centuries B.C.[13] After the fourth century B.C., the sensate system in Greece became dominant. The anarchy of the transition was over, and the values were reintegrated into a new sensate system. Hence the decline of the war curves of Greece in the third and second centuries B.C.

In Rome, the minima of war occurred in the fourth century B.C. and the first and second centuries A.D. These were the centuries of comparatively high integration of the Roman value system. The great expansion of Rome did not begin until after the fourth century, and it was accomplished in all essentials by the beginning of our era.

A similar explanation holds for the comparatively low level of warfare in the medieval Europe before the thirteenth century. During the

12. See Wright, *A Study of War,* esp. vol. 2. See my criticism in *Ethics* (April 1943): 202–7.
13. Detailed factual data on wars in Greece, Rome, and Europe can be found in my *Dynamics* and in Wright's *A Study of War.*

Middle Ages, the Christian system of values was highly integrated and universal for the whole of Europe. Sociocultural anomie was at its lowest ebb. Hence the small amount of warfare throughout these centuries. The relative recession of warfare in the eighteenth and nineteenth centuries followed the ending of the transition from the ideational to a settled sensate system of values.

Thus, the minima of war have fallen in the periods in which they should have occurred according to our hypothesis. This conclusion is further reinforced by the corresponding data for eight European nations studied separately. These include England, France, Russia, Austria, Italy, Spain, the Netherlands, and Poland-Lithuania.[14]

B. The minima of murder likewise fall in the periods of strong integration of the system of values. "Commercial murders" flourish uniformly in the societies where the value system is in an anomic state. Conversely there is a notable increase of murders in periods of transition, anomie, and great calamities. The groups that permit such crimes are desocialized and demoralized, controlled mainly by disorganized biological impulses. On the other hand, in the periods of great and sudden increase in integration, murders notably decrease.[15]

C. A well-established fact is the periodic mitigation and humanization of punishment imposed on one part of the society by the other. Such relaxations of severity of punishment have regularly happened during epochs of social integration.[16]

The Conditions of a Lasting Peace in the Postwar Period

A lasting peace after this war is possible only if the cause of war is either eliminated or greatly diminished. Without this central step, no plans can succeed. Many suggested measures for the organization of a stable peace do not touch the real cause of war. For this reason they are doomed to failure. Indeed, many of these plans actually reinforce rather than remove the cause of war. They repeat the tragic errors of the Versailles treaty. It is high time to stop this gambling with the lives of millions of human beings and to begin the organization of a lasting peace with the measures that really eliminate or limit the cause of war.

1. The first great step is the reintegration of the basic values so as to terminate the existing anomie and its consequences. To offset the

14. See the data in my *Dymanics*.
15. See the facts in my *Man and Society in Calamity*, chaps. 10–12.
16. *Dynamics*, vol. 2, chap. 15.

current atomization and relativization, the process of universalizing the main values and their norms of conduct must be energetically pushed. Purely sensate values without the supersensate, spiritual values cannot be universal. They can only be increasingly atomized. Hence a transvaluation of the present sensate norms by coalescence with more spiritual principles as end values becomes inescapable. It is clear that a profound mental and moral revolution to make the dominant mentality more idealistic and spiritual is urgent. Those who do not like these terms can substitute more neutral ones such as the *categoric imperative, unconditional social duty,* and the like. When a given norm of conduct is regarded as obligatory and sacred, it becomes a transcendental value over and above utilitarian and hedonistic standards.[17]

2. We cannot make identical all the religious, ethical, and juridical norms, aesthetic values, or economic and political organizations of peoples with diverse cultures. But we can make them compatible by universalizing their basic norms of conduct. If this cannot be effected in terms of the Sermon on the Mount, it surely can be based on the Golden Rule: "Do not do unto others as you would not have others do unto you." Such norms can be universalized by promulgation in all the constitutions and by ingrafting them into the conduct of all peoples and persons. They furnish the common ground for eliminating the irreconcilable values and for making the rest harmonious. It was pointed out above that heterogeneity of values does not necessarily mean incompatibility. Nations and classes can have different religions, aesthetic standards, and economic and political regimes and yet live peacefully side by side.

3. Of the necessary supplementary steps, two are particularly important. First, we must limit the sovereignty of all states with respect to questions of war and peace. Second, we must create an international body to handle conflicts among the participant nations. Its decisions must be obligatory and enforceable. The body itself should be composed not only of the representatives of the states but also of the representatives of the great religions, occupations (agriculture, labor, management), and professions (science, art, and philosophy).

Without these three steps no project for a stable peace can succeed. But if our leaders and their followers will begin to build the temple of a lasting peace along these lines, we have for the first time in history a fighting chance to achieve this great objective.[18]

17. For details see my *Crisis of Our Age.*
18. See for elaboration of these conditions and the possibility of realization of a lasting peace my paper on "Conditions and Possibility of a Lasting Peace" in *A Righteous Faith for a Just and Durable Peace* (New York, 1942), 60–68.

20

The Conditions and Prospects
for a World without War

No Lasting Peace within Contemporary Culture
and Society

Within the framework of contemporary (sensate) culture and with the
type of society and man that express it, no enduring peace is possible.
Regardless of what economic and political modifications may be made
within such a framework, they cannot abolish international and civil
wars, nor can they substantially decrease their magnitude or destructive ferocity. This gloomy statement is the only possible conclusion to
be drawn from the relevant empirical facts, as well as from an analysis
of the "heart and soul" of modern culture, society, and man. Empirical
evidence shows that, with the emergence and growth of this sensate
culture, society, and man, beginning with the thirteenth century and
extending on to the twentieth century, the frequency and intensity of
war have followed a clearly discernible trend. The data show that war
steadily increased from the thirteenth to the seventeenth centuries, remained high throughout the eighteenth and the early nineteenth, decreased to the level of the sixteenth century during the period 1820–
1910, and then soared up to an unprecedented height during the twentieth century—the bloodiest century in all the thirty centuries of
Greco-Roman and Western cultures.[1] This movement of war, together
with the unrivaled destructiveness and bestiality of the present war,
convincingly demonstrates that modern culture, society, and man are
belligerent in their very sociocultural nature, that their avowed pacifism is a mere illusion, and that interindividual (crime), civil, and international war is their inalienable characteristic.

Originally published in the *American Journal of Sociology* 49 (March 1944): 441–49.
© 1944 University of Chicago. All rights reserved. Reprinted by permission of the
publisher.
    1. See the data on the movement of the magnitude of war and revolution in my
Social and Cultural Dynamics (New York, 1937), vol. 3, and in Quincy Wright, *A Study
of War* (Chicago, 1942).

An examination of the main properties of this culture, society, and man leads to the same conclusion and makes the above movement of war comprehensible.[2]

Being an articulation of its major premise that the true reality and values are sensory, this modern culture cannot help being preeminently empiricistic, positivistic, economically minded, and materialistic in its mentality; utilitarian and hedonistic in its ethics and law; sensualistic in its fine arts; and dynamic and relativistic in all its values. In accordance with its major premise, it puts the highest premium upon sensory values, beginning with wealth, material comfort, kisses, copulation, and popularity and ending with a thoroughly hedonistic, more rarely eudaemonistic, notion of happiness. In its decadent phase, its scientific, religious, ethical, and sociocultural relativism develops to such an extent that there results an extreme atomization of values, which to an ever increasing degree become devoid of any universal validity, universal acceptance or rejection, and universal binding and controlling power. The clear boundary line between truth and falsity, right and wrong, the beautiful and the ugly, the just and the unjust, tends progressively to disappear, every group and individual becoming the supreme arbiter in all these matters. This leads to an enormous increase in the number of interindividual and intergroup conflicts over these issues. Such a situation results in a veritable sociocultural anomie, with all its mental, moral, social, and behavioral anarchy. This anomie makes inevitable the emergence of sheer brute force, assisted by fraud, as the supreme ruler of human behavior. This is uniformly accompanied by an extraordinary explosion of wars, revolutions, and crimes. Inasmuch as this relativization of values in our present-day culture has reached such a stage of anomie, the upsurgence of war and of bloody revolution in this century is a natural and inevitable consequence.

There are other processes as well by which sensate culture, particularly in its stage of extreme relativism, leads to war and revolution. By putting a premium upon sensory values it molds in its own image the personality and conduct of its members. Each of these is impelled by it to secure a maximum share of sensory and material values, ranging all the way from wealth, kisses, freedom, popularity, and power on up to a maximum of *Lebensraum*, natural resources, markets, and world domination. An interindividual and intergroup struggle for these values develops and becomes the dominant drive in the life of

---

2. See a detailed analysis of the characteristics of modern sensate culture, society, and man and the pertinent evidence in my *Dynamics* (4 vols.) and *The Crisis of Our Age* (New York, 1941). Here I mention merely those traits most relevant to the topic.

individuals and groups, the main ethos and pathos of their existence. As long as universal values with their universally binding norms are active, they are able to moderate the ferocity of this struggle and inhibit the use of extremely antisocial means. But, as these values become relativized and atomized, their "brakes" cease to function, and eventually any means and any way becomes permissible as long as one is able to "get away with it." The result is an explosion of violence in various forms, with the rise to power of pressure groups and of dictatorships and with an upsurge of crime, civil war, and international war. "To suppose that men who are filled individually with every manner of restlessness, maddened by lust of power and speed, votaries of the god Whirl, will live at peace either with themselves or others, is the vainest chimera," rightly remarks one of the eminent American humanists.[3]

This conflagration of war and violence is hastened along by the general degradation of man's value by sensate culture. Quite consistently with its major premise, it views man as a mere empirical "electron-proton complex," a "reflex mechanism," a mere "animal organism," a "psychoanalytical bag filled with libido," devoid of anything supersensory, sacred, or divine. No wonder that in such a culture man is treated in the same manner as we treat all the other sensory "complexes," "mechanisms," and "animals": any individual or group that hinders the realization of one's wishes is eliminated in the same way in which we liquidate a mosquito or a snake or "neutralize" any organic or inorganic object that impedes the fulfilment of our desires. This explains why, in spite of all the vociferous claims by our culture as to its humanistic, humane, and humanitarian mission, it is, objectively, in its decadent phase, one of the most inhuman of all cultures, killing, mutilating, and degrading human beings by the tens of millions.

Similarly, the basic institutions of contemporary society are permeated by the same militarism and are incessantly generating interindividual, civil, and international conflicts. Private property, with its inevitable differentiation into the excessively rich and the utterly miserable, generates persistent criminality, class antagonism, and class war. The state, with its naked power policy of the Machiavellian *raison d'état,* is an openly militaristic institution unrestrained by any of the ethical norms that are obligatory for private conduct. The same is true of our political parties: first and foremost they are fighting machines, using the spoils system, bribery, vituperation, murder, and civil war as in-

3. Irving Babbitt, *The Breakdown of Internationalism* (a reprint from the *Nation,* June 1915), 25.

struments in their struggle for spoils and power. Our occupational unions, beginning with labor unions and ending with capitalists' associations, are organized primarily for militant purposes, namely, the successful defeat of antagonistic organizations by whatever means may be necessary, whether there be strikes and lockouts or revolution and civil war. Even the family, so far as it imbues the children with the cult of family egotism, power, and "success," is shot through with the same militaristic spirit. Finally almost all our institutions glorify sensate power and success as the highest virtues. They methodically inculcate a "fighting spirit" into everyone from the day of his birth to the day of his death. Our heroes are invariably fighting persons who successfully crush their rivals, whether on the football field, in cutthroat business rivalry, on a battlefield, in political machinations, or in class war; and they are typified by our "world champions" in tennis, swimming, coffee-drinking, pole-sitting, and jitterbugging. Even our "Superman" is the superman only because he "is faster than a bullet, more powerful than a locomotive," and more militant than Mars: he is forever in a fighting mess.

Thus, whether we study the objective movement of war that has accompanied the emergence and growth of modern culture or whether we study the essential characteristics exhibited by it and the society and man expressing it, we cannot fail to see their preeminently militant sociocultural nature. War in its various forms, and especially the war for sensory values, is their ethos, soul, and heart. Within their framework no lasting national or international peace has ever been or ever will be possible.

This means also that most of the contemporary plans for a lasting peace are doomed to failure so far as they hope to achieve it within this framework by a mere job of repatching. Elementary inductive considerations will show this unequivocally. As patented panaceas against war, these plans offer an enlightened self-interest; a specious "utilitarian rationality"; emancipation from religion and absolutistic ethics; a greater and more extreme relativism of all values; a still greater dose of positivism, empiricism, materialism, utilitarianism, and mechanisticism in all their varieties; a further expansion of literacy, schools, universities, newspapers, magazines, movies, the radio, and other "educational" instrumentalities; a still more rapid increase in scientific discoveries and technological devices; a replacement of all monarchies by republics, of all autocracies by democracies, of capitalism by communism, socialism, and other sensate "-isms"; dismemberment and disarmament of the vanquished; a bigger and better "balance of powers" and various "Unions Now" in the form of diverse double, triple, and quadruple alliances on up to the League of Nations, armed with a crushing military and police force; a higher economic plane of living, at least for the victorious nations; a more just distribution of natural resources; and so on and so forth. The hopelessness of all these hopes is unquestionably shown by "an ugly fact" that with the emergence and growth of our modern culture and society from the thirteenth on to the twentieth century all these panaceas have been growing also; and yet their growth has been paralleled during these centuries by an increase of war instead of the decrease for which the plans contend. From such a "concomitant variation" only an idiot can conclude that these panaceas are suffocating war and that, when applied in a still greater dose, they could kill it forever. The only sound conclusion is that either the panaceas are perfectly impotent in the eradication of war or that, within the framework of this modern culture, society, and man, they work in favor of war rather than against it. For this reason these plans, especially those that call themselves "practical," "realis-tic," and "scientific," are nothing but an illusion and self-delusion. Within a different framework, as we shall see, some of these measures can be helpful; within the contemporary one, they cannot and will not build a temple of enduring peace.

The Culture and Society Necessary for an Enduring Peace

These gloomy conclusions do not mean that an enduring peace is gen-erally impossible. They signify only that for its realization a new cul-ture, with an appropriate kind of society and man, different from the contemporary one, is in order. The essential characteristics of these can be briefly summed up.[4]

1. The new culture will put less emphasis upon purely sensory real-ity value and more upon the truly rational and upon the supersensory-metarational reality value, viewing the true reality value as an infinite manifold with three main aspects: sensory, rational, and supersensory-metarational, each within its sphere being a true reality and a true value. This conception of the true reality value, sponsored by Plato and Aristotle, Erigena, Thomas Aquinas, and Nicolas of Cusa, to men-tion but a few names, will replace the major premise of our sensate

4. See a more detailed analysis of this new culture, society, and man in my paper "The Task of Cultural Rebuilding," to be published in a volume to be entitled "Intellec-tual and Cultural Foundations of World Order," by the Institute for Religious Studies.

culture. Accordingly, the new culture will be an articulation of this new major premise in all its main compartments: in its science, philosophy, religion, fine arts, ethics, law, and forms of social organization on up to the manners, mores, and ways of living of its individual and group members.

2. Its science will study, through sensory observation, the empirical aspects of the infinite manifold; its philosophy will investigate through mathematical and syllogistic logic the rational and logical aspects of the true reality value; its intuitive wisdom will give us the notion of the supersensory-metalogical aspects of it through the intuition of great religious and ethical seers, great scientists like Sir Isaac Newton, great philosophers like Plato, great artists like Beethoven and Shakespeare, and great technological inventors inspired to their achievements by intuition.[5] The history of human knowledge is a cemetery filled with wrong empirical observations, false logical reasonings, and misleading intuitions. This means that, taken separately, each of these ways of cognition is fallible and that if it is to achieve a less fallibility it must have the cooperation and mutual verification of the other two ways of cognition. The outlined integralist system of truth gives us precisely this organic integration, cooperation, and mutual verification of all three ways of cognition. As such, it promises to give a more valid, richer, and better-tested truth than that which the dominant, one-sided sensory cognition can give. It eliminates also the contemporary antagonism between, and mutual undermining of, science, philosophy, and religion.

3. Instead of the excessively relativized and atomized utilitarian and hedonistic pseudonorms of our culture—devoid of their universal binding power, transgressed at every suitable occasion, and degraded to the level of mere Paretian "derivations," Freudian "rationalizations," Marxian "ideological beautifications" of the economic, sexual, and other sensate "residues," "complexes," "drives," and "inter-

5. Many self-appointed pseudoempiricists in their attack against intuition as a way of cognition of *sui generis* display a complete ignorance of how most of the great scientific, philosophical, technological, ethical, religious, and artistic discoveries and inventions have really been made. If they were real empiricists and had empirically studied this problem, they would have learned the empirically undeniable fact that most of these discoveries and inventions have been initiated and inspired by intuition (see the facts and literature on that in my *Dynamics,* 4:746ff.; see also I. Sikorsky, *The Story of the Winged-S* [New York, 1942], chap. 22; T. Langmuire, "Science, Common Sense and Decency" [presidential address of this Nobel Prize winner to the American Association for the Advancement of Science, delivered in 1942], *New York Times,* 27 December 1942).

ests"—the ethics and law of the new culture, in accordance with its major premise, will be embodied in a set of universal norms binding and effectively controlling the behavior of all, unquestioned and undisputed in their ethical prestige by any other conflicting norm. In their content these universal norms will be a variation of the main ethical norms of practically all great religions and moral codes, from the elemental Golden Rule and Ten Commandments on up to the norms of the Sermon on the Mount as their sublimest expression. Such an ethics and law will stop the atomization of moral values, eliminate ethical and legal cynicism, and abolish the dictatorship of rude force and fraud as the supreme arbiters of human conduct.

4. Again in accordance with its major premise, the painting and sculpture, literature and music, drama and architecture of the new culture will be quite different from contemporary fine arts. Integralist beauty will be reunited with truth and goodness, so that the new fine arts will become a value-laden art instead of being an empty art for art's sake. Instead of debunking the immortals, the new art will immortalize the mortals, ennoble the ignoble, and beautify the ugly. Instead of being negativistic, centered around the police morgue, criminals' hideouts, insane asylums, and sex organs, it will reflect mainly the eternal values, positive ideals, heroic events, and great tragedies and dramas. Like the comparable art of Greece in the fifth century b.c. and of Europe in the thirteenth century a.d., it will be an inspiring, ennobling, educating, and truly beautifying art instead of being a degrading, demoralizing, and enervating cult of social pathology, as contemporary art largely is.

5. In such a culture man will again be regarded as an end value, as an incarnation of the divine manifold rather than as a mere biological organism, reflex mechanism, or psychoanalytical libido, as he is usually regarded now. The value of man will again be lifted far above the utter degradation into which he is now thrown. Accordingly, the practices, institutions, and relationships that turn man into a mere means for predominantly sensate ends will largely disappear.

6. Most of the social institutions that contradict the total character of this new culture will be eliminated. The dominant form of social relationships in such a society will be neither contractual nor compulsory but familistic, similar to the relationships among the members of a good family. The economic and political regimes of such a society will be neither capitalistic nor communistic nor socialistic but familistic. The enormous contrast between multimillionaires and paupers, the rulers and the ruled, will disappear. Private property will be limited and will be turned into a kind of public trusteeship. A decent minimum

of the necessities will be secured for all. The main motives for a socially useful economic and political life will be neither profit nor power but the motive of creative service to the society—similar to the motivation of great artists, religious leaders, scientists, and true philanthropists. Social institutions that contradict these purposes will largely disappear; those that serve them will be established and reinforced.

7. The practical consequences of the establishment of such a culture will be immense, especially in the field of human mentality, conduct, and interrelationships. The new system of values and truth will abolish the contemporary antagonism between science, philosophy, and religion; they will all be inseparable organs of a unified system of truth, all pointing toward the same verities, validities, and values. The contemporary atomization and relativization of truth, goodness, and beauty will have been terminated. With this there will be an end to the contemporary mental, moral, and social anarchy. An age of certainty will replace our present age of uncertainty. Liberated from the gnawing tortures of uncertainty, the sapping poison of contradictions, and the weariness of confusion, the human mind will once more regain an inner harmony, peace, and happiness. With these qualities its creative vigor, self-confidence, and self-control will be restored. In such conditions most of the contemporary psychoneuroses will evaporate. Universalized truth will unite into one mind all of mankind.

The general devaluation of that which is purely sensate will greatly weaken the contemporary struggle for existence and for material values and will reinforce the quest for the rational and metarational values. As a result interindividual and intergroup antagonisms will greatly decrease, their brutal forms will wither, and man's conduct will be ennobled and made truly social. The same result will follow from the universalized ethical norms rooted into the heart and soul of men. Not so much by external sanctions as by inner power they will inhibit most of the antisocial actions and relationships, particularly the bloody mistreatment of man by man, of group by group. The most brutal forms of crime, civil strife, and international warfare cannot thrive in such a cultural climate and will greatly decrease. The same is true of brute force and fraud as the arbiters of human conduct.

The new fine arts will contribute their share to the same effect. By virtue of their positive beauty they will educate, inspire, instruct, fascinate, and control human beings fully as much as the new science and religion, philosophy, and ethics. Primarily devoted to eternal beauty, the fine arts will serve also, as a by-product, the task of true socialization of *Homo sapiens*. In this way they will contribute generously to an elimination of antisocial activities, relationships, and institutions in the human universe.

Finally, through its regained harmony, peace, and happiness of mind, the new culture will make human beings less egoistic, irritable, quarrelsome, violent, and antisocial. Through a release of new creative forces in all fields of sociocultural activity it will make everyone a partner and participant in the most sublime form of happiness—the happiness of a creative genius.

In these and thousands of other ways the new culture will develop a new man—happy, generous, kind, and just to himself and to all his fellow men. Within the framework of such a culture, society, and man neither interindividual war (crime) nor civil war nor international war can flourish. If they do not disappear entirely, they will certainly decrease to the lowest minimum known in human history.

8. Such are the essential traits of the culture, society, and man necessary for an enduring peace in interindividual, intergroup, and international relationships. Without this framework, as the main condition of peace, all the other panaceas against war are futile. With it, many of these will facilitate its realization. For instance, with this sociocultural foundation the League of Nations and other forms of superstate government will faithfully and fruitfully serve the cause of peace. Without it, such a superstate government will be either as impotent as the defunct League of Nations or, what is still worse, may turn into a world tyranny as cruel as some of the "world empires" of the past. Without it the military and police forces of such a world government will certainly be misused and will eventually serve the cause of war instead of the cause of peace. With it, all the state and superstate governments, no matter what may be their technical forms, will be true familistic democracies. As such they will actively facilitate the maintenance of peace. Without it, no formal republican or democratic regime, even if universally diffused, can ever help—no more so than in the past, when the democratic and republican countries were at least as belligerent as the monarchical and autocratic nations and when the growth of republican and democratic regimes for the last few centuries has been followed by an increase, rather than by a decrease, of war.[6] Without this framework the further increase of scientific discoveries and tech-

6. See the data on the comparative belligerency and revolutionism of republican, democratic, and monarchical-autocratic countries in my *Dynamics*, vol. 3, chaps. 12, 13, 14; also A. Toynbee, *A Study of History* (London, 1939), 4:141ff.; Wright, op. cit., chap. 22.

nological inventions will be of just as little avail as in the past, during which, beginning with the thirteenth century, they have steadily and rapidly increased up to the present time and have been followed by an almost parallel increase of war. The same is true of the development of schools, universities, books, magazines, papers, movies, radio, theaters, and all the other means of contemporary education. Beginning with the thirteenth century, they have been steadily increasing without any resulting decrease of war, revolutions, or crime. This is still more true in regard to such panaceas as a more equitable distribution of the natural resources or a higher material standard of living or a more enlightened self-interest and utilitarian "rationality." Without the foregoing framework, any truly equitable distribution of the natural resources throughout all mankind is impossible, just as it has been impossible in the past. The states and nations will remain as egotistic and rapacious as they have hitherto been. Those who believe that a diffusion of democratic forms of government would change this forget that the so-called democracies of the past and the present have been fully as imperialistic as the autocracies. They forget also the unpleasant but unquestionable fact that almost all such democracies, beginning with the Athenian and ending with the contemporary ones, have been based upon the severest exploitation of colonies and "spheres of influence" or have consisted of a vast layer of semifree and unfree population many times larger than the full-fledged citizenship of such democracies.

Likewise an "enlightened self-interest" and utilitarian "rationality" have been growing ever since the thirteenth century, without being accompanied by any decrease of war. One of the reasons for this is the fact that from a deeper standpoint this self-interest turns out to be a blind egotism and utilitarian "rationality" a most irrational illusion. Utilitarian rationality is defined as the use of the most efficient means for the realization of an end desired. Typically, it has in view only the rationality of the means, and it neglects the rationality of the ends. The present war, which uses the most efficient and scientific means available for the defeat of the enemy, is perfectly rational from this standpoint; so also is the activity of a gang of efficient murderers, armed with the best techniques of murder, which is never caught or punished. These considerations show clearly that the truly rational action is that in which the ends as well as the means are rational. An action that uses rational means to irrational ends is particularly irrational. For this reason the utilitarian rationality of our society cannot regard war as irrational, and still less is it able to achieve the abolition of war.

Likewise, without this framework, the panaceas suggested for the eradication of crime, rioting, revolution, and civil war cannot be effective. These irrational phenomena will remain and may even grow in spite of the panaceas, just as they have remained and grown during the centuries of the domination of modern culture. Notwithstanding the fact that these panaceas have been applied with especial liberality in the twentieth century, the glaring fact remains that neither crime, rioting, nor revolution has decreased; nor has the family become any better integrated; nor have suicide and mental disease declined; nor has the intensity of the interindividual and intergroup struggle for existence diminished; nor, if we can measure happiness by the movement of suicide, has man become any more happy. If anything, the objective results have been exactly opposite to what might be expected from the application of the panaceas.

The net result of the preceding analysis is that the suggested framework of the new culture, society, and man is not the manifestation of a preacher's complex, nor is it the "impractical" indulgence of an armchair philosopher in his pet preoccupation, but rather is it a most practical, scientific, and matter-of-fact indication of the necessary conditions for a realization of the objective—a lasting peace. Without it, all the other means to building a temple of lasting peace are bound to be impotent or will only produce even bigger and more terrible wars.

Prospects

To this conclusion may be raised the objection that the new sociocultural framework is itself unrealizable and utopian. If such an objection were valid, it would only mean that an enduring peace is impossible. In that case all rational persons should stop fooling themselves and others with the utopia of a mankind without war, bloody revolution, and crime and should resignedly accept them as inevitable in the same manner in which we accept death. However, after a careful scrutiny, the objection turns out to be far less axiomatic and unquestionable than it appears at first glance. In other words, the chances for a realization of the new framework, with the enduring peace that it implies, are not at all nil.

First, if mankind is going to live a creative life and is not going to sink either into the somnolence of "a benumbed and ruminating human herd" or into the tortuous agony of decay, the new framework is the only way that is left. The existing framework is so rotten and is progressively becoming so destructive and painful that mankind cannot creatively and contentedly live within it for any length of time. If it cannot be replaced by the new framework, then the end of mankind's creative history, in one of the two ways just indicated, is inescapable. But such a conclusion is far more fantastic in its pessimism than the facts of human history warrant: in spite of the gravity of many of the great crises that have beset mankind throughout history, human beings have always been able somehow to create new forms of culture and society that have eventually terminated the crisis. For the present, there is no evidence whatsoever that a new sociocultural renaissance is impossible.

Second, the shift from a withered sensate culture to a form of culture somewhat akin to that just outlined has happened several times in the history of Greco-Roman, Western, and certain other great cultures. If it has been possible of occurrence in the past, there is every reason to suppose that it can recur in the future.

Third, if the birth of the new culture were dependent entirely upon contemporary "utilitarian rationality," its emergence and growth would be uncertain indeed. But fortunately such is not the manner in which one form of culture is ordinarily replaced by another. The replacement is usually a result of the historical process itself, of gigantic, impersonal, spontaneous forces immanent in a given sociocultural framework; and only at a later stage does it become facilitated by truly rational forces that plan and endeavor to build the new culture with all available scientific means. The spontaneous forces immanent in our modern culture have already brought about its phase of decline and crisis; they have already undermined its prestige and fascination to a considerable degree; they have already alienated from it a considerable portion of the population; they have robbed it of most of its charms: its security, its safety, its prosperity, its material comfort, its happiness, its sensate freedom, and all of its main values. Not in the classroom but in the hard school of life millions of people are being incessantly taught by these forces an unforgettable and indelible lesson, comprehensible by the plainest human being, that the existing framework is going to give them "stones" and bullets instead of bread; gigantic destruction in place of creative construction; misery instead of prosperity; regimentation in lieu of freedom; death, mutilation, and suffering instead of security of life, integrity of body, or bigger and better pleasure. With these charms progressively evaporating, this modern culture of ours has no other great values by which to hold the allegiance of humanity. Like a pretty woman whose bodily charms have gone, it is destined to lose more and more the adherence of humanity until it has been entirely forsaken and dethroned from its dominant position in favor of a different sociocultural framework. This point has about been reached by our culture. Its magnificent creativeness, its prestige, and its charms are about over.

Parallel with this defection of humanity from contemporary culture, the same spontaneous forces are generating and increasing the quest for a different sociocultural framework, one which is more creative and adequate and less destructive and painful. This quest is at the present moment the main item in the order of the day: almost everyone is busy with the problems of the future society and culture. Only a few, who nothing forget and nothing learn, still cherish ideas of a restoration of the past and a revitalization of a withered framework. The overwhelming majority understand—if not by calculation and logical analysis, then by plain horse sense—that this is impossible. They recognize the necessity of some framework different from that which we have now.

At this stage the truly rational forces enter the play and take a guiding hand in it. With all the available wisdom and knowledge and with a sense of supreme duty they endeavor to create various systematic blueprints of the new sociocultural framework—to test them, to improve them, rejecting the less adequate ones and perfecting the better ones. New plans, with their philosophies, ideologies, and ways and means of realization, multiply, become more and more coordinated, more and more diffused, continually accumulate a momentum and an ever increasing legion of adherents, until they become a tangible social force. This force grows and in thousands of ways begins significantly to influence human mentality and conduct, science and religion, philosophy and ethics, fine arts and social institutions. The process is slow, develops erratically from day to day, and has many deviations, mistakes, and miscarriages of its own. Altogether, it takes several decades, even a few centuries, for its full realization. Sooner or later, however, it terminates in a dethronement of the previously dominant sociocultural framework and in a rise to ascendancy of the new framework.

In the case of our contemporary culture we have reached the point at which the rational forces are about ready to enter the play. Together with the spontaneous forces of the historical process itself, they will be able to create a new sociocultural framework that will be a rough approximation to the one outlined above. When this objective has been reached, the utopia of a lasting peace will become a reality.

Love, Altruism, and
Social Reconstruction

21

Sociology and Ethics

Logical Interrelations or Sociology and Ethics

The principal task of ethics in the past has been an elaboration of the prescription of what ought to be and what ought not to be. Since the ethics of the Bible and the sacred books of India and China, since the works of Plato and Aristotle, up to the contemporary treatises in ethics, this task has been and still is regarded as the principal task of ethics.[1] So far as sociology professes that its scientific task consists in the study of social phenomena as they have existed, do exist, and will exist, there is no direct connection between the two disciplines. The reason for this is that the world of what ought to be and what really is, or has been, or will be are quite different and lie in quite different planes. The judgments of *ought to be* are not aimed to find the truth, whereas the cognitive judgments of existence have the truth as their only objective. "Love they neighbor," "kill thy enemy," and other similar expressions are neither true nor non-true. They do not pretend to state that between *a* and *b* there exists such a relation. They simply demand an obedience regardless of whether their *what ought to be* really exists or not. On the other hand, cognitive judgment always says

---

Originally published in *The Social Sciences and Their Interrelations*, ed. William F. Ogburn and Alexander Goldenweiser (New York: Houghton Mifflin Co., 1927), 311–17. Reprinted by permission of the publisher.

1. This is recognised by all prominent ethicists, even by those who do not limit the task of ethics by this prescription of "what ought to be." Cf. W. Wundt, *Ethik*, 1:8–10; R. Stammler, *Theorie der Rechtswissenschaft* (Halle: Buchhandlung des Waisenhauses, 1911), 23ff; Binding, *Handbuch des Strafrechts*, 1–10; Birkmeyer, *Studien zu dem Hauptgrundsatz*, 166ff; H. Rickert, *Zwei Wege der Erkenntistheorie, Kantsstudien* 14, and *Die Grenzen der Naturwissenschaftlichen Begriffsbildung*, last part; P. Natorp, *Sozialpädagogik*, 1–190ff; W. Windelband *Praeludien* (Tubingen: J. Mohr Publishers, 1911); H. Sidgwick, *Methods of Ethics*, 4th ed., 4; T. H. Green, *Prolegomena to Ethics*, 3d ed., 9; J. Dewey and J. Tufts, *Ethics*, 1–3; H. Höffding, *Ethik* [German trans.], 24; B. Croce, *Philosophy of the Practical*, 42ff; R. Eucken, *Ethics and Modern Thought*, passim; E. Boutroux, *Education and Ethics*, introduction and 53ff; G. T. Ladd, *What Ought I to Do*, passim; E. C. Hayes, *Sociology and Ethics*, 30ff. With still greater reason this may be said of almost all "pure and philosophical" ethicists, like Lotze and Kohen.

what does exist or does not exist, and never what ought to be. Natural science and other real sciences study the reality as it is, irrespective of whether it is "good" or "bad." The phenomena of death, plague, murder, and war are recognised by many as something "bad"; and yet science studies them as carefully as any "good" phenomena.[2] In our cognitive judgments we are free from the judgments of *ought to be*. And, vice versa, our judgments of valuation (*ought to be*) are independent logically from the judgments of existence and from the existing reality itself. In spite of the existence of plague and war, one may say that they ought not to exist, or that they are evil. In spite of the nonexistence of universal love, one may say that it ought to exist. The same idea is well expressed by the great French mathematician and philosopher, H. Poincaré. He says:

> There is no and cannot be any scientific ethics as there is no and cannot be an unmoral science. The reason is very simple: namely, grammatical. If both premises of a syllogism are in the indicative, the conclusion will be also in the indicative. All postulates and judgments of science are and can be only in the indicative. The most sophisticated dialecticians may manipulate these principles as they like: all that they can obtain will be in the indicative also. They never can obtain judgment which would run: do this or don't do that. This is the difficulty which all ethicists always find. They try to prove scientifically a "moral principle." They must be excused because it is their business.[3]

Correspondingly, scientific law which describes the existing relations among phenomena, and moral law, which prescribes a definite form of conduct and valuates the phenomena as good or bad, moral or immoral, are laws quite different and do not have logically anything

---

2. This was well understood by St. Thomas Aquinas: "*In scientiis nor quaeritur aisi cognitio veritatis. In scientiis operativis, finis is operatio.*" (*Summa Theologica*, Ia, q. 14, art. 16).

3. H. Poincaré, *Dernières Pensées*, essay "*La Moral et la Science.*" Cf. for detailed analysis of the above statements V. Pareto, *Traité de Sociologie Générale* (Paris: Payot & Cie, 1917–19), chaps. 1–5 et passim; K. Pearson, *The Grammar of Science* (London: W. Scott, 1892), chap. 3; H. Kelsen, *Hauptprobleme der Staatslehre* (Tubingen: J. C. B. Mohr, 1923), 1–94; E. Durkheim, *Règles de la Méthode Sociologique*, 2d ed. (Paris: Alcan, 1927), 51; *L'Annee sociologie* 9:324; L. Lévy-Bruhl, *La Moral et la Science des Movers* (Paris: Alcan, 1903), chap. 3 et passim; Boutroux, op. cit., chap. 3; E. Husserl, *Logische Untersuchungen*, 1:29ff; P. Sorokin, "Are Ethics a Normative Science and Does Any Normative Science Exist?," in *Crime and Punishment*, introduction; P. Sorokin, "The Category of Ought to Be and Its Application in Science," *Juridichesky Vestnik* (January 1917); cf. also Sigwart's analysis of "Sollen" in his *Logic*, 2 vols. (London: S. Sonnenschein & Co., 1895).

in common.[4] Similarly, as poetry represents a kind of social thought quite different from science, judgments of valuation represent a kind of social thought quite different from the scientific judgments. Similarly, as there is neither scientific nor nonscientific poetry, there is neither scientific nor nonscientific ethics. Each of them—poetry, science, and ethics—has its own criteria of valuation. To try to measure them with the same criteria is no better than to measure a distance by the unit of weight, and vice versa.

If this point is clear, then it is very easy to distinguish scientific statements from ethical evaluations wherever they are given. Their mixture is logically inadmissible. Such are the logical interrelations of sociology and ethics as a discipline which prescribes what ought to be.

Factual Interrelations of Sociology and Ethics

If we turn now to the problem as to what are the factual interrelations between the sociological and the ethical treatises and between the sociologists and the ethicists, the picture appears very different from the above logical interrelations. In the first place, the great ethicists happen to be the great social thinkers or sociologists too; and vice versa.[5] Confucius, Mencius, Plato, Aristotle, Cicero, Seneca, Dante, St. Thomas Aquinas, Machiavelli, Hobbes, Locke, B. Spinoza, Rousseau, Montesquieu, Ferguson, Malthus, A. Smith, Kant, Hegel, Fichte, S. Simon, Auguste Comte, Bentham, J. S. Mill, Spencer, to mention but a few of the leaders, have been ethicists as well as social thinkers or sociologists. In the second place, their works have been dedicated to the study of the social phenomena as they existed and at the same time to the valuation of the phenomena from the standpoint of how they ought to be. It is hard to find any work of these authors in which the cognitive judgments are not intermingled with those of *ought to be*. This situation continues to exist up to the present time. There are very few if any sociological works that are free from ethical valuations like "this is desirable or undesirable," "useful or harmful," "progressive or regressive," "just or unjust," "moral or immoral," "social or antisocial." Whole divisions of sociology, such as "theory of progress," "applied

4. Though the judgments of valuation like "this is good" have an appearance similar to cognitivo statements, nevertheless, their nature is quite different. Cf. the analysis in the indicated works of Poincaré, Pareto, Kelsen, Husserl, Pearson, Sorokin, and others.

5. The same is true in regard to economists, political thinkers, and ethicists. Cf. C. E. Ayres, *The Nature of the Relationship Between Ethics and Economics* (Chicago: University of Chicago Press, 1918), chap. 3.

sociology," and "social control," are in essence nothing but the discussions from the standpoint of what ought to be. Almost any textbook in sociology not only teaches but at the same time preaches, and preaching sometimes occupies a much greater place than teaching.[6] There is no need to point out the fact that the great majority of political and journalistic writings represent nothing but preaching. On the other hand, it is equally difficult to find a treatise in ethics which does not represent a mixture of the ethical valuations with the cognitive judgments. The traditional division of ethics into "the physics of mores" and "the metaphysics of mores" shows this clearly. There has not been a single system of ethics, not excluding even that of Kant, that has succeeded in building a "pure ethics" without consideration, analysis, study, and description of facts as they have existed or were thought of as existing. Such has been and is the real situation.

The Present Trend in the Relationship Between Sociology and Ethics

Everyone who has studied the recent trend in both disciplines cannot but notice that ethical treatises are becoming more and more saturated with the factual materials supplied by sociology, anthropology, and other social sciences. The reasons for this are at hand. In the first place, the last few decades in sociology and other social sciences have been marked by an enormous work in the collecting and analysis of mores, customs, ceremonies, moral opinions, and prescriptions as they have existed among the most widely differing peoples and at different times. Thanks to this procedure, it has become impossible for even the most ardent partisan of a "pure ethics" to ignore the obtained data. When these data were lacking, an ethicist could speculate as he pleased. Now, under existing conditions, to continue to build "a system of pure ethics" means practically nothing but to be busy with a childish work which can scarcely bring any credit to its author or be influential in practice.

In the second place, any ethicist may postulate anything as the highest moral principle or moral value—happiness, solidarity, human welfare, "the Golden Rule," the categoric imperative, oneness, harmony,

---

6. It is curious to note that even those sociologists who, like Durkheim and Lévy-Bruhl, have tried to put out of the science of sociology all judgments of valuation did not accomplish this. See S. Deploige, *Le Confit de la Moral et de la Sociologie,* i–xvi; G. Richard, "*Sociologie et Metaphysique,*" in *Foi et Vis* (June and July 1911).

or whatnot—but in order to show that his formula is right he must explain why his postulate is the highest principle or moral value. To give reasons means, practically, to turn to facts and to try to show that they really prove the validity of his contention. This is necessary because at the present time references to "God's will" or to a metaphysical principle of nature are not sufficient.

In the third place, the formula of the highest moral principle in all ethical systems is so broad and indefinite that it is practically meaningless. Being so, it does not and cannot give any concrete indication as to what one ought to do in a given situation. To say that "the highest goodness is happiness" is nothing but a substitution of one unknown for another. What is happiness? What forms of conduct lead to it? When? Under what conditions? The general formula does not give any answer to such concrete problems. This may also be said of all highest moral principles given by the ethicists. Therefore such formulae are practically useless. In order to be able to indicate what ought to be done, ethics must give some concrete rules. To formulate such rules, the ethicist must know customs, mores, mechanism of human behavior and its stimuli, causal relations between different factors that influence human behavior and social life, the concrete circumstances of each case, and so forth. These data are given by sociology, anthropology, psychology, biology, and by other sciences. Without a knowledge of these data, an ethicist can give only purely theoretical and useless recipes or the prescriptions which instead of curing may poison, instead of improving may aggravate individual or social sickness. Hence, an increasing dependence of ethics, as an applied art, upon science. As in the growth of biology the time of the ignorant medicine man passed by, so in the growth of the social and psychological sciences the time of the metaphysical ethicist is also passing by.

In the fourth place, I admit that any ethicist may postulate an ideal of *ought to be* if he pleases. But if he is free from facts in this respect, he is bound to know their casual relations in order to realize his ideal in the easiest and the most efficient way. Whether he chooses a communistic or a capitalistic type as an ideal of social organization, he must know the forces, means, and ways which may lead to a realization of his ideal. Otherwise there is no use of his metaphysical theorizing. The same may be said of any plan of social reconstruction—improvement of family, diminution (or even increase) of crimes, modification of religion or political constitutions. These reasons account for an increasing dependence of ethics or any social applied discipline on sociology and other sciences. Future ethics is likely to be an elaborated discipline which, like the science of medicine, will indicate the concrete ways and means of doing what ought to be done under any given situation. At the basis of these prescriptions will lie the causal relations indicated and discovered by other sciences which study the reality as it is.

Ethical Elements in Contemporary Sociology

As I have already stated, the contemporary sociology still contains in abundance ethical evaluations and similar preaching judgments. Nevertheless, during the last two decades there appeared the tendency, which seems to be growing, to abolish, or at least to reduce, these elements as much as possible. Durkheim, Lévy-Bruhl, de Roberty, Waxweiler, W. G. Sumner, F. H. Giddings, and recently V. Pareto, not to mention many other names, represent this tendency. In my opinion it must be supported. Logically, as I have endeavored to show, all this valuation lies outside of the realm of science. Psychologically, moralizing considerably hinders an objective study of the real situation and leads to partiality and one-sidedness. Factually, in the majority of the cases it remains still purely metaphysical, not being based on a really scientific scrutiny of the corresponding facts and their causal relations.[7] Under such conditions, a moralizing sociologist is no better leader of the social reconstruction movement than a medicine man of the past or a speculative ethicist. Through his speculative preaching, he compromises the science of sociology, and, like a speculative reformer, he may facilitate an aggravation of social situation instead of an improvement. These reasons are sufficient to understand the urgent necessity for getting rid of moralizing and valuation within the realm of sociology as a science. If sociology and other social sciences are going to grow they must follow the natural sciences in this respect. This does not mean any underappreciation of moral values. But it does mean that everything is proper in its own place. Moreover, I am convinced that the greater the purely scientific progress of these sciences, the greater power they will have to serve our practical needs and ethical purposes. The natural sciences, being already free from ethical elements, serve our needs more efficiently than any social and political discipline. "Discovery of causal regularities is a self-sufficient and primary task of sociology. When this is done the results may serve other needs. To mix this and ethical tasks means to do harm to both of

---

7. See a series of appropriate remarks in F. H. Giddings, *The Scientific Study of Human Society* (Chapel Hill: University of North Carolina Press, 1924), chap. 3.

them," rightly says Pareto.[8] "Facing the facts the physical and biological sciences have made known to us has enabled us to live more comfortably and longer than men once did. Facing the facts that the social sciences are making known to us, and will make better known, should enable us to diminish human misery and to live more wisely than the human race has lived hitherto. It will be discovered one day that the chief value of social science, far from being academic, is moral," no less rightly says Professor Giddings.[9]

8. Pareto, op. cit., 1599–1600.
9. Giddings, op. cit., 37–38.

22

Amitology as an Applied Science of Amity and Unselfish Love

Almost all sane persons prefer life to death, love to hate, friendship to enmity, cooperation to conflict, creativity to destruction, peace to war. These preferences are especially strong now when mankind painfully suffers from the bloodiest mass murders, hate, and destruction threatening its very existence. Now more than before, we all want peace, love, and constructive creativeness.

In spite of our wishes, these boons somehow are not coming through. On the horizon there is no sign of clearing. The tornadoes of bloodiest wars are still sweeping in an endless procession. Our prayers for peace seem to find no response. Our knowledge to realize these boons is insufficient. We seemingly know little about how to make friends and build a harmonious universe.

The time has come when this knowledge must be obtained and fully developed. The historical moment has struck for building a new applied science or a new art of amitology—the science and art of cultivation of amity, unselfish love, and mutual help in interindividual and intergroup relationships. A mature amitology is now the paramount need of humanity. Its development tangibly determines the creative future of *Homo sapiens*.

Such a science is an antidote to the Machiavellian *Prince*. Machiavelli's little volume is a guidebook for the power-crazy and predatory princes, kings, revolutionary dictators, and military conquerors who are willing to use all means, foul and fair, for satiation of their lust for power.

Mankind has had enough of these power-drunk "saviors." In spite of millenia of their predatory efforts, counseled by thousands of Machiavellis, they failed to build a harmonious and creative human universe. At the present time these "saviors" begin to threaten the very existence of mankind by setting a hellish fire to the whole house of

Originally published in *Soziologische Forschung in Unserer Zeit*, ed. Karl G. Specht (Kohn: Westdeutscher Verlag, 1951), 277–79. Reprinted by permission of the publisher.

humanity and by pushing mankind to a universal fratricide, patricide, homicide, and suicide.

The time has come when these murderous maniacs must be replaced by the leaders of amity, love, and creativity. Machiavellian "guidebooks" for subjugation, extermination, and domination need to be replaced by "guidebooks" of mutual service and free cooperation.

Now let us look into what sort of science is amitology. Since its purpose is a cultivation of a creative amity and unselfish mutual service in human relationships, its main tasks are about as follows: first, a careful analysis of the main aspects, properties, and basic forms of altruistic relationships or of love energy. When this preliminary task is roughly cleared, the main problems of amitology follow from the basic constituents of social relationship or interaction. An amicable social relationship consists of: (1) two or more individuals or two or more organized groups that are in friendly relationships. They can be called the subjects of amicable interaction or relationships. (2) The friendly relationship itself manifesting in the actions–reactions and instrumentalities of the interacting parties. (3) Other individuals who by their mere existence (as catalytic agents) or by passive or by active participation, tangibly influence the interaction between the subjects of amicable relationships. (4) The cosmic, vital, and sociocultural environment in which the parties and other individuals interact. These components are present in all social interactions, amicable as well as inimical. In accordance with these components, the main divisions of amitology fall under the following headings:

1. A study of personality structure of the subjects of interaction: what sort of personality is necessary, most favorable, and most unfavorable for a fruitful development of a creative amity in human relationships. This part of amitology must give a sound theory of personality structure generally and of the mental structure demanded by successful cultivation of creative friendship.

2. An investigation, discovery, and invention of the most fruitful means and most efficient techniques for altruistic transformation of and for development of creative friendly relationships between the individuals and groups. Put in the terms of energy, this task consists in finding and inventing the most efficient ways of production, accumulation, and circulation of love energy in the human universe. The techniques imply also their efficiency in transformation of the inimical into amical relationship, of hate into friendship. This is the most important, and the most difficult, part of amitology.

3. A study of the other persons' roles and functions facilitating or hindering the development of creativity and unselfish love between the

subjects of the interaction. The functions of *pater spiritualis,* of guru, or moral or religious instructor, of parents, of agents of social institutions, of psychiatrist, friend or enemy, and so on, play an instrumental role in amicable relationships between the parties. They can notably help or hinder the establishment and development of friendship.

4. A research into the kind of the cosmic, biological, and sociocultural environment, inimical or necessary or most favorable for the maximal development of amical relationships.

Such appear to be the main five tasks (including the preliminary one) of amitology. If and when they are sufficiently developed, amitology becomes a mature applied science and effective practical art developed for a successful amelioration of the human universe in all important respects but particularly in its moral and social and creative aspect.

As one of the first steps in this direction, a recent establishment, in 1949, of the Harvard Research Center in Creative Altruism can be mentioned. Its main task is to study the chief properties and functions of creative, altruistic love and, especially, to investigate and invent efficient techniques for the creative altruization of persons and groups, or find efficient ways for the production, accumulation, and circulation of creative love in the human universe.

Just as medical science assumes that life and health are preferable to death and sickness, so the Research Center presupposes that love and free cooperation are greater values than hateful strife and coercion. A preliminary exploration of the phenomena of altruistic love, carried on by the Center, has well confirmed the age-old belief in love's enormous creative and therapeutic potentialities.

23

Studies of the Harvard Research Center in Creative Altruism

The Harvard Research Center in Creative Altruism was established in 1949. It has been supported by a grant of $15,000 annually ($120,000 for eight years) by Mr. Eli Lilly and the Lilly Endowment. As the basis of the Center's establishment there were two main assumptions, already vindicated by the minimum necessary evidence. The first of these assumptions is that none of the prevalent prescriptions against international and civil wars and other forms of interhuman bloody strife can eliminate or notably decrease these conflicts. By these popular prescriptions I mean, first, elimination of wars and strife by political changes, especially by democratic political transformations. Tomorrow the whole world could become democratic and yet wars and bloody strife would not be eliminated because democracies happen to be no less belligerent and strife-infected than autocracies. Still less pacification can be expected from autocracies. Neither the United Nations nor the world government can give a lasting internal and international peace if the establishment of these bodies is not reinforced by notable altruization of persons, groups, institutions, and culture.

The same goes for education in its present form as a panacea against war and bloody strife. Tomorrow all grown-up persons in the world could become Ph.D.'s and yet this enormous progress in education would not eliminate wars and bloody conflicts. Since the tenth century on up to the present century, education has made an enormous progress—the number of schools of all kinds, the percent of literacy, the number of scientific discoveries and inventions have greatly and almost systematically increased, and yet the international wars, the bloody revolutions, and the grave forms of crime have not decreased at all. On the contrary, in the most scientific and most educated twentieth century, they have reached an unrivaled height and made this century

Originally a privately printed and circulated publication of *The Harvard Research Center in Creative Altruism*. Reprinted by permission of Dr. Sergei Sorokin.

the bloodiest among all the preceding twenty-five centuries of Greco-Roman and European history.

The same goes for religious changes, if by religion is meant a purely ideological belief in God or in the credo of any of the great religions. One of the evidences for that is given by our investigation of seventy-three Boston converts "brought to Jesus" by two popular evangelical preachers. Of these seventy-three converts, only one changed his overt behavior in an altruistic direction after his conversion. Thirty-seven converts slightly changed their speech reactions; after their conversion they began to repeat more frequently the words "Our Lord Jesus Christ" and similar utterances, but their overt behavior did not change tangibly. The remaining converts changed neither their actions nor their speech reactions. If by religious revival and "moral rearmament" are meant this sort of ideological and speech reactional transformation, it would not bring peace or decrease interhuman strife, because it represents mainly a cheap self-gratification for psychoneurotics and sham-religious persons.

The same goes for communist, socialist, or capitalist economic remedies, for scientific, artistic, legal, or other ways of establishing and maintaining lasting peace in the human universe when these are not backed by increased altruization of persons and groups. In my *Reconstruction of Humanity* (1948), I have given the minimum of evidence to substantiate these statements. The assumption positively signifies that without a notable increase of unselfish, creative love (as ideally formulated in the Sermon on the Mount) in overt behavior, in overt interindividual and intergroup relationships, in social institutions and culture, there is no chance for a lasting peace and for interhuman harmony, internal or external. This, then, was our first assumption, already vindicated to a considerable degree by the existing body of inductive evidence.

Our second assumption was that this unselfish, creative love, about which we still know very little, potentially represents a tremendous power—the veritable *mysterium tremendum et fascinosum*—provided we know how to produce it in abundance, how to accumulate it, and how to use it; in other words, if we know how to transform individuals and groups into more altruistic and creative beings who would feel, think, and behave as real members of a mankind united into one intensely solidary family. Viewed in this light, love appears to be one of the highest energies, which contains in itself enormous creative and therapeutic possibilities.

With these hypotheses the Center started to investigate scientifically this unknown or little-known energy. At the start we were quite aware of the gigantic disparity between our limited capacities and meager material resources, on the one hand, and the tremendous difficulty of the problem on the other. We did not and do not expect to contribute more than the proverbial drop in a bucket. But since governments, big foundations, and better brains seem to be absorbed mainly in the promotion of wars and in the invention of increasingly destructive means for the extermination of man by man, someone, somehow and sometime, had to engage in the study of the phenomena of unselfish love, no matter how inadequate were his capabilities or how low the esteem of his colleagues for his engaging in such a "foolish research project."

During the six years of the Center's existence, our studies have had two phases or two main topics. Our first step consisted in delineating and formulating a working definition of unselfish creative love and in finding out what was the state of this problem in contemporary science. These studies were published in a *Symposium* volume, *Explorations in Altruistic Love and Behavior* (1950), and in my volumes *Reconstruction of Humanity* (1948) and *Altruistic Love* (1950). The *Symposium* attempts to give a delineation of the main aspects, forms, and dimensions of love and of the place of this problem in contemporary science and philosophy. The *Symposium* opens with my study of a multidimensional universe of love in its physical, religious-ontological, biological, ethical, psychological, and sociological aspects, subdividing each aspect into two forms: love as eros and as agape. Concentrating on the empirical, psychosocial love, the study reduces observable and partly measurable aspects of empirical love to five "dimensions"—the intensity of love, its extensity, its duration, its purity, and its adequacy—and then explores the uniformities in the relationships, covariations, and correlations of these "dimensions" with one another. It also outlines the problems of production, accumulation, and distribution of love energy.

Subsequent chapters of the *Symposium* deal with a mathematical theory of egoism and altruism (N. Rashevsky); with biological foundations and factors of cooperation, conflict, and creativity (M. Ashley Montagu, Trigant Burrow, Therese Brosse); with a psychological approach to the study of love and hate (G. W. Allport); with scientific, philosophical, and social foundations for altruism (F. S. C. Northrop, L. Dechesne); with altruism in the psychotherapeutic relationship and interactions in the mental hospital (M. Greenblatt, H. Eichorn, R. W. Hyde); among the college students and nursery school children (P. Sorokin, D. Cove); with parapsychological (extrasensory) perception and friendly relationships (J. B. Rhine, S. D. Kahn); with electroencephalographic aspects of normal, homicidal, and friendly personalities (M. Greenblatt, B. Sittinger); with the techniques of emotional integration (Swami Akhilananda); and with the problems of labor harmony (G. K. Zipf). The result of this "stocktaking" is not very cheerful. It shows that this gigantic problem is largely neglected by modern science. Professor A. H. Maslow confirms this result by finding out that the word "love" does not appear in the indexes of most psychological, sociological, and anthropological texts. G. Allport sees "a persistent defect of modern psychology in its failure to make a serious study of the affiliative desires and capacities of human beings." While many a modern sociologist and psychologist view the phenomena of hatred, crime, and mental disorders as the legitimate objects of scientific study, quite illogically they stigmatize as theological preaching or nonscientific metaphysics any investigation of the phenomena of love, friendship, heroic deeds, and creative genius. There is no need to argue the patently unscientific nature of such an attitude. It is but one of the manifestations of the prevalent concentration on the negative, pathological, and subhuman phenomena which is typical for the disintegrating phase of our sensate culture.

My volume *Altruistic Love* is an unpretentious, preliminary study of some of the tangible characteristics of all Christian saints (some 4600 about whom the necessary data are available) and of some 500 living American "good neighbors." It is the first "census" of all Christian saints: their age and sex composition; their marital and family status; their parental families; their occupational, economic, and social positions; their education and school intelligence; their longevity and health; their ways to sainthood; their rural–urban and national distribution; their political ideologies and group affiliations; and so on. Side by side with this census, the study also investigates the changes in all these characteristics which the group of saints has undergone during the twenty centuries of Christianity.

Of several results of this census, one or two can be mentioned here. First, the extraordinary longevity and vigorous health of the saints is remarkable. In spite of the ascetic mode of living followed by a great number of saints, the unhygienic conditions, and often physical self-torture, including some 37 percent premature deaths as martyrs, their average duration of life turns out to be far longer than that of their contemporaries and somewhat longer than even the longevity of contemporary Americans or Europeans. Second, the proportion of the women saints grows fairly steadily as we pass from the first to the twentieth century. While the proportion of the saints from the royalty, the nobility, and, later on, from the bourgeoisie has been steadily decreasing, the proportion of the saints from lower and poorer classes has been rising during the last few centuries. These changes reflect those in the social organization of Christian societies: growing equalization of the status of women with that of men, the declining importance of royalty and aristocracy, and bourgeoisie strata. Finally, after the seventeenth century, the "production" of saints declines sharply and reaches almost a zero line at the end of the nineteenth and at the beginning of the twentieth century.

Along somewhat similar lines are studies of 500 living American altruists. All in all, the study gives some concrete material about the biological, mental, and social "makeup" of the saintly and secular altruists, contrasted with the "makeup" of criminals, aggressively selfish, and subhuman types of the individuals.

In this first, orientative phase, we have also had to make some studies of the problem of the power of love. Since we assumed that love was power, we had to test this assumption. Our investigations have been carried along diverse lines and by different methods, beginning with a mere collection of the existing historical and individual facts recording this power and ending with semiexperimental and experimental testing of the hypothesis on students of Harvard and Radcliffe College, on the patients of the Boston Psychopathic Hospital, and on several groups of mutually antagonistic persons. These studies (published in my volume *The Ways and Power of Love: Types, Factors, and Techniques of Moral Transformation* [1954]) uncovered a sufficient body of evidence to show that unselfish, creative love is a power which (*a*) can stop aggressive interindividual and intergroup attacks, (*b*) can transform inimical relationships into amicable ones, (*c*) begets love, and (*d*) can tangibly influence international policy and pacify international conflicts. Additionally, an unselfish and wise (adequate) love manifests itself as (*e*) a life-giving force, necessary for physical, mental, and moral health; (*f*) a longer life for altruistic persons; (*g*) a positive force in the moral and social development of children; (*h*) a powerful antidote against criminal and suicidal tendencies, against hate, fear, and psychoneuroses; (*i*) an important cognitive and aesthetic force; (*j*) the loftiest and most effective educational force for moral enlightenment and ennoblement of humanity; (*k*) the heart and soul of freedom and of moral and religious values; (*l*) an absolutely necessary factor for a harmonious social order and for creative progress; (*m*) finally, at this present catastrophic moment of human history, a necessary condition for the prevention of new wars and for the alleviation of enormously increased interindividual and intergroup strife.

With notable increase of our knowledge of love, its potentialities can be used for the service of mankind in immeasurably greater proportions.

Having thus validated our starting assumptions, we have passed to the second phase of our research. In this stage we concentrated on the investigation of the effective techniques for altruistic formation and transformation. We have analyzed and, when possible, tested experimentally the efficacy of various methods of altruistic education. For example: the ancient techniques of Yoga, Buddhism, Zen Buddhism, Sufism, and somatophysic techniques of Orthodox Christianity (the studies of R. Godel, J. H. Masui, A. Migot, P. Masson-Oursel, M. Eliade, G. E. Monod-Herzen, A. Bloom, E. Dermenghem, R. Kita, K. Nagaya, H. Benoit, P. Marinier, published in the *Symposium: Forms and Techniques of Altruistic and Spiritual Growth* [1954]); the techniques invented by the founders of great religions and monastic orders, Oriental and Occidental (the techniques of St. Basil the Great, St. Benedict, St. Francis of Assisi, St. Bernard, Ignatius Loyola, and others, published in my volume *The Ways and Power of Love*); then the techniques of the eminent secular educators, such as Montessori, Froebel, and others; and ending with the techniques of contemporary education, psychology, psychiatry, sociology, and those used in such contemporary Christian altruistic communities as the Society of Brothers in Paraguay and the Mennonite, Hutterite, and Quaker communities in the United States (studies of E. C. H. Arnold, C. Krahn, J. W. Fretz, R. Kleider, in the *Symposium: Forms and Techniques,* mentioned, and my studies in *The Ways and Power of Love*). A careful analysis of the ancient techniques of Yoga, Buddhism, and monastic orders has been made because of the unexcelled—possibly even unrivaled—ingenuity, subtlety, and efficacy of these techniques. Their known and unknown inventors perhaps knew more about the effective methods of moral transformation than we know at the present time. They certainly have been successful moral educators of humanity.

As indicated, we did not limit our study of these techniques to a mere theoretical analysis but wherever possible tried to test them empirically and experimentally. Do these techniques work, and in what social and cultural conditions? The following examples give an idea of our experimental testing. One of the techniques in Raja-Yoga is *pranayama,* or training in voluntary control of respiration. It is paralleled by the voluntary "suspension" of heart activity. It is well known that the real Yogi can voluntarily "suspend" or reduce to an almost intangible degree his heart and breathing activities for hours, days, and weeks. Eminent specialists, cooperating with the Center, tested in the light of modern science the authenticity, the mechanism, and the therapeutic consequences of voluntary regulation of respiration. Other eminent cardiologists of the Center made objective, instrumental-cardiographic, encephalographic, girographic, etc. investigations on the suspension of heart activity by the Yogi, as well as instrumental recordings of all the important changes in the functions of all the important organs of the human organism that occur when a person concentrates and deconcentrates his thought, when he experiences hate and love, when the Yogi reaches the state of *samadhi,* and so on (the studies of W. Bischler, F. P. Jones, Therese Brosse, J. S. Bockoven, and M. Greenblatt in the *Symposium: Forms and Techniques*).

Further on, for testing the efficacy of the "techniques of good deeds," we looked for five pairs of students. The partners of each pair hated each other. We set for ourselves the task to change (within the period of three months) these hateful relationships into amicable ones by the techniques of "good deeds." We convinced one partner of each pair to try to render friendly actions (invitations to lunch, to movies, to dances, etc.) to his disliked partner, and then we observed what changes, if any, the repeated good deeds produced in both partners. To make a long story short, we changed four pairs into friends and one into indifferent partners. A similar experimental transformation of inimical into amicable relationships between the nurses and patients at the Boston Psychopathic Hospital was made by the method of good deeds and had similar success (studies of J. M. Thompson, R. W. Hyde, R. H. Kandler in the *Symposium: Forms and Techniques*). These examples give a notion of our experimental testing of the various techniques studied. Similar analysis and testing of various techniques for reducing group prejudice, of group therapy techniques for altruization of "the hardened prisoners" in the Iowa penitentiary and for making friends among the students of Harvard and Radcliffe, of "the psychodramatic production techniques," have been done for the Center by G. W. Allport, [myself], J. L. Moreno, W. A. Lunden, B. Davis, and A. Miller (their studies are published in the *Symposium: Forms and Techniques*). F. S. C. Northrop and M. Engleson investigated the kind of international law and of the New Declaration of the Rights of Man and Citizen necessary for realization of altruistic values in mankind.

All in all, some thirty different techniques for the altruistic transformation of persons and groups have been analyzed, and several of these have been experimentally tested.

In trying to unravel the mystery of the how and why of altruistic transformation, we have also made a detailed analysis of the process of altruization in the lives of the great apostles of unselfish love, like Buddha, Jesus, St. Francis of Assisi, M. Gandhi, and many others.

Since they succeeded in becoming the living incarnation of love, they evidently had successfully solved the problem. How did they solve it? What techniques, what factors, and what sociocultural conditions were involved? These "case studies" formed a large slice of our research. Here again we have tried to be as empirical, experimental, and scientific as possible.

These detailed case studies yielded several results. First was the three types of altruists: (*a*) "fortunate" altruists, who [from] early childhood display a well-integrated set of "egos," values, and social affiliations centered around the values of love and who, like grass, quietly and gracefully grow in their altruistic creativity without any catastrophe or sharp conversion. A. Schweitzer, John Wollman, B. Franklin, Dr. T. Haas, and many others exemplify this type. (*b*) "Catastrophic" and "late" altruists, whose life is sharply divided into two periods: prealtruistic and altruistic. The latter is precipitated by a catastrophic event (sickness, death of their beloved, etc.) in their lives that transforms them. The process of transformation is difficult, painful, and lasts from a few months to several years. During this tortuous period, the respective persons have to perform the difficult operation of a basic rearrangement of the "egos," "values," and "group affiliations." When this operation is completed and well interiorized, a new altruistic personality emerges and grows up to the end of its life. G. Buddha, St. Francis of Assisi, St. Augustine, St. Paul, Simone Weil, and others exemplify this type. (*c*) Finally, the intermediary type is marked by some of the traits of the fortunate and the late–catastrophic types. St. Theodosius, St. Basil the Great, M. Gandhi, St. Theresa, Sri Ramakrishna, and others give examples of this type.

Second, these investigations led to confirmation of the *law of polarization* previously formulated in my volume *Man and Society in Calamity* (1942). Contrary to the Freudian claim that calamity and frustration uniformly generate aggression, and contrary to the old claim—reiterated recently by Toynbee—that "we learn by suffering" and that frustration and catastrophes lead uniformly to the moral and spiritual ennoblement of human beings, the law of polarization states that, depending upon the type of personality, frustrations and misfortunes are reacted to and overcome now by an increased creative effort (deafness of Beethoven, blindness of Milton, etc.) and by altruistic transformation (the positive polarization of St. Francis of Assisi, Ignatius Loyola, etc.) and by the negative polarizations of suicide, mental disorder, brutalization, increase of selfishness, dumb submissiveness, and cynical sensualism. The same polarization occurs on a mass scale when catastrophes and frustration fall upon a large collectivity. Some of its members mentally and morally disintegrate, while the other parts of the collectivity become more religious, moral, and altruistic, as shown also by our "catastrophic altruists." This law explains also why the periods of catastrophes are marked on the one hand by disintegration of the value system of a given society and on the other by a creative reintegration of a new value system, especially of religious and ethical values. As a rule, all great religious and moral systems have emerged and then have been ennobled, mainly in catastrophic periods of a respective society, be it ancient Egypt, China, India, Israel, the Greco-Roman, and the Western nations. A vast body of other empirical evidence well supports the validity of the law of polarization (roughly outlined here and more precisely analyzed in my *Ways and Power of Love*).

The third result of these studies has been a revision of the prevalent theories of personality structure and personality integration. Investigation of the relevant theories shows them entirely untenable. The first blunder of these theories is found in their merging into the category of the "unconscious" or "subconscious" (E. von Hartmann, P. Janet, S. Freud, and others) two radically different "energies" of man: the *biologically unconscious* that lies below the level of the conscious state of mind and the *supraconscious* ("genius," "creative elan," the *nous* of the Greeks, the "pneuma" of the Church Fathers, etc.) that lies above the level of any conscious or rational thought or "energy." The "depth psychology" of the prevalent theories is in fact quite shallow. It either flattens the mental structure almost exclusively to the level of the unconscious or subconscious "id," with a sort of epiphenomenal and ineffective "ego" and "superego" (S. Freud) or just depicts it as a "two-story building"—the unconscious (subconscious), and the conscious (rational).

Instead of these utterly inadequate theories, we have been forced— by logical and factual reasons—to construct a four-fold framework of personality structure: (1) the biologically unconscious (subconscious); (2) the biologically conscious; (3) the socioculturally conscious; and (4) the supraconscious. The unconscious and the supraconscious mental levels are devoid of any sense of "ego," while the socioculturally conscious level has as many different "egos" as there are groups with which the individual is associated ("ego" of his family, occupational group, political party, religious group, and other organizations in which he holds a membership). If the groups with which the individual is affiliated are in harmonious relationship with one another and "dictate" similar ideas, beliefs, tastes, values, and imperatives of conduct, all the "egos" and "values" of the individual will be in harmony with each other, merging together into one integrated ego and one system of values. As a result, such an individual will have peace of mind, strong convictions, unclouded conscience, and a consistent conduct. If the groups of the individual's affiliation are mutually contradictory in their values and in their demands on the individual, his "egos" and "values" will be at war with one another; the individual will become a house divided against itself, devoid of peace of mind, of consistency of thought and conduct, suffering from incessant inner conflicts, dissatisfied, and psychoneurotic. A large part of the neuroses are due to the inner tensions and wars of the "egos"—the results of an unfortunate affiliation of the individual with mutually contradictory groups. This last hypothesis has been tested in various ways by us and by other psychiatrists and is becoming increasingly accepted. This pluralistic theory of "egos" as a microcosm reflecting the macrocosm of group affiliations explains why the fortunate altruists, since early childhood placed amidst harmonious and altruistic group affiliations, have a harmonious set of "egos," "values," and actions and therefore in their altruistic growth do not need to pass through painful crises accompanying rearrangement of the "ego," "values," and group affiliations. And why the persons (catastrophic altruists) who happened to be affiliated with mutually discordant groups and having, therefore, a set of discordant "egos," "values," and actions have to pass through the painful process of their disintegration and reintegration, if they do not commit suicide, or become mentally ill, or "regress" to the state of a brutal or decadently sensual human animal.

Finally, as to the supraconscious in man, we collected and analyzed a considerable body of empirical evidence showing its reality, its creative functioning in men of genius, and some of its characteristics. Though this evidence is still meager, it is about sufficient to establish the reality of this highest form of man's creative energy. It seems to be the main source (working in cooperation with rational thought) of all the greatest creative achievements in all fields of culture, from science and the fine arts up to religion and ethics. It is also a condition necessary for becoming a genius of altruistic love.

Among the tests of the supraconscious, T. Brosse carried on an experimental cardiographic, encephalographic, girographic, etc. verification. Her pioneering study instrumentally confirmed the tangible effects of the supraconscious upon the activities of heart, lungs, and other organs of some 213 persons experimented with. (Brosse's study is published in the *Symposium;* the theory of the personality structure and of the supraconscious is published in my *Ways and Power of Love.*)

Fourth, in studying the types of altruistic rearrangement of group affiliations and of "egos," "values," and actions, we investigated in some detail the strategies used to accomplish this difficult task: (*a*) the self-isolationist, eremitic solution, when an altruist cuts off all his previous group affiliations, isolates himself in a desert, and, face to face with himself (like St. Anthony, St. Jerome, or other "desert hermits"), painfully labors over a new reintegration of his personality; (*b*) the solution of the unattached pilgrims or seekers of goodness, going from place to place like Buddha, Jesus, and others who cut off almost all their previous affiliations and until "the enlightenment" wandered either alone or with disciples and coseekers; (*c*) the solution through establishment of their own group and institution (monastery, cloister, special school, etc.) dedicated to spiritual and altruistic training; (*d*) the solution through living in the ordinary "sinful" world but avoiding membership in all selfish groups and affiliating only with the mutually harmonious altruistic collectivities and their values.

All in all, the process of a real altruistic transformation for persons who were not altruistic in their early life is a very difficult and painful operation, taking a fairly long time and hardly ever happening momentarily. This explains why almost all momentary religious or moral "conversions" are superficial and why today's "religious revival," so widely advertised in the United States and elsewhere, is a mere surface ripple, hardly changing deeper currents of social life and moral conditions of nations and mankind.

A deep comprehension of the nature and workings of unselfish, creative love is impossible without an adequate knowledge of the society, culture, and value system in which human beings live and act. This explains why, besides investigating the basic problems of altruism, we also had to study the structure and the historical dynamics of social, cultural, and value systems. In addition to attention given it in [my] previously published sociological and historico-philosophical works— *Social and Cultural Dynamics; Society, Culture, and Personality; Social Mobility; Crisis of Our Age,* and others—this task is dealt with in [my] *Social Philosophies of an Age of Crisis,* devoted to a comparative analysis of the sociology and philosophy of history of Danilevsky, Spengler, Toynbee, Northrop, Kroeber, Schweitzer, Berdyayev, Schubart, [myself], and others; and in *Fads and Foibles in Modern Sociology and Related Sciences* which contains a critical analysis of today's "physicalistic and mechanistic" sociology, psychology, psychiatry, and other "behavioral sciences."

An assessment of today's knowledge in values is given in the *Symposium: New Knowledge in Human Values,* edited by A. H. Maslow. The volume consists of the papers read and discussed at the Conference on New Knowledge in Human Values organized by the Center and the Research Society for Creative Altruism in October 1957. The papers of G. W. Allport, L. von Bertalanffy, J. Bronowski, T. Dobzhansky, E. Fromm, K. Goldstein, R. S. Hartman, G. Kepes, D. Lee, H. Margenau, A. Maslow, [myself], D. T. Suzuki, P. T. Tillich, and W. A. Weisskopf summarize the existing knowledge in this field.

Finally, *S.O.S., American Sex Revolution,* and *Power and Morality* explore particularly dangerous traits and trends in today's sex behavior, marriage, and family life and in the behavior and policies of governments; they point out the best possible ways of altruistic reconstruction of these relationships and institutions.

The above gives an idea of the studies of the Research Center.

Selected Publications by and about Pitirim A. Sorokin

Several exhaustive bibliographies of Professor Sorokin's English works are available, and compilations of his Russian works are underway at this writing in the new Russian republics. The best summaries of the American period are found in *Pitirim A. Sorokin in Review*, edited by Philip J. Allen (Durham, N.C.: Duke University Press, 1963), 497–506; and *Sociological Theory, Values, and Sociocultural Change: Essays in Honor of Pitirim A. Sorokin*, edited by Edward A. Tiryakian (New York: The Free Press, 1963), 295–302. This volume includes a small number of Sorokin's Russian publications. *Sorokin and Sociology: Essays in Honour of Pitirim A. Sorokin*. edited by C. C. Hallen and R. Prasad (Agra, India: Satish Book Enterprises, 1972), is a very comprehensive work. It includes an extensive list of books, chapters, and articles about Sorokin's ideas. Yuri Doykov, *"Modern Thought" of P. A. Sorokin* (Arkhangelsk: Arkhangelsk Regional Studies Museum, Emigration History Research Center, 1966), lists many of Sorokin's articles under his real name as well as his pen names (L. N. Chadayev, V. V. Vigon, P. S.). For a listing and annotation in English of his selected Russian works, see Barry V. Johnston, Natalia Mandelbaum, and Nakita E. Pokrovsky, "Commentary on Some of the Russian Writings of Pitirim A. Sorokin," *Journal of the History of the Behavioral Sciences* 30 (January 1994): 28–42.

Books

1924   *Leaves from a Russian Diary*. New York: E. P. Dutton and Co.
1925   *The Sociology of Revolution*. Philadelphia: J. B. Lippincott.
1927   *Social Mobility*. New York: Harper and Brothers.
1928   *Contemporary Sociological Theories: Through the First Quarter of the Twentieth Century*. New York: Harper and Row.
1929   *Principles of Rural–Urban Sociology* (with Carle C. Zimmerman). New York: Henry Holt.
1930–   *A Systematic Source Book in Rural Sociology* (with Carle C. Zim-
32   merman and Charles J. Galpin). 3 vols. Minneapolis: University of Minnesota Press.
1937   *Social and Cultural Dynamics*. 3 vols. New York: American Book Company.
1941   *The Crisis of Our Age*. New York: E. P. Dutton.

1941 *Social and Cultural Dynamics.* Vol. 4. New York: American Book Company.
1942 *Man and Society in Calamity.* New York: Dutton.
1943 *Sociocultural Causality, Space, Time.* Durham, N.C.: Duke University Press.
1947 *Society, Culture, and Personality: Their Structure and Dynamics: A System of General Sociology.* New York: Harper and Brothers.
1948 *The Reconstruction of Humanity.* Boston: Beacon Press.
1950 *Altruistic Love: A Study of American Good Neighbors and Christian Saints.* Boston: Beacon Press.
1950 (ed.) *Explorations in Altruistic Love and Behavior: A Symposium.* Boston: Beacon Press.
1950 *Leaves from a Russian Diary and Thirty Years After.* Boston: Beacon Press.
1950 *Social Philosophies of an Age of Crisis.* Boston: Beacon Press.
1951 *S.O.S.: The Meaning of Our Crisis.* Boston: Beacon Press.
1954 (ed.) *Forms and Techniques of Altruistic and Spiritual Growth: A Symposium.* Boston: Beacon Press.
1954 *The Ways and Power of Love.* Boston: Beacon Press.
1956 *Fads and Foibles in Modern Sociology and Related Sciences.* Chicago: Henry Regnery.
1957 *The American Sex Revolution.* Boston: Porter Sargent.
1959 *Power and Morality: Who Shall Guard the Guardians?* (with Walter A. Lunden). Boston: Porter Sargent.
1963 *A Long Journey: The Autobiography of Pitirim A. Sorokin.* New Haven, Conn.: College and University Press.
1964 *The Basic Trends of Our Times.* New Haven, Conn.: College and University Press.
1966 *Sociological Theories of Today.* New York: Harper and Row.
1975 *Hunger as a Factor in Human Affairs.* Gainesville: University of Florida Press.

Articles

1925a "American Millionaires and Multimillionaires." *Social Forces* 4: 627–40.
1925b "Monarchs and Rulers: A Comparative Historical Study." *Social Forces* 4: 22–35.
1927 "Russian Sociology in the Twentieth Century." *Publication of the American Sociological Society* 31: 57–69.
1932 "An Experimental Study of the Influences of Suggestion on the Discrimination and Valuation of People." *American Journal of Sociology* 37: 720–37.
1933 "*Recent Social Trends:* A Criticism." *Journal of Political Economy* 4: 194–210.

1936	"Forms and Problems of Cultural Integration and Methods of Their Study." *Rural Sociology* (September 1936): 121–41.
1938a	"Histrionics." *Southern Review* 4: 555–64.
1938b	"A Neglected Factor of War." *American Sociological Review* 3: 475–86.
1940	"Arnold J. Toynbee's Philosophy of History." *Journal of Modern History* 12: 374–87.
1945	"War and Post-War Changes in Social Stratification of the Euro-American Population." *American Sociological Review* 10: 294–303.
1949	"The Real Causes of the Russian–American Conflict." *World Affairs* (April).
1957	"Integralism Is my Philosophy." In *This Is My Philosophy*, ed. Whit Burnett. New York: Harper and Brothers.
1960a	"How Are Social Theories Conceived, Developed, and Validated?" *Social Science* (April): 78–91.
1960b	"Three Basic Trends of Our Time." *Main Currents in Modern Thought*, nos. 3–4: 58–81.
1963	"Sociology of My Mental Life." In *Pitirim A. Sorokin in Review*, ed. Philip J. Allen, 3–36. Durham N.C.: Duke University Press.
1964	"The Mysterious Energy of Love." In *The Basic Trends of Our Time*, Ed. Pitirim A. Sorokin. New Haven, Conn.: College and University Press, 160–208.

Commentaries on Pitirim A. Sorokin's Works

Coulborn, R., and W. E. B. DuBois. 1942. "Mr. Sorokin's System." *Journal of Modern History* 14: 500–521.

Cowell, F. R. 1952. *History, Civilization and Culture: An Introduction to the Historical and Social Philosophies of P. A. Sorokin.* Boston: Beacon Press.

———. 1967. *Values in Human Society: The Sociology of P. A. Sorokin.* Boston: Porter Sargent.

Fan, Winston C. P. 1950. *Introduction to P. A. Sorokin's Theories.* Hong Kong: Freedom Press. [Chinese]

Ford, Joseph B., Michel Richard, and Palmer Talbutt, eds. 1996. *Sorokin and Civilization: A Centennial Assessment.* New Brunswick, N.J.: Transaction Books.

Ford, Joseph B. 1971. "The Life and Works of Pitirim Alexandrovitch Sorokin (1889–1968)." *International Review of Sociology* 7: 820–37.

Jaworski, Gary Dean. 1993. "Pitirim A. Sorokin's Sociological Anarchism." *History of the Human Sciences* 6(3): 61–77.

Johnston, Barry V. 1995. *Pitirim A. Sorokin: An Intellectual Biography.* Lawrence, Kans.: University Press of Kansas.

———. 1986. "Sorokin and Parsons at Harvard: Institutional Conflict and the Origin of a Hegemonic Tradition." *Journal of the History of the Behavioral Sciences* 22: 107–27.

———. 1987. "Pitirim Sorokin and the American Sociological Association: The Politics of a Professional Society." *Journal of the History of the Behavioral Sciences* 23: 103–22.

Maquet, Jacques J. 1951. *The Sociology of Knowledge.* Boston: Beacon Press.

Nichols, Lawrence T. 1989. "Deviance and Social Science: The Instructive Career of Pitirim A. Sorokin." *Journal of the History of the Behavioral Sciences* 25: 335–55.

———. 1992. "The Establishment of Sociology at Harvard: A Case of Organizational Ambivalence and Scientific Vulnerability." In *Science at Harvard University: Historical Perspectives,* ed. Clark A. Elliott and Margaret W. Rossiter, 191–222. Bethlehem, Pa.: Lehigh University Press.

———. 1996. "Intergenerational Solidarity in the Creation of Science: The Ross-Sorokin Correspondence, 1921–1931." *Journal of the History of the Behavioral Sciences* 32: 135–50.

Talbutt, Palmer. 1986. *Reanimation in Philosophy.* Lanham, Md.: University Press of America.

———. Forthcoming 1998. *Rough Dialectics: Sorokin's Philosophy of Value.* Amsterdam: Rodopi.

———. 1980. "Sorokin versus American Thought." *Sociologia Internationalis* 18. heft 1–2: 5–20.

Tiryakian, Edward A. 1988. "Sociology's Dostoyevsky: Pitirim A. Sorokin." *The World & I* (September): 569–81.

Index